KOREA JOONGANG DAILY

NEW
READING
Spectrum | 자연과학편 |

인문·사회·자연과학 및 예술·문화 전영역을 다룬 **영어신문 원문 독해 시리즈 ❸**

Jonghap Books

Introduction

| 기획 의도 / 구성과 특징 |

기획 배경과 의도

- '리딩 스펙트럼'은 「코리아 중앙데일리」 발행 초기부터 현재까지 독자의 각별한 관심 속에 연재되고 있는 칼럼 코너 내용 중 읽기, 독해연습 자료로 가장 적당한 것을 선별해서 이를 토대로 제작됐습니다.

- 원문 내용이 그야말로 모든 분야에 걸쳐 아주 다양한 주제로 된 유용하고 재미있는 관련 지식·정보 등을 담고 있으므로 독자들의 흥미와 지적 호기심을 끌어내고 또, 동시에 각종 영어 독해 시험에 자주 나오는 수준 있는 문제 유형들을 첨부해서 문제를 풀어봄으로써 이에 대비하기에도 충분하리라 판단되어 이 책을 기획했습니다.

구성 및 특징

- 신문에 게재되는 글이라는 특성상 내용의 유용함은 물론 원문의 단어, 문장 하나하나까지도 원어민 에디터들의 철저한 감수 등, 검증 과정을 거치므로 그만큼 신뢰할 수 있다.

- '리딩 스펙트럼'은 인문·사회·자연과학 그리고 문화·예술 분야 관련 내용을 모두 4권의 책으로 나눠 실었는데, 각 권에 해당 영역에 따른 각기 다른 주제로 된 원문 100개씩을 수록하여 다뤘다.

- 따라서 모든 영역에 따른 다방면에 걸친 다양한 주제로 된 내용을 두루 접함으로써 유연하고 균형 잡힌 사고력의 발달과 함께 지적 갈증을 해소시켜 나갈 수 있다.

- 한편, 수능을 비롯한 토플·텝스·편입·공무원 등 영어 독해시험에서 이런 류의 원문들이 장문 독해지문으로 출제되는 경향이 많은 점을 감안, 실제 시험에 자주 나오는 문제 유형과 동일한 형식의 문제들로 구성해서 각 권의 원문마다 다뤄놓아 각종 시험에 대비한 학습이 되도록 했다.

- 또한 원활한 학습을 돕기 위해서 매 지문(원문)의 어휘해설, 해석은 물론, 중요 구문과 각 문제별 해설도 다뤘다. 특히, 각각의 지문에 추론 문제를 넣어 생각하는 힘과 글 속에 담긴 뜻을 정확히 파악하는 연습도 되도록 했다. (문제의 난이도는 수능보다 좀 더 어려운데 토플·공무원·편입 중위권 정도 수준)
- 학습의 편의성, 효율성을 위하여 각 권에 원문(지문), 문제, 어휘 및 중요 구문 해설은 본 책에, 정답을 포함한 원문 해석·문제 해설은 별책에 각각 나눠 실었다.
- 이 밖에 이 책을 독해 연습용으로 일차 사용한 후 원문 해석 부분을 원문(지문)과 비교하면서 작문을 시도해보면 아주 좋은 영작 연습이 될 것이다.

끝으로 이 책(리딩 스펙트럼 총 4권)은 기존 일반 독해 교재와는 달리 원문 지문 하나하나에 완결성이 있고, 우리의 현실적인 측면과도 접목될 수 있는 외국의 사례에 따른 내용들이 적재적소에 배치되었기 때문에 더욱 흥미롭게, 또 친근감을 가지고 원문 내용을 즐기며 독해연습을 할 수 있다.

이렇게 좋은 자료를 독해 교재로 만들 수 있도록 허락해 주신 코리아중앙 데일리 社에 감사드린다.

홍준기

Contents

unit 1	A dark omen settles over Korea |일조량 천재지변|	8
unit 2	Turning yellow dust into gold |녹색 계열|	10
unit 3	Racing toward a dissonant drive |전기자동차와 소음|	12
unit 4	The weird thing about warming |글로벌 위어딩|	14
unit 5	Calming the fires on our planet |지구가 뿔났다|	16
unit 6	The unwinnable war on germs |슈퍼박테리아|	18
unit 7	The benefits of bug science |곤충 테크놀로지|	20
unit 8	Patriotism perverts science |과학과 우상|	22
unit 9	Hackers and crackers |해커와 크래커|	24
unit 10	Gender and the courts |성전환증|	26
unit 11	The footprint of food |로컬 푸드|	28
unit 12	A cure for obsessions |강박장애|	30
unit 13	Out for blood |헌혈|	32
unit 14	The year of the Earth |지구의 해|	34
unit 15	Medicine and poison |탈리도마이드|	36
unit 16	Fish story |참치|	38
unit 17	Chips on shoulders, too? |생체 칩|	40
unit 18	Bogus complaints |가짜약|	42
unit 19	UN World Water Day |물의 날|	44
unit 20	Potent pill |비아그라|	46
unit 21	The captive mammoth |매머드|	48
unit 22	Up to the challenge |파란 장미|	50
unit 23	Written in wrinkles |보톡스|	52
unit 24	Astro trash |케슬러 신드롬|	54
unit 25	Food for thought |GMO(유전자변형)|	56
unit 26	Temperamental children |라니냐|	58
unit 27	New materials, old weapons |다마스쿠스 검|	60
unit 28	Shame on Volkswagen |폭스바겐의 사기극을 보며|	62
unit 29	Surveillance has a role |CCTV|	64

unit 30	Joining the space club |우주인|	66
unit 31	Flying pandemics |조류 인플루엔자|	68
unit 32	Mobile gold rush |도시광업|	70
unit 33	Risk management |위험사회|	72
unit 34	Remembering the day before yesterday |기억력|	74
unit 35	Life on Mars |화성|	76
unit 36	Unfounded fears |공포의 문화|	78
unit 37	Bad branding |낙인|	80
unit 38	Chain reactions |연쇄 반응|	82
unit 39	Power paralyzed |뇌졸중|	84
unit 40	Gold rush |우주의 금|	86
unit 41	Breast is best |모유|	88
unit 42	Refugee plants |난민 식물|	90
unit 43	Insane or sane? |정신분석 요법의 귀환|	92
unit 44	Hearing voices |목소리 무늬|	94
unit 45	The silent organ |간|	96
unit 46	Countering counterfeits |위조지폐 방지책|	98
unit 47	History in color |피부색|	100
unit 48	Addicted to speed |속도|	102
unit 49	Man's best friend |사람과 개|	104
unit 50	The capitalist line |포드주의|	106
unit 51	Under the microscope |다이옥신|	108
unit 52	Carbon not always to blame |탄소를 위한 변명|	110
unit 53	Government stuck in a rut |경로 의존성|	112
unit 54	Silence leads to true inspiration |미래를 여는 힘, '깊은 침묵'|	114
unit 55	Weather not an exact science |수치예보|	116
unit 56	A rose by any other name |구인배율|	118
unit 57	Dangers of tunnel vision |터널시야|	120
unit 58	Joining in the game |지구 온난화|	122
unit 59	Corny economics |옥수수 쟁탈전|	124
unit 60	That weather is a killer |기상병|	126
unit 61	Thunderstruck |벼락|	128
unit 62	Going ape |찜통더위|	130
unit 63	Percentage point |1%의 힘|	132
unit 64	A different side to drones |드론|	134
unit 65	A depressing future |우울증|	136

unit 66	An unnatural disaster |인공지진과 자연지진|	138
unit 67	Are electric cars eco-friendly? |전기차가 친환경적이라고?|	140
unit 68	UN tide turns against North |지구촌|	142
unit 69	Dark clouds hang over the peninsula |먹구름|	144
unit 70	Food for thought for a desolate land |바오밥|	146
unit 71	Wrangling with nuclear risk |핵실험|	148
unit 72	A high-tech, brain-shrinking future |진화하는 인간|	150
unit 73	Helping turtles get back on their feet |달려라 거북|	152
unit 74	All that glitters is not 'green' growth |'그린 랜드'|	154
unit 75	Painful patent protection |특허의 역설|	156
unit 76	Humility in the face of pandemics |전염병|	158
unit 77	Modern-day Medusa stings |해파리|	160
unit 78	Lawmakers eclipsed |일식|	162
unit 79	Hats off to Naro's blastoff |우주 개발|	164
unit 80	High hopes for hothouses |비닐하우스|	166
unit 81	X and Y |성별|	168
unit 82	Statistics use and misuse |통계의 사용과 오용|	170
unit 83	Reinventing the wheel |볼펜 · 아이팟 · 신문|	172
unit 84	Sweetening up lethal diseases |프랑스병|	174
unit 85	The life-saving act of washing |팬데믹(pandemic)|	176
unit 86	Seeking signs of aliens in universe |외계인|	178
unit 87	The high cost of the patent wars |복제약|	180
unit 88	The empty seat |빈자리|	182
unit 89	Scarier than genetic diseases |유전질환보다 더 두려운 것|	184
unit 90	Listeria hysteria |리스테리아|	186
unit 91	The joy of leaving your car behind |차 없는 날|	188
unit 92	A critical look at global warming |온난화 회의론|	190
unit 93	Repent, ye carbon emitters |환경 면죄부|	192
unit 94	Undersea calamity omen of greater ills |온난화 부메랑|	194
unit 95	Sky-high dreams |마천루|	196
unit 96	Turn off the lights |빛 공해|	198
unit 97	Political deja vu |기시감|	200
unit 98	Planet's apes in peril |고릴라|	202
unit 99	Kimchi in space |우주식품|	204
unit 100	A cry for the wolf |늑대의 죽음|	206

NEW READING Spectrum

자연과학편

Unit 1 — A dark omen settles over Korea
|일조량 천재지변|

• 지구과학 •

One day of sunshine can make a big difference in May and June. It's time for farmers to finish planting the rice, and for rice plants to grow quickly. Around this time, the amount of sunshine is no less important for plants than the nutrients they get from the soil. If, however, they do not get enough sunshine, their leaves get long and thin, and their chlorophyll levels and cellular tissue mass decrease, along with the plant's ability to photosynthesize. Consequently, there are empty heads of grain and the crop goes bad. And that is how a day can make a difference in the life of a plant.

Changes in the amount of sunshine were said to be the direct cause of the extinction of the dinosaur. A study conducted by a group of international specialists including 41 geologists and paleontologists says that the dinosaur era ended when an asteroid 10 kilometers (6.2 miles) in diameter landed on the Yucatan Peninsula in Mexico some 65 million years ago. Although all living things within a 1,500-kilometer radius perished due to the enormous earthquake and tsunami caused by the collision, the biggest disaster was that the Earth had to go through a

prolonged period of winter because dust and sulfurous elements created by the impact blocked out light. About two-thirds of animals and plants on Earth ultimately disappeared due to a severe shortage of sunshine. The study was published in the March edition of the journal "Science."

When Mount Pinatubo, an active volcano in the Philippines, erupted in 1991, some 20 million tons of sulfur dioxide soared up to the stratosphere some 40 kilometers above the ground. The fine particles of smoke and fog wrapped around the Earth and blocked the sun. For a year after that, the average temperature was 0.58 degrees Celsius lower than it had been in the 10 preceding years. That, too, was a consequence of the decrease in the amount of sunshine.

1. What's the passage about?

   (a) The extinction of the dinosaurs

   (b) The changes in sunshine levels

   (c) The health benefits of sunshine

   (d) Events that change the Earth

2. What can you infer about the Yucatan Peninsula asteroid?

   (a) It caused massive damage and change to the Earth at the time.

   (b) It killed lots of dinosaurs.

   (c) It brought a long summer to the Earth.

   (d) Its effects only lasted a short time before receding.

3. Which of the following is true?

   (a) People were killed in the eruption of Pinatubo and others lost their homes.

   (b) The sulfur dioxide from Mount Pinatubo killed many plants, making them extinct.

   (c) Mount Pinatubo erupts frequently and always causes this temperature change.

   (d) Mount Pinatubo caused the Earth to get a little bit colder.

4. What happens when plants do not get enough sunshine?

   (a) They do not have energy to grow becoming stunted and short.

   (b) They change color and their grain tastes bitter.

   (c) They produce low-grade crops.

   (d) They cannot go through photosynthesis and they die.

Words & Phrases

make a big difference 큰 차이를 가져오다   nutrient n. 영양분, 영양소   chlorophyll n. 엽록소   cellular a. 세포의
photosynthesize v. 광합성하다   head of grain 쭉정이(속이 빈 곡식의 열매)   extinction n. 멸종
paleontologist n. 고생물학자   perish v. 소멸하다   prolonged a. 연장된   sulfurous a. 유황의   erupt v. 분출하다
sulfur dioxide 이산화황   stratosphere n. 성층권   fine a. 미세한   particle n. 입자, 분자   consequence n. 결과, 결말
preceding a. (시간, 장소의) 이전의, 앞선

문장분석

■ Around this time, the amount of sunshine is no less important for plants than the nutrients they get from the soil. → ⟨A is no less 형용사 than B⟩ 구문으로 'A는 B 못지않게 ~하다'는 의미를 지닌다. '못지않게'란 의미를 지니기 때문에 no less 뒤에 오는 형용사는 긍정의 의미를 지닌 형용사가 오게 되고, 반대로 no more라면 뒤에는 부정의 의미를 지닌 형용사가 온다.

Unit 2 Turning yellow dust into gold |'녹색 계열'|

• 환경 •

A poet from the Tang Dynasty (618-907) once wrote that a "sandstorm covered the sun." Tales of the yellow dust storms that blow down from China and spread out over Asia every year date back that far. Today, even the boundaries of the storms' influence have been blurred. Hong Kong, which was thought to be safe from the yellow dust, was recently blanketed with the stuff. The chalky debris regularly makes its way into the Korean Peninsula, out across the Korean Strait and on to Japan. According to Beijing's state-run weather agency, the damage from the yellow dust this year will be the worst of its kind thus far.

The dust originates from three places in China — the southern parts of Xinjiang and Neimenggu (Inner Mongolia), as well as Gansu Province. Of China's 27 provinces and autonomous regions, 21 provinces lie within a "damage zone" as the dusty cloud sweeps across the country. One-fifth of China is desert, and one-fifth of the population suffers the dust's effects. The person credited for exacerbating the dust problem should be Mao Zedong, who ordered trees cut down at random to get iron for arms, created terraced fields by leveling mountains and destroyed grassland to grow grain.

But the yellow dust is only a part of the environmental destruction going on in China. The entire country is overflowing with contaminated water and garbage. To stop the desertification of China's grasslands and slow the movement of the yellow dust, Premier Wen Jiabao recently announced the state's "Green Policy Guidelines." The guidelines, which will apply to all industries, stipulate that forestry and water resources be protected for the next 100 years. The Chinese government has also announced a plan to create windbreak forests and has established special task forces on renewable energy development and climate change.

1. What's the passage about?

    (a) China's position in the world

    (b) The yellow dust problem in China

    (c) The desertification of China

    (d) A new China

2. Which of the following statements is true?

    (a) Wen Jiabao is tackling the environmental problems in China with the Green Policy Guidelines.

    (b) China blames its desert communities for not doing more to help.

    (c) China is continuing to ignore its environmental problems.

    (d) Yellow dust is a fairly recent phenomenon, created from modern environmental problems.

3. What can you infer about yellow dust?

    (a) It is the result of a lack of hygiene.

    (b) It no longer appears in China but in surrounding Asian countries.

    (c) It is the cause of much illness in China.

    (d) Its effects are being felt on an ever widening scale.

4. What made the yellow dust worse?

    (a) Wen Jiabao

    (b) The Chinese farmers

    (c) The actions of Mao Zedong

    (d) Contaminated water and garbage surpluses

Words & Phrases

yellow dust 황사   date back (시점이) 거슬러 올라가다   blur v. 흐리게 하다, 희미하게 하다   blanket v. 완전히 뒤덮다
chalky a. 백악질의   debris n. 파편   state-run a. 국영의   originate v. 기원하다   autonomous a. 자치의
sweep across 전역을 휩쓸다   credit v. ~의 공으로 돌리다   exacerbate v. 악화시키다   level v. 평평하게 하다
contaminated a. 오염된   desertification n. 사막화   windbreak forest n. 방풍림   renewable energy 재생에너지
climate change 기후변화

문장분석

■ <u>Of</u> China's 27 provinces and autonomous regions, 21 provinces lie within a "damage zone" as the dusty cloud sweeps across the country. ➡ 문장을 보다보면 of로 시작하는 경우를 볼 수 있다. 이때 of는 '~중에서'라는 의미를 지니며 out of에서 out이 생략되었다고 생각할 수 있다. 위의 문장에서 원래 21 provinces (out) of China's 27 provinces and autonomous regions가 주어가 되는데 주어가 지나치게 길어져 문장이 가분수가 되는 것을 방지하기 위해 of 이하를 앞으로 도치했다고 생각하면 이해하기 쉽다.

Unit 3 Racing toward a dissonant drive
|전기자동차와 소음|

•기술•

The distinctive feature of Harley-Davidson motorcycles is the roaring sound of their engines. It is said that the cycle of engine combustion is built to match the rhythm of human heartbeats. As soon as the engine is started, it roars up like the heartbeat of a young person in love. Harley-Davidson Motor Company had even applied for a patent for its peculiar engine sound in 1944 but gave up on the idea because of the complicated paperwork. The engine sounds of Harley-Davidson bikes imported to Korea are adjusted to below 80 decibels in accordance with the local law. Therefore, it is not possible to hear the original roaring sound of its engine unless it's readjusted. The manufacturers of Ferrari, one of the most prominent sports-car makers, pay close attention to the roar of an engine as they put their final touches to a vehicle. Sports-car lovers will recognize a Ferrari's deep metallic growl and sigh in envy of the Italian marvel. Race fans will tell you that one of the most exciting moments of Formula One is hearing the deafening vroom of the racing cars.

Of course, engine noise has a practical purpose beyond its romantic charms. Luxury sedans are so quiet that drivers often make the mistake of thinking the engine is off and turning the key again. Jaguar has gotten around this problem by having the car play a tenor C note when the engine is turned on. Electric vehicles, on the other hand, do not make any noise because they run on electric motors, not combustion engines. They do not even make noise from the friction between the car wheels and the surface of the road when traveling at speeds less than 40 kilometers per hour (25 miles per hour). This lack of noise has proved dangerous to both car passengers and pedestrians. Other cars and people crossing the street cannot hear the car coming, so the chances of an accident occurring increases greatly. A quiet engine, once the source of pride of luxury carmakers, has become a safety problem. The United States Congress is even considering forcing carmakers to create vehicles with a minimum noise level.

1. What is the main idea of the passage?

   (a) Sound is important to those who deal with motor vehicles.
   (b) Harley Davidson motorcycles are too loud.
   (c) Congress doesn't want to have electric cars on the road.
   (d) Electric engines are better than regular combustion engines.

2. Which of the following is not untrue according to the passage?

   (a) Jaguar cars play a song in C major when the car starts.
   (b) Electric cars running below 40 kilometers per hour are nearly completely silent.
   (c) Electric car drivers cause many accidents due to their driving.
   (d) The best Formula One cars are made by Ferrari.

3. What is the most likely topic for the next paragraph?

   (a) The practical purposes for making cars sound loud.
   (b) How the car makers deal with cars that make either too much or too little noise.
   (c) The quietest cars in production today.
   (d) The new laws being proposed in Congress for electric cars.

4. What can be inferred from the passage?

   (a) Electric cars are plagued with safety issues.
   (b) There is a great importance to the level or lack of sound vehicles make.
   (c) Car makers will start making cars that are quieter.
   (d) Electric cars are not better than regular motor cars.

Words & Phrases

distinctive a. 독특한   feature n. 특징   roaring a. 으르렁거리는, 굉음의   patent n. 특허   complicated a. 복잡한   paperwork n. 서류 작업   in accordance with ~에 맞춰   growl n. 으르렁거리는 소리   deafening a. 귀청이 터질 듯한   vroom n. (차량이 주행 중 내는 소리인) 부웅   combustion n. 연소   friction n. 마찰   pedestrian n. 보행자

문장분석

■ As soon as the engine is started, it roars up like the heartbeat of a young person in love. ➡ as soon as는 '~하자마자'라는 뜻의 구문으로 뒤에는 절이 온다. 비슷한 뜻을 지니는 the moment, the instant 등으로 대체할 수 있다.

Unit 4 The weird thing about warming
| 글로벌 위어딩 |

· 환경 ·

Former U.S. vice president turned environmental evangelist Al Gore likes to say, "The Earth has a fever." The "fever" of which he speaks is global warming. However, there is considerable skepticism about global warming. For example, when the Northern Hemisphere was hit by abnormal cold waves and extraordinary snow storms last winter, skeptics sarcastically said that climate change is more like global cooling than warming. Jim Inhofe, the senior senator from Oklahoma, slammed Al Gore and urged him to return the Nobel Peace Prize, which Gore had won for raising awareness about climate change. To mock him, Inhofe built an igloo on the National Mall near Capitol Hill and put up a sign saying, "Al Gore's New Home."

Nevertheless, many experts say that the cold waves and snow storms are not unrelated to global warming. As the temperature over the North Pole rises, the jet stream surrounding the cold air has been weakened and the cold air moved southward, bringing unusually cold weather all over Asia, Europe and North America. Meanwhile, as the temperature of the Pacific Ocean increased, the resulting vapor led to great snowstorms when it met the cold wave. Considering that the Southern Hemisphere suffered from extreme heat and heavy rain last winter, it is too rash to call the global warming a scam.

Now the Northern and Southern Hemispheres are experiencing completely opposite ordeals. The Northern Hemisphere is in summer, and many countries are suffering from a severe heat wave, which has resulted in a number of deaths. In contrast, the Southern Hemisphere is experiencing a harsh winter. It would be a misconception to think of global warming as a long, hot summer and a short, warm winter. Also, heavy snow, heavy rain and extreme drought are occurring here and there all at once. Floods, storms and wild fires have become much more frequent and intense.

Now, global warming alone is certainly not enough to explain such comprehensive climate changes. So people have started using the newly coined phrase "global weirding." But no matter what we call it, the cause remains the same: a rapid increase in energy consumption. By 2050, the world's consumption of energy is expected to double. I, for one, cannot begin to fathom how weird the climate will become and what kind of damage the world will suffer. This summer, hundreds of penguins died in Brazil and South Africa, and that should be taken as a significant warning to the world. At this rate, one-fifth of the creatures on Earth are expected to disappear in three decades. Do you think we will manage to remain unharmed even after having explained all of the causes for the "weirding?" Now that would truly be weird.

1. What's the passage mainly about?

    (a) Global warming

    (b) Global cooling

    (c) Al Gore

    (d) Global weirding

2. What can you infer from the creatures on the Earth?

    (a) They are consuming more energy than before, contributing to global weirding.

    (b) Their destruction is already affecting humans.

    (c) They are able to withstand the weird weather.

    (d) They are being adversely affected by the weird weather that is occurring.

3. Choose the false statement from the following.

    (a) Inhofe built an igloo to commemorate Al Gore's efforts.

    (b) Al Gore won the Nobel Peace Prize.

    (c) The cold weather has made people doubt global warming.

    (d) Weather incidents such as floods, storms and wild fires are becoming more frequent.

4. Why did skeptics turn against Al Gore?

    (a) They didn't like the way he put forward his information.

    (b) He lost fans by his lack of scientific knowledge about global warming.

    (c) Some places were hit by extremely cold weather instead of warmer conditions.

    (d) They thought he was just trying to gain political points.

Words & Phrases

evangelist *n.* 복음 전도사   skepticism *n.* 회의론   cold wave 한파   sarcastically *ad.* 비꼬는 투로   senator *n.* 상원의원
mock *v.* 조롱하다   rash *a.* 성급한   ordeal *n.* 시련   heat wave 열파, 혹서   misconception *n.* 오해
comprehensive *a.* 포괄적인, 종합적인   newly coined 새로 만든, 신조어인   weird *a.* 이상한   consumption *n.* 소비
fathom *v.* 헤아리다, 가늠하다   creature *n.* 생명체

문장분석

■ But <u>no matter what</u> we call it, the cause remains the same: a rapid increase in energy consumption.

→ no matter what은 〈no matter + 의문사〉 형태의 양보구문의 접속사로 '무엇을 ~하더라도'의 의미를 지닌다. 즉 what 이하의 내용은 중요하지 않다(no matter)는 뜻을 내포하기 때문에, 우리가 그것을 무엇이라 부르는지는 중요하지 않고 상관없다는 뜻이 된다.

Unit 5 Calming the fires on our planet

|지구가 뿔났다|

• 환경 •

The Earth is bleeding to salve its festering wounds. There is no way to explain this other than to say that we humans have brought these catastrophic changes upon ourselves with our indiscriminate use of fossil fuels and greenhouse gas emissions. In his 2006 documentary "An Inconvenient Truth," the former U.S. Vice President Al Gore emphasized that it will not be possible to revive the Earth if we do not reduce fossil fuel consumption immediately. We need an alternative to oil and gas, synthetics and plastics. That's a fine notion, but we may already be beyond the point where we can solve the problem with a pledge like the one Martin Luther made when he said, "Even if I should learn that the world would end tomorrow, I would still plant this apple tree today."

Scientists are now turning to geo-engineering to manipulate the climate and to temper the effects of global warming. They found a clue following the eruption in 1991 of Mount Pinatubo, an active volcano on Luzon Island in the Philippines. They discovered that the Earth's temperature had decreased because the enormous amount of ash from the volcano created a haze of sulfuric acid droplets, which in turn decreased the amount of sunlight in the area. It has been reported that Intellectual Ventures, a private company claiming to invest in "pure invention," plans to launch "a garden hose to the sky." They intend to spray liquefied sulfur dioxide from a base station, which is fixed by a helium gas-filled balloon, through a 29-km-long hose stretching from the ground to the stratosphere. The firm estimates that construction of the device will take about three years; it has an initial investment of about $150 million and an annual budget of around $100 million. Opposition from environmentalists could prevent the project from being realized. But it's nice to know that people are still trying.

1. What can be inferred from the passage?

   (a) Al Gore doesn't use fossil fuels.

   (b) Other projects are under way to help reverse global warming.

   (c) Intellectual Ventures will solve the Earth problems.

   (d) Environmental groups are preventing progress to save the planet.

2. Which of the following is not true according to the passage?

   (a) Geo-engineering is a possible way to save the planet.

   (b) Nature has given scientists ideas on how to save the planet.

   (c) Fossil fuel and plastics are a cause of global warming.

   (d) Creating eruptions around the world would help lower the Earth's temperature.

3. What according to the passage does sulfur dioxide have to do with global warming?

   (a) It has the ability to block out the sun partially, lowering localized temperatures.

   (b) It causes acid rain to cover an area.

   (c) It has the ability to cause an eruption that will lower surface temperatures.

   (d) It has nothing at all to do with global warming.

4. What would be the best title for the passage?

   (a) Sulfur Dioxide and its value to the Earth

   (b) Al Gore and his beliefs for the future

   (c) When will we stop using fossil fuels

   (d) How to save the world through geo-engineering

Words & Phrases

salve v. (상처 등에) 연고를 바르다   festering wound 곪은 상처   catastrophic a. 대변동의; 파멸의
indiscriminate a. 무차별적인   fossil fuel n. 화석 연료   alternative n. 대안   synthetic n. 합성 물질
pledge n. 약속, 맹세, 서약   turn to ~에 의지하다   geo-engineering 지구공학   manipulate v. 조작하다
temper v. 누그러뜨리다, 완화시키다   eruption n. 분출, 폭발, 분화   sulfuric a. 황의   acid a. 산성의   droplet n. 작은 물방울
liquefied a. 액화된   sulfur dioxide n. 이산화황   stratosphere n. 성층권   environmentalist n. 환경보호론자

문장분석

■ They discovered that the Earth's temperature had decreased because the enormous amount of ash from the volcano created a haze of sulfuric acid droplets, which in turn decreased the amount of sunlight in the area. ➡ in turn은 '차례차례'라는 뜻이 있지만 '결국, 결과적으로'의 뜻으로도 사용된다. 이런 의미로 사용되는 경우 앞에는 'A라는 사건으로 인해 B가 일어난다(A→B)'는 내용이 나오며, in turn 뒤에는 'B로 인해 다시 C라는 사건이 일어난다(B→C)'는 내용이 등장한다. 간단히 다시 표현하면 〈A→B, in turn, B→C〉의 내용이 된다. 이런 흐름을 연결하는 연결어가 in turn이 되는 것이다. 위의 예문을 보면, 화산재(A)가 이산화황 입자(B)를 만들었고, 다시 이 이산화황 입자(B)가 태양광의 양을 줄게 했다(C)는 내용이 된다.

Unit 6 The unwinnable war on germs
|슈퍼박테리아|

• 의학 •

A big fire broke out at a night club in Boston on Nov. 19, 1942. The fate of several hundred victims who were badly burned in the conflagration initially looked grim. Most of the patients developed staphylococcus infections and began passing away, as a treatment for the bacteria had not yet been developed at the time. But doctors began treating the burn victims with something called penicillin, a relatively untested drug that had not yet been refined. The medicine wound up saving the lives of about 200 patients. It was a historic event, marking one of the first times penicillin was used on infected patients.

The history of the human race is filled with constant struggles against bacteria. It should come as no surprise as there are more than 600 trillion germs and microorganisms that live in the human body. The first major victory for humans in the war against bacteria was penicillin. And that was just 70 years ago. Before that there was virtually nothing humans could do to fend off germs. The plague that killed roughly a quarter of Europe's population in the 14th century was the result of bacteria.

But the medical effects of penicillin, which was once called a "miracle drug," did not last long. New germs that destroy and neutralize the molecular structure of penicillin soon appeared. According to medical experts, about 50 percent of staphylococcus bacteria acquired a tolerance to penicillin by the 1940s. That means penicillin surrendered to the counterattack of germs less than 10 years after its introduction. Although humans have responded by developing second and third-generation antibiotics, it is difficult to put an end to the war, as the bacteria continue to mutate into germs that are resistant to the latest drugs.

These types of "super" bacteria are more formidable an enemy than AIDS. In 2005, AIDS claimed the lives of 12,500 people in the United States, while the death toll from methicillin-resistant Staphylococcus aureus hit 18,650. Deaths tied to super bacteria are making headlines. A few days ago, news broke in Japan that nine people died from a super bacteria called acinetobacter baumannii. There are reports that four people died in Korea two years ago from the same germ. And last month, health officials across the world issued warnings about the spread of a new bacteria called NDM-1.

The appearance of super bacteria is in part the result of the abuse of antibiotics. In the war against germs, therefore, we should look to prevent such abuse before releasing new drugs. It's been said that too much of something is as bad as too little. If the human race does not want to return to pre-penicillin era, we should take this to heart.

1. Why according to the passage are people in danger from bacteria yet again?

   (a) They do not take their antibiotics when they should.

   (b) Because the use of antibiotics has been abused allowing resistances to occur.

   (c) Because there is a lack of effective antibiotics available to them.

   (d) Because the new bacteria that exist are not discovered in time to treat properly.

2. What can be inferred from the passage?

   (a) Using drugs to prevent infections is bad.

   (b) There is a large gap between how fast people develop antibiotics and how quickly bacteria mutate.

   (c) Japan will be the epicenter for the next big super bacteria outbreak.

   (d) People are on the verge of suffering a period similar to that of pre-penicillin times.

3. What is meant by the term super bacteria according to the passage?

   (a) A bacteria that is extremely strong physically

   (b) A bacteria that can survive outside of the human body

   (c) A bacteria that has become resistant to all known antibiotics

   (d) A bacteria that has the ability to do several things

4. What is the most likely topic of the next paragraph?

   (a) How Japan dealt with its super bacteria outbreak

   (b) What research and steps are being taken to prevent a return to a pre-penicillin era

   (c) What caused the growth of super bacteria around the world

   (d) How people will deal with super bacteria in the future

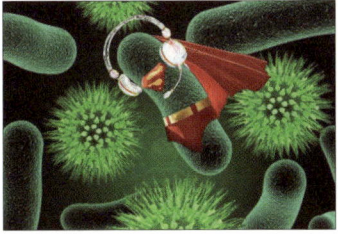

Words & Phrases

break out 발생하다   fate n. 운명   victim n. 희생자   conflagration n. 큰 불, 대화재   grim a. 암울한, 음침한
refine v. 정제하다   wind up 처하게 되다, 마무리 짓다   struggle n. 투쟁, 몸부림, 고군분투   germ n. 세균
microorganism n. 미생물   virtually ad. 사실상   fend off ~의 공격을 막다   plague n. 전염병   neutralize v. 중화하다
molecular a. 분자의   tolerance n. 내성   counterattack n. 반격, 역습   antibiotics n. 항생제
mutate v. 돌연변이를 하다   formidable a. 가공할   claim v. 목숨을 앗아가다   death toll 사망자 수

문장분석

■ The medicine <u>wound up saving</u> the lives of about 200 patients. → wind up은 '어떤 상황에 처하게 하다'는 의미이며, 보통 좋지 않은 상황으로 마무리되는 것을 의미한다. ⟨wind up doing something⟩의 형태로 사용되며 wind up in jail/court처럼 전치사구를 동반하기도 한다. end up도 같은 의미이므로 같은 의미 그룹으로 알아두면 좋다.

Unit 7 The benefits of bug science
|곤충 테크놀로지|

• 기술 •

What material is as light as fluff, as strong as steel and as durable as nylon? It is the spider web. The thickness of a spider silk strand is one-tenth that of a human hair, but when it is pressed together, it is five times stronger than steel of the same thickness. Unlike silkworms, which have been used to make silk for 5,200 years, spiders have not made a contribution for mankind. The amount of silk strands a spider can produce through its lifetime is limited, and because of a tendency of preying on one another, spiders cannot be reared. Instead, it is possible that artificial spider silk will be commercialized soon. A few years ago, a Canadian biotech venture transplanted genes related to spider silk to a goat's mammary glands and successfully extracted the material needed to produce spider silk from the goat milk.

A cockroach carries more than 100 germs and is a target of extermination at home. However, to the robot scientists, it is a creature to model after. They study the cockroach to imitate the stable and speedy movement of its six legs. American scientists made a robot by applying the anatomical structure of the cockroach, and it can travel 50 times its body length in a very short time. This small, multi-legged robot can be equipped with a remote controlled chip to penetrate rooms that cannot be reached by humans. It can also be used for military reconnaissance.

Using and imitating the abilities of insects is called "insect technology." Insects can produce substances that cannot be artificially synthesized and have outstanding senses and functions that cannot be imitated by humans. With over 1 million varieties living on earth, scientists claim that insects are a great resource.

According to foreign news last week, a U.S. national research institute is conducting a study, training honeybees with a highly developed olfactory sense for explosive detection. The U.S. Forces have already used the honeybees in actual battles of the Iraq War to detect mines and bombs. Japan turned to the insect industry early and developed the technology to apply the coloring structure of the jewel beetle, which boasts seven brilliant colors including gold and green, on cars and other metallic surfaces. It is an environment-friendly coloring technology.

1. What is insect technology?

   (a) Using insects in the U.S. military

   (b) The ways that insects use objects for their own benefit

   (c) The technological implications of testing insects for vaccines

   (d) Artificially creating the skills and expertise that insect possess for human use

2. Which of the following is false about the cockroach?

   (a) The cockroach has been used to create a robot.

   (b) Scientists studied the cockroach to find out how it lives for so long.

   (c) The speed of a cockroach is admirable.

   (d) The cockroach robot is able to enter places that humans cannot.

3. What can you infer about spider silk?

   (a) It is of much inferior quality to silkworm silk.

   (b) It will be as popular as silkworm silk soon.

   (c) It has not been used commercially because it is expensive to farm.

   (d) It is frequently destroyed when the spiders fight each other.

4. Which of the following is not an example of insect technology in use?

   (a) The speed and stability of a cockroach have been used to make a robot.

   (b) A goat can make spider silk with its milk.

   (c) Japan uses the coloring of jewel beetles to color metal.

   (d) The US uses the sense of smell of honeybees to search for mines and bombs.

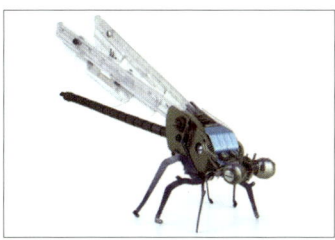

Words & Phrases

fluff n. 보풀   durable a. 내구성이 좋은   strand n. 가닥, 실, 섬유   silkworm n. 누에   tendency n. 경향
prey v. 잡아먹다   rear v. 기르다   artificial a. 인공의   transplant v. 옮겨 심다, 이식하다   mammary gland 젖샘
extract v. 추출하다   cockroach n. 바퀴벌레   extermination n. 박멸   anatomical a. 해부의   penetrate v. 침투하다
reconnaissance n. 정찰   substance n. 물질   synthesize v. 합성하다   olfactory a. 후각의   detect v. 탐지하다
mine n. 광산, (광산의) 갱

문장분석

■ What material is as light as fluff, as strong as steel and as durable as nylon? → as ~ as는 두 대상의 특성을 동일하게 비교하는 원급 비교이다. 〈A is as 형용사 as B〉로 사용되며 A와 B가 동일하게 형용사의 성질을 지닌다는 뜻이다. 원급 비교이므로 as 사이에 들어오는 형용사는 비교급이나 최상급이 아닌 원급을 사용해야 한다.

Unit 8 Patriotism perverts science |과학과 우상|

• 과학철학 •

The principle behind the atomic bomb was first discovered in Germany during the days of Hitler. Chemist Otto Hahn reported that slowly bombarding uranium with neutrons creates an enormous amount of energy along with nuclear fission. However, he refused Nazi orders to create an atomic bomb. Hahn poured his energy into developing a peaceful nuclear reactor. After Germany lost the war, Hahn was confined in a P.O.W. camp by allied forces. The chief of the camp was nervous that Hahn might commit suicide at the news that an atomic bomb had been dropped.

Hungarian scientist Leo Szilard had a unique love for his home country. When Hitler invaded Hungary, Szilard voluntarily joined the Manhattan Project. On July 16, 1945, a truck driver who was crossing the Nevada desert reported, "All of a sudden a thousand suns rose above the ground and disappeared." When Szilard learned the power of atomic bombs, he opposed them. Szilard told his fellow scientist Enrico Fermi, "Today will be written as the saddest day in history."

"Is science a friend or enemy of mankind?" This is the question British chemist Max Ferdinand Perutz asked the world. Fritz Haber is the person who synthesized ammonia from nitrogen and set mankind free from the fright of hunger by developing nitrogenous fertilizer. However, this German was also the person who developed poison gas, which put the allied forces in great fear during the First World War. After Germany lost the war, he was obsessed by research to extract gold from sea water in hopes of helping his country pay war compensation. Haber also met a miserable death after the Nazis branded him a "Jewish scientist."

In a private girls high school in Hiroshima Japan, there is a statue of three girls. It is a memorial to the people who died in the atomic attack. Einstein's "$E=mc^2$" formula is carved on the chest of one of the girls. It wordlessly warns how humanity should approach science. Now the stem cell debate has become a social issue. We should first calm down. Whenever science becomes an idol, it can turn into a deadly weapon.

1. What is the purpose of this passage?

   (a) To explain why there is a statue of 3 girls in Japan
   (b) To show how the Manhattan project was an international effort
   (c) To explain the necessity of creating nuclear fission
   (d) To illustrate the negative side effects of scientific advancement

2. What can be inferred from the passage?

   (a) Nuclear fission is the greatest invention of the last century.
   (b) Not all advances in science and technology are positive ones.
   (c) Einstein is held responsible for the atomic bomb attacks on Japan.
   (d) The allied forces would have won the war just as quickly without the atomic bomb.

3. Why should people be wary of science according to the passage?

   (a) It can be hazardous to your health.
   (b) It is a thankless job where you are blamed for the applications of your work by others.
   (c) It sometimes has results that are not desired or enjoyable.
   (d) It can cost you your life.

4. What would be the best title for this passage?

   (a) The negative side of science
   (b) Einstein and the atomic bomb
   (c) Why nuclear fission is bad
   (d) The best places to do research

Words & Phrases

bombard v. 폭격하다   uranium n. 우라늄   neutron n. 중성자   nuclear fission 핵분열   pour v. 쏟아 붓다
confine v. 구금하다   P.O.W. n. 전쟁포로 (= prisoner of war)   voluntarily ad. 자발적으로   synthesize v. 합성하다
ammonia n. 암모니아   nitrogenous a. 질소의   fertilizer n. 비료   extract v. 추출하다   war compensation 전쟁 배상금
miserable a. 비참한   brand A as B A를 B라고 낙인찍다   statue n. 동상   idol n. 우상   deadly a. 치명적인

문장분석

■ Fritz Haber is the person who synthesized ammonia from nitrogen and set mankind free from the fright of hunger by developing nitrogenous fertilizer. → 〈by -ing〉라는 구문은 '~함으로써'의 의미를 지닌다. 즉 'by 이하의 내용을 실행해서 어떤 일을 수행하다'는 뜻이기 때문에 by 이하의 내용이 원인이나 이유가 되며 by 앞의 내용은 결과가 된다. 위의 예문을 보면 질소 비료를 개발한 것이 원인이고, 이를 통해 인류를 기아의 공포에서 해방한 것이 결과가 된다.

Unit 9 Hackers and crackers
|해커와 크래커|

•기술•

ENIAC, or the "Electronic Numerical Integrator and Computer" was developed in 1946 in the United States and is generally thought to be the first computer in the world. It actually was not the first of its kind. The British mathematician Alan Turing rightfully deserves the honor of the visionary who brought about the digital society. Mr. Turing was a member of the British intelligence team Ultra, which decrypted the Enigma ciphers that Germany used during World War II.

He developed an electronic computing device called "Colossus" that could read Enigma-encrypted messages, which could once be decrypted mechanically but which then were improved to the point that mechanical devices were simply too slow to crack in an acceptable length of time.

The Colossus machine was fast and accurate, and the Allies went to great pains to disguise the fact that they were reading the German's military traffic, even to the point of pretending they were not aware of bombing raids planned and executed by the Nazis.

The Ultra team was disbanded after the war, and all the machines and their blueprints were destroyed. Mr. Turing got no recognition for his accomplishments and had to watch ENIAC bask in its electronic glory despite having appeared two years after Colossus.

It might have been a little comfort for Mr. Turing had he known that he would be acknowledged as the world's first hacker. Ever since Mr. Turing's invention, computers have fascinated creative brains around the world. Some programmers enjoy making software purely for the fun of it. They came to be known as "hackers" in 1961 when the Massachusetts Institute of Technology purchased the second-generation computer PDP-1. Members of the Tech Model Railroad Club, a student organization studying train systems at MIT, secretly played with school computers at night. They enjoyed creating the programming tools, environments and related jargon that we use today.

1. What can be inferred from this passage?

   (a) Colossus was responsible for winning the second World War.
   (b) Discoveries are not always going to make the person responsible for them famous.
   (c) Computers like Colossus are very common in today's society.
   (d) MIT has the best hackers in the world.

2. What is another way of saying the word "jargon" as it is used in the passage?

   (a) Specific written and spoken language
   (b) Skills
   (c) Specialized symbols
   (d) Words

3. Which of the following is not true according to the passage?

   (a) The Germans were unaware of the existence of Colossus.
   (b) Students at MIT made a lot of money creating the languages that are used today.
   (c) Computers are capable of performing mathematical calculations faster than people.
   (d) MIT had some of the first hackers as students.

Words & Phrases

rightfully *ad.* 당연히   deserve *v.* ~할 만하다, ~받을 가치가 있다   decrypt *v.* (암호문을) 해독하다   enigma *n.* 수수께끼
cipher *n.* 암호   Colossus *n.* 콜로서스(세계 최초의 프로그래밍 가능 전자 계산기)   mechanically *ad.* 기계적으로
to the point that ~할 정도까지   disguise *v.* 위장하다   pretend *v.* ~인 체하다   execute *v.* 실행하다   disband *v.* 해체하다
blueprint *n.* 설계도, 청사진   bask in (관심·칭찬 등을) 누리다, (특히 햇볕을 기분 좋게) 쪼이다   comfort *n.* 위안
come to ~하게 되다   jargon *n.* 전문용어

문장분석

■ He developed an electronic computing device called "Colossus" that could read Enigma-encrypted messages, which could once be decrypted mechanically but which then were improved <u>to the point that</u> mechanical devices were simply too slow to crack in an acceptable length of time. ➡ to the point

구문은 〈to the point that 절〉 혹은 〈to the point of something〉의 형태로 사용되며, '~할 정도까지'의 뜻을 지닌다. 예문에서는 Enigma를 이용한 암호문이 향상되었다고 나오는데, 어느 정도까지 향상되었냐면 that 이하의 내용까지라고 설명하고 있다. 따라서 '~할 정도로, ~할 정도까지' 향상되었다고 해석하면 된다.

Unit 10 | Gender and the courts
|성전환증|

• 의학 •

The medical world began to pay academic attention to transsexualism in the 1950s. George Jorgenson, then 26, who was suffering from a gender identity crisis, became one of the first people to have sex change surgery in 1952. A Roman emperor named Elagabalus was said to have had an operation to cut his genitalia and became a woman, but that cannot be confirmed. Starting at Johns Hopkins University after it set up a sexual disorder clinic, sex change operations were being performed around the world by the 1960s. In 1994, the World Health Organization defined transsexuals as "those who have a desire to live and be accepted as a member of the opposite sex, usually accompanied by a sense of discomfort with, or inappropriateness of, one's anatomical sex, and a wish to have surgery and hormonal treatment to make one's body as congruent as possible with one's preferred sex."

Due to their deep-rooted Confucian tradition, Koreans used to look at transsexuals with reproachful eyes. Depending on the tendency of a court, suits pursued by transsexuals to change their genders were treated differently. A transsexual in her 50s who finally went through a sex change operation was told by a court that she deserved to live a decent life as a human being and was allowed to change her gender on the census registry. But some religious and legal groups criticized the court for playing God by determining the gender of human beings.

1. What can be inferred from the passage?

    (a) Transsexuals are now a more accepted social sector of society than in the past.

    (b) Transsexuals are not a naturally occurring group in society.

    (c) People have only recently really desired to change their sexual orientation.

    (d) Confucianism disagrees with the concept of transsexuals.

2. Which of the following is incorrect according to the passage?

    (a) Some courts in Korea allow sex change and registry changes.

    (b) The W.H.O. recognizes transsexuals as a group.

    (c) Transsexualism is an abomination against God.

    (d) Sex change operations are now much more common place than in the 50's or 60's.

3. What is the next paragraph most likely to be about?

    (a) Korean courts and how they feel about sex change

    (b) The process of having a sex change operation

    (c) Why some groups disagree with the courts being involved in the issue of sex and gender

    (d) Where the desire to become a transsexual comes from

Words & Phrases

transsexualism *n.* 성전환   gender *n.* 성별   identity crisis 정체성 위기   emperor *n.* 황제   genitalia *n.* 성기
accompany *v.* 동반하다   inappropriateness *n.* 부적절함   anatomical *a.* 해부학의   congruent *a.* 일치하는; 적합한
reproachful *a.* 꾸짖는, 비난하는   go through a operation 수술을 받다   decent *a.* 괜찮은, 품위 있는
census registry 호적   play God 신처럼 행동하다   abomination *n.* 혐오

문장분석

■ Due to their deep-rooted Confucian tradition, Koreans used to look at transsexuals with reproachful eyes. ➡ due to는 '~때문에'라는 뜻으로, 뒤에어 이유에 해당하는 명사가 등장한다. 동의어로는 because of, owing to, thanks to 등이 있으며, 뒤에 절이 나오기 위해서는 〈due to the fact that 절〉 형식으로 사용할 수 있다.

Unit 11 The footprint of food |로컬 푸드|

• 환경 •

The rate of conversion of rainforests to farmland and pastures, which once remained stable at 7 percent 300 years ago, has seen a remarkable increase to more than 40 percent in recent years. With over 40 percent of the Earth's rainforests already destroyed, the capacity for absorbing greenhouse gases is decreasing. The transport of foods over hundreds or thousands of kilometers also poses a significant threat to the environment by the amount of greenhouse gases emitted from shipping. Cod caught off Norway is shipped to China to be turned into fillets, and then shipped back to Norway for sale. It costs only $0.50 in China, much cheaper than $2.99 per kilogram in Europe.

In this process, there are no binding regulations on greenhouse gas emissions. Under the 1944 Convention on International Civil Aviation, commonly known as the Chicago Convention, there is no simple way to impose levies on fuel consumed in carrying commercial cargo on various international routes by air or by water. Environmentalists are insisting that governments should take regulative measures by imposing relevant taxes on fuels or preventing emission of greenhouse gases. The European Union plans that all cargo-carrying commercial aircraft coming to and from Europe be required to purchase the right to emit greenhouse gases.

Some people are also insisting that consumers should have the final say, rather than regulations. One way is to indicate each product's "greenhouse footprint" on its label showing the total amount of greenhouse gases emitted in the process of producing and transporting the product. Currently, people are initiating local food movements in many places as collaborative efforts to build more locally based, self-reliant food economies. It is gaining widespread popularity among consumers. For example, the "100 Mile Diet" movement in New York is spreading rapidly. People only buy foods produced within 100 miles from their home, at least during harvest season.

1. What's the main idea of the passage?

   (a) The steady rise in greenhouse emissions by everyone
   (b) The greenhouse emissions from transportation around the world
   (c) The lack of concern of the airline companies over greenhouse gases
   (d) The efforts of researchers to find a solution to the crisis
   (e) The fight between businessmen and environmentalists

2. Which of the following is true?

   (a) The 100 Mile Diet is an attempt by consumers to reduce greenhouse emissions from transporting food.
   (b) The idea of the 100 Mile Diet is rapidly spreading throughout the U.S. as consumers become more aware of the environmental problems.
   (c) Environmentalists want all commercial aircraft to be grounded immediately.
   (d) The European Union has had success with a program that forces airline companies to buy permission to fly.
   (e) Our greenhouse emissions are decreasing because the rainforests are disappearing.

3. What can you infer about the Norwegian cod fillets?

   (a) They have a large greenhouse footprint.
   (b) They are considered the tastiest in the world.
   (c) They are too expensive for the average person to buy.
   (d) They lose their freshness when traveling.
   (e) Chinese people love to consume Norwegian cod fillets.

4. Which of the following is the best paraphrase of the meaning of greenhouse footprint?

   (a) The method by which food is transported around the world
   (b) The movement to make food consumption local once again
   (c) The number of miles covered when a product is flown to another country
   (d) The place where the product originally comes from
   (e) The quantity of greenhouse gases that are produced when something is transported

Words & Phrases

conversion *n.* 변환, 전환   pasture *n.* 목초지   rainforest *n.* 열대우림   greenhouse gas *n.* 온실가스   transport *n.* 수송
pose a threat to ~에 위협을 주다   emit *v.* 방출하다   cod *n.* 대구   fillet *n.* (육류·생선의 뼈를 발라내고 저민) 살코기
binding regulation 구속력 있는 규제   aviation *n.* 비행, 항공   convention *n.* 규약, 조약   impose levy 세금을 부과하다
take regulative measures 규제적 조치를 취하다   relevant *a.* 관련 있는, 연관된   emission *n.* 방출   initiate *v.* 시작하다
movement *n.* 운동   collaborative *a.* 협동의, 협력의   gain popularity 인기를 얻다

문장분석

■ Environmentalists are <u>insisting</u> that governments <u>should take</u> regulative measures by imposing relevant taxes on fuels or preventing emission of greenhouse gases. ➡ 〈insist/demand/require/recommend that + 주어 + (should) 동사원형〉 구문으로 의미상 that 절 이하의 동사에는 should가 사용되어야 한다. 의미상으로 ~해야 한다고 주장하거나, 요구하거나 추천하고 있기 때문이다. 그리고 이때 should는 생략 가능하다.

Unit 12 A cure for obsessions
|강박장애|

• 의학 •

What happens in your brain when you cannot feel at ease unless you take a certain action? Scholars claim that those suffering from obsessive-compulsive disorder have an abnormally faster metabolism in the brain, which means that energy is consumed at an excessively high rate by the brain. According to the theory, people with obsessive-compulsive disorder have relatively smaller brains than other controlled groups of people.

Dr. Judith Rapoport of the U.S. National Institute of Mental Health says that obsessive-compulsive disorder is characterized by a feeling of relief when ceaselessly repeating a certain action over and over again. The disorder can be categorized into three types: checkers, exacters and washers. The checkers constantly repeat the same action to confirm something while the exacters spend time keeping things arranged in a certain symmetrical pattern. The washers believe that they have to wash themselves repeatedly and clean things around them. Dr. Rapoport said that obsessive-compulsive disorder distorts one's perception of reality, and it is almost like magic.

When disturbed by the condition, the brain gets lost and wanders about. Once the brain operates abnormally, it leads to a series of strange behaviors. Brain malfunction can not only harm the individual but also negatively influence those around him and the organization he belongs to.

The problem is that a serious case of obsessive-compulsive disorder requires long-term treatment. There is a risk that a patient might fall into complete despair. They are tremendously frustrated and tormented when they cannot achieve certain tasks that might be easy for other people because of their mental condition. Combined with social criticism and derision, they can even feel psychological devastation. The cure for obsessive-compulsive disorder is to help the patients get over the object of obsession and build understanding, tolerance, compassion and mercy. However, it is not easy to recover a brain reduced by obsessive-compulsive disorder, and a patient might perceive it as a failure or surrender.

1. What's the main topic of the passage?

   (a) Various treatments for obsessive-compulsive disorder
   (b) New research into mental health
   (c) What happens to obsessive-compulsive disorder sufferers
   (d) How we can cure obsessive-compulsive disorder

2. Which best paraphrases the opinion of Dr. Rapoport?

   (a) You need a magic cure to recover from obsessive-compulsive disorder.
   (b) Obsessive-compulsive disorder cannot be cured.
   (c) Obsessive-compulsive disorder sufferers are strange people to be around.
   (d) Sufferers perceive a different kind of reality to everyone else.

3. What can you infer about sufferers?

   (a) They often are on the receiving end of some negative societal attitudes.
   (b) They lose large periods of time when they don't know what they were doing.
   (c) They find it hard to maintain relationships.
   (d) They are cured by taking medication.

4. Which of the following is a symptom of someone with obsessive-compulsive disorder?

   (a) Washing hands or parts of the body over and over again, even when they appear clean.
   (b) Someone who likes to say the same thing to the same person repeatedly.
   (c) Being competitive to the point that it causes problems in personal relationships.
   (d) Eating too much because the sufferer feels depressed.

Words & Phrases

feel at ease 편안함을 느끼다   obsessive-compulsive disorder *n.* 강박장애   metabolism *n.* 신진대사
characterize *v.* 특징짓다   ceaselessly *ad.* 쉴 새 없이   symmetrical *a.* 대칭의   distort *v.* 왜곡하다   perception *n.* 지각
disturb *v.* 방해하다, 건드리다   wander *v.* 배회하다   malfunction *n.* 고장   tremendously *ad.* 엄청나게
frustrated *a.* 좌절감을 느끼는   tormented *a.* 고통 받는   derision *n.* 조롱, 조소   devastation *n.* 황폐   tolerance *n.* 관용
compassion *n.* 동정   mercy *n.* 자비   surrender *n.* 굴복

문장분석

■ The cure for obsessive-compulsive disorder is to help the patients get over the object of obsession and build understanding, tolerance, compassion and mercy. ➡ 〈help + 목적어 + (to) 동사원형〉 구문으로 help 뒤에 오는 동사는 원형부정사, to부정사 모두 가능하다. 따라서 to가 상황에 따라 생략되어 표현된다. 위 예문에서는 help 뒤에 이어지는 동사로 get over와 build가 병렬 구조로 배열되어 나타나고 있다.

Unit 13 Out for blood |헌혈|

William Harvey is an English physician who discovered the true nature of the circulation of blood. He also discovered that the heart functions as a pump. He also realized, in 1628, the fact that blood circulates inside the human body. He rejected Galen's theory, which had dominated medical theory for the previous 1,500 years. Claudius Galenus was a physician to the Roman Emperor Marcus Aurelius. He believed the liver produced blood, which sent it to the outer parts of the body to form flesh. He also said blood leaks out of the body in the form of human waste, such as sweat and urine.

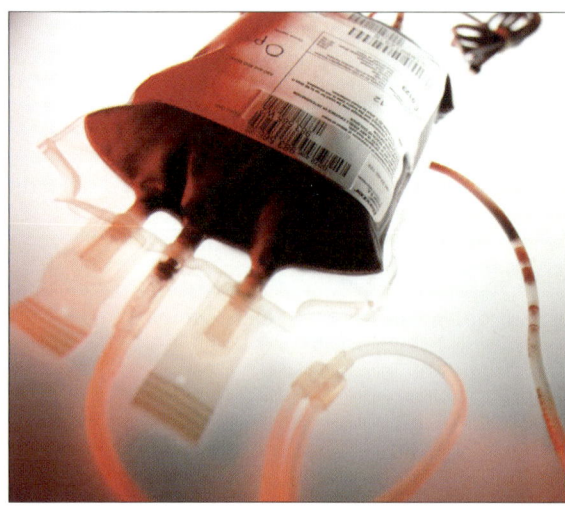

By a close shave, Harvey's theory about "blood circulation" was formally recognized as an established theory, but it took another 190 years for a successful blood transfusion to occur. The British obstetrician James Blundell performed the first successful transfusion of blood to a patient to treat a hemorrhage. In 1818, he succeeded in saving a patient by transfusing 400cc of blood. At that time, blood transfusions were conducted with the artery of the blood donor directly linked to the patient's vein to prevent the blood from solidifying.

Modern medicine, which has succeeded in developing an artificial heart, has not yet been able to create the perfect artificial blood. Artificial blood that carries oxygen produces serious side effects, such as high blood pressure. We cannot receive artificial blood which carries waste and immunity. People who need a blood transfusion have to anxiously wait for blood to be donated. However, blood only can be preserved three weeks, on average, and never more than 35 days.

1. What's the passage mainly about?

   (a) The distinguished career of James Blundell

   (b) The discovery of blood circulation

   (c) The dangers of receiving a blood transfusion

   (d) The fight to replace Galen's theory

2. What can be inferred about William Harvey?

   (a) Harvey's theory has never been fully accepted by the medical community.

   (b) Harvey made his discovery while giving the first successful blood transfusion.

   (c) He worked hard all his life and finally discovered the truth about blood circulation shortly before his death.

   (d) He was brave to speak out against Galen's theory which was largely accepted.

3. Which of the following is true?

   (a) More than one of Galenus' medical theories were wrong.

   (b) Harvey's theory was recognised immediately by the medical world.

   (c) Blundell performed a blood transfusion on himself when he suffered a hemorrhage.

   (d) Blood transfusion are still today sometimes performed by directly linking the veins of two patients.

4. What has still defied modern medicine?

   (a) Modern medicine has still not been able to perform a successful blood transfusion.

   (b) Modern medicine has not yet found the technology to create artificial blood.

   (c) It has not discovered a way to remove waste from the body.

   (d) It has not created an artificial heart that works.

Words & Phrases

physician n. 내과 의사   nature n. 본질   circulation n. 순환   reject v. 퇴짜 놓다, 버리다   theory n. 이론
dominate v. 지배하다   liver n. 간   leak v. 새다, 유출되다   urine n. 소변   by a close shave 간신히, 아슬아슬하게
established theory 정설   blood transfusion n. 수혈   obstetrician n. 산과 의사   hemorrhage n. 출혈
artery n. 동맥   blood donor n. 혈액 기증자   vein n. 정맥   solidify v. 응고하다   immunity n. 면역
preserve v. 보존하다

문장분석

■ It took another 190 years for a successful blood transfusion to occur. → ⟨it takes + (사람) + 시간 + to do something⟩ 혹은 ⟨it takes + 시간 + (for 사람) + to do something⟩ 구문으로 'to 이하를 하는 데 ~만큼의 시간이 걸리다'는 뜻이다. 이때 it 은 가주어이고 to부정사가 진주어가 된다. 그리고 take 뒤에 오는 목적어인 '사람'은 종종 생략되거나 to부정사 앞에 for와 함께 사용되어 가주어를 이끈다.

Unit 14 The year of the Earth |지구의 해|

• 환경 •

Some say this planet should not be called Earth, but Water. The oceans are 360 million km² (95 million acre) wide, and account for two-thirds of the entire surface of the planet. The average depth of the ocean is about 3,800 meters (12,500 feet). Until very recently, people did not know a lot about the sea. The crew of the HMS Challenger, a British oceanic research ship, was surprised to learn, when they extended a rope in the Pacific Ocean on missions between 1872 and 1875 to calculate ocean depth, that the bottom of the sea was more than 8 kilometers from the surface. This wide and deep sea is now facing multiple threats. The inland seas and gulfs, in particular, which are surrounded by lands are turning into dead seas without any oxygen due to severe levels of pollution.

The sky is wider and higher than the ocean. The troposphere, the lowest atmospheric layer of the Earth and the determinant of the weather, reaches 10 to 15 kilometers on average, although it expands or decreases based on the altitude and seasonal changes. On top of the troposphere lies the stratosphere. But to humans, that wide sky seems claustrophobic. That's why they made a hole in the stratosphere, even though the decrease in the use of freon gas means it might be refilled within 50 years. Carbon dioxide has increased its occupancy from 0.028 percent to 0.038 percent of the Earth's atmosphere over the last two centuries, enough to cause the greenhouse effect that is warming the world.

The year 2008 is the year of the planet Earth, as declared by the United Nations. The Village Earth, which witnessed the tsunami that hit Southeast Asia in December 2004, decided to memorialize this year for studies about the Earth to prevent natural disasters and tie scientists' research to actual policies. However much we study the Earth, though, we might not be able to maintain the health of the planet unless we curb human desires, which are higher than the sky and wider than the sea. Just as the UN Development Program warned in November, even nine planets Earth would not be able to harbor humankind if all 6.5 billion people consumed energy and emitted greenhouse gases like the people in developed countries.

1. What's the main idea of the passage?
   (a) How pollution of the oceans is causing the human population to gradually decrease
   (b) The rivalry between the oceans' scientists and the scientists of the atmosphere
   (c) The progress the scientists of the world are making to cure the problem
   (d) To describe how the planet is still heading towards crisis, despite some attempts to spread awareness of the problems
   (e) The extent of human desire for consumption and material things

2. What can you infer about Earth?
   (a) People on Earth still have little desire to help it and turn the problem around.
   (b) It is being destroyed mainly by the developed countries and their way of living.
   (c) A small number of people will survive the eventual destruction of Earth's atmosphere.
   (d) If pollution continues, Earth will experience more and more natural disasters.
   (e) Earth has a special ability to save itself, so all is not lost.

3. Choose the incorrect one from the following.
   (a) The level of carbon dioxide in the atmosphere is increasing.
   (b) Pollution of the oceans is having a deadly affect on those creatures that live off the oceans.
   (c) The natural world is winning the battle because the size of the atmosphere and the oceans is smaller than human desire.
   (d) If developing countries were able to live like developed countries the world would surely be doomed.
   (e) Human learned the extent of the oceans and the intricate part they play in the health of the planet.

4. Which of the following best paraphrases how we can save the world?
   (a) Saving the Earth requires not study alone but also looking to ourselves to change the way we live.
   (b) By financially supporting scientists in their studies, we can produce quicker results.
   (c) By learning why and how natural disasters take place, they become more easily preventable in the future.
   (d) Scientists need to start suggesting policies for the future instead of merely doing research.
   (e) Humans have to learn about the Earth first in order to fully understand what they must do to change.

Words & Phrases

planet n. 행성   account for ~을 차지하다   face v. 직면하다   threat n. 위협   inland n. 내륙   gulf n. 만
oxygen n. 산소   pollution n. 오염   troposphere n. 대류권   atmospheric a. 대기의   determinant n. 결정 인자
altitude n. 고도   stratosphere n. 성층권   claustrophobic a. 밀실 공포의   occupancy n. 점유, 점령   tsunami n. 쓰나미
curb v. 억제하다, 구속하다, 제한하다   harbor v. 품다, 숨기다   emit v. 방출하다

문장분석

■ However much we study the Earth, though, we might not be able to maintain the health of the planet unless we curb human desires, which are higher than the sky and wider than the sea. ➡ ⟨however + 형용사/부사 + 주어 + 동사⟩ 구문으로 양보절을 이끈다. 이때 however는 'no matter how'로 대체해서 표현할 수 있다. 예문의 양보절을 해석하면, '우리가 아무리 지구를 연구한다 하더라도', 혹은 '우리가 얼마나 많이 (much) 지구를 연구한다고 하더라도 그건 중요한 것이 아닌'이라는 의미가 된다.

Unit 15 Medicine and poison |탈리도마이드|

Thalidomide, which caused horrific birth defects in children whose mothers took the drug in the 1960s, seemed likely to disappear permanently due to its catastrophic side effects. However, it has returned from the grave. Recently a medical journal in New England published an article saying that thalidomide can effectively treat chronic lymphocytic leukemia. Medicine can be poison, and poison can be medicine.

Thalidomide was first sold in Germany in 1958, initially as a sedative. Soon, however, it was sold as an antiemetic for pregnant women to relieve morning sickness. Until 1961 pregnant women in 48 countries had taken this medicine. But two to three out of every 10 children of women who took the pill early in pregnancy were born with severe defects, including missing limbs. These "Thalidomide babies" numbered about 10,000.

The front page headline of the Washington Post on July 15, 1962 read: "'Heroine' of FDA Keeps Bad Drug Off of Market." A young doctor named Francis Kelsey, who had been hired by the FDA just two years earlier, did not approve thalidomide for sale in the U.S. due to lack of sufficient documentation. As a result, the U.S. suffered very few cases from the drug, and the FDA was praised worldwide.

1. What's the idea of the passage?

    (a) Who is responsible for thalidomide babies

    (b) The assimilation of thalidomide babies into society

    (c) How to prevent the re-emergence of thalidomide babies

    (d) The case of thalidomide babies in the 1960s and why it may return

2. Which of the following paraphrases the quote, "medicine can be poison, and poison can be medicine"?

    (a) The properties of medicine can change from safe to harmful very quickly.

    (b) Medicine, while making us better in one way, can make us sicker in another way.

    (c) A medicine can be a poison to one person and a cure to another.

    (d) Taken in the wrong dosage, medicine can be poison.

3. What can you infer about thalidomide babies?

    (a) Their defects arose directly from consumption of the drug by their mothers and for no other reason.

    (b) They lived the same kind of lives as any other child at the time.

    (c) The era of thalidomide babies will never return again.

    (d) The babies that were affected received huge compensation for the mistake.

Words & Phrases

birth defect 선천적 결손증   permanently *ad.* 영구적으로   catastrophic *a.* 파국적인, 파멸의   effectively *ad.* 효과적으로
chronic *a.* 만성의   lymphocytic *a.* 림프구성의   leukemia *n.* 백혈병   initially *ad.* 처음에는   sedative *n.* 진정제
antiemetic *n.* 구토 방지제   relieve *v.* 완화하다   limb *n.* 팔이나 다리   sufficient *a.* 충분한

문장분석

■ But two to three <u>out of every</u> 10 children of women who took the pill early in pregnancy were born with severe defects, including missing limbs. ➡ 〈숫자 + out of (every) 숫자 + 명사〉 형태로 사용되며, '몇 명 중에서 몇 명'이 해당한다는 뜻을 지닌다. every가 들어가면 비율을 지닌다. 예를 들어 예문처럼 10명의 아이 중 2~3명이라고 하면 아이들 중 20~30%에 해당하기 때문이다.

unit 15 탈리도마이드

Unit 16 Fish story |참치|

There are about 20 different types of tuna — including bluefin tuna, bigeye tuna and yellowfin tuna. Even bluefin tuna has two categorizations: Northern bluefin tuna and southern bluefin tuna, depending on which hemisphere, north or south, they live in. North Atlantic bluefin tuna can reach up to 3 meters, or 10 feet, in length, also weighing 560 kilograms (1,230 pounds). Every year, more than 4 million tons of tuna are caught in the oceans and seas. Japan, the world's largest consumer of tuna, eats one-quarter of the total catch. Korea also consumes 250,000 to 300,000 tons of tuna each year. Japan consumes 480,000 tons of bluefin and bigeye tuna. The United States eats from 30,000 to 50,000 tons.

Tuna is a food high in omega-3 fatty acids and selenium, which can help prevent heart disease and colon cancer. Backed by people's growing awareness of a healthy lifestyle, there has been a growing demand for tuna. Greenpeace, the world's most effective environmental activist group, maintains that bluefin tuna will most likely be extinct sometime in the next five years. As the resource becomes depleted, the price of one bluefin tuna has soared, equivalent to the purchase price of a compact car in Japan. Japan is making big efforts to replace the sushi ingredient with other ones.

Recently, The New York Times wrote an article saying that high levels of mercury had been found in tuna sushi sold in Manhattan stores and restaurants. If you consume just six pieces of tuna sushi per week, your blood mercury levels could easily exceed U.S. government safety limits. The Food Standards Agency of the United Kingdom has already recommended that pregnant women avoid eating tuna. The issue seems to be a warning to humans: If people eat too much tuna, it could ruin both their health and the ecosystem, no matter how good it tastes.

1. What's the passage mainly about?

   (a) The financial side of the fish market

   (b) The argument for eating more sushi

   (c) The many species of tuna

   (d) The advantages and disadvantages of consuming tuna

2. What's the danger of eating too much tuna sushi?

   (a) You body's mercury levels will soar to a dangerous level.

   (b) Your weight will rise dramatically.

   (c) You can grow accustomed to the taste very fast.

   (d) It's expensive so your bank balance will suffer.

3. Choose the false one from the following.

   (a) Tuna has both health benefits and health warnings.

   (b) Asia has cut back on the amount of tuna it consumes, which has negatively affected the tuna market.

   (c) People have been eating more tuna because it has been marketed as a healthy food.

   (d) Pregnant women should steer clear of tuna to avoid any problems during pregnancy.

4. What can you infer about people who eat bluefin tuna?

   (a) They are looking for alternatives to endangered tuna.

   (b) They are rich people who do not care if the bluefin tuna disappears forever.

   (c) They are becoming more and more unhealthy as they eat the tuna.

   (d) They eat a lot of tuna sushi every week.

Words & Phrases

tuna n. 참치   hemisphere n. 반구   catch n. 어획량   fatty acid n. 지방산   selenium n. 셀레늄
colon cancer n. 대장암   back v. 지지하다   awareness n. 자각, 각성   maintain v. 주장하다   extinct a. 멸종한
depleted a. 고갈된, 소모된   soar v. 치솟다   equivalent a. 상당하는   ingredient n. 재료, 원료   mercury n. 수은
ruin v. 망치다   ecosystem n. 생태계   steer clear of ~에 가까이 가지 않다

문장분석

■ The Food Standards Agency of the United Kingdom has already recommended that pregnant women avoid eating tuna. ➡ 〈insist/demand/recommend that + 주어 + (should) 동사원형〉 구문으로 의미상 that 절 이하의 동사에는 should가 사용되어야 한다. 의미상으로 ~해야 한다고 주장하거나, 요구하거나 추천하고 있기 때문이다. 그리고 이때 should는 생략 가능하다. 위의 예문에서는 should가 생략되어 있다.

Unit 17 Chips on shoulders, too? |생체 칩|

•기술•

This could actually happen when radio frequency identification technology will be used in daily life. Tracking is simple. An electronic chip is loaded with information and attached with a tiny antenna to send and receive information. Data on the chip can be sent and in some models new data can be added. These chips can be inserted into the human body.

The Associated Press reported in July 2004 that the Mexican government had electronic chips inserted in some 160 civil workers, including the minister of justice, prosecutors and police officers. The government said they were for security and identification purposes when the workers enter major information agencies. The chips were products of the U.S. company VeriChip. A 12-millimeter-long and 2.1-millimeter-wide chip was inserted under the skin, using a syringe.

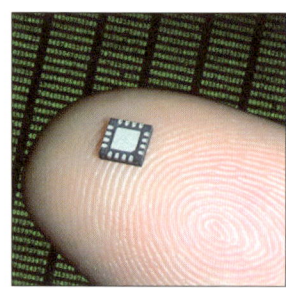

The Independent reported that the British government was considering using electronic chips as a tool to monitor prisoners on parole. A chip would be inserted in the body and the person could be monitored by satellite wherever he goes.

In the United States in 2006, Scott Silverman, VeriChip's board chairman, maintained that electronic tags should be inserted into the bodies of immigrants living in America. This was suggested when President George W. Bush said that for national security reasons, officials must know who lives in the United States, and where.

A bionic microchip is an advanced version. In February 2002, a research team at the University of California-Berkeley announced that it developed a bionic microchip combining a human cell with an electronic chip circuit. According to a study by a U.S. intelligence agency, the forehead or the back of the hand are good places to insert a semiconductor containing a battery which can be recharged through changes in temperature on the human skin. The Biblical "Book of Revelations" by St. John, while predicting idolatry on the last day, wrote about tags on people's right hand or forehead. This is the background of a conspiracy theory opposing electronic tags.

1. What's the main idea of the passage?

    (a) The use of electronic chips to monitor humans
    (b) The moral argument against bionic microchips
    (c) Using electronic chips for security purposes
    (d) Why we need to use electronic chips these days

2. Which of the following is correct, according to the passage?

    (a) The electronic chips have already been used in Mexico for the purposes of security.
    (b) The American government wants to make it mandatory for all citizens to wear a chip.
    (c) The bionic microchip has to be removed to be recharged.
    (d) The British government is watching America closely and will follow their lead on chip usage.

3. What can you infer about bionic microchips?

    (a) Most governments do not want to use them because the general population does not want them.
    (b) The development of the microchip was hazardous.
    (c) Moral issues have been identified over the use of bionic microchips.
    (d) They will shortly be made available for over-the-counter purchase.

4. Why do some top officials in America want electronic tags for immigrants?

    (a) Officials don't trust immigrants and they are waiting for them to commit a crime.
    (b) The electronic tags are used to find out personal information that will help the government.
    (c) They want to begin a program of expelling all immigrants.
    (d) Officials want to know who is living in the country at any given time and where in the country they are.

Words & Phrases

frequency n. 주파수   RFID 전파식별(Radio Frequency Identification), 전파를 이용해 물체를 식별하는 기술   tracking n. 추적
be loaded with ~이 담기다   civil worker 공무원   prosecutor n. 검사   security n. 보안; 안보   syringe n. 주사기
on parole 가석방 중인   bionic a. 생체 공학적인   circuit n. 회로   intelligence n. 기밀, 정보; 지능   forehead n. 이마
Revelation n. [성경] 요한계시록   idolatry n. 우상 숭배   conspiracy n. 음모   over-the-counter a. (약을) 처방전 없이 살 수 있는

문장분석

■ The Independent reported that the British government was <u>considering</u> using electronic chips as a tool to monitor prisoners on parole. ➡ ⟨consider -ing⟩ 구문은 '~을 고려하다'는 뜻을 지닌다. 형태에서 볼 수 있듯이 consider는 동명사만을 목적어로 취하는 동사에 속한다. 참고로 이런 동사로는 avoid, finish, enjoy, deny, mind, practice, keep 등이 있다.

Unit 18 | Bogus complaints |가짜약|

There are four types of bogus medicines that have no therapeutic effect. If they are listed in their order of creation, the oldest one is a placebo. A placebo looks like ordinary medicine, but has no pharmaceutical effect. It has more of a psychological effect because a doctor prescribes it. The second type is a treatment, which has no medicinal value but is promoted as having miraculous effects. The third is a copy of an existing formula. A bogus form of Amodipine, a high blood pressure remedy, was stopped from being sold shortly before it entered the domestic Korean market. The World Health Organization said 10 percent of the treatments sold in the world, or one out of four pills on the market in developing countries, are bogus. As we can expect, bogus Viagra keeps coming out; most bogus drugs copy blockbuster brand medicines such as Novask, Dioban, Cialis and Propecia. The fourth type contains poison or harmful ingredients. Heparin may have killed 19 people in the United States recently, and cold medications also may have killed 200 in Panama and Haiti. It turned out that Heparin contained irregularities and the cold remedies contained glycerin intended for industrial use. The two instances have something in common: The medicines were produced by chartered pharmaceutical companies 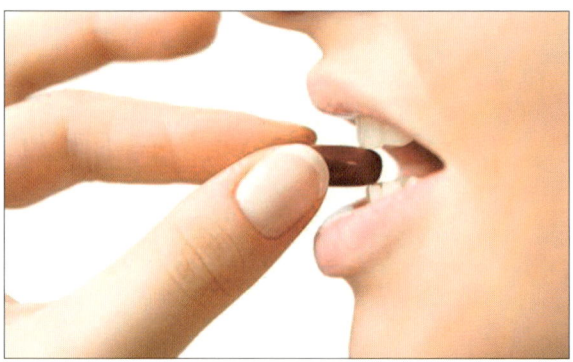 but poisoned ingredients imported from China were used. Among the four, placebos are harmless because they are simply sugar pills, distilled water or a saline solution. The other three types risk people's lives. Of drugs sold under the name of Artesunate, an anti-malarial agent, up to 53 percent are bogus, which clearly shows the danger and lack of ethics in the production of fake medicines. About 1 million people die from malaria each year and the World Health Organization estimates that if genuine drugs were used, 200,000 would have survived.

1. What can be inferred from the passage?

   (a) The World Health Organization is going to fight against corrupt drug companies.

   (b) Drug companies are now being held responsible for their actions.

   (c) The use of bogus drugs is a serious issue that can have disastrous effects.

   (d) China cannot be trusted to produce any products used for consumption.

2. According to the passage what are the major differences between the 4 bogus types of medications?

   (a) One is medical, one is pharmaceutical, one is poisonous, and one is made of sugar.

   (b) One is bogus, one is harmless, one is fake, and one is a remedy.

   (c) One is genuine, one is a placebo, one is useful, and one is a toxin.

   (d) One is psychological, one is non-medical, one is a duplicate, and one is a toxin.

3. Which of the following could be a possible reason for the occurrence of third and fourth types?

   (a) Companies are attempting to create a higher amount of profit.

   (b) There is a lack of proper ingredients so they use whatever they can.

   (c) They are attempting to create new placebos for doctors to use.

   (d) They are simply clerical errors that allow small mistakes to happen in production.

4. Which of the following is incorrect according to the passage?

   (a) Bogus medications can have very negative effects on people.

   (b) Placebos can be dangerous to patients that take them do to their psychological effects.

   (c) Some companies use improper ingredients when manufacturing drugs.

   (d) Bogus drugs are responsible for a large amount of deaths that could be partially prevented.

Words & Phrases

bogus a. 가짜의   therapeutic a. 치료의   placebo n. 위약   psychological a. 심리의   prescribe v. 처방하다
remedy n. 치료, 의료   domestic a. 국내의, 자국의   ingredient n. 재료, 원료   turn out ~로 밝혀지다
irregularity n. 불규칙한 것, 변칙, 이상   glycerin n. 글리세린   have something in common 공통점이 있다
chartered a. 인가받은, 공인된; (항공기나 배가) 전세 낸   distilled water 증류수   saline solution n. 식염수
agent n. (특정한 효과·목적을 위해 쓰이는) 물질   ethic(s) n. 윤리   estimate v. 추산하다   genuine a. 진짜의

문장분석

■ It turned out that Heparin contained irregularities and the cold remedies contained glycerin intended for industrial use. ➜ 〈turn out that 절〉은 '~로 밝혀지다'라는 뜻을 지닌다. 〈turn out to be 형용사〉 형태로도 사용된다. 참고로 위 예문의 it은 가주어이고, that 이하가 진주어이다. 따라서 예문은 that 이하의 내용이 사실로 밝혀졌다는 뜻이 된다.

Unit 19 | UN World Water Day |물의 날|

• 환경 •

A 154-pound person is almost half water. If our body's water drops by 1 percent, we get thirsty; if we lack 5 percent, we get dizzy. If 10 percent goes, walking becomes difficult. A 12 percent decrease in body water puts our very lives in danger. It's impossible to last more than a few days without water.

Each person in a Korean family uses an average of 47 gallons of water every day. On the other hand, in sub-Saharan Africa and parts of Mongolia, one must take care of all one's needs with 1.3 gallons a day. Although the United Nations proclaimed in 1992 that every person should have access to 11 gallons of water a day, about 1.1 billion people still suffer due to lack of water. Many must walk more than half a mile to obtain clean water or end up drinking heavily contaminated water from close by. In Somalia, where people suffer from droughts, there are sometimes killings between tribes for access to wells.

March 22 is United Nations World Water Day. Every year at around this time, there are debates as to whether Korea is a water-scarce country or not. According to Swedish scholar Malin Falkenmark, a nation with less than 449,000 gallons of water per person annually is water-scarce. This definition is widely used internationally. Water annually available to Koreans amounts to 393,000 gallons, making Korea a water-scarce country by this measure. However, it is true that other than water shortages in certain regions in the spring, we don't feel the shortage.

This is because South Korea imports the water it lacks. Of course, it is not real water, but "virtual water" in the form of food. To produce one ton of wheat, 343,000 gallons of water are needed; one ton of beef takes 4 million gallons. If we

import food, we are saving that much water used in agriculture. According to UNESCO, Korea imported 10.3 trillion gallons of virtual water and exported 1.8 trillion gallons between 1997 and 2001. That meant a net import of 8.5 trillion gallons of virtual water. Korea is the fifth-largest importer of water after Japan, Italy, the United Kingdom and Germany.

1. What can be inferred from the passage?

   (a) Some countries must rely on trade to provide enough water for all their citizens.

   (b) Japan has less actual water than Korea, so they have to import more virtual water.

   (c) Koreans use far more water than they should considering the water shortages in the country.

   (d) World Water Day does little to help those without clean water.

2. What is meant by the phrase "virtual water"?

   (a) The water that is found in video games

   (b) The total amount of water that a country should have in reserve in case of drought

   (c) The total water; other than that directly used by people, to produce food and other consumables

   (d) The average amount of water used every day by livestock and farms to produce food

3. Which of the following is correct according to the passage?

   (a) Korea uses more water than it is capable of supplementing through importing.

   (b) Countries like the UK and Germany are water-scarce due to their wastage of water.

   (c) Most places that lack water don't have many people living in them.

   (d) The level of access to water is very diverse for people in different countries.

4. Why is Korea both a water-scarce and non-water-scarce country according to the passage?

   (a) Because they export a lot of their virtual water rather than keeping it.

   (b) They lose most of their actual water to agriculture so there is a discrepancy in the amounts.

   (c) Because it is on the border so sometimes it's above; sometime it's below.

   (d) It doesn't actually have enough water but imports secondary water produced consumables.

Words & Phrases

thirsty *a.* 목마른, 갈증 나는　dizzy *a.* 현기증이 나는　put ~ in danger ~을 위험에 처하게 하다　last *v.* 지속되다
proclaim *v.* 선언하다, 공포하다　have access to ~에 접근하다, ~을 이용하다　end up 결국 (어떤 처지에) 처하게 되다
contaminated *a.* 오염된　drought *n.* 가뭄　tribe *n.* 부족　well *n.* 우물　as to ~에 관해서　scarce *a.* 부족한
shortage *n.* 부족　virtual *a.* 가상의　wheat *n.* 밀　agriculture *n.* 농업　net import 순수입

문장분석

■ Every year at around this time, there are debates as to whether Korea is a water-scarce country or not.

→ 〈as to something〉 구문은 '~에 대하여, ~에 관해서는'이라는 의미를 지닌다. 동의어로는 as regards something이 있다. 여기서 to는 전치사이기 때문에 뒤에 명사가 와야 한다. 예문에서는 '~인지 아닌지'를 나타내는 whether ~ or not을 이용한 명사절을 사용했다. 따라서 예문의 해석은 '한국이 물 부족 국가인지 아닌지에 대해서 논의가 진행된다'는 뜻이 된다.

Unit 20 Potent pill |비아그라|

• 의학 •

In the late 1990s, a research team from multinational pharmaceutical company Pfizer ended clinical trials on sildenafil, an angina drug that was shown to have little effect on the disease it was meant to treat. Told the trials had been terminated, male patients complained, some even refusing to hand in their leftover medicine. Probing a little deeper, researchers discovered an unexpected side effect. Sildenafil wasn't that effective against angina, but it turned out that it did work against male erectile dysfunction.

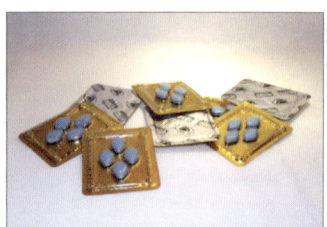

Sensing the drug could be a blockbuster, Pfizer focused on the side effect of the drug. It eventually came up with Viagra, the first pill to treat erectile dysfunction. The name is a portmanteau of "vigor" and "Niagara."

The drug was approved for sales by the U.S. Food and Drug Administration on March 27, 1998. Viagra soon became an unprecedented success in the drug market, propelling Pfizer to the heights of the global pharmaceutical industry. Over the past 10 years, 1.8 billion pills have been consumed. According to official data, 35 million men around the world have taken the medicine. Six pills are consumed every second.

Viagra is regarded as the drug that completed the sexual revolution of the 20th century. The first revolution was contraceptive pills which came into the market in the 1950s. Known simply as "The Pill," it stops women from worrying about pregnancy. The second revolution was accomplished by Viagra. Amid the many aging societies of the world, the drug drastically improved the lives of elderly citizens. The British newspaper *The Independent* called Viagra "the blue miracle" after the color of the pill.

Viagra is also known to have an effect on heart failure, diabetes, memory loss and stroke. Some even say the drug works like aspirin, the universal panacea. Viagra does have a variety of side effects, such as sneezing, headache, dyspepsia, palpitations, photophobia, priapism, hypotension and heart attack. More serious cases of vision impairment and even death have been reported. Still, few refuse to take the medicine.

1. Which of the following is correct according to the passage?

    (a) The little blue pill has caused a lot of trouble for older people.

    (b) The discovery of this pill completed the sexual revolution of the 20th century.

    (c) The drug company wasn't sure what to do with the pill when it first discovered the side effects.

    (d) Only a few people are able to take the pill due to health risks.

2. What cannot be inferred from the passage?

    (a) The pill has probably enhanced the private lives of people.

    (b) People will be using this pill for a long time for various reasons.

    (c) The company that produced this pill is now very wealthy.

    (d) The risks from side effects make taking the pill a very unsafe decision, even though people do.

3. What would be the best title for this passage?

    (a) How a miracle was found

    (b) Pill research in the 1990's

    (c) The sexual revolution

    (d) How medical discoveries are made

4. Why is it called a miracle in the phrase "the blue miracle"?

    (a) It appeared from nowhere to solve problems it wasn't supposed to fix.

    (b) It brought men and women back to equality in the revolution.

    (c) It was only found by mistake.

    (d) It just happened to solve problems that had no solution before, hence a miracle for some.

Words & Phrases

pharmaceutical *a.* 제약의   clinical trial 임상 실험   angina *n.* 협심증   have little effect on ~에 거의 효과가 없다
terminate *v.* 종료하다   leftover *n.* 잔여물, 나머지   probe *v.* 조사하다   side effect *n.* 부작용
erectile dysfunction 발기부전   come up with ~을 내놓다, 생산하다   portmanteau *a.* 여러 가지로 이뤄진
unprecedented *a.* 전례가 없는   contraceptive *a.* 피임(용)의   pregnancy *n.* 임신   drastically *ad.* 대폭, 과감하게, 철저하게
diabetes *n.* 당뇨   stroke *n.* 뇌졸중   panacea *n.* 만병통치약   sneezing *n.* 재채기   dyspepsia *n.* 소화 불량
palpitation *n.* 가슴 떨림   photophobia *n.* 빛 공포증   priapism *n.* 지속 발기증   hypotension *n.* 저혈압

문장분석

■ Viagra is also known to <u>have an effect on</u> heart failure, diabetes, memory loss and stroke. → 〈have an effect/impact on something〉 구문은 '~에 효과가 있다'는 뜻을 지닌다. 효과가 없다고 할 때는 〈have no/little effect on something〉이라고 표현한다. 또한 effect나 impact 명사 앞에 형용사를 사용해 뜻을 강조하거나 더 분명하게 나타낼 수 있다. have a significant/profound/negative/detrimental/dramatic/negligible effect/impact 등으로 사용해 엄청난 효과가 있다거나, 미미한 수준의 효과가 있다는 식으로 나타낸다.

Unit 21 The captive mammoth |매머드|

• 동물 •

The carcass of a young mammoth was found frozen and preserved in permafrost, in the northwest part of Russia's Siberia in May of last year. Kicked by a ranch hand's boots, the mammoth finally revealed itself to the world after being concealed beneath a wall of ice for 10,000 years. The 6-month-old female mammoth is the most well-preserved example yet found of the beasts. It looked as if it were still alive.

Experts in Russia and Japan have great expectations that if they attempt to inject cells from the carcass into an elephant's ova, they might be able to succeed in cloning the mammoth species. If their dream comes true, dinosaur cloning as seen in the movie "Jurassic Park," a 1993 science-fiction film directed by Steven Spielberg, will be a reality in the near future.

Mammoths are regarded as a symbol of enormity. Fossils of huge mammoths that had towered as high as five meters (16 feet) from ground to shoulder and weighed 12 tons when they were alive have been found occasionally. The mammoths first appeared in Africa approximately 1.6 million years ago and thrived 50,000 years ago, at the end of the diluvial epoch. The species lived in Africa, Europe, Asia and North America until 10,000 years ago. Some of them survived until 3,600 years ago. However, they ended up extinct.

Recent sample analyses by Spanish scientists regarding climate, different mammoth species and populations, showed that the number of mammoths saw a rapid decline due to climate change beginning 8,000 to 6,000 years ago. In the long run, the study indicated, the ultimate killer of the mammoths was found to be hunting by humans. However, mammoths are still caught in the fatal ties that bound them to humankind and led to their demise.

As the permafrost melts away at a swift pace because of global warming, the search for mammoth fossils is all the rage at the moment. In addition to professional hunters searching for mammoth ivory, reindeer hunters and laborers in oil and gas fields have jumped on the bandwagon. Mammoth fossils have emerged as a major Russian export and are sold everywhere. Mammoth ivory exports, which remained at no more than two tons per annum in 1989, reached more than 40 tons last year. A mammoth-head fossil with well-preserved three-meter-long tusks is worth roughly $20,000, and a perfectly restored mammoth fossil is quoted at between $150,000 to $250,000 or higher.

1. What can be inferred from the passage?

   (a) Mammoths will roam the world again in the near future.

   (b) More mammoths will immerge at an increasing rate as the Earth warms and more people hunt them.

   (c) Mammoths will be bred for their ivory in the future.

   (d) Climate change will cause the extinction of other species as well.

2. Which of the following is untrue according to the passage?

   (a) Mammoths became extinct due to several contributing factors.

   (b) Ivory export is a very profitable business for some.

   (c) The rate of Mammoth ivory being sold will probably continue to increase.

   (d) Mammoths will become extinct again if they are cloned because of climate change.

3. Which of the following is the most likely topic of the next paragraph?

   (a) How Mammoths were used by humans in the diluvial epoch

   (b) Where mammoth ivory is sold and what it is used for

   (c) Where the best places to discover mammoths are

   (d) How to recover a mammoth fossil from the ice

4. What is the passage mainly about?

   (a) The sale of mammoth ivory

   (b) The extinction of mammoths by man

   (c) Mammoths and the reasons for their death and recent discovery

   (d) Who hunts for mammoth fossils today

Words & Phrases

carcass n. (동물의) 시체, 죽은 동물   permafrost n. 영구 동토층   ranch hand n. 목장 종업원, 목동   conceal v. 감추다
ovum n. 난자 (pl. ova)   clone v. 복제하다   thrive v. 번성하다   diluvial epoch 홍적세
end up 결국 (어떤 처지에) 처하게 되다   in the long run 결국에는   fatal a. 치명적인   bind v. 묶다   demise n. 사망
swift a. 신속한   pace n. 속도; 보폭   all the rage 성행하다   jump on the bandwagon 우세한 편에 붙다; 시류에 편승하다
tusk n. 상아   quote v. 견적을 내다

문장분석

■ It looked as if it were still alive. → 〈as if + 가정문〉 구문으로 '마치 ~인 것 같다'는 뜻을 지닌다. as if 뒤에는 가정법이 오는 것이 특징이다. 의미상의 시점에 따라 주절의 시제와 같은 경우에는 가정법 과거가 오고, 주절의 시제보다 한 시제 앞서는 경우 가정법 과거완료가 온다. 예문에는 가정법 과거인 were를 사용했기 때문에, 주절의 looked의 시제와 의미가 같다. 따라서 매머드를 발견했을 때 마치 살아있는 것처럼 보였다는 뜻이 된다.

Unit 22 | Up to the challenge |파란 장미|

• 식물 •

Cleopatra, the legendary beauty from Egypt, was crazy about roses. She used roses to make men remember her for a long time. The idea was that they would think of her any time they smelled the scent of a rose. When Cleopatra tried to seduce Mark Antony, or Antonius of the Roman Empire, she used rose perfume, which has an aphrodisiac effect. Antonius could not forget the scent of the rose. He even ordered the people to spread rose petals over his grave before he died fighting against Caesar's army. The petals were from a red rose. That is why the red rose signifies desire, love and passion.

The Thirty Years' War is also known as the War of the Roses, since the noble Yorks used the white rose as their crest and the Lancaster used the red rose as their crest. The War of the Roses ended as Henry the VII started the Tudor Dynasty. The House of Tudor's royal standard, which is made of a red and white rose, is still used as the crest of England's royal family. That is why the "Tudor Rose" represents both water and fire as well as unification and peace.

There are up to 25,000 kinds of roses, in 3,000 colors. The flower has more than 60 meanings, including both the English and French languages. The term "blue rose" means impossible in English. That comes from the fact that no roses are naturally blue, nor could one be created even with plant breeding. Although the whole world has tried continuously since the 12th century to grow a blue rose, efforts have proved useless. A blue rose has only been possible in dreams.

But the Japanese liquor company Suntory has announced it has received approval from its government to sell blue roses, starting next year. By transplanting the pansy gene that carries the delphinidin blue pigment into the rose, the company was able to produce the impossible blue rose. It took 14 years. The founder of Suntory, Shinjiro Torii, had a favorite catchword, "Challenge." That finally resulted in achievement. Out of the 260 billion yen ($2.4 billion) rose market, the blue rose is expected to grab about 20 percent. During the past 14 years, however, Suntory only invested about 3 billion yen. What is most interesting is that a liquor company started the research and succeeded in results. Maybe the common link is that roses, like alcohol, can make people spellbound.

1. What's the main idea of the passage?

    (a) The search for the impossible blue rose

    (b) The role of roses throughout time and into the future

    (c) The problems caused by human's love of roses

    (d) The strange connection between roses and liquor

2. What can you infer about Cleopatra?

    (a) Cleopatra ordered Mark Antony to take roses into battle.

    (b) She attended his funeral wearing rose perfume.

    (c) She was well aware of the effect roses had on men and used it to her advantage.

    (d) She invented rose perfume.

3. Which of the following best paraphrases the meaning of the blue rose?

    (a) Folklore said that the side that carried the blue rose would be impossible to beat.

    (b) Blue roses do not bloom often so it is impossible to find one in bloom.

    (c) The blue rose is so rare that is it considered impossible to find.

    (d) Blue roses have proven impossible to create, despite centuries of trying.

4. Choose the false one from the following.

    (a) The red rose is a symbol of the passionate love of Cleopatra and Antonius.

    (b) The War of the Roses refers to the two families at war who each had a rose as their family symbol.

    (c) Suntory managed to find a blue rose that had not been artificially tampered with.

    (d) Suntory will gain much more profit than they invested in the quest for the blue rose.

Words & Phrases

legendary *a.* 전설적인   scent *n.* 향기   seduce *v.* 유혹하다   aphrodisiac *a.* 최음의   petal *n.* 꽃잎
signify *v.* 의미하다, 뜻하다   passion *n.* 정열   crest *n.* (오랜 역사를 지닌 가문을 상징하는) 문장
represent *v.* 표현하다, 상징하다; 대표하다, 대변하다   unification *n.* 통일   breeding *n.* 품종 개량   transplant *v.* 이식하다
pansy *n.* 팬지(꽃)   pigment *n.* 색소   grab *v.* 잡다, 차지하다   spellbound *a.* 마음을 다 빼앗긴, 넋을 잃은
tamper with (허락도 받지 않고 마음대로) 손대다[건드리다/조작하다]

문장분석

■ The Thirty Years' War is also <u>known as</u> the War of the Roses, since the noble Yorks used the white rose as their crest and the Lancaster used the red rose as their crest.　➡ 〈A is known as B〉 구문으로 'A가 B로 알려졌다'는 뜻이다. 따라서 30년 전쟁을 다른 말로는 장미전쟁이라고도 한다는 뜻이 된다. known 뒤에 오는 전치사에 따라 서로 다른 의미를 지니게 되는데, 예를 들어 be known to somebody는 '~에게 알려졌다'는 뜻이고, be known for something은 어떤 일로 잘 알려져 있으므로 '~로 유명하다'의 뜻을 지닌다.

Unit 23 Written in wrinkles |보톡스|

• 의학 •

These days, Botox is the most well-known substance of the anti wrinkle wonder drugs. Botox is a brand name but it often refers to all types of botulinum toxin cosmetic treatments. The problem is that this medicine is only effective for three to six months. A person who receives this treatment also has trouble making facial expressions. But Botox costs less than surgery and people now want to appear younger than they actually are, so the product is popular. Botox has a strong brand power, second only to Viagra.

The last syllable in Botox comes from toxin. Botulinum toxin occurs naturally and causes food poisoning. Dioxin is known to be the most poisonous artificial substance, and botulinum toxin is 100 times more toxic. Ordinary poisoning causes diarrhea and stomach ache but a botulinum poisoned patient has a 50 percent risk of death. In short, it is the most dangerous kind of poison.

Late last month, the U.S. Food and Drug Administration expressed concerns over the safety of Botox after the U.S. civic group Public Citizen announced that 16 people have died from side effects of Botox treatments since the drug was commercialized. The Korea Food and Drug Administration also took measures because it believes that an overdose of Botox might cause difficulty in breathing and swallowing food, thus putting lives at risk. The key word here is overdose. Most of the victims were cerebral palsy patients and they tried to temporarily ease muscle spasms with Botox. The injection they took was 28 times more than the amount used for cosmetic treatments.

Wrinkles on the face are traces of the person's life. In the late 20s, wrinkles start to form around people's eyes, then on the forehead in the late 30s and then around the mouth in the late 40s. There is a saying that wrinkles around the eyes form when a person starts to understand reason and rationality, on the forehead when he understands life and around the mouth when he grasps the laws of nature.

1. What's the passage mainly about?

   (a) Growing old gracefully

   (b) Why Botox has become so popular

   (c) The toxicity and danger of Botox

   (d) The future ban of Botox

2. Which of the following is true?

   (a) Those who have died from Botox have mostly done so because they overdosed on the poison.

   (b) The Korea Food and Drug Administration is unconcerned about Botox and supports its use for cosmetic procedures.

   (c) Botulinum toxin is not very dangerous if you handle it with care.

   (d) Deaths have occurred because the toxin is being sold to people who are not aware of the danger.

3. What can you infer about people who have Botox injected for cosmetic reasons?

   (a) They don't have any of the side effects that are commonly reported.

   (b) They put up with the sickness that comes with it, in order to look younger.

   (c) They might delay wrinkles, but even more will appear when the toxin wears off.

   (d) Their primary aim is to make wrinkles disappear and avoid the onset of aging.

4. What are the effects of injecting Botox?

   (a) In most cases death, but usually just severe stomach cramps

   (b) Wrinkles disappear temporarily as facial muscles cease moving.

   (c) The permanent removal of all facial wrinkles

   (d) Sickness until the toxin wears off

Words & Phrases

substance *n.* 물질   refer to ~을 지칭하다   toxin *n.* 독소   cosmetic *a.* 미용의, 화장의   facial expression 표정
food poisoning *n.* 식중독   artificial *a.* 인공적인   toxic *a.* 독성의, 유독한   diarrhea *n.* 설사
express concerns over ~에 대해 우려를 표명하다   civic group 시민단체   side effect 부작용
take measures 조치를 취하다   overdose *n.* 과다복용   swallow *v.* 삼키다   put ~ at risk ~을 위험에 처하게 하다
victim *n.* 희생자   cerebral palsy *n.* 뇌성마비   temporarily *ad.* 일시적으로   ease *v.* 완화시키다
muscle spasm *n.* 근육 경련   wrinkle *n.* 주름   trace *n.* 흔적, 자취   saying *n.* 속담   rationality *n.* 합리성, 순리성

문장분석

■ A person who receives this treatment also has trouble making facial expressions. ➔ 〈have trouble -ing〉 구문은 '~하는 데 어려움을 겪다'는 뜻을 지닌다. 이때 trouble 은 무관사 명사로 사용되어야 한다. 바로 뒤에 -ing 대신 명사가 나오는 경우 with를 사용해 〈have trouble with something〉 형태로 표현된다. 형태는 비슷하지만 뜻이 다른 경우로 〈have the trouble to do something〉이란 구문이 있는데, 이것은 '~하기 위해 무척 노력하다'는 뜻이 된다.

Unit 24 Astro trash |케슬러 신드롬|

•기술•

On Jan. 11, last year, China launched a missile to destroy its weather satellite, the Fengyun-1C which was orbiting at an altitude of 863 kilometers above the country. The satellite was launched into space in 1999 and had been continuing to orbit despite having gone out of service. After the destruction of the satellite, China officially became a state that possesses ballistic missile technology, after the United States and Russia. The problem is the debris from the destroyed satellite has now become space litter. The trash orbits the Earth at a speed of 5 to 7 kilometers per second, so it is not much different from bullets or bombs.

Space litter has been increasing as human-launched spacecrafts and satellites from the past decades leave behind or drop empty fuel tanks, tools, pieces of metal and debris. NASA monitors 3,100 satellites launched by 47 countries, along with 9,300 chunks of space trash of larger than 5 centimeters in diameter. Among the debris, 2,600 pieces are known to be bits of a Chinese satellite that was destroyed last year. There are hundreds of thousands of pieces of space debris that are 1 centimeter in diameter, but it is impossible to find or monitor them. Even a piece of debris of this size is capable of breaking a satellite.

Thus, the Kessler syndrome is now drawing attention. This is a scenario in which space debris collides with satellites or each other, increasing the debris to such an enormous amount that it covers the entire Earth orbit. In that case, it would be impossible to launch spacecraft or a satellite. Nonetheless, *The Associated Press* reported on Feb. 13 that the U.S. Department of Defense plans to shoot down a broken spy satellite this week. The stated reason was that if the satellite is left alone, it will fall to Earth next month and toxic substances in the fuel could cause human casualties.

1. What is the main idea of the passage?

    (a) China has become a major super power.

    (b) Space junk is becoming a serious problem.

    (c) How to deal with old space equipment

    (d) Tracking space debris to prevent accidents

2. What cannot be inferred about the passage?

    (a) Space debris will be a serious problem in the future.

    (b) The problem of space debris will have to be dealt with before it causes serious damage.

    (c) Countries will have to find ways to destroy all their satellites safely.

    (d) Not many countries have the capability to destroy satellites.

3. Which of the following is not correct according to the passage?

    (a) Many countries have contributed to the scenario known as the Kessler syndrome.

    (b) The destruction of the Chinese satellite has contributed to a large amount of space debris.

    (c) Space junk is comprised of a wide variety of objects and other man-made particles.

    (d) In a few more years the entire Earth will be surrounded with nothing but junk.

4. If space debris is such a problem, why do countries like China and the US destroy satellites?

    (a) The immediate risk from their re-entry into Earth is greater than future concerns.

    (b) The governments like to show that they have the capability to do it.

    (c) They do not want to risk another country recovering their broken technology.

    (d) The countries want their debris to damage other countries' satellites.

Words & Phrases

launch *v.* 발사하다   altitude *n.* 고도   out of service 수명이 다한, 퇴직한   officially *ad.* 공식적으로
ballistic missile *n.* 탄도 미사일   debris *n.* 파편, 잔해   litter *n.* 쓰레기   orbit *v.* 궤도를 돌다   bullet *n.* 탄환
leave behind 남기다   collide *v.* 충돌하다   toxic *a.* 유독한   casualty *n.* 사상자, 희생자

문장분석

■ The trash orbits the Earth <u>at a speed of</u> 5 to 7 kilometers per second, so it is not much different from bullets or bombs. ➔ ⟨at the speed/rate/altitude of + 숫자⟩라는 표현에서는 전치사 at에 주의하도록 한다. 어떤 비율로 변하거나, 어떤 속도로 이동한다고 할 때는 항상 전치사 at과 함께 사용된다. 전치사 at은 특정 지점이나 위치를 가리키는 전치사이기 때문이다. 따라서 시계가 진행하다 특정 시각에 멈춰있는 모습을 표현할 때 at을 쓰고, 특정 장소에 있다고 할 때도 at을 쓴다. 마찬가지로 특정 속도로 이동하거나, 특정 비율로 변화하고 있다고 할 때도 at을 사용한다.

Unit 25 Food for thought | GMO(유전자변형) |

Of all the developments that have revolutionized food, two must always be disclosed when they are employed. They are radiation examination and genetic modification (GMO). Because the government cannot yet verify their safety, it is basically leaving it up to the people to decide. In the past, GMOs were the darling of the Green Revolution. This enthusiasm contributed to making genetic engineering and bioengineering favorite fields of study in the '70s and '80s. GMOs disproved Thomas Malthus' theory of population, which claims that food supply grows at an arithmetic rate while the population grows at an exponential rate, leaving many hungry. Thus GMOs provided hope for the end of hunger. However, since the U.S. company Calgene in 1994 introduced the genetically modified "Flavr Savr" tomato, which is resistant to rotting, opinions have reversed. Civil society and certain media organizations labeled the new tomato as potentially unsafe "Franken-food." Since then, the idea that GMOs are harmful has taken root in the minds of many. At present, it is too early to expect any verdict on the safety of GMOs. There has been no conclusion to the debate between GMO advocates, who ask people to report any damage incurred from GMOs, and their opponents, who ask for proof that GMOs do no harm if it cannot be directly proven that they are harmful.

1. What can be inferred from the passage?

    (a) Media organizations will never allow these types of food to be developed in the future.

    (b) If Calgene had succeeded there would now be a large market for GMOs.

    (c) If GMOs can be proven safe they could help feed many hungry people.

    (d) GMOs are most likely harmful to humans, but we just can't prove it yet.

2. What, according to the passage, is the difference between GMO tomatoes and regular ones?

    (a) GMO tomatoes are able to ripen on the vine because they won't get damaged.

    (b) GMO tomatoes are able to feed more people than regular tomatoes.

    (c) GMO tomatoes are far too expensive compared with regular tomatoes.

    (d) GMO tomatoes are more resistant to decomposition than regular tomatoes.

3. What does the phrase "Franken-food" mean from reading the passage?

    (a) It is likening genetic manipulation of food to that of the creation of a monster.

    (b) That the tomatoes are all murdering monsters.

    (c) It is saying that the tomatoes are a new kind of food unlike any other on the planet.

    (d) That it will have many enemies because of its differences from regular tomatoes.

4. What is the passage mainly about?

    (a) The production process of GMOs in the late 20th century

    (b) The development of bioengineered food and its impact on society

    (c) How the media can alter people's perceptions about things

    (d) Ways in which world hunger can be eliminated

Words & Phrases

revolutionize v. 혁명을 일으키다   disclose v. 공개하다   employ v. 사용하다   radiation n. 방사선   genetic a. 유전의
modification n. 조작   verify v. 입증하다, 확증하다   darling n. 특히 사랑받는[인기 있는] 사람, 총아
enthusiasm n. 열심, 열중, 열광   disprove v. ~이 그릇됨을 증명하다, 논박하다   exponential a. 기하급수적인
label A as B A에 B라는 딱지를 붙이다   take root 뿌리 내리다   verdict n. 판단, 결정   advocate n. 지지자
incur v. 초래하다   do no harm ~에게 피해를 입히지 않다

문장분석

- This enthusiasm <u>contributed to</u> making genetic engineering and bioengineering favorite fields of study in the '70s and '80s. → 〈A contribute to B〉 구문은 'A가 B에 기여하다'는 의미로, A라는 이유로 인해 B라는 결과가 생긴다는 인과 관계를 설명하는 구문이다. 비슷한 뜻으로 lead to, result in, cause 등이 사용된다.

Unit 26 Temperamental children |라니냐|

On March 24, 1989, the Exxon Valdez oil tanker hit a reef off the coast of Alaska and spilled a huge amount of crude oil into the sea. The accident happened because the ship had gone off course in an attempt to avoid icebergs. The flow was blocked because La Niña had caused the current to shift. El Niño

and La Niña are opposite phenomena — in most cases the former is followed by the latter. When water temperatures in the eastern Pacific near the equator rise by more than 0.5 degrees for five months or longer, the phenomenon is called El Niño. When the temperatures decrease by 0.5 degrees, we get La Niña. In Spanish, a "nino" is a little boy, often referring to the Christ child, and a "nina" is a little girl. Fishermen in Peru in the 19th century knew about El Niño. When the water temperature rose, their catch shrank.

El Niño was first scientifically defined in 1923 by the British mathematician Gilbert Thomas Walker. He collected 40 years' worth of atmospheric data and found that the difference in air pressure between the south Pacific east of Tahiti and the Indian Ocean west of Darwin, Australia, fluctuated like a seesaw. When the air pressure in one area went up, it went down in the other. Walker called it the Southern Oscillation. The Southern Oscillation and El Niño and La Niña are two sides of a coin. The Southern Oscillation is the fluctuation of air pressure and El Niño and La Niña are changes in the ocean temperatures. When the air pressure in the Indian Ocean goes up, El Niño starts. If trade winds strengthen, cold ocean water rises and the water temperature decreases, signs of La Niña. El Niño causes floods in Peru and Ecuador and droughts in Southeast Asia and Australia. La Niña brings rainy spells in Southeast Asia and dry periods in South America.

1. What is the main purpose of the passage?

    (a) To illustrate how Spanish fishermen have bad fishing seasons

    (b) To explain about the effects of a specific weather phenomena

    (c) To defend the crew of the Exxon Valdez

    (d) To demonstrate how floods or droughts happen in parts of the world

2. According to the passage what is the difference between El Niño and La Niña?

    (a) They are two weather conditions that have an inverse relationship based on the Southern Oscillation.

    (b) One is a little boy; the other a little girl.

    (c) + 0.5 degrees over 5 months.

    (d) - 0.5 degrees over 5 months.

3. From reading the passage, what is the most likely reason why it is named after a word meaning little boy and not after its 20th century discoverer?

    (a) Because the Spanish published the results first.

    (b) The Spanish names sounded better.

    (c) South Americans speak Spanish so they understand the Spanish names.

    (d) Spanish fisherman had already named the phenomena in the 19th century.

4. Which of the following is incorrect according to the passage?

    (a) El Niño and La Niña are opposites of each other.

    (b) The two weather conditions cause reverse conditions in the areas they affect.

    (c) They are conditions that happen very rapidly.

    (d) These weather conditions can cause major economic damage.

Words & Phrases

reef *n.* 암초   spill *v.* 쏟아져 나오다, 유출하다   crude oil 원유   current *n.* 해류   phenomenon *n.* 현상 (*pl.* phenomena)
the former 전자   the latter 후자   refer to ~을 지칭하다   catch *n.* 어획량   shrink *v.* 줄어들다   atmospheric *a.* 대기의
fluctuate *v.* 요동치다   trade wind 무역풍   rainy spell 우기

문장분석

■ The accident happened because the ship had gone off course in an attempt to avoid icebergs. ➡ 〈in an attempt to do something〉 구문은 '~하기 위해서'라는 의미로, in order to do something, so as to do something, with the aim of doing something, with a view to doing something 등 다양한 동의어가 존재한다.

Unit 27 New materials, old weapons
|다마스쿠스 검|

Damascus swords are considered one of the world's most mysterious weapons. Made in Syria using imported Indian steel, the swords are believed to be the strongest swords ever made in history. Owing to the Damascus swords' reputation, the Roman army didn't dare attack the Sassanid Empire. Even an entire army of European Crusaders were defeated in Jerusalem by Arab armies led by Saladin. In contrast, European swords from this period were bulky and dull. They were no match for Damascus swords, famed for their lightness and sharpness. Historical records even describe Damascus swords as cutting enemy swords in two and penetrating armor.

Damascus swords feature a beautiful pattern of lateral bands, often called "Muhammad's Ladder." Despite their beauty, however, the manufacturing process was horrible. As written records describe, "The blade was heated until it turned into a peach color like the king's clothes, and then cooled by inserting it into the muscle of a healthy slave. So a sharp, strong sword was created from a slave's power and soul."

The swords are so rare now that we are practically unable to find any traces of them. By the 1750s, Indian iron resources dried up, creating a sense of intrigue and curiosity that exist to this day. Modern scholars of metallography categorize Damascus swords as carbon alloys containing a minimum of vanadium and molybdenum. They suggested that the combination of these impurities with carbon greatly contributed to increasing the degree of strength.

However, a discovery published two years ago in the science journal Nature caused a stir. Using electron microscopes, scientists at the Technical University in Dresden, Germany, discovered carbon nanowires and nanotubes within the molecular structure of a Damascus sword. And so a mysterious 800-year-old sword was found to contain high-tech new materials.

1. How were Damascus swords better than European swords?

    (a) They were lighter and sharper; their blades even being able to cut the enemys' swords in half.

    (b) They were a good match for the armor of the Syrians.

    (c) They were much heavier which caused more damage when used against an enemy.

    (d) The blade was prettier so worked psychologically on the enemy, who were in awe of the blades.

2. Which of the following paraphrases the manufacturing process of a Damacus sword?

    (a) Slaves who are already dying are used to make the blades strong.

    (b) The blade takes a very long time to make because of the high temperatures needed.

    (c) The same slave who heats the metal commits suicide with the blade to bring more power to it.

    (d) After heating the metal to an extremely high temperature, it is quickly cooled by plunging it into the muscle of a slave.

3. What can you infer from the discovery reported in the science journal Nature?

    (a) The technology used to make the Damascus sword seems advanced but is actually quite simple.

    (b) Damascus swords were not as advanced as the swords we have now are.

    (c) The materials used to make the swords were very common at the time.

    (d) The technology used to make the blades is very advanced; more advanced than the Syrians were thought to possess.

4. Choose the correct one from the following.

    (a) Muhammad's Ladder refers to the shape of the blade on the sword.

    (b) Damascan swords are still easily available today but they are expensive to buy.

    (c) Even the reputation of the Damascan sword could win battles for the Syrian army.

    (d) The Damascan swords are some of the strongest swords in the world, second only to Indian swords.

Words & Phrases

Damascus n. 다마스쿠스 (Syria의 수도)   reputation n. 명성   Crusader n. 십자군   bulky a. 부피가 큰   dull a. 무딘
in comparison 비교해 보면   match n. 상대, 적수   penetrate v. 뚫고 들어가다, 침투하다, 관통하다   armor n. 갑옷
feature v. 특징을 지니다   lateral a. 측면의   peach a. 복숭아 빛의   practically ad. 사실상   trace n. 자취, 흔적
intrigue n. 강한 흥미, 호기심   metallography n. 금속학   alloy n. 합금   impurity n. 불순물   cause a stir 파문을 일으키다
electron n. 전자   molecular a. 분자의

문장분석

■ Damascus swords <u>are</u> also <u>considered</u> one of the world's most mysterious weapons. ➡ 〈A is considered B〉 구문은 'A가 B로 생각되다'는 뜻을 지닌다. 비슷한 구문으로 〈A is regarded/seen as B〉가 있는데 이때는 as가 같이 사용되며, 〈A is thought of as B〉도 동일한 의미를 지닌다. consider는 as와 같이 사용되지 않으므로 주의하도록 한다.

Unit 28 Shame on Volkswagen
|폴크스바겐의 사기극을 보며|

• 환경 •

"Were we deceived because we really didn't know?" I thought when the Volkswagen emissions scandal was revealed. We all remember that German carmakers, including Volkswagen, promoted the "clean diesel" technology in the mid-2000s. European automobile companies introduced diesel cars in Korea with aggressive marketing campaigns.

Diesel cars had a bad image at the time, as Koreans remember diesel-powered buses that produced exhaust fumes. Did they really have clean diesel? It is common sense that diesel has better fuel efficiency and power than gasoline and produces less carbon dioxide but also emits nitric acid and fine dust, which the World Health Organization classified as Group 1 carcinogens. If anyone raises a question how diesel can be clean, automakers refuted by presenting various test results proving how clean diesel engines can be. They argued that world-class German automobile technology accomplished complete combustion of fuel while controlling exhaust fumes, and Europe's shift to diesel engines proves the reliability of clean diesel technology.

In fact, since the mid-1990s, EU members presented various policies encouraging diesel engines, offering lower tax rates or long-term tax benefits. Diesel cars had been a small portion in European market until the early '90s, but today 35 percent of the cars in the EU have diesel engines. Perhaps, we abandoned common sense as we were blinded by the prestige of German technology and environmentally friendly Europe.

Some mention the reflected advantage for Hyundai Motors. But just as the cold reaction of the stock market shows, the crisis won't bring any benefits to Korean carmakers that aggressively introduced diesel models. If the diesel technology is abandoned altogether, Korean carmakers will also suffer. As Volkswagen's diesel cars have been revealed to produce pollution on the road while test results were manipulated, and the investigation is expanding to all diesel models, some already switched over to the alternative of electric cars as the true clean vehicles. Some researches show that the electric cars have little effect in improving the air quality when the pollution from the process of power generation was taken into account. Also, the electric cars are equipped with large-capacity batteries, which need to be replaced after reaching certain charging cycles. The batteries are composed of various materials including lithium, and commercialization of electric cars would lead to pollution from battery waste.

In the end, there is no completely clean vehicle. An American automobile magazine featured a confession from a former Volkswagen executive that a clean diesel engine at a reasonable price was an unrealistic goal. When there is no fuel-powered vehicle that benefits the environment, the company fabricated that it could be overcome by technology to mitigate the guilt of pollution, and consumers and the carmakers spread the myth of a clean car. Perhaps, we had reasonable doubts that clean diesel didn't make sense. But we may have turned a blind eye to drive a powerful, efficient and brand-name German car and claim to be environmentally friendly at the same time. As we condemn Volkswagen's dishonesty,

_____ .

1. What is the purpose of the passage?

   (a) To attempt to hold the dishonest carmakers responsible for environmental pollution.

   (b) To reflect on what makes us ignore the hard data and follow something we know is wrong.

   (c) To make readers question themselves and their own complicity in the dupe of clean diesel.

   (d) To accuse the carmakers of deliberately deceiving consumers because of their greed.

2. Which of the following is correct, according to the passage?

   (a) People were happy to believe whatever Volkswagen said because they wanted to support German manufacturing.

   (b) Clean fuel is readily available, but there are no carmakers that support its use in our vehicles.

   (c) Electric cars are much better than diesel cars when it comes to the amount of pollution they cause.

   (d) The carmakers were adept at producing evidence to counter any accusations that clean diesel was a myth.

3. What can you infer from the passage?

   (a) Hyundai will surely follow Volkswagen's lead.

   (b) German cars will never be as reliable again.

   (c) Volkswagen never thought the lie would work.

   (d) We wanted to believe the carmakers' falsifications.

4. Which best completes the sentence?

   (a) we also need to reflect on our consumer awareness

   (b) there is also the question of why they wanted to do it

   (c) they should be aware of how angry the public feels toward them

   (d) it is necessary to make them admit their error

Words & Phrases

deceive *v.* 속이다   emission *n.* 배기; 방사, 발산   scandal *n.* 추문, 스캔들   automobile *n.* 자동차   aggressive *a.* 공격적인
exhaust *n.* 배기; 고갈시키다   fume *n.* 가스   carcinogen *n.* 발암물질   combustion *n.* 연소   prestige *n.* 명성
environmentally-friendly 친환경적인

문장분석

■ It is common sense that diesel has better fuel efficiency and power than gasoline and produces less carbon dioxide but also emits nitric acid and fine dust, which the World Health Organization classified as Group 1 carcinogens. → It은 가주어 that절은 진주어이다. diesel과 gasoline을 비교하는 비교구문으로, better fuel efficiency and power than 비교급이 쓰였다. and는 주어 diesel을 공통으로 하고, 동사 has와 produce를 연결한다. but also는 역접 접속사 but이 앞 절의 내용과 반대되는 내용을 기술함을 보여주며, also는 부사로 또한, 역시의 의미이다. which는 계속적용법의 목적격 관계대명사로, 선행사는 nitric acid와 fine dust이다.

Unit 29 Surveillance has a role |CCTV|

The global non-governmental organization working to protect privacy, the Global Internet Liberty Campaign divides privacy into four categories: information, physical, telecommunication and space privacy. Among the main violators of spatial privacy are CCTVs installed around homes, the workplace and public spaces. They are surveillance systems to protect against strangers and theft. Worldwide, the United Kingdom is one of the countries with many CCTVs. About 4.2 million are installed. There are about 20 million CCTVs worldwide, meaning that a country that has only 1 percent of the global population has 20 percent of the systems. They are installed in ordinary public spaces, major buildings and on streets. As a CCTV stronghold, the United Kingdom is continuously developing its technology. The British police introduced a flying CCTV. On a pilotless reconnaissance plane produced for military use, they have installed a CCTV, making it possible to take high-resolution videos from 1,640 feet. They are also testing an intelligent CCTV that can recognize people who are likely to commit a crime. It has software that can detect suspicious behavior by observing people from eight cameras. There is even a CCTV that scolds a person who has committed a crime or misbehaves. In reality, it is a speaker warning from a watchman monitoring the camera speaker. There are endless debates on the violation of privacy, but public sentiment about CCTVs is not all negative. Since a CCTV played a critical role in capturing terrorists suspected of the July 2005 London bus and subway bombings, technology has evolved so that when there is a crime, on the same evening, the BBC broadcasts the CCTV footage. Some people say one CCTV plays the role of 10 policemen. Coincidentally, George Orwell, who warned against Big Brother surveillance systems in his book "1984", is British.

1. From the passage, what is the most likely meaning of "Big Brother"?

   (a) A bully that makes sure you don't do anything he doesn't like

   (b) The government watching over you like a big brother would for siblings

   (c) An intelligent computer system that watches over everyone

   (d) A lot of cameras watching everyone committing crimes

2. What can be inferred from this passage?

   (a) The British government feels that CCTV cameras are good for crime prevention.

   (b) CCTV cameras will replace the regular police force.

   (c) Terrorist attacks will decrease because of the use of CCTV cameras.

   (d) CCTV camera use will increase worldwide until all countries are like Britain.

3. What is the main theme of the passage?

   (a) The arrival of Britain's Big Brother

   (b) Whether the CCTV cameras in Britain are doing better work than police

   (c) Whether the extensive use of CCTV cameras is worth loss of privacy

   (d) The high crime rate in Britain that requires so many CCTV cameras

4. Which of the following is correct according to the passage?

   (a) British CCTV technology is much more advanced than other countries.

   (b) British police have incorporated military hardware in their surveillance technology.

   (c) All CCTV cameras in Britain can take High resolution video.

   (d) Britain has developed an AI computer system for identifying and arresting terrorists.

Words & Phrases

non-governmental organization 비정부 조직(NGO)   spatial *a.* 공간의   install *v.* 설치하다   public space 공공장소
surveillance *n.* 감시   stranger *n.* 낯선 사람   theft *n.* 절도   stronghold *n.* 근거지, 중심지   reconnaissance *n.* 정찰, 수색
high-resolution *a.* 고해상도의   suspicious *a.* 수상한   scold *v.* 꾸짖다   misbehave *v.* 못된 짓을 하다, 비행을 저지르다
sentiment *n.* 감정, 정서   play a critical role 중요한 역할을 하다   evolve *v.* 진화하다   footage *n.* 장면, 화면
coincidentally *ad.* 동시적으로   Big Brother *n.* 독재자(조지 오웰(George Orwell)의 소설 '1984년'에 나오는 독재자 Big Brother에서 유래)

문장분석

■ Since a CCTV <u>played a critical role in</u> capturing terrorists suspected of the July 2005 London bus and subway bombings, technology has evolved so that when there is a crime, ➡ ⟨play a (형용사) role/part in -ing⟩

구문은 '~하는 데 있어서 …역할을 하다'는 뜻을 지닌다. play a key/vital/major/critical/leading role 등의 형용사는 모두 중요한 역할을 뜻하며, 형용사 없이도 사용 가능하다.

Unit 30 Joining the space club |우주인|

Space development was the only field in which the Soviet Union was ahead of the United States during the Cold War. In 1957, the Soviet Union sent a satellite, Sputnik, into orbit. Four years later, it sent the shuttle Vostok 1 into space, with the cosmonaut Yuri Gagarin becoming the first human to orbit Earth. Lieutenant Gagarin reported to the people on Earth what he had seen: "The Earth is green." Then he said, "I looked hard, but there was no God in space." This was a typical statement for a soldier reared in dialectical materialism.

The United States was chagrined. It was the biggest shock since Pearl Harbor was attacked by Japanese forces, because the Soviet Union, was thought to be only good at ballet and making vodka, as the first country to enter space. Sergei Korolyov was the scientist in charge of the Soviet space program that made Gagarin's feat possible. However, he was a hero without a name. Since the Soviets feared he might be assassinated, his name was kept top secret until his death in 1966. They even refused a Nobel Prize for the person who succeeded in launching the first manned spacecraft.

At the time, the world powers staked their destinies on space development. That is because the technology and skills deployed are inseparable from military ones. The reason China was able to succeed in launching manned spaceships, only the third country in the world to do so, is its long history of military ability. The bonanza from those technical skills in the private economic fields is also very large. That is another reason that powerful countries are not forthcoming in sharing their skills in this field.

1. What was meant by the phrase "I looked hard, but there was no God in space."?

   (a) He did not believe in God and wanted to proclaim that there was no such thing.

   (b) He wasn't a believer so was unable to see God.

   (c) There wasn't enough time to travel to where God was.

   (d) God exists somewhere else other then in space.

2. What can be inferred from the passage?

   (a) Countries capable of space flight are also very militarily advanced compared to others.

   (b) The Chinese stole military secrets from the Soviets.

   (c) The U.S. took the advances by the Soviets as a challenge.

   (d) The U.S. would have assassinated the Soviet lead scientist if they had known who he was.

3. What could be inferred as the importance of putting a person in space according to the passage?

   (a) It is a way to assert dominance over others without having to go to war.

   (b) It is a matter of national pride among the leading nations.

   (c) It is a demonstration of a country's military might and economic resources.

   (d) It is the easiest way to receive a Nobel Prize.

4. What would be the best title for the passage?

   (a) The Nobel Prize for Space exploration

   (b) How the Soviets outpaced the Americans

   (c) The space race of the 20th century

   (d) China's rise among the space capable nations

Words & Phrases

satellite n. 위성   cosmonaut n. 우주비행사   orbit v. 궤도를 돌다   rear v. 기르다, 양육하다   dialectical a. 변증적인
materialism n. 물질주의   chagrined a. 유감스러운   overtake v. 추월하다, 따라잡다   assassinate v. 암살하다
stake A on B B에 A를 걸다   destiny n. 운명   deploy v. 효율적으로 사용하다; 배치하다   inseparable a. 양분할 수 없는
bonanza n. 노다지, 대성공   forthcoming a. 기꺼이 말하는; 다가오는   field n. 분야

문장분석

■ Four years later, it sent the shuttle Vostok 1 into space, with the cosmonaut Yuri Gagarin becoming the first human to orbit Earth. → 〈with + 목적어 + 현재분사/과거분사/형용사/전치사구〉라는 구문이 있는데, with 이하 구의 동작이 주절의 동작과 거의 동시에 일어나기 때문에 이를 '부대상황'의 with라고도 한다. 이 구문은 사실 동시에 진행되는 두 개의 문장 중에서 with로 연결된 문장을 단순하게 표현하기 위한 것이다. 두 개의 절을 접속사로 연결해 놓으면 문장이 길어지기 때문이다. 그리고 주절의 주어와 with 구에 속한 목적어(이때 목적어는 구 안에서 의미상 주어의 역할을 한다)는 서로 다른 대상을 지칭한다. 예문에서 주절의 주어는 소련이고, 구의 목적어는 유리 가가린이다. 이처럼 주어가 서로 다를 경우 한 문장을 분사구문의 형태로 바꾼 후 이를 with로 연결해서 두 가지가 동시에 벌어지고 있는 상황을 간략하게 서술한다.

Unit 31 Flying pandemics
|조류 인플루엔자|

• 의학 •

On March 11, 1918, a military hospital at Camp Funston in Fort Riley, Kansas, United States, treated an unusual number of patients who had similar symptoms all day long. "I feel a cold coming on," they said, by the hundreds. Some of them were shipped off to Europe a few days later to fight in the First World War. By May of that year, the flu had infiltrated the French army trenches. In June of that year, more than 8 million were brought down by influenza in Spain. It was referred to as "Spanish flu" by the French, while the Spanish called it the "French flu." Influenza was far more dreaded than the shells the French army rained down upon the German enemy. By the time that summer came to a close, influenza had overtaken the German barracks; at least 400,000 German civilians lost their lives. The disaster spread to Asia and swept India and China. The 1918 influenza pandemic, which continued into the following year, caused genuine panic throughout the world. The more surprising fact is that the memory of the calamity left people's minds so 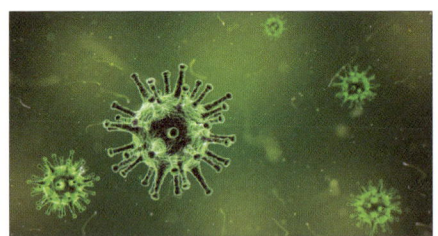 quickly. Many people know about the black plague, one of the deadliest pandemics during the Medieval Period, but have no idea about the "spanish flu," which broke out in the 20th Century. A major culprit behind the calamity was not a cold virus, but an influenza virus. In 2005, Dr. Jeffrey Taubenberger of the U.S. Armed Forces Institute of Pathology succeeded in mapping the genetic material of the virus that caused the devastating 1918 influenza pandemic. He is well-known for his work extracting samples of the 1918 virus from preserved tissue and sequencing its genome. He conducted an in-depth study on the corpse of an aboriginal man who died the same year as the flu pandemic and was buried in the ice for 80 years in Alaska. He initially believed a pig was the major culprit behind the epidemic; people and animals can be infected with the pig influenza virus. However, after a close investigation of virus genes extracted from corpses, he reached the conclusion that the disease originated from birds.

1. What cannot be inferred from the passage?

   (a) The influenza virus was a devastating disease.

   (b) Scientists eventually developed a cure for the influenza outbreak of 1918.

   (c) It would not have been as severe if there had not been a war.

   (d) It was shadowed by the tragedy of the war, while the black plague was not.

2. What is the most likely reason the French called it the "Spanish Flu"?

   (a) The Spanish actually gave them the flu.

   (b) A Spanish doctor was the first one to identify it.

   (c) They wanted to blame another country for the introduction of the flu to their people.

   (d) They were told it was called that by the German army.

3. How did Dr. Taubenberger believe the flu was spread to humans?

   (a) He believed it was transmitted from birds to people.

   (b) He believed it was a cold that new troops brought with them.

   (c) He thought it was contracted by being too close to pigs.

   (d) He felt it was spread through long times spent in trenches during the war.

4. Which of the following is true according to the passage?

   (a) The virus was first unlocked after it melted out of 80 year old ice.

   (b) The first person to die from the disease was an aboriginal man in Alaska.

   (c) The Spanish gave the flu to the French.

   (d) The genome of the 1918 influenza was discovered to be different from what was originally thought.

Words & Phrases

symptom *n.* 증상   infiltrate *v.* 침입하다, 침투하다   trench *n.* 참호   A is referred to as B A가 B로 지칭되다
dreaded *a.* 두려운, 무서운   shell *n.* 포탄   overtake *v.* 불시에 닥치다   barrack *n.* 막사, 병영   civilian *n.* 민간인
disaster *n.* 재난   sweep *v.* 휩쓸다   pandemic *n.* 전국[전 세계]적인 유행병   calamity *n.* 재난, 재해, 참화
medieval *a.* 중세의   culprit *n.* 범인, 장본인   pathology *n.* 병리, 병리학   devastating *a.* 황폐시키는, 파괴적인
extract *v.* 추출하다   sequence *v.* 순서대로 나열하다   corpse *n.* 시체   aboriginal *a.* 원주민의   initially *ad.* 처음에는
originate *v.* 유래하다

문장분석

■ However, after a close investigation of virus genes extracted from corpses, he <u>reached the conclusion</u> that the disease originated from birds. ➡ 〈reach the conclusion that ~〉이라는 표현은 '결론에 도달하다'는 뜻으로, 동격의 that을 사용해 that 이하라는 내용의 결론에 도달하다는 뜻이 된다. '결론에 도달하다'는 다른 표현으로는 arrive at the conclusion, come to the conclusion 등이 있다.

Unit 32 | Mobile gold rush |도시광업|

During a gold rush in the mid-19th century in Victoria, Australia, a hotel bar in Bendigo was popular among miners looking to celebrate after gold was found in the area. Workers assigned to clean the floor may have grumbled about the job at first, but they soon stopped complaining. This is because while cleaning, they found that they were able to sweep up gold that had fallen off the miners' boots. At the time, workers came from all around the world to help dig up what was then 40 percent of the world's gold output. Nowadays, people rushing to find gold in backwater regions can only be seen in Charlie Chaplin movies. The number of unmined gold reserves has dramatically shrunk.

Instead, the 21st century gold rush is in the city. In advanced countries, the trend has shifted to urban mining, finding useful minerals within industrial waste such as discarded electronic devices. One cellular phone has an average of 6.8 milligrams of gold. That means 1,000 cellular phones contain around 6.8 grams of gold. Lighter and smaller is the gold standard of high-tech electronic devices. Most cell phones use gold in their circuit boards, as it is high in connectivity. The amount used is not negligible. While only 5 grams of gold can usually be extracted from 1 ton of ore, 1 ton of mobile phones yields 150 grams of gold, 30 times the amount from ore. Moreover, from 1 ton of cellular phones, 100 kilograms of copper and 3 kilograms of silver can be extracted, along with other precious metals such as iridium.

1. What can be inferred from the passage?

   (a) Junk yards will become the new mines of the future.

   (b) The world has run out of naturally occurring gold reserves.

   (c) The modern age has opened up a new source of precious metals.

   (d) The price of gold will drop as more electronics are harvested for reusable gold.

2. Which of the following is incorrect according to the passage?

   (a) There are few unmined reserves in the world.

   (b) Gold is not the only precious metal found in electronic devices worth large amounts of money.

   (c) Miners in Victoria were angry at the hotel bar for stealing their gold.

   (d) The only source of gold in the near future will be cell phones and circuit boards.

3. What is the main purpose of the passage?

   (a) To illustrate the dangerous levels our gold reserves have reached

   (b) To get people to invest in gold

   (c) To inform the reader of alternate sources for metals

   (d) To encourage people to enter the metal salvage business

4. What would be the best title for this passage?

   (a) Urban mining

   (b) Cell phones made of gold

   (c) The deteriorating gold supplies of the world

   (d) Gold mining; a history

Words & Phrases

miner *n.* 광부   celebrate *v.* 축하하다   assign *v.* 할당하다   grumble *v.* 불평하다   backwater *n.* 벽지, 후미진 곳
shrink *v.* 줄어들다   trend *n.* 경향   shift *v.* 변하다   urban *a.* 도시의   mineral *n.* 광물   discard *v.* 버리다
circuit *n.* 회로   extract *v.* 추출하다   yield *v.* 산출하다   copper *n.* 구리

문장분석

■ While only 5 grams of gold can usually be extracted from 1 ton of ore, 1 ton of mobile phones yields 150 grams of gold, 30 times the amount from ore. ➡ 접속사 while은 '~하는 동안'이란 뜻의 '시간'을 의미하는 접속사로도 쓰이지만, 위의 예문에서와 같이 두 대상을 '비교/대조'하는 '~하는 반면'이란 의미로도 사용된다.

Unit 33 Risk management |위험사회|

• 과학철학 •

The biggest nuclear accident happened at the Chernobyl nuclear power plant in the former Soviet Union (now Ukraine) in April 1986. Reactor No. 4 exploded, leaking 10 tons of radioactive material. The leak was much stronger than that of the nuclear bomb dropped on Hiroshima. Afraid of exposing secret information and civilian unrest, the Soviet government kept the accident silent while the damages widened. Nearby countries also were fearful.

German sociologist Ulrich Beck, who observed the shock of the Chernobyl nuclear accident, published "Risk Society." It is a theory on risk that stipulates that industrialization and modernization brings technological development and material prosperity, but also greater risk. Beck's theory on risk purports that there are not only more calamities, but that calamities are a structural part of modern society. It is a society that encompasses catastrophic disaster in its daily life.

The risks include biological calamities, nuclear accidents, unemployment, financial commotion, environmental destruction and global warming. Thus risks are repeatedly produced and our awareness of the dangers become muted, as does their control. As risks become globalized, everyone is affected. As shown in the oil spill, accurate calculation of the damage and compensation are not easy. Beck wrote, "It is important for the state to carefully discuss with the people what risks they can handle and what risks it would first manage and thus come up with an agreement."

1. What can be said to mean the same as the phrase "It is a society that encompasses catastrophic disaster in its daily life."?

   (a) It plans for terrible things to happen.

   (b) It has encountered disasters in the past and is now able to deal with them.

   (c) It regularly does things that could realistically bring about major disasters.

   (d) It includes disaster preparation in its daily life.

2. What does the passage say about our perception of calamities?

   (a) We no longer fear them as we once did.

   (b) We have the ability to prevent most of them and can recover quickly from the rest.

   (c) We feel that they are only a temporary thing that passes quickly.

   (d) They have become so common place that we do not even notice the obvious threat they pose.

3. What can be inferred from the passage?

   (a) We as a society have come to accept risk as a price we must pay to live the way we want to.

   (b) We will eventually cause the destruction of our planet.

   (c) The Russians no longer are allowed to use nuclear power.

   (d) People are no longer made aware of disasters, if they were they would stop.

4. What would the next paragraph most likely be about?

   (a) How we have come to expect the worst

   (b) How to better prepare for the inevitable

   (c) Risk assessment and action plan procedures

   (d) The different types of calamities and their effects

Words & Phrases

nuclear *a.* 핵의   explode *v.* 폭발하다   leak *v.* 새다   radioactive *a.* 방사능의   expose *v.* 노출시키다
civilian *a.* 민간의   unrest *n.* 소요   sociologist *n.* 사회학자   observe *v.* 관찰하다   theory *n.* 이론
stipulate *v.* 규정하다, 명기하다   industrialization *n.* 산업화   modernization *n.* 현대화   prosperity *n.* 번영, 번성
purport *v.* 주장하다, 칭하다   calamity *n.* 재난, 참사   encompass *v.* 포함하다   catastrophic *a.* 재난의
unemployment *n.* 실업   commotion *n.* 소란, 소요   muted *a.* 약해진, 잠잠해진   compensation *n.* 보상
come up with (해답·돈 등을) 찾아내다[내놓다]

문장분석

■ <u>It</u> is important <u>for</u> the state <u>to</u> carefully discuss with the people what risks they can handle and what risks it would first manage and thus come up with an agreement. → 〈it is 형용사 + for + 의미상주어 + to do something〉 구문으로 흔히 'it ~ for ~ to ~' 구문이라고 한다. 이때 it은 가주어이고 to 이하가 진주어이며, to부정사의 주어를 전치사 for를 이용해 표현한다.

Unit 34 Remembering the day before yesterday
|기억력|

As a human grows old, the brain gradually loses the ability to convert short-term memories into long-term memories for storage. In order to delay the deterioration of memory, Japanese doctor Takuji Shirasawa recommended writing journal entries by recalling what happened the day before yesterday. I began my journal of the day before yesterday in early June.

But I struggled from the beginning. I didn't expect it would be so hard to recall what my day was like just two days ago — not one month ago. I often couldn't remember with whom I had lunch or how my evening went. I recalled I went to lunch with four colleagues to meet another person, but I could only remember three of them.

After roaming around the corridor of my memories for more than an hour, it occurred to me that the other person gave a bunch of books to one of my colleagues, and he had taken them to the office. When I recalled the conversation and the scene, the name and the face became very clear. I was pleased, as if I got a full mark on an exam, but at the same time, I felt sad about my deteriorating memory. I have to confess that I had to refer to my schedule book for one-third of my journal entries.

Zoologists say chimpanzees and orangutans can remember three years back. A group of Danish scientists showed 15 chimpanzees and four orangutans where to find tools that help them obtain food. Three years later, the primates were brought to the same environment, and they immediately remembered where the tools were. Primates surely share their ancestors with humans. While humans have the best memories among the creatures living on earth, we cannot be overly confident because memories can be distorted, lost, modified or implanted.

1. What do we learn about the writer of the passage?

   (a) He became fearful for his overall health when he found that his memory was poor.

   (b) He initially was amused at the thought that writing a journal could help people with memory loss.

   (c) He did not believe that the test would teach him anything about himself but it did.

   (d) He realized that he did not have as good a memory as he thought he had when he began to test it.

2. Which of the following could replace the underlined?

   (a) While taking an hour-long walk to try to jog my memory, I came to the realization that

   (b) Since I had to waste an hour of my time searching in vain for my memories, it was clear that

   (c) I spent over an hour trying to recall the information I wanted when I remembered that

   (d) In spite of the fact that I prowled the corridors for an hour vainly trying to recall things, I knew that

3. Choose the true statement.

   (a) From the very beginning this task was hard.

   (b) The task began easy but became harder.

   (c) The task was not as hard as was expected.

   (d) By the end the task was harder than it had been.

4. What final comment does the writer give?

   (a) Primates may have overtaken us with better memories.

   (b) We need to be careful about protecting our precious memories.

   (c) Messing with our brains could destroy our memories forever.

   (d) Humans will soon possess memories akin to those of mice.

Words & Phrases

delay v. 늦추다   deterioration n. 악화, 하락, 저하   journal n. 일기   roam v. 헤매다, 두리번거리다   corridor n. 복도(미로)
a bunch of 한 다발의   full mark 100점   zoologist n. 동물학자   primate n. 영장류

문장분석

■ I was pleased, as if I got a full mark on an exam, but at the same time, I felt sad about my deteriorating memory. ➜ please는 감정을 나타내는 타동사이므로, be pleased는 '나는 ~에 의해 기뻐졌다'라는 수동표현이 된다. as if는 유사 구조를 나타내며 '마치 ~처럼'이란 뜻이다.

Unit 35 Life on Mars |화성|

• 천문학 •

The question of whether aliens actually exist has long stimulated people's imaginations. People began to explore space by launching space probes. The Viking 1 and 2 were sent to explore Mars, 78 million kilometers (48.5 million miles) away from Earth, as part of NASA's Viking program in 1975 and 1976, respectively, in order to find out whether aliens exist there, and transmit data back to Earth. NASA's robotic spacecraft Phoenix is currently on a mission at the Martian North Pole and continues to send pictures back to Earth. Scientists say that Mars could potentially sustain life due to large, frozen lakes. Even though Mars is similar to Earth in terms of distance to the Sun and how long it takes to revolve, it cannot sustain life due to its brutal climate. Mars' average surface temperature is 53 degrees below zero, far lower than that of the Earth, which is a balmy 13 degrees above. The Gaia hypothesis of Earth formulated by Dr. James Lovelock proposes that the different elements of our world, such as the atmosphere, land and water, are all joined together to form a complex system. Dr. Lovelock says the system is able to support life because it tends to maintain a balance of climactic and other conditions through the interaction of its different elements. The main underlying idea is that the Earth is a single organism, and that everything on it is a part of that larger being. Many people still fear that the Earth's ecosystem is in serious condition due to global warming.

1. What can be inferred from the passage as the main reason why probes are being sent to Mars?

    (a) To determine what the temperature of the planet was
    (b) To find a suitable place for future probes to land
    (c) To determine the elemental makeup of the planet
    (d) To determine if aliens exist there.

2. What is the most likely topic of the next paragraph?

    (a) How we will colonize Mars
    (b) How global warming may be affecting the ecosystem
    (c) How the Earth's ecosystem will be maintained
    (d) The contributing factors to the destruction of our ecosystem

3. Which of the following is correct according to the passage?

    (a) Viking 1 landed on Mars in 1975, Viking 2 in 1976, and the Phoenix is there now.
    (b) Viking 2 landed in 1976, Viking 1 in 1975, and Phoenix is there now.
    (c) Viking 1 were launched to Mars in 1975, Viking 2 in 1976, and the Phoenix is there now.
    (d) The Phoenix explored Mars in 2010, Viking 1 in 1976, and Viking 2 in 1975.

4. According to the passage what is the main reason Mars, unlike Earth, cannot sustain life?

    (a) The planet is too cold to allow the proper mix of conditions to support life.
    (b) There is no water on Mars.
    (c) The planet is too close to the sun and is therefore too hot.
    (d) The elemental makeup of Mars is too different from that of Earth.

Words & Phrases

alien *n.* 외계인   stimulate *v.* 자극하다   explore *v.* 탐험하다   launch *v.* 발사하다   probe *n.* 탐사선
respectively *ad.* 각각   potentially *ad.* 잠재적으로, 어쩌면   sustain *v.* 유지하다, 지탱하다   brutal *a.* 모진, 잔인한, 가차 없는
hypothesis *n.* 가설   underlying *a.* 근원적인, 밑에 있는   organism *n.* 생명체   ecosystem *n.* 생태계

문장분석

■ Mars' average surface temperature is 53 degrees below zero, far lower than that of the Earth, ➡ 비교급에서 비교의 대상을 맞추기 위해 that/those를 이용한다. 예문의 주어는 화성이 아닌 화성의 표면 '온도'이므로 뒤에 나온 비교 대상으로 지구가 아닌 지구의 '온도'가 되어야 하는데, 중복되기 때문에 대명사 that을 사용했다. 앞의 주어가 복수라면 those를 사용한다.

Unit 36 Unfounded fears |공포의 문화|

On April 19, 1982, U.S. TV network NBC aired a one-hour program called "DPT: Vaccine Roulette." It was a story about how the whooping cough vaccine could cause death by critically damaging the nerves. It was a story about a child with serious disabilities and his worried parents. The story was later featured on NBC's Today Show and in newspapers for several weeks. This led to mass phone calls to pediatricians nationwide, all because parents wanted to know whether their children would soon die.

In response, the U.S. Food and Drug Administration distributed a detailed 45-page document assuring that rarely does vaccination lead to death or complications. However, most news organizations ran condensed stories. In weeks, victims organized to systematically fundraise and publicize their anger. By 1984, unable to bear the demonstrations, testimonies of victims at public hearings and multiple litigations, two of the three DPT vaccine producers closed down. Years later, research on 1 million children showed that the threats had been hugely exaggerated.

The damage? In the U.S., parents feared having their children vaccinated, leading to an increase in the number of children with whooping cough. Be it vaccines or not, why are people so afraid even if the real threats are minimal? The American sociologist Barry Glassner, who wrote "The Culture of Fear" points to the "merchants of fear." Media organizations promote fear to increase sales of their newspapers and TV shows' ratings, politicians create a sense of fear to win votes and shift people's attention from really important issues and all kinds of groups use fear for their own marketing. All are responsible.

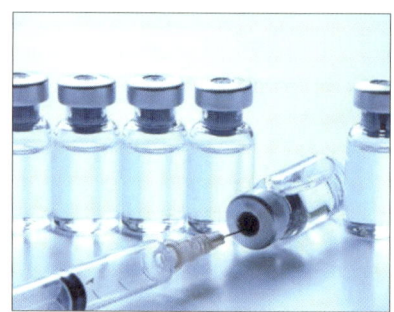

1. What does the last portion of the passage on "Culture of Fear" mean?

   (a) People grow up in a society that is based on fear of the unknown.

   (b) TV shows use fear to increase their ratings.

   (c) People are afraid of dangerous vaccines that are not tested properly.

   (d) Ordinary people are told partial truths to scare them into doing what others want them to do.

2. What can be inferred from the passage?

   (a) Vaccines are inherently dangerous and shouldn't be used.

   (b) Fear is an effective motivator to make people act in a certain way.

   (c) Fear is the best motivator to get things done.

   (d) Whooping cough is a very serious illness that cannot be prevented.

3. Which of the following is true according to the passage?

   (a) DPT was actually not as dangerous as it was made out to be.

   (b) The U.S. government uses fear to control its people.

   (c) DPT was one of the most dangerous vaccines made in recent history.

   (d) People only fear threats that are truly dangerous.

4. What would be the best title for this passage?

   (a) DPT; death by vaccine

   (b) Fear as a tool

   (c) Manipulation of mass media

   (d) The Whooping cough

Words & Phrases

air *v.* 방영하다   whooping cough *n.* 백일해   nerve *n.* 신경   feature *v.* 특집 기사를 싣다   pediatrician *n.* 소아과 의사
assure *v.* 안심시키다   complication *n.* 합병증   condensed *a.* 압축된, 축약된   threat *n.* 위협   exaggerate *v.* 과장하다
minimal *a.* 최소의   sociologist *n.* 사회학자   promote *v.* 장려하다

문장분석

■ This <u>led to</u> mass phone calls to pediatricians nationwide, all because parents wanted to know whether their children would soon die. → 〈A lead to B〉 구문은 'A라는 원인으로 B라는 결과가 발생하다'는 뜻으로 인과관계를 설명할 때 자주 사용되는 표현이다. 비슷한 표현으로는 앞서 나왔던 contribute to를 포함해 result in, cause, give rise to, translate to 등이 있다.

Unit 37 | Bad branding |낙인|

• 기술 •

During the 1960s, the U.S. army discovered a new way to store food longer in the field. After being exposed to weak gamma rays, the food could be stored for extended periods, its freshness maintained far longer than before. The newly developed method, called radiation exposure, was designed to sterilize food before it was packed. Unlike earlier chemical treatments, it left no dangerous substances. The World Health Organization classified the process as harmless to human health, and the Food and Drug Administration allowed for food so treated to be provided to school children.

But environmental organizations are still insisting that radiation exposure should be banned. Compulsory regulations have been devised to ensure that the food is labelled with a five-centimeter disclosure, "Food exposed to radiation," on the package. Consumers recognize it as an indication that they should avoid the food. That is because radiation reminds us of the damage caused by World War II atomic bombs.

However, gamma rays are used far more frequently than generally known in hospitals. Disposable syringes and burn gauze are sterilized with gamma rays. There are many cases where a saline solution for cleansing contact lenses can be used to kill germs with radioactive rays. The gamma knife is gaining popularity as it can kill brain tumors and cancer cells by emitting gamma rays.

1. What is the passage about?

    (a) The link between the U.S. army and techonological advances

    (b) The campaign by environmentalists to ban radiation exposure

    (c) The growing use of radiation in everyday life

    (d) The use of radiation in food storage and the medical field

2. Which of the following is true?

    (a) When we go to hospital, we probably come into contact with some form of radiation.

    (b) Radiation causes home appliances to work better.

    (c) New advances in the understanding of gamma rays signal danger in using them.

    (d) If you eat some food that has been exposed to radiation, you will end up in hospital.

3. What can you infer about radiation exposure?

    (a) Recently, more and more children are showing signs of damage linked to radiation exposure.

    (b) It is cheap and used by most companies these days.

    (c) It has a bad image due to its destruction in World War II.

    (d) It causes long term damage to anything that touches it.

4. Why was radiation exposure first used by the U.S. army?

    (a) Because they didn't like the local food they were forced to eat when they were in the field.

    (b) The soldiers always complained that their food lacked taste.

    (c) They wanted to find something that would make the enemy afraid of them.

    (d) They needed to find a way to make food stay fresh for longer so they could eat well during missions.

Words & Phrases

expose v. 노출시키다   radiation n. 방사선, 방사선 치료   sterilize v. 살균[소독]하다   pack v. 포장하다
substance n. 물질   classify v. 분류하다   compulsory a. 의무적인, 강제적인   regulation n. 규제   devise v. 고안하다
ensure v. 확실히 ~하게 하다, 보장하다   label v. 라벨을 붙이다   disclosure n. 공개, 폭로   consumer n. 소비자
indication n. 표시   disposable a. 일회용의   syringe n. 주사기   burn gauze 화상용 거즈   saline solution n. 식염수
germ n. 세균, 병균   radioactive ray 방사선   tumor n. 종양   emit v. 방출하다

문장분석

■ That is because radiation <u>reminds</u> us <u>of</u> the damage caused by World War II atomic bombs. → 〈remind A of B〉 구문은 'A에게 B가 생각나도록 하다'의 의미를 지닌다. 여기서 보통 A는 사람이 되고, B는 사물이 된다. 비슷한 표현으로 〈inform A of B〉는 'A에게 B를 통보하다'는 뜻이고, 〈convince A of B〉는 'A에게 B를 확신시키다'는 뜻이다.

Unit 38 Chain reactions |연쇄 반응|

• 의학 •

In 1996, international pharmaceutical company Abbott started selling Ritonavir, an antiretroviral drug to treat HIV and AIDS. Abbott faced a difficult situation two years later after having invested $200 million to develop the new medicine. Ritonavir's polymorphs, unknown till then, appeared in a pharmaceutical company in Illinois. (Just like black lead and diamonds, polymorphs refer to crystals that have the same chemical element but different physical structures.) Thereafter, the basic structure of the pills consecutively changed into new polymorphs. The problem was that the new pills are unable to treat the disturbing protein cohesion of the AIDS virus.

Fortunately, the new pill was not discovered at the company's Italian factory. However, shortly after the Illinois scientists visited the site, the same phenomenon occurred. The microcosmic polymorphs stuck to the scientists' clothes were the seed.

The company had to recall all of the pills produced at the factory during this time. The chain reaction of spreading new seeds that alter the basic structure brought drastic consequences. The modified prion protein that causes the mad cow disease is another example. It has the same ingredient as a normal prion, but its amino acid crystal structure is different, making it impossible to function properly inside the body. If this goes into the brain, normal prions change into the same structure as the modified ones and cause mad cow disease.

1. What can be inferred from the passage?

   (a) Mad cow disease is very easy to contract.
   (b) Pharmaceutical companies must be very careful not to allow contamination of their products.
   (c) Antiretroviral drugs now require little research investment, unlike in the past.
   (d) The scientists intentionally contaminated the drugs to cost Abbott large amounts of money.

2. Which of the following is true according to the passage?

   (a) Lead and diamonds are identical in element and structural shape.
   (b) Polymorphs can very easily change or be changed into a different variant of themselves.
   (c) All prion proteins from cows cause mad cow disease.
   (d) AIDS antiretroviral drugs are readily available; being made by many companies.

3. Which of the following is the most likely title for the passage?

   (a) The problem with polymorphs
   (b) How to create a polymorph
   (c) How to prevent the spread of alternate polymorphs
   (d) How to prevent mad cow disease

4. What is the main purpose of the passage?

   (a) To explain how AIDS medications can be altered
   (b) To show how people contract mad cow disease
   (c) To explain the issues that arise when dealing with polymorphs
   (d) To show how different crystalline structures can be completely different

Words & Phrases

pharmaceutical *a.* 제약의   polymorph *n.* 다형체   consecutively *ad.* 연속하여
disturbing *a.* 충격적인, 불안감을 주는   protein *n.* 단백질   cohesion *n.* 결합, 응집   microcosmic *a.* 축소판의
drastic *a.* 극단적인, 격렬한, 맹렬한   consequence *n.* 결과   modified *a.* 변형된
prion *a.* [생물] 프리온(광우병, 크로이츠펠트 야콥병 등의 유발 인자로 여겨지는 단백질 분자)   mad cow disease 광우병
ingredient *n.* 재료, 성분   function *v.* 작동하다   contract *v.* 병에 걸리다

문장분석

■ Its amino acid crystal structure is different, making it impossible to function properly inside the body.

→ 〈동사 + it + 목적보어 + to부정사〉 형태의 구문으로, to부정사 명사적 용법에서 가주어/진주어, 가목적어/진목적어 등을 설명할 때 등장한다. 여기서는 it이라는 가목적어와 부정사구인 진목적어를 구별하는 것이 핵심이다. 예문의 부정사구처럼 목적어로 사용되기에는 내용이 길어질 때 가목적어 it을 사용해 진목적어를 맨 뒤로 도치시킨다.

Unit 39 Power paralyzed |뇌졸중|

The "Big Three" of World War II Franklin D. Roosevelt, Winston S. Churchill, and Joseph Stalin convened the wartime Yalta Conference in February 1945. The three leaders later also all died from strokes. Roosevelt passed away just two months after the meeting. A year before his death, he often suffered from shortness of breath, as his high blood pressure considerably weakened his heart. At Yalta, he made many concessions to Stalin, often attributed to his illness. Owing to his poor health, in dealing with a matter of great consequence, he did a slovenly job that he was ashamed of, leaving a stain on his reputation in American history and diplomacy.

Stalin died eight years after the conference. A year before his death, his 165-centimeter frame began gaining much weight. After his doctor was arrested for being involved in a "conspiracy of doctors," he no longer trusted medical professionals. In March 1953, Stalin failed to emerge from his bedroom following an all-night dinner at his dacha. He was later discovered partially paralysed. He fell into a coma and died three days later. Even though there are no "what ifs" in history, had he received timely medical treatment, the Cuban missile crisis of 1963 might have escalated into full-scale nuclear war.

Churchill had been long plagued with obesity and high blood pressure, and attended the Yalta Conference with the aid of a respiratory device. However, he lived for 21 years more after the meeting. Churchill was a heavy smoker, seldom seen without a pipe in his mouth. He was definitely a high risk candidate for a stroke. However he was actively involved in politics until he was 81 years old, thanks to medication developed in the 1960s and his positive personality. He also lived to the ripe old age of 91. After his third stroke, however, he failed to recover his health.

1. What's the topic of the passage?

    (a) The final outcome of the negotiations at the Yalta Conference

    (b) The deaths of the three men who met at the Yalta Conference

    (c) Idiosyncrasies of the top leaders of the world after World War II

    (d) The secret relationships between Roosevelt, Stalin and Churchill

2. Choose the false one from the following.

    (a) Churchill did not deserve to die young since he led a healthy life for as long as possible.

    (b) Churchill benefitted from new advances in medicine.

    (c) While at Yalta, Churchill was already in bad health.

    (d) Churchill lived to an old age, despite his unhealthy lifestyle.

3. What can you infer about Roosevelt?

    (a) His behavior at the Yalta conference caused much concern to the other participants.

    (b) His death came as a surprise to everyone, including himself.

    (c) He strongly fought many times with Stalin during the negotiations at Yalta.

    (d) Had he been healthier just prior to his death, the outcome of the Yalta conference might have been different.

Words & Phrases

convene v. 회의를 소집하다   conference n. 회담   stroke n. 뇌졸중   pass away 사망하다
considerably ad. 상당히   concession n. 양보   of great consequence 매우 중요한   slovenly a. (외모·행실이) 지저분한
stain n. 오점, 자국   reputation n. 명성   diplomacy n. 외교   conspiracy n. 음모   dacha n. (러시아의) 시골 저택, 별장
partially ad. 부분적으로   paralyzed a. 마비가 된   what if (만약에 과거에 이러했더라면 현재 어떻게 되었을까 하는) 가정(의 문제), 만약의 문제
timely a. 시기적절한, 때맞춘   be plagued with ~으로 고통을 겪다   obesity n. 비만   respiratory a. 호흡의, 호흡 기관의
personality n. 성격, 인격   ripe old age 고령   idiosyncrasy n. 특이한 성격[방식]

문장분석

■ Even though there are no "what ifs" in history, had he received timely medical treatment, the Cuban missile crisis of 1963 might have escalated into full-scale nuclear war. ➔ ⟨if + 주어 + had p.p., 주어 + might/could have p.p.⟩ 구문으로 전형적인 가정법 과거완료의 형태이다. 예문에서는 if가 생략되어 주어와 had가 서로 도치되어 있다. 1963년 핵전쟁으로 비화할 수 있었던 쿠바 미사일 위기는 다행히 발생하지 않았다. 과거의 시점에서 발생할 수 있었던 일이 발생하지 않았기 때문에, 이런 경우 가정법 과거완료의 표현을 사용해 '~했었다면 쿠바 미사일 위기가 핵전쟁으로 발생했을 수도 있었을 텐데'라는 의미를 지닌다. 가정법 주절의 시제인 'might/could have p.p.'에 주의하도록 한다.

Unit 40 Gold rush |우주의 금|

• 지질학 •

The astrophysical origin of heavy metals such as gold and platinum has long been a mystery. The situation is as follows. Our universe was created by a huge explosion about 14 billion years ago. Ordinarily a star transforms hydrogen into helium as the result of a simple nuclear reaction, and heavier elements, like carbon, oxygen, magnesium, silicon, sulfur, nickel and iron are formed from the nuclear fusion and fission in the life cycle of stars. Through this process, some of the stars explode as supernovas, and if the debris is scattered far and wide, it becomes material for another star. However, the energy of a supernova doesn't play a pivotal role in fusing such heavy metals as gold or platinum. British and Swedish researchers suggested a new solution to this question when they presented the theory of neutron star collision. Matter in neutron stars is extremely dense — a mass 1.6 times more than that of the sun. Through supercomputers, researchers calculated that two neutron stars colliding into each other will explode to form a black hole. At that time, iron and nickel absorb the neutron elements which are transformed into gold and platinum, thanks to a 1 billion degree heat and enormous density. After the explosion, pieces are consequently scattered throughout the universe. However, such a phenomenon can occur only once every 100,000 years in the universe. Hence, the scarcity of gold is natural. The occurrence of gold on the Earth's crust remains just five billionths, with a smaller amount recovered through mining. According to the World Gold Council, the total amount of gold discovered on Earth over the past 6,000 years does not exceed 125,000 tons.

1. What's the main topic of the passage?

    (a) How heavy metals like gold and platinum form

    (b) How to find gold deposits on Earth

    (c) How our universe was created

    (d) The difference between stars and the sun

2. What can you infer about gold?

    (a) It is easier to create gold than platinum.

    (b) It is rare because the process of creating it doesn't happen very often.

    (c) Most of the gold in the world can be found in one place.

    (d) The amount of gold on Earth is decreasing and may not be replaced.

3. Which of the following is not needed to produce gold or platinum?

    (a) 2 neutron stars

    (b) Iron and nickel

    (c) 1 billion degree heat

    (d) A supernova

4. Choose the true one from the following.

    (a) A black hole is created when 2 neutron stars crash into each other.

    (b) Scientists have always known how gold is made, but they cannot recreate the process.

    (c) A supernova will create the climate needed for gold or platinum to form.

    (d) The phenomenon that creates gold happens once a century.

Words & Phrases

astrophysical *a.* 천체 물리학의   heavy metal *n.* 중금속   hydrogen *n.* 수소   helium *n.* 헬륨   carbon *n.* 탄소
oxygen *n.* 산소   sulfur *n.* 황   nuclear fusion 핵융합   nuclear fission 핵분열
supernova *n.* [천문] 초신성(보통 신성보다 1만 배 이상의 빛을 내는 신성)   debris *n.* 파편, 잔해   scatter *v.* 흩뿌리다
pivotal *a.* 중요한, 중추적인   neutron *n.* 중성자   collision *n.* 충돌   consequently *ad.* 결과적으로   exceed *v.* 초과하다

문장분석

■ The astrophysical origin of heavy metals <u>such as</u> gold <u>and</u> platinum has long been a mystery. ➡ 〈대상 + such as A and B〉는 '예를 들어 A와 B 같은'의 의미를 지니며, 앞에 나온 대상에 대한 구체적인 예시를 들 때 such as를 사용한다.

Breast is best |모유|

Breast-feeding is the greatest gift any mother can give her child. However, despite studies testifying to its benefits, the rate of breast-feeding among Korean women is very low — only 37.4 percent. It fell to as low as 6.5 percent in 2002, but is showing a steady increase these days. Even though there seems to be some controversy, many research findings suggest that breast-fed infants are smarter than formula-fed infants.

Colostrum is produced in the breasts in the seventh month of pregnancy and is the first milk in the first few days after birth. It is rich in protein and antibodies. Foremilk, first drawn during breast-feeding, is reported to contain vitamin A and DHA, which affect brain cell development. Research findings in 2005 suggested that the economic effect of breast-feeding was worth 2.2 billion Australian dollars (2 trillion Korean won) per annum in Australia.

Even though breast-feeding can be very inconvenient, it is beneficial to the mother as well. The practice of exclusive breast-feeding helps mothers lose the weight accumulated during pregnancy, by consuming about 500 kilocalories more energy on average a day. In addition, the latest results suggest that breast-feeding has added health benefits for mothers, such as lower risk of contracting ovarian and breast cancers, diabetes and rheumatoid arthritis.

Last year, scientists at Copenhagen University in Denmark discovered that a mother's breast milk can be flavored by the foods she eats. Mothers can influence the flavor of their breast milk by simply eating a particular fruit, such as a banana, an hour or less before they breast-feed their baby. Accordingly, if a mother eats something harmful to health, it can be transferred directly to the child.

1. What's the passage mainly about?

    (a) The benefits to both mother and child of breast feeding

    (b) How to make sure that your child is smart

    (c) Getting past the social stigma of breast-feeding

    (d) How to influence your child by breast-feeding

2. Which of the following is an advantage of breast-feeding?

    (a) Mothers will pass both nutrients and toxins to the baby through breast milk.

    (b) Breast-feeding is quite an inconvenience to mothers who have to find an appropriate place to do it.

    (c) Bottle milk contains important nutrients that will encourage brain cell growth.

    (d) You can lose your body weight more quickly by breast-feeding.

3. What can you infer from the passage?

    (a) You can influence the likes and dislikes of your child by eating certain things before breast-feeding.

    (b) Most Korean women do not like to breast-feed despite research that shows it is better than using bottle milk.

    (c) Babies must have colostrum in order to develop fully and grow healthily.

    (d) Women with heart problems are advised to breast-feed.

4. What opinion does the writer of the passage appear to have?

    (a) The writer has mixed feelings about breast-feeding, providing a balanced argument of both sides.

    (b) The writer supports the decision of women to reject breast-feeding in favor of formula.

    (c) The writer feels that women should look to the advantages of breast-feeding when making their decision.

    (d) The writer is more concerned with economic repercussions than the personal benefits to the participants.

Words & Phrases

breast-feeding *n.* 모유 수유   testify *v.* 증언하다   steady *a.* 꾸준한   controversy *n.* 논쟁   formula-fed *a.* 분유를 먹은   colostrum *n.* 초유   antibody *n.* 항체   foremilk *n.* 초유   per annum *ad.* 매년, 연간   beneficial *a.* 유익한   exclusive *a.* 전면적인, 배타적인   accumulate *v.* 축적하다   consume *v.* 소비하다   contract *v.* (병에) 걸리다   ovarian *a.* 난소의   diabetes *n.* 당뇨   rheumatoid arthritis 류머티스성 관절염   flavor *v.* 맛을 내다   stigma *n.* 오명   repercussion *n.* 영향

문장분석

■ It is rich in protein and antibodies. → 〈사람/사물 is rich in something〉 형태의 구문으로 '사람/사물에 ~가 풍부하다'는 뜻을 지닌다. 'He is rich in experience.'처럼 사람이 올 수도 있고, 주어진 예문과 같이 특정 물질에 특정 성분이 많이 들어있다는 뜻으로도 사용된다. rich 대신에 high를 써도 의미가 같다. 'Eat a diet that is high in fiber.'라고 하면 '섬유질이 풍부한 음식을 먹어라'라는 뜻이 된다.

Unit 42 Refugee plants |난민 식물|

Official statistics in the United States show that 67 million people, about one percent of the world's population, are classified as refugees who have been forced out of their homes. Refugees are persons who live outside their country of nationality, in a constant state of stress, anxiety, fear or panic due to political persecution or natural disasters such as earthquakes and cyclones.

Climate change is another culprit behind displacement, not of people, but of animals and plants. In Europe, the number of mountain birds has been reduced by nearly 20 percent over the past two decades. The number has dropped by as much as three-quarters in the United Kingdom. This is because as temperatures rise, the number of natural habitats has been shrinking.

Plants are no exception. The natural boundary which divided plants in the U.S. was reported to have moved 300 kilometers (186 miles) northward compared to the past. This means that animal species which live in warmer climates are able to migrate further northward as well.

European winemakers have been scouring mountains in search of cool places. Growing grapes in traditional farming areas has become more difficult due to warmer temperatures. According to research conducted by French experts comparing growth altitudes of 171 plant species in the mountainous areas of Western Europe, it was confirmed that they have relocated upward an average of 29 meters per decade because of global warming.

1. What's the main idea of the passage?

    (a) The displacement of refugees from country to country for a variety of reasons

    (b) A positive way of looking at climate change

    (c) Global warming causes the displacement of plants and animals

    (d) The consequences on the wine industry if global warming continues

2. What is the impact of global warming on winemaking?

    (a) Many species of grape have died due to their inability to grow in the warmer climate.

    (b) Winemaking is decreasing in France as there are less places to do it.

    (c) The location of grape cultivation is constantly moving upward as the temperature rises.

    (d) European farmers are looking to alternative grape species that can withstand warmer temperatures.

3. Choose the false one from the following.

    (a) The number of refugees is increasing as climate change increases.

    (b) One cause of refugee status is a volatile political situation in the home country of the refugee.

    (c) The number of mountain birds is decreasing as their habitats are disappearing.

    (d) The locale of specific plant species is changing as the climate changes.

4. What can you infer about global warming?

    (a) Human population shift is already starting as an effect of global warming.

    (b) Humans have no cause for concern since global warming is slowing down.

    (c) It is causing the world to change in a variety of ways.

    (d) Plants are not affected by global warming and have given no indication of any change in behavior.

Words & Phrases

statistics *n.* 통계   classify *v.* 분류하다   refugee *n.* 난민   nationality *n.* 국적   persecution *n.* 박해
disaster *n.* 재난   climate change 기후 변화   culprit *n.* 범인, 장본인   displacement *n.* (제자리에서 쫓겨난) 이동, 이주
decade *n.* 10년   habitat *n.* 서식지   shrink *v.* 줄어들다   exception *n.* 예외   migrate *v.* 이주하다, 이동하다
scour *v.* 샅샅이 뒤지다; 문질러 닦다   conduct *v.* 실시하다   altitude *n.* 고도   relocate *v.* 이전하다, 이동하다
volatile *a.* 불안한, 변덕스러운   locale *n.* (사건 등의) 현장[무대]

문장분석

■ Climate change is another <u>culprit behind</u> displacement, not of people, but of animals and plants.

→ 〈the (main) culprit behind something〉 구문은 '어떤 사건 배후의 주범'이란 뜻을 지닌다. 원래 culprit은 범죄를 저지른 범인을 말하지만 비유적으로 어떤 현상을 일으키는 진짜 원인(cause)이란 의미를 지닌다. 언론에서 자주 등장하는 표현이다.

Unit 43 Insane or sane? |정신분석 요법의 귀환|

Is it possible for psychologists to accurately diagnose psychological disorders? In 1970, an unknown American psychologist conducted an experiment to test this. David Rosenhan and seven of his friends went to psychiatric hospitals all over the United States and falsely declared, "I hear voices and thudding sounds." By just stating this symptom, they were all hospitalized in psychiatric hospitals. But upon being hospitalized, they acted just like normal people, expressing their satisfaction and dissatisfaction with daily life to their doctors. By the end of the experiment, seven had been diagnosed with schizophrenia and one with bipolar disorder. After an average of 19 days, they were released from hospitals on the grounds that they had temporarily recovered upon treatment. Based on the experiment, Rosenhan published the paper, "On Being Sane in Insane Places." In reaction to the negative publicity, one psychiatric hospital challenged Rosenhan to send more pseudo-patients over the next three months, claiming "We will find them." Three months later, the hospital proudly declared that they had found 41 such patients. In reality, not a single pseudo-patient had been sent.

But perhaps this style of treatment could make a comeback. The Internet version of the New York Times on Oct. 1 carried the story "Psychoanalytic Therapy Wins Backing." According to the article, "Intensive psychoanalytic therapy, the 'talking cure' rooted in the ideas of Freud, has all but disappeared in the age of drug treatments and managed care. But now researchers are reporting that the therapy can be effective against some chronic mental problems, including anxiety and borderline personality disorder." The study, based on more than 1,000 patients, was published in the Journal of the American Medical Association on Friday. The return of psychoanalytic therapy must be proof that it has developed more effective methods after Rosenhan's attack. Just like civilization, doesn't science develop by taking up challenges?

1. What can you infer from the experiment of David Rosenhan?
   (a) The psychiatric hospitals were proven right in their diagnosis of their pseudo-patients.
   (b) Schizophrenia and bipolar disorder are much more common than previously thought.
   (c) Psychiatric hospitals and their employees have little knowledge of what they are doing and make mistakes.
   (d) Psychiatric doctors need to be more careful in prescribing drugs to patients.

2. How many pseudo-patients did the psychiatric hospital find?
   (a) None because the patients all acted like normal sane people.
   (b) All of them because it was obvious who was faking it.
   (c) None because there was none to find.
   (d) All 41 were found and sent away from the hospital.

3. According to the passage, what caused the disappearance of intensive psychoanalytic therapy?
   (a) The ideas of Freud brought about a change and intensive psychoanalytic therapy was used less and less.
   (b) The experiment of Rosenhan directly brought about a lack of trust in psychiatric hospital treatment.
   (c) People became more able to self-diagnose and self-treat themselves.
   (d) The global reliance on drug treatments rather than talking about what is wrong.

4. What's the main topic of the passage?
   (a) The attack on intensive analytic therapy in the 1970s and its subsequent evolution into a more reliable mode of therapy
   (b) The motivation of Rosenhan and his colleagues in conducting this experiment
   (c) The never-ending rivalry between psychoanalytic therapy and simple drug treatment
   (d) The change in civilization from the 1970s to present day and our attempts to keep up with it

Words & Phrases

psychologist n. 심리학자   diagnose v. 진단하다   disorder n. 질병   conduct v. 실시하다   experiment n. 실험
psychiatric a. 정신 의학의, 정신 질환의   thud v. 쿵하고 떨어지다   symptom n. 증상   schizophrenia n. 정신분열증
bipolar disorder n. 조울증   on the grounds that ~라는 근거로   temporarily ad. 일시적으로   sane a. 제정신인
insane a. 미친   publicity n. 공개, 공표, 널리 알려짐   pseudo-patient n. 가짜 환자   backing n. 지원, 지지
intensive a. 집중적인, 철저한   all but 거의   chronic a. 만성   borderline personality disorder n. 경계선 인격장애
take up a challenge 도전을 받아들이다

문장분석

■ But upon being hospitalized, they acted just like normal people, expressing their satisfaction and dissatisfaction with daily life to their doctors. → 〈on/upon -ing〉 구문은 '~하자마자'의 뜻을 지닌다. 앞서 나온 as soon as 와 같은 의미를 지니지만, on -ing는 구로 사용되고 as soon as 뒤에는 절이 오는 차이가 있다.

Unit 44 Hearing voices |목소리 무늬|

In 1970, former Soviet leader Nikita Khrushchev's memoirs, "Khrushchev Remembers," were published in the United States. But immediately after being released, debate raged over the authenticity of the tape recordings of the memoirs, amid rumors that the U.S. Central Intelligence Agency had fabricated them. The publisher claimed that it got hold of tapes that Khrushchev secretly recorded after he was thrown out of power in 1964. But questions lingered over how the tapes, recorded while under house arrest, could leak through the Iron Curtain. The issue was solved when the voiceprint was analyzed. The voice in the tapes and Khrushchev's 1960 speech at the United Nations were compared and found to be identical.

A voiceprint visually shows the wavelengths that display a voice's rise and fall, volume and resonance. Just like a fingerprint, each person has distinctive vocal characteristics. Lawrence Kersta at Bell Labs developed the first machine to analyze voiceprints in 1963. He recorded and analyzed the voices of 50,000 people and proved that each person has a clearly different voiceprint. Nowadays, the analysis of voiceprints has been scientifically adopted as a decisive tool in identifying individuals. When taped messages from Osama bin Laden in 2001 and Saddam Hussein, in 2003, were broadcast, the CIA could verify that they were indeed authentic by analyzing their voiceprints.

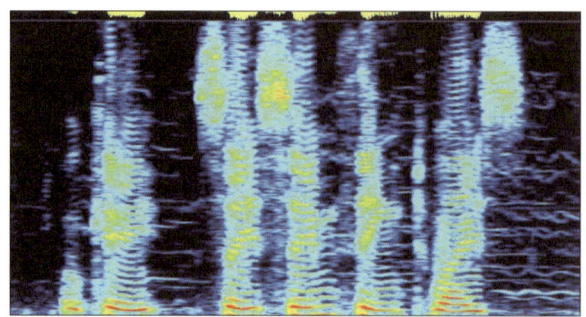

1. What can be inferred from the passage?

   (a) The voiceprint can narrow identification down to a family but no further.

   (b) The capture of Saddam Hussein occurred as a result of identifying his voiceprint.

   (c) Voiceprints could be used to accurately identify criminals on recordings.

   (d) Technology is still being developed whereby voiceprints can be trusted one hundred percent.

2. What's the passage mainly about?

   (a) The public reaction to the publishing of the memoirs of Khrushchev

   (b) The long struggle to prove the usefulness of voiceprints

   (c) The similarities and differences between voiceprints and fingerprints

   (d) The use of voiceprints to prove the authenticity of a recording and attribute the voice to the correct person

3. Which of the following is correct, according to the passage?

   (a) Bell Labs got the idea for voiceprints in 1963 but did not proceed with creating the machine until much later.

   (b) The authenticity of the Khrushchev tapes was disputed because it seems impossible to imagine how someone had got hold of the tapes.

   (c) Lawrence Kersta was working for the CIA when he made his discovery of voiceprints.

   (d) The Khrushchev tapes were validated when Khrushchev himself admitted they had been made by him.

Words & Phrases

memoir *n.* 회고록   publish *v.* 출판하다   immediately *ad.* 즉시   rage *v.* 맹렬히 계속되다, 맹위를 떨치다
authenticity *n.* 진짜임   fabricate *v.* 조작하다   linger *v.* 계속되다, 오래 머물다
under house arrest 가택연금 중인   voiceprint *n.* 성문   identical *a.* 동일한   wavelength *n.* 파장   resonance *n.* 공명
distinctive *a.* 독특한   characteristic *n.* 특징   adopt *v.* 채택하다   decisive *a.* 결정적인   identify *v.* 지목하다, 식별하다
authentic *a.* 진본인, 진짜인   validate *v.* 입증하다, 인증하다

문장분석

■ Just like a fingerprint, each person has distinctive vocal characteristics. ➡ 수량형용사 중에서 each와 every는 의미상 복수이지만 뒤에 단수명사와 단수동사가 와야 한다. 단 every two hours, every five days 등과 같이 빈도수를 나타내는 경우엔 복수가 올 수 있다.

Unit 45 The silent organ |간|

According to a dissertation in Science magazine, Volume 276, the mythical story about Prometheus is an indication that ancient Greeks knew that the liver can regenerate itself if surgically removed or injured. The liver is one of a few internal human organs capable of natural regeneration of lost tissue; as little as 15 percent of a liver can regenerate into a whole liver in two or three months. Even if the liver is impaired by excessive drinking or hepatitis, it can be easily restored after a short period of abstinence or if the hepatitis is completely cured.

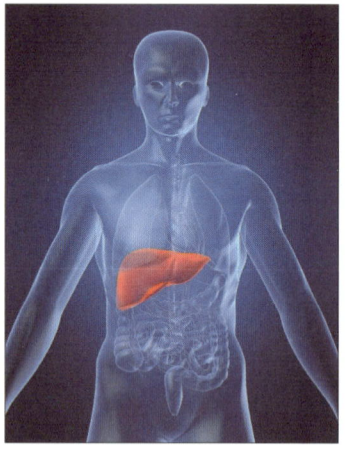

The adult human liver normally weighs 1.5 kilograms, the largest internal organ in the human body, and has several important functions. As we know, the liver is the key organ that metabolizes or breaks down alcohol; counteracting such poisoning is a process that transforms potentially toxic substances into less dangerous forms and pushes them out of the body. However, the liver is not able to detoxify or remove all toxic substances. It passes through hazardous substances that it is unable to neutralize.

The role of the liver in the human body can be compared to a link player in football. The food is broken down into the basic components, dextrose, amino acids and fatty acids, and gets fully digested in the body. All of these substances enter the liver via the portal vein and are changed into each required cell. When we do not have enough food to satisfy our appetite, the old axiom "Not the slightest hint to the liver," is actually scientifically accurate.

Unlike other organs that send distress signals directly, it serves well without uttering any complaints — until 70 percent of the liver is impaired, living up to its nickname, "the silent organ." Therefore, when the liver does give a cry of pain, it is likely to be already in an unrecoverable situation. We need to take care of it, before it sends a distress signal.

1. What's the topic of the passage?

    (a) Why we should treat the human liver delicately

    (b) How much poison the human liver can take

    (c) The least important of the human organs

    (d) An overview of the characteristics of the human liver

2. How did the liver receive the nickname "the silent organ"?

    (a) The liver does not notify the body when it is becoming unhealthy until it is probably too late.

    (b) The name is used ironically because the liver tells the body straight away when there is a problem.

    (c) It can recover quickly from a poisonous substance.

    (d) The liver works hard and never complains until the moment when it effectively stops functioning.

3. What cannot be inferred from the passage?

    (a) The liver might be considered by some to be the hardest working organ in the human body.

    (b) We shouldn't forget to take care of our liver because it is not going to warn us of ill-health.

    (c) The liver will treat any substance that enters your body and neutralizes anything dangerous to health.

    (d) You can treat your liver extremely badly and still it can repair itself given some time of healthy living.

4. Which of the following is false?

    (a) The human liver has one function: to remove the toxins in alcohol from the human body.

    (b) If you are not eating enough, your liver will be affected.

    (c) Not all of the organs in the human body can regenerate.

    (d) If your liver starts hurting, you need to see a doctor immediately.

Words & Phrases

dissertation n. 논문   mythical a. 신화의   liver n. 간   regenerate v. 재생되다[재생시키다]   hepatitis n. 간염
abstinence n. (도덕·종교·건강상의 이유로 인한 음식·술·섹스의) 자제, 금욕   organ n. 장기   metabolize v. 대사 작용을 하다
toxic a. 유독한   detoxify v. 해독하다   hazardous a. 위험한   neutralize v. 중화하다
dextrose n. 덱스트로오스(포도당의 일종)   amino acid n. 아미노산   fatty acid n. 지방산   portal vein n. 간문맥
axiom n. 격언   live up to ~의 기대에 부응하다   distress signal 조난 신호

문장분석

■ <u>Unlike</u> other organs that send distress signals directly, it serves well <u>without</u> uttering any complaints. ➔ 〈unlike + 명사〉는 '~와는 달리'라는 의미이며, 〈without -ing〉는 '~하는 것 없이'라는 뜻이다. unlike와 without이 모두 전치사이기 때문에 뒤에 모두 명사가 와야 한다는 것에 주의한다. without은 바로 뒤에 동사가 와야 할 때 명사가 위치해야 하므로 -ing 형태의 동명사가 오게 된다.

Unit 46 Countering counterfeits |위조지폐 방지책|

The most notorious counterfeit bank note in modern society is the "supernote." The fake dollars earn their "super" tag because the technology used to produce the bills is superior to that of the original. They have broken through counterfeit deterrence technology so thoroughly that even experts have difficulty distinguishing counterfeit notes from real. It is estimated that one in 10,000 one dollar bills currently in circulation is a supernote. Who produced them is still a mystery. The U.S. government's claim that North Korea is the culprit is convincing, but Iran, Syria, and even the U.S. CIA are being suspected. The supernote may be the only counterfeit bank note that is practically impossible to detect, but with a multitude of high-tech color copiers, scanners and computers, it has now become possible to produce counterfeit bank notes that outwardly look similar to the real ones. It is no longer necessarily the work of organized criminals or those with a great level of expertise.

Governments in all countries are mobilizing technology to prevent such counterfeits. A prime example is the EURion anti-copying mark. The Orion stars imprinted on the front and back of our 10,000 won bills are an example. The latest copiers are also programmed not to be able to copy bank notes with such marks. Most countries have adopted this mark. The second technology used against computer software programs that handle images, such as Photoshop, is the counterfeit deterrence system that blocks computers from scanning and amending digital identification transparently printed on bank notes. This technology has been supplied to member countries of the Central Bank Counterfeit Deterrence Group in which 30 central banks of major Western countries are participants. Unfortunately Korea is not a member. The Bank of Korea's counterfeit deterrence measures against computers are weak.

1. What can you infer from the passage?

   (a) It appears that the only viable suspect for the influx of counterfeit U.S. dollar bills is North Korea.
   (b) Producing successful counterfeit notes is easier in Korea than many other countries because Korea is not a part of the Central Bank Counterfeit Deterrence Group.
   (c) The supernote can be easily spotted by anyone, not only experts, as long as you know what to look for.
   (d) The CIA is closing in on the producers of the counterfeit dollar bills.

2. What's the passage mainly about?

   (a) The efforts being made to hinder the flow of counterfeit money
   (b) The superiority of the supernote and some of the ways to prevent the production of it
   (c) The mission of the Central Bank Counterfeit Deterrence Group
   (d) The use of Korean technology in the fight against counterfeiting

3. What is so special about the supernote?

   (a) It was produced using high-quality materials.
   (b) It will soon be more common than the actual dollar bill.
   (c) It is virtually impossible for anyone to detect its falseness.
   (d) It is made by organized criminals and professional counterfeiters.

4. Choose the incorrect one from the following.

   (a) Korean 10,000 won bills have some protection, such as the EURion mark, but it may not be enough.
   (b) The Bank of Korea will be able to fight counterfeiting when it joins the Deterrence Group next year.
   (c) Modern technology has made it easy for anybody to produce counterfeit notes.
   (d) The supernote got its name as a result of the superior quality of the technology used to make it compared to that which makes a real bank note.

Words & Phrases

notorious *a.* 악명 높은   counterfeit *a.* 가짜의, 위조의   superior *a.* 우수한   deterrence *n.* 저지, 억제
estimate *v.* 추산하다   circulation *n.* 유통, 순환   culprit *n.* 주범   practically *ad.* 사실상   detect *v.* 탐지하다
organized *a.* 조직화된   expertise *n.* 전문 지식   mobilize *v.* 동원하다   prime example 전형적인 예
imprint *v.* 인쇄하다, 각인시키다   transparently *ad.* 투명하게   viable *a.* 실행 가능한, 성공할 수 있는   influx *n.* 유입
close in on 포위망을 좁혀 들어오다

문장분석

■ The fake dollars earn their "super" tag because the technology used to produce the bills is superior to that of the original. → 〈A is superior/inferior to B〉라는 구문은 'A가 B보다 더 우월하다/열등하다'는 뜻을 지닌다. 비교급의 의미를 지니지만 원급의 형태를 취하고 있으며 비교의 대상 앞에 than 대신 전치사 to가 사용된다. 라틴어 계열의 형용사들이 이런 형태를 보이는데, 비슷한 예로는 be senior/junior to, be preferable to 등이 있다.

Unit 47 History in color
|피부색|

Science explains that skin color depends principally on the following three elements: melanin, hemoglobin and carotene. Among them, carotene has a temporary effect on skin color. Excessive consumption of foods high in carotene, such as carrots and tangerines, may turn one's skin yellow for a short time. If hemoglobin is abundant on the surface of the skin, it may appear reddish. But the important factor in determining race and skin color is the amount of the dark brown pigment melanin in the skin. The number of melanin cells is not determined by race, but by the density of centrioles in a melanin cell.

The theory that skin color adapts to the level of ultraviolet radiation makes some sense. The ancestors of modern humans who lived predominantly near the equator in Africa had darker skin because it was more effective at reflecting heat, helping the body cool down and preventing the skin from receiving harmful ultraviolet rays. When receiving the same amount of sunlight, white people are 10 times more likely to develop skin cancer than black people. However, less exposure to ultraviolet rays can lead to a deficiency in vitamin D, also known as the "sunshine vitamin." This is the main reason why black people are at higher risk of contracting rickets, rheumatoid arthritis, cardiovascular diseases and colon, lung and prostate cancer, due to vitamin D deficiency.

After migrating from Africa and settling into areas of Asia and Europe, these humans may have needed to receive more vitamin D, thus their skin became yellow or white in order to survive. An exception to this theory are the original inhabitants of Alaska who had black skin, despite living in a polar area, which has scarce sunlight. Experts explained that their diet of fish high in vitamin D removed the need for their skin tone to lighten.

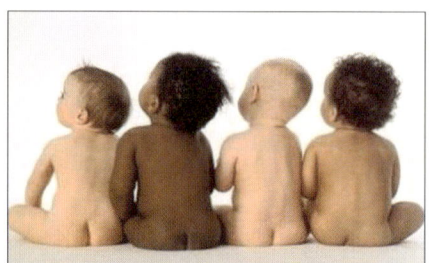

1. Which of the following is not discussed in the passage?
   (a) The problems that can arise in the body as a result of not receiving enough vitamin D
   (b) The evolution of skin color to adapt to the environment
   (c) How melanin, hemoglobin and carotene affect the color of our skin
   (d) The effect that race has on skin color

2. What cannot be inferred from the passage?
   (a) A diet which contains a lot of fish will provide all of your vitamin D needs.
   (b) White people don't get diseases which are associated with vitamin D deficiency.
   (c) Darker skin can reflect heat better; therefore a darker skinned person will feel cooler in the desert than a white skinned person.
   (d) A temporary skin color change can come about from eating certain foods high in carotene.

3. What's the passage mainly about?
   (a) The reasons for the migration of African people to Asia and Europe
   (b) The importance of diet in choosing a skin color
   (c) The theory that skin color is determined directly by contact with ultraviolet rays, specifically vitamin D
   (d) What to eat to remain healthy

4. Choose the correct one from the following.
   (a) Alaskans retained their darker skin because their diet gave them the vitamin D that was missing from the atmosphere.
   (b) Everyone is at the same high risk of skin cancer regardless of skin color.
   (c) The skin of people who live far the equator is darker to protect it from dangerous rays and to keep the body cool more effectively.
   (d) Your race will have a direct correlation with your skin color because melanin appears in different numbers in different races.

Words & Phrases

melanin n. 멜라닌 (색소)   hemoglobin n. 헤모글로빈, 혈색소   carotene n. 카로틴(당근 등에 들어 있는 적황색 물질)
temporary a. 일시적인   excessive a. 과도한   tangerine n. 탄제린(껍질이 잘 벗겨지는 작은 오렌지)   abundant a. 풍부한
factor n. 요인   pigment n. 색소   ultraviolet a. 자외선의   predominantly ad. 대개, 대부분   equator n. 적도
reflect v. 반사하다   exposure n. 노출   deficiency n. 부족   contract v. 병에 걸리다   rickets n. 구루병
rheumatoid arthritis 류머티즘 관절염   cardiovascular disease 심혈관 질환   colon n. 결장   prostate n. 전립선
inhabitant n. 거주자   scarce a. 부족한

문장분석

■ When receiving the same amount of sunlight, white people are <u>10 times</u> <u>more likely</u> to develop skin cancer <u>than</u> black people. →
〈배수사 + 비교급 + than = 배수사 + as ~ as〉 구문에서는 배수사(0.5배, 3배, 10배 등)의 위치에 주의해야 한다. 원급 비교에서는 as ~ as 앞에 위치하며, 비교급에서는 비교급 바로 앞에 위치한다. 예문에서 be likely to는 '~할 가능성이 크다'는 의미이며, be more likely to ~ than이라고 하면 '~할 가능성이 …보다 더 크다'는 뜻이 된다. 이때 가능성이 몇 배가 더 크다고 표현할 때는 앞서 말한 위치에 배수사가 놓이게 된다.

Unit 48 Addicted to speed |속도|

•기술•

The world's fastest passenger rail service, Alstom's TGV Est, runs between Paris and Strasbourg at a top speed of 575 kilometers per hour (357 miles per hour). With its successful debut in April 2007, the upgraded French bullet train outshined its competitors, ICE of Germany and Shinkansen of Japan. In speed, Shinkansen still holds the world record of 581 kilometers per hour, set in 2003. But at that time it ran on the maglev system, which is impractical for commercial use due to engine overheating and weight problems. The French high-speed train normally shoots through Europe at 300 kilometers per hour.

The world's fastest car, the GTBO, is designed and manufactured by Britain's Acabion. The concept car showcased a top speed of 547 kilometers per hour in February. The 360-kilogram (794-pound) dolphin-shaped two-seater is capable of a scorching 480 kilometers in just 30 seconds, but remains out of reach for most petrol-heads at a price tag of over $2 million. In the sky, Lockheed's SR-71, or the Blackbird, stands out. The long-range strategic reconnaissance aircraft can reach a speed of Mach 3.3, (4,000 kilometers per hour for laymen) much faster than the Concorde's once-proud cruising speed of Mach 2.23.

The 21st century is an era of speed. History substantiates that speed corresponds with power. Genghis Khan built his Mongol Empire with the help of his efficient horseback archers while German military hero Erwin Rommel roamed North African deserts with his Afrika Korps tanks during World War II. Greater speed can take mankind to higher and farther places. We can attain more information and get more work done in less time. Speed can accelerate growth while growth presses on for more speed. Today some talk of a "speed virus." They complain that people having difficulty keeping up with society's obsession with speed are being left behind and neglected. Meanwhile, Mother Nature and her resources are falling victim to the human thirst for greater speed. One year's worth of global energy consumption eats up a 1-million-year accumulation of fossil fuel. Excessive consumption of fuels like oil and coal are fanning global warming.

1. What does the term "speed virus" not refer to, according to the passage?

    (a) A quick acting virus that leaves people disabled and unable to keep up with others

    (b) People's inability to keep up with the need for speed in today's society

    (c) The need to keep going at a quicker and quicker pace that some cannot maintain

    (d) The accelerated growth that presses us to work faster, doing more in less time

2. What cannot be inferred from the passage?

    (a) People will eventually use up fossil fuels if they continue to use them at the rate they do.

    (b) Speed has been the key element to many important events.

    (c) The speed record set by the Japanese train will remain intact for the remainder of this century.

    (d) Our obsession with speed will not end anytime in the near future.

3. Which of the following is not true, according to the passage?

    (a) People like Rommel owe much of their achieved goals to their ability to utilize speed.

    (b) Fossil fuels are used to a great degree and are causing environmental issues.

    (c) The British made GTBO can travel faster than the average traveling speed of the French bullet train.

    (d) The British have built the fastest passenger vehicle in the world.

4. What could be a possible subject for the next paragraph?

    (a) How the French will succeed in developing a train faster than the Japanese

    (b) Possible cures for those infected with the speed virus

    (c) The alternative sources of fuel energy in the future to maintain our obsession with speed

    (d) What will be the fastest machines in the next century

Words & Phrases

bullet train n. 고속 열차　outshine v. ~보다 더 뛰어나다　competitor n. 경쟁자　maglev n. 자기 부상
showcase v. 나타내다, 전시하다, 진열하다　strategic a. 전략적인　reconnaissance n. 정찰　era n. 시대
substantiate v. 입증하다　roam v. 돌아다니다, 배회하다　attain v. 획득하다　keep up with (시류[유행]를) 뒤따르다
be left behind 뒤처지다　fall victim to ~의 희생물이 되다　thirst n. 갈증　accumulation n. 축적
fossil fuel n. 화석 연료　excessive a. 과도한　fan v. 부채질하다　intact a. (하나도 손상되지 않고) 온전한, 전혀 다치지 않은

문장분석

■ The long-range strategic reconnaissance aircraft can reach a speed of Mach 3.3, <u>much</u> faster than the Concorde's once-proud cruising speed of Mach 2.23.

➡ 비교급을 강조할 때 흔히 사용되는 부사가 much이다. 이때 주의할 점은 비교급 앞에 more가 올 수 없다는 점이다. 그렇게 되면 비교급이 이중으로 들어가기 때문이다. much 말고도 even, still, far, a lot 등도 같은 의미로 사용될 수 있다.

Unit 49 Man's best friend |사람과 개|

Pompeii was completely buried during a catastrophic eruption of Mount Vesuvius in 79 A.D. The city was lost for nearly 1,700 years before its accidental rediscovery in 1748. Since then, its excavation has provided an extraordinarily detailed insight into life at the height of the Roman Empire. Of particular interest is the warning, "Cave Canem," which adorns many ancient dog mosaics at the thresholds where houses open to the streets. The Latin Cave Canem means "Beware of the dog."

It was long ago that domesticated dogs began to live with humans. The earliest fossil of what is believed to be one of the first domesticated dogs was found along with human remains in a cave in the Middle East, about 14,000 years ago. Recently, however, some scientists said that the world's first dog lived with humans 30,000 years ago or even earlier, since remains of a dog thought to be 31,700 years old were discovered in a cave in Belgium.

Experts estimate that dogs were domesticated from wolf ancestors in East Asia about 15,000 years ago, based on DNA analysis of more than 500 dog species worldwide. Dogs were probably the first animals to be tamed. They provided humans with fur, leather and meat, and shouldered the responsibility of hunting or carrying loads. Dogs have achieved huge success in terms of evolution. Wolves have been reduced to around 100,000 and are considered one of the world's most endangered species.

Dogs were wise to take up residence with humans, and were smart enough to learn right from wrong. A recent study by Austrian scholars showed that dogs can feel jealousy or envy when they become aware of unfair circumstances. For example, if one dog gets no reward, and then sees another get a treat for doing the same trick, it suffers stress and frustration. A homeless dog is Chile's newest hero after it risked its life to help a canine companion. A surveillance camera caught the dog running past speeding cars on a busy Santiago freeway to grab the body of another dog that had been fatally hit by a vehicle.

1. What's the passage mainly about?

    (a) The discovery of dog fossils in the excavation site of Pompeii
    (b) The history of dogs' association with humans
    (c) The many ways that humans can use dogs to survive
    (d) Why dogs became domesticated in the first place

2. Choose the false one from the following.

    (a) It has been discovered that dogs share some feelings with humans, such as jealousy and envy.
    (b) In recent times, a discovery has shown that the relationship between dog and human dates further back than previously thought.
    (c) Dogs evolved from wolves, their numbers flourishing where wolf numbers have diminished.
    (d) The excavation of Pompeii occurred by chance when experts found a dog skeleton when digging.

3. What can be inferred from the passage?

    (a) Roman civilization worshipped the dog and built statue idols with which to worship them.
    (b) Humans like dogs better than cats because dogs can do more than cats.
    (c) Dogs are quite unintelligent and this contributed to their domestication by humans.
    (d) There may be more ways, yet to be discovered, where dogs mirror the personalities and emotions of humans.

4. What have dogs supplied humans with in the past?

    (a) A meal when no other meat can be found
    (b) A pack animal that can bear the brunt of transporting heavy things around
    (c) Material that can be used to keep humans warm in cold weather
    (d) All of the above

Words & Phrases

bury v. 묻다   catastrophic a. 비극적인, 파멸의   eruption n. 분출   excavation n. 발굴
at the height of ~의 절정에, ~이 한창일 때에   adorn v. 꾸미다, 장식하다   threshold n. 문지방, 문간
domesticated a. 사육된, 길들여진   tame v. 길들이다   shoulder the responsibility 책임을 지다
endangered species 멸종 위기 동물   take up residence 주거를 정하다   learn right from wrong 옳고 그름을 알다
jealousy n. 질투   envy n. 시기   reward n. 보상   treat n. 특별한 대접   frustration n. 좌절, 불만   canine a. 개의
surveillance n. 감시   fatally ad. 치명적으로   pack animal 짐을 나르는 동물   bear the brunt of 가장 큰 타격을 받다

문장분석

■ It was long ago that domesticated dogs began to live with humans. → ⟨it is + 강조할 + 대상 that …⟩ 구문은 강조용법으로 it is와 that 사이에 강조하고자 하는 대상이 들어간다. 일반적으로 주어나 목적어, 부사구 등이 온다. 'it is ~ that …'이 강조를 위해 쓰였기 때문에 없어도 문장이 성립한다.

Unit 50 The capitalist line |포드주의|

Fordism is a modern assembly line used in mass production developed by Henry Ford, the founder of Ford Motor Company. Every stage of a car assembly process was subdivided into simpler steps, minimizing the amount of time spent by one laborer on handling components on an automotive assembly line operated on a conveyor system. It has achieved remarkable success in production efficiency, high wages and a reduction in normal working hours.

Left-leaning economists expressed their concerns about the possibility of isolating laborers in a mass production line. However, as mass consumption was fostered as a natural consequence of mass production, this played a pivotal role in generating economic prosperity for Western countries. In the wake of the economic turmoil of 1970s and 1980s, the concept of "post-Fordism" began to appear, reflecting globalization, rapid developments in information technology, post-industrialization and destatization.

American automobile giants such as Ford are now reeling under a heavy blow amid widespread financial turmoil. This has led to the suggestion that cutthroat competition is bad. The 1936 comedy film by Charlie Chaplin presented his deepest cynicism about Fordism. Even though the scene that Chaplin was force-fed by a "modern" feeding machine exaggerated reality, we need to bear in mind the proposition that what is most important in the era of capitalism is a human face at all times.

1. What can be inferred from the passage?

   (a) Fordism met with great resistance when it was first introduced into industry.

   (b) Charlie Chaplin was a close friend of Ford and thought it would be funny to make a movie about Fordism.

   (c) Although industrialization of industry has had benefits there is also a negative effect on humanity.

   (d) Globalization will cause the downfall of the Ford motor company and all other similar industries.

2. Which of the following is not discussed in the passage?

   (a) What is most important in the era of capitalism is a human face at all times

   (b) The ways in which mass production introduced by Ford changed businesses and their employees

   (c) The process by which Henry Ford developed mass production in his factories

   (d) The after effects on Fordism as it met with the globalization of the world's economies

3. Which of the following could not be the topic of the next paragraph?

   (a) The human factor when discussing and dealing with capitalism in the future

   (b) Charlie Chaplin's rise to movie stardom during the time of Fordism

   (c) The results of the economic turmoil on post Fordism industries

   (d) The developing effects of globalization on companies

Words & Phrases

Fordism n. 포드 방식[주의], 대량 생산 방식(Henry Ford가 자동차 생산에 처음 도입)   assembly line 조립 라인
mass production 대량 생산   founder n. 창립자, 설립자   laborer n. 노동자   component n. 부품
efficiency n. 효율성   wage n. 임금   left-leaning a. 좌경의   isolate v. 고립시키다   foster v. 조성하다, 발전시키다
pivotal a. 중요한, 중심축이 되는   prosperity n. 번영   in the wake of ~가 발생한 이후   turmoil n. 혼란, 소란
reflect v. 반영하다   reel under a heavy blow 큰 펀치를 한방 맞고 비틀거리다   widespread a. 널리 퍼진
cutthroat competition 치열한 경쟁   exaggerate v. 과장하다   bear in mind 명심하다   proposition n. 제안, 주장
era n. 시대   capitalism n. 자본주의

문장분석

■ In the wake of the economic turmoil of 1970s and 1980s, the concept of "post-Fordism" began to appear. → 〈in the wake of something〉 구문은 '~을 뒤따라'라는 뜻이다. 배가 지나간 흔적을 wake라고 하는데, 배가 지나간 것처럼 마치 어떤 것이 지나가고 그 뒤를 다른 것이 뒤따른다는 뜻을 지닌다. 비슷한 관용 표현으로 〈on the heels of something〉이 있다.

Unit 51 | Under the microscope |다이옥신|

Our intellectual curiosity for the infinitesimal world is limitless. Scientific development satisfies our desire to seek knowledge. Viruses and prions are seen under an electron microscope. Extremely minute amounts of chemical substances can be analyzed by methods such as GC-MS or HPLC-MS. People in their 40s and over were interested to discover the concept of "micro." The "nano" terminology was popular in the '90s, while the scientific prefix "pico" has become familiar to us today.

Nowadays the food industry is under the microscope. They have to contend with vCJD, norovirus, dioxin and PCB, which were too small to be seen under detection technology in the past. In this context, the U.S. Food and Drug Administration abolished the 1958 Delaney Clause [of the Food, Drugs and Cosmetic Act of 1938], the zero cancer risk standard, on the sly.

With the development of analytical chemistry, the most hazardous substance revealed by the assessment processes was dioxin. Recently, some Irish pork has been found to contain dioxins. Toxins such as dioxin bio accumulate up the food chain so the dioxin levels for the final consumer are far higher than that of primary consumers. Organisms such as plankton can accumulate these toxic chemicals at much higher concentrations than are found in the water. As the plankton is eaten by fish, the toxic chemicals are further concentrated in the bodies of the fish.

Breast-fed infants are at the top of the food chain. Naturally, the highest level of dioxin is detected in breast milk, outside of man-made incidents including the Belgian dioxin crisis in 1999. However, despite the presence of dioxins in human milk, breast-feeding should be encouraged and promoted on the basis of convincing evidence of its benefits to the overall health and development of the infant.

1. What's the main topic of the passage?

    (a) The presence of toxins, especially dioxins, in our food

    (b) The ways that technology can eradicate toxins from our food and drink

    (c) The importance of breast-feeding babies

    (d) Hope for the future through the advances made in food science

2. Which of the following is incorrect?

    (a) The U.S. Food and Drug Administration secretly tried to get rid of the Delaney Clause.

    (b) These days the food industry has a lot to deal with, more than in the past.

    (c) Dioxins increase as they pass up the food chain, becoming more dangerous to those who ingest it.

    (d) Breast-feeding is being discouraged by the writer due to the dioxins present in it.

3. What has progress in analytical chemistry allowed us to do, according to the passage?

    (a) We can now identify toxins which we were previously unable to pinpoint.

    (b) We have discovered which foods are healthy to eat and which are not.

    (c) It is possible to cause the decrease in dioxins in food through chemical processes.

    (d) Food must be labeled to display its dioxin levels clearly to consumers.

4. What can we infer from the passage?

    (a) Irish pork doesn't sell well throughout the world because of its association with dioxins.

    (b) We are able to consume certain amounts of dioxin before any harm is done to our health.

    (c) Dioxins are a main cause of death to plankton.

    (d) We are going to find more hazardous substances in the future in our food.

Words & Phrases

infinitesimal *a.* 극미한   prion *n.* 프리온   electron *n.* 전자   minute *a.* 미세한   terminology *n.* 전문 용어
prefix *n.* 접두사   contend with ~와 씨름하다   detection *n.* 탐지   abolish *v.* 폐지하다   on the sly 은밀히
hazardous *a.* 위험한   reveal *v.* 드러내다   assessment *n.* 평가   toxin *n.* 독소   accumulate *v.* 축적하다
concentration *n.* 농도   concentrate *v.* 농축시키다   convincing *a.* 확실한   eradicate *v.* 근절하다
get rid of ~을 없애다

문장분석

■ People <u>in their 40s and over</u> were interested to discover the concept of "micro." → 〈in the early/mid/late 40s〉라는 표현은 나이가 40대임을 나타내는 말로, 40대 초빈/중빈/후반이냐에 따라 early/mid/late 등을 사용한다. 그리고 40대는 40~49까지의 숫자들이 모여서 하나의 단위를 이루고 있다고 생각해서 정관사 the(위의 예문처럼 소유격도 가능)와 복수의 s를 앞뒤로 사용해서 표현한다. 심슨 가족이라고 할 때 'the Simpsons'처럼 성을 이용해 the와 s를 붙이는 것과 같다고 할 수 있다. 마찬가지로 1990년대 혹은 2000년대도 같은 방식으로 the 1990s 혹은 the 2000s로 표현한다.

Unit 52 Carbon not always to blame
|탄소를 위한 변명|

• 화학 •

Carbon nanotubes have been hailed as the "new dream material of the 21st century." When Sumio Iijima of NEC discovered this material while conducting research on graphite carbon in 1991, no one could have predicted the infinite possibilities this material presented; it became the foundation for the latest modern equipment like semiconductors, flat panel televisions, super tough fibers and biosensors. It may overtake semiconductors, which have been exalted as the "rice of industry." For his work, Sumio Iijima is regularly nominated as a candidate for the Nobel Prize.

Carbon is the chemical element that has the symbol C and atomic number 6. Carbon is a derivation of the Latin word "carbo," which means charcoal. This contributes to the dull and somber image people have of carbon. However, chemists view carbon as being "bright and gregarious." Carbon reacts with other elements easily; regardless of its formation, a chain or ring formation, it creates an infinite amount of chemical compounds. Carbons are also very adept at sticking together. Diamonds are the crystallization of carbon. Relating carbon to human beings, carbon would be the ideal student who leads a model life at home and in society; that is not all — it would be impossible to discuss biochemistry or organic chemistry, which examine the mystery of life, without mentioning carbon compounds such as proteins and carbohydrates. Revolutionary substances like nylon, aspirin and phenol that revamped our economy are made of carbon compounds.

Perhaps the greatest job of carbon is the circulation of the world's ecosystems through photosynthesis. Carbon dioxide (CO_2) creates dextrose and oxygen when encountering water and air, and carbon dioxide returns to the earth as a carbon ingredient through the life cycles of plants and animals. Global warming occurs when carbon dioxide, a greenhouse gas, is made in excess. Last year, the British government proposed an idea called the "carbon credit card." The card would be swiped every time a person bought gas; it would penalize people who overconsume carbon. Environmentalists propose to end the "carbon economy" based on fossil fuels and urge rapid changes to a "hydrogen economy" based on clean energy. Carbon nanotube researchers may flinch at this proposal.

1. What's the main topic of the passage?

    (a) The invention of carbon nanotubes

    (b) The push to reduce carbon use and increase use of alternative resources

    (c) The work of Sumio Iijima and why he should receive the Nobel Prize

    (d) The qualities of carbon and its intrinsic role in the world

2. Which of the following best explains the difference in opinion of people towards carbon?

    (a) People usually see carbon as boring, but actually carbon is a very sociable and adaptable element.

    (b) Carbon is not considered important; however chemists have discovered just how important it is to us.

    (c) The black color of carbon means that it is limited in what it can do.

    (d) Everyone knows that carbon is essential but only chemists see the disadvantages to using it.

3. What is the idea of the carbon credit card?

    (a) The card is used every time a person buys gas and if they are using too much gas they will be penalized.

    (b) The card is used when buying gas and will penalize too much and reward buying very little.

    (c) Users can collect points every time they buy gas and get free gifts and incentives to buy more.

    (d) Card users can track how much carbon they come into contact with during the day.

4. What can't you infer about carbon?

    (a) Carbon can make so many different products and materials because it reacts with other elements so easily.

    (b) Carbon levels will be reduced as people are encouraged to stop using so much carbon.

    (c) Carbon has a dark side also, contributing to global warming.

    (d) Carbon is an integral part of biochemistry and organic chemistry.

Words & Phrases

be hailed as ~로 환영받다   conduct v. (특정한 활동을) 하다   graphite n. 흑연   semiconductor n. 반도체
derivation n. 어원   charcoal n. 숯   somber a. 어두침침한, 칙칙한   gregarious a. 사교적인   revamp v. 개조하다
ingredient n. 성분   swipe v. 읽다   intrinsic a. 고유한   integral a. 필수적인, 필요불가결한

문장분석

■ Carbon nanotubes have been hailed as the "new dream material of the 21st century." ➡ ⟨hail A as B⟩ 구문은 'A를 B라고 칭송하다/환영하다'는 뜻이다. 원래 hail은 명사로 '우박'을 의미하며, 우박이 쏟아지는 것처럼 박수갈채를 보내며 어떤 것을 환영한다는 의미의 동사로 발전했다. 예문에서는 이 구문이 수동태로 전환되어 ⟨A is hailed as B⟩ 구문이 됐다.

Unit 53 Government stuck in a rut
|경로 의존성|

All objects are predisposed to maintain their state of motion. Suspended objects want to remain suspended and moving objects want to travel in the same direction at their original speed. Galileo discovered and Newton formulated the first law of motion — the "law of inertia." Objects in the natural world cannot stop or change direction on their own. External forces govern inertia. A flying baseball drops to the ground because of the external forces of air resistance and gravity, not because it wants to.

Inertia in human life refers to a tendency to stick to old routines and shy away from change. Just as the inertia of an object increases with mass, human beings have a difficult time breaking free from inertness the more time passes, giving rise to sayings like, "A leopard cannot change its spots," or, "What is learned in the cradle is carried to the tomb." Inertia can be discovered in societal systems and organizations. If a certain system or organization is formed, it becomes very difficult to eliminate or change. When they grow in size and become historic, the method of management becomes habitual, and they even display a tendency to expand and reproduce themselves.

Social science refers to this as "Path Dependency," a phenomenon where a series of events progresses in a specific direction from the onset; the system and organization become set in their ways to the point that they become unchangeable. Path traveled in the past decides the future. In the British Commonwealth of Nations, the location of the steering wheel and the traffic system conform to driving on the left side of the road, which makes it an unchangeable system. The QWERTY keyboard layout devised in 1868 by Christopher Sholes remains the standard for the simple reason that it was the first layout. The established keyboard layout, which has become systematized, remains immutable regardless of new proposals.

1. What's the passage mainly about?

    (a) The struggle that took place to ensure the law of inertia became accepted in the world of science

    (b) The opinion that people can become set in their ways and resist all attempts at change

    (c) How the law of inertia can be applied to tangible objects as well as more abstract ideas, such as organizations

    (d) Attempts and failures to change some processes that are ingrained in society from the moment of invention

2. "What is learned in the cradle is carried to the tomb." What does this phrase mean?

    (a) The first way of doing something remains the only way of doing something, regardless of pressure to change.

    (b) A lesson that you learn early on in life will not be forgotten, but it is possible to adapt to better ways of doing things.

    (c) Society places more importance on ideas from a long time ago compared to more recent ideas.

    (d) Babies are likely to be more flexible to different ideas than old people.

3. Which of the following can you infer?

    (a) If a book falls from a high shelf, its fall is due to gravity and air resistance rather than because the book wants to fall from the shelf.

    (b) It is human nature to oppose to Path Dependency.

    (c) Everything is moving in the world because it wants to and the desire of objects to travel is underestimated.

    (d) The more humans do the same thing, the more bored they become and look for change.

4. Choose the incorrect one from the following.

    (a) Once a system or organization is formed, it is almost impossible to modify or remove it.

    (b) All objects would remain on their course if there were no external forces to change it.

    (c) When you stick to the same routine and habits that you have always followed, you are reinforcing the law of inertia.

    (d) The QWERTY keyboard layout may not have been the first layout, but remains the most popular.

Words & Phrases

predispose v. ~하게 만들다   formulate v. 만들어 내다   inertia n. 관성   govern v. 통제하다
shy away from ~을 피하다   cradle n. 요람   onset n. 시작   devise v. 창안하다   immutable a. 불변의
struggle n. 투쟁   tangible a. 유형의, 만질 수 있는   ingrained a. 깊이 몸에 밴

문장분석

■ Inertia in human life refers to a tendency to stick to old routines and shy away from change. ➡ shy away from은 '(불안하거나 무서워서) ~을 피하다'는 뜻이다. shy는 형용사로 '수줍은, ~을 두려워하는, 꺼리는' 등의 의미를 지니는데, 동사로도 사용된다는 것에 유념한다.

Unit 54 Silence leads to true inspiration
|미래를 여는 힘, '깊은 침묵'|

• 발명 •

A boy was born on Feb. 11, 1847. As he grew up, he did not receive any attention at school. His teacher did not hesitate to address him by saying "You stupid." His official schooling ended in less than half a year. What's worse, he lost much of his hearing in his adolescence. However, he still invented the phonograph, not to mention light bulbs. By the time he died, he had as many as 1,093 patents filed under his name — Thomas Edison.

Edison's inventions in the 19th century created a better life in the 20th century and opened up a new future. What encouraged him in his work? The long and deep silence to which he confined himself when he was focusing on his experiments.

There is a famous quote by Mr. Edison. "Genius is 1 percent inspiration and 99 percent perspiration." Of course inspiration sparked his creativity and he supplied sufficient perspiration when he tried more than 300 materials before finding the right one for the filament of a light bulb.

But there is one thing that we should not overlook. His inspiration and perspiration would never have been if it had not been for his deep silence. The inventor found inspiration when he had time to himself. Because he locked himself in his laboratory, he was able to invent many devices. Thanks to his inventions, the 20th century was radically different from the 19th. When Mr. Edison blocked out noises and complications from the outer world, he found the creative ideas that led to inventions.

A future is not something that comes to us. It is something that we go to. We should not idly wait for the future. Instead, we can shape our future through our own will and efforts. A future is decided by what you look for and where you want to go. We should remember that the real driving force to make a better future is the inspiration found in deep silence.

1. What can be inferred about the childhood of Mr. Edison?

    (a) He often impressed his teachers with his creativeness and innovative nature.

    (b) He was mercilessly bullied by the other schoolchildren to the point where he could not continue in school.

    (c) He was not considered particularly intelligent by anyone, even teachers and classmates.

    (d) He had a terrible illness that left him isolated for much of his childhood, unable to play or communicate with other children.

2. What's the main topic of the passage?

    (a) The life and times of Edison

    (b) The achievements of Edison, in spite of a number of misfortunes

    (c) The secrets to inventing something truly innovative and fresh

    (d) Isolation and silence can give birth to inspiration and creativity.

3. Which of the following is NOT discussed in the passage?

    (a) The circumstances of his death

    (b) The working style of Edison

    (c) The change between the 19th and 20th centuries brought about by his inventions

    (d) Some inventions of Mr. Edison

4. Choose the one that matches best to the philosophy of Edison?

    (a) People should live solitary lives without wives and other distractions to ensure great achievements.

    (b) A genius is someone whose work is achieved mostly by effort and a little bit of inspiration.

    (c) If you try enough you can beat anyone who just has natural talent but no dedication.

    (d) More work now will prepare you for the future.

Words & Phrases

address *v.* 호칭으로 부르다   adolescence *n.* 청소년기   phonograph *n.* 축음기   not to mention ~은 말할 것도 없고
light bulb 백열전구   open up 열다   confine *v.* 가두다   quote *n.* 인용문   inspiration *n.* 영감
perspiration *n.* 노력   overlook *v.* 간과하다   complication *n.* 문제   idly *ad.* 하릴없이   mercilessly *ad.* 무자비하게
bully *v.* 괴롭히다   distraction *n.* 오락

문장분석

■ What's worse, he lost much of his hearing in his adolescence. ➡ what's worse는 '더 안 좋은 것은, 설상가상으로'라는 뜻이다. 비슷한 표현으로는 '더 좋은 것은, 금상첨화로'라는 뜻의 what's better와, '더군다나'라는 뜻의 what's more가 있다.

Unit 55 Weather not an exact science |수치예보|

•기상•

Increasing the accuracy of weather forecasts, is not a simple task because, fundamentally, weather forecasts are destined to be fallacious. The science of forecasting weather has been in existence for only a short time. Before people invented equipment that could accurately observe meteorological conditions, people predicted weather through experience and human senses. Galileo invented a crude thermometer in the early 1600s, and Benjamin Franklin discovered in 1773 that meteorological phenomena moved regionally. Weather charts that display expansive regional meteorological patterns were used in forecasting weather only after the wireless telegraph was invented in the 19th century. During the middle of the 20th century, high-tech meteorological equipment like artificial satellites and meteorological radar were invented, along with a supercomputer that could process vast amounts of meteorological information. The era of "numerical forecasting" began; forecasters used current meteorological data to calculate future weather.

Using a supercomputer to analyze the prodigious amount of information that can influence the weather to increase the accuracy of forecasts has its limits because of the so-called "butterfly" effect, a term coined in 1961 by American scholar Edward Lorentz. "The flap of a butterfly's wing in Brazil can set off a tornado in Texas." This suggests that small early meteorological conditions produce large variations. Regardless of how elaborate a weather forecasting model may be, if the initial data is slightly off, the forecast results will change dramatically. Augmentation of weather information and more elaborate models for forecasting do not guarantee weather forecasts that are more accurate. Precise numbers do not ensure precise forecasts. Human beings are left with the task of analyzing the numbers produced by computers and forecasting the weather.

1. What is the butterfly effect?

   (a) Butterflies in Brazil are extremely intelligent and able to tell what weather is coming.

   (b) Even small, and seemingly unimportant things, can produce enormous changes elsewhere.

   (c) Weather conditions in one particular country can be duplicated almost exactly in another country at the same time.

   (d) It is impossible to make weather forecasts accurately.

2. What jumpstarted the era of numerical forecasting?

   (a) 20th century technology that could process larger than ever amounts of information and calculate future weather

   (b) The inventions of Benjamin Franklin in the field of meteorology

   (c) A change in attitudes that meant society was beginning to rely more heavily on human forecasters.

   (d) There had been mistakes where society had wrongly trusted human senses, so people began looking for other ways to predict the weather.

3. What can you infer about the supercomputer used to forecast weather?

   (a) It took many years and a lot of scientists to develop it.

   (b) If used correctly it can predict the weather perfectly, but if used incorrectly it fails.

   (c) The job of forecasting weather is done completely by the computer and humans do not have input.

   (d) Despite all the data it uses, it cannot predict the weather exactly because there are unknown variables which affect it.

Words & Phrases

accuracy *n.* 정확도   fundamentally *ad.* 근본적으로   be destined to ~로 운명 지어지다   fallacious *a.* 틀린
meteorological *a.* 기상의   crude *a.* 대강의, 대충 만든   thermometer *n.* 온도계   telegraph *n.* 전보
artificial *a.* 인공의   satellite *n.* 위성   prodigious *a.* 엄청난   coin *v.* 신조어를 만들다   set off 유발하다
variation *n.* 변화   regardless of ~와 관계없이   elaborate *a.* 정교한   augmentation *n.* 증가, 증대

문장분석

■ During the middle of the 20th century, high-tech meteorological equipment like artificial satellites and meteorological radar were invented, along with a supercomputer that could process vast amounts of meteorological information.   → along with는 '~와 함께, ~와 더불어'라는 뜻의 표현이며, 비슷한 표현으로는 together with, coupled with 등이 있다.

Unit 56 — A rose by any other name |구인배율|

•수학•

Rate and ratio are commonly used when comparing quantities. They are similar in that one quantity is divided by another. Both measurements reveal the degree of difference between two comparative quantities.

Although ratio and rate are both calculated the same way, they display a subtle difference in their usage. Rate has a standard quantity; it looks at the difference that exists between the standard quantity and the compared quantity. For example, the unemployment rate is the proportion of unemployed people among the economically active population. The rate is usually below 1 because the comparison quantity is rarely higher than the standard quantity. In particular, composite rates are always below 1. However, the increasing rate is a rare example of the rate being over "1" because the amount of increase is higher than the standard quantity.

Ratio does not have a standard quantity but examines how many times greater one quantity is over another. The magnification ratio is the relationship between the size of an object seen through telescopes and microscopes and its actual size; therefore, the ratio is usually greater than 1, and the term "times" is usually used. As is the case with reduction ratios on copy machines, some rare instances exist when the ratio is below 1, but in most instances, ratio is used when the comparison quantity is much higher than the quantity to which it is being compared.

1. What is the main point of this passage?

   (a) To explain how unemployment rates can vary because of ratios

   (b) To distinguish the difference between rate and ratio in their basic and alternate forms

   (c) To show the comparative relationships between different ratios and "1"

   (d) To elaborate on the proportionality of rates in comparison to "1"

2. What cannot be inferred from the passage?

   (a) That although rates and ratios are different they operate on similar mathematical principles.

   (b) Ratios and rates, although appearing to be similar, are in fact different.

   (c) The use of rates can be applied to any situation where there is at least one standard.

   (d) If you know the rate at which something increases you can determine its ratio to another.

3. What is a suitable title for this passage?

   (a) The similarities and differences between rates and ratios

   (b) A description of the difference between rate and ratio

   (c) The different forms of rates and how they apply to ratios

   (d) The similar forms of ratios and their application to rates

4. Which of the following is not true?

   (a) Rates and ratios are different forms of mathematical relationships.

   (b) Rates are dependant on the ratio of the standard by which they are measured.

   (c) Ratios are a factor of how many times something is greater or smaller than something else.

   (d) Rates are entirely dependant on the relationship with the standard by which they are measured.

Words & Phrases

rate *n.* 비율   ratio *n.* 배율   quantity *n.* 양   similar *a.* 유사한   comparative *a.* 비교의   subtle *a.* 미묘한
proportion *n.* 비율   comparison *n.* 대조   reduction *n.* 축소

문장분석

- As is the case with reduction ratios on copy machines, some rare instances exist when the ratio is below 1. → ⟨as is the case with somebody/something⟩ 구문은 '~에게 흔히 있는 일이지만, 흔히 있듯이'라는 뜻이다. 이때 as를 문법적으로 주격 유사 관계대명사라고 하며, 앞이나 뒤의 절 전체를 선행사로 취한다.

Unit 57 Dangers of tunnel vision |터널시야|

• 의학 •

Extreme gravity can cause a fighter or stunt pilot to experience tunnel vision, where central vision is retained and peripheral vision is lost. It is an optical illusion — when traveling at high speeds through a dark tunnel, the exit of the tunnel appears bright and round while the periphery grows dark. It is similar to looking through a telescope; the world is reduced to the boundaries of the cylindrical circle. Judgment is bound to suffer as anything outside of the circle cannot be recognized.

There are many medical explanations for the occurrence of tunnel vision. A person's vision can be curtailed because of injuries or staining of the cornea through eye diseases. Cerebral hemorrhaging or oxygen toxicity of the central nervous system can cause tunnel vision, as well. There are also reports that altitude sickness, hypoxia and migraine headaches can induce tunnel vision.

Tunnel vision is also commonly experienced when drinking excessively. Eye muscles become lax and focusing becomes difficult. Vision narrows as objects become blurry and the drinker experiences double vision. The danger of accidents increases with the onset of tunnel vision. One can suffer a fatal accident if experiencing tunnel vision while piloting a plane, driving a car, working heavy machinery or crossing the street.

1. What can you infer about people experiencing tunnel vision?

   (a) They should lie down in a dark room in silence.

   (b) They should not do anything that may put themselves or another person in danger.

   (c) They should drink lots of water to counteract the effects.

   (d) They should sleep to help their bodies rejuvenate themselves.

2. Which of the following is not thought to be a cause of tunnel vision?

   (a) Having a bad hangover

   (b) Experiencing sickness and dizziness in high places

   (c) Suffering a serious eye disease

   (d) Traveling at exceptionally high speeds

3. All of the following are correct except...

   (a) Drinking over your personal limit for alcohol can cause tunnel vision.

   (b) When you experience tunnel vision you are unable to see anything except what is directly in front of you.

   (c) Tunnel vision is only dangerous for those people with dangerous jobs.

   (d) The experience of tunnel vision mirrors the experience of looking through a telescope.

4. What's the most likely title of the passage?

   (a) What to do when you get tunnel vision

   (b) Accidents that happen when people unexpectedly get tunnel vision

   (c) Reasons for and effects of getting tunnel vision

   (d) The signs that you may be a tunnel vision sufferer

Words & Phrases

tunnel vision *n.* 터널 시야, 좁은 시야   retain *v.* 유지하다   peripheral *a.* 주변적인   optical *a.* 시각적인
illusion *n.* 환각   be bound to ~하게 돼 있다, ~하게 마련이다   cornea *n.* 각막   cerebral hemorrhaging 뇌일혈, 뇌출혈
altitude sickness *n.* 고산병   hypoxia *n.* 저산소증   migraine *n.* 편두통   lax *a.* 느슨한   blurry *a.* 흐릿한
counteract *v.* (무엇의 악영향에) 대응하다   rejuvenate *v.* 활기를 되찾게 하다   hangover *n.* 숙취

문장분석

■ <u>There are</u> many medical explanations for the occurrence of tunnel vision. ➔ ⟨there is + 단수명사⟩,   ⟨there are + 복수명사⟩ 구문은 '~가 있다'는 뜻으로, 뒤에 오는 명사의 수에 따라 be동사의 수도 결정되므로 주의한다.

Unit 58 Joining in the game |지구 온난화|

Is global warming a blessing to humankind? Some 100 years ago when fossil fuel was not as massively consumed as it is these days, eminent scientists in Europe believed it was. In 1890, Svante Arrhenius, a chemist who won the Nobel Prize in 1903 for his study on ions, found that an increase in carbon dioxide in the atmosphere caused greenhouse effects. But he did not realize the seriousness of the issue. In his book "World in the Making," he described a pastoral view of the future. He wrote that the greenhouse effects caused by the increase in carbon dioxide will make cold regions warmer and increase the volume of harvest around the world, which will be a great help in sustaining the world's surging population.

Now everybody knows that greenhouse gas is harmful. The United Nations Intergovernmental Panel on Climate Change recently made a conclusion on this issue. The panel decided that excessive emissions of carbon dioxide are the culprit ruining the Earth and that the increase in carbon dioxide must be curbed within eight years for humankind to survive.

The general idea is clear, but particular issues are complex. The warming is more serious in middle and high altitudes. Because of the word "warming," many imagine heat waves and droughts, but global warming will cause a variety of disasters from floods to tsunamis to hurricanes. There will be a huge difference between rich countries and poor ones in their ability to respond to such possible events.

As Antarctic glaciers melt, raising the sea level, Tuvalu, a Polynesian island-nation in the South Pacific, is in danger of sinking into the ocean. Some 90 percent of Mongolia could become desert. Many countries exposed to dangers caused by global warming have no defense. But advanced countries protect themselves with financial power and high technology, such as a carbon exchange and green technology.

1. What's worrying about the effects of warming from greenhouse gases?
   (a) Richer countries can adequately deal with the problems that arise but poorer countries do not have the means to copy them.
   (b) Most countries are going to experience severe droughts and heat waves when the climate changes.
   (c) Many people welcome these changes to a warmer era.
   (d) Anyone living at a high altitude will almost certainly be wiped out and the population shift to low altitude places will be huge.

2. How did Svante Arrhenius view the greenhouse effect?
   (a) He felt that humans would not benefit well from the climate change and suffer a multitude of medical problems.
   (b) Arrhenius believed that humans would embrace climate change as he did, if only they understood everything he did.
   (c) He thought that all the different races around the world would be brought closer together.
   (d) He felt it would be a positive change, aiding the climate of extremely cold places and increasing food production.

3. Choose the correct from the following.
   (a) Many advanced countries around the world will be destroyed by extreme weather conditions.
   (b) The UN panel on climate change have given a maximum of 8 years before greenhouse gases begin to harm us.
   (c) Tuvalu and Mongolia are in danger of becoming submerged countries.
   (d) The opinions of scientists towards global warming have dramatically altered in the last century or so.

4. What's the purpose of the passage?
   (a) To look at both sides of the arguments concerning global warming
   (b) To warn about the very real and disturbing effects of greenhouse gases
   (c) To encourage people to use their cars less and public transportation more
   (d) To jumpstart an international campaign to save Tuvalu

Words & Phrases

global warming 지구 온난화   eminent a. 저명한   pastoral a. 목가적인   sustain v. 유지하다, 지탱하다
surging a. 불어나는, 밀려오는   emission n. 배출   culprit n. 범인, 주범   ruin v. 망치다   curb v. 억제하다
altitude n. 고도   drought n. 가뭄   respond to ~에 대응하다   Antarctic n. 남극지역   glacier n. 빙하
adequately ad. 충분히   be wiped out 전멸하다   submerged a. 물 아래로 가라앉은, 수중의

문장분석

■ In 1890, Svante Arrhenius, a chemist who won the Nobel Prize in 1903 for his study on ions, found that an <u>increase in</u> carbon dioxide in the atmosphere caused greenhouse effects. ➡ ⟨increase/decrease/change/hike/drop + in⟩에서 볼 수 있듯이 증가/감소/변화 등과 관련된 명사 뒤에는 전치사 in이 주로 오는 것에 유의한다.

Unit 59 Corny economics |옥수수 쟁탈전|

Today's news is that Mexico, where corn originated, is having a hard time because of the sudden rise in the price of corn. Last spring, about 120,000 people gathered to protest in the center of Mexico City, raising the government's tension level. During the past year, the price of a tortilla has risen to three times its original price. That is because it has gotten hard to secure the cheap American corn that had been imported ever since the two countries signed the North American Free Trade Agreement, or NAFTA. The shortage is not due to a bad corn harvest. It is because of the Bush government's bio-energy policy planning.

Refining fermented corn makes ethanol. When it is combined with gasoline, ethanol can be used as fuel for automobiles. Because of the record-high oil prices and the unstable situation in the Middle East, the United States is working harder than ever to create bio energy. President George W. Bush announced in his annual State of the Union address to Congress that the country will reduce its gasoline consumption by 20 percent in the coming decade through the use of bio-fuels. With bio-fuels factories and gas stations increasing in great numbers, the price of corn is climbing fast, too. In an effort to meet the national demand, the amount of corn exports has decreased greatly. This is why the Mexicans, who have been a great beneficiary of NAFTA for the past 10 years, are demonstrating and calling for a renegotiation of the deal.

Mexicans are not the only ones having a hard time. The Japanese, across the sea, are also affected by the bio energy boom. Livestock farms are closing due to the high price of feed. There is no need to mention that the price of pork and ham has also risen. Besides corn, the price of other grains has also risen. That is because most farmers have switched to growing corn because they can earn much more, so the production of other grains has declined. As a result, Japanese factories that made tofu or natto with American bean have reduced the portion of bean in their product and raised its price. In Germany, the price of beer has risen. This is also because barley farms have switched to corn.

1. What has caused the sudden rise in corn prices?

    (a) The bad corn harvest of the year when NAFTA was signed

    (b) A decrease in corn farmers throughout the US in favor of alternative farming

    (c) A shortage of corn caused by the rise in the use of bio-energy

    (d) A rise in the use of corn in cooking due to its health benefits

2. What can you infer about corn?

    (a) Corn is staying inside the country to be of use to American citizens.

    (b) Corn is being used to make more natto and tofu in Japan.

    (c) The price of corn has been set very high due to NAFTA.

    (d) More and more corn farmers are giving up their corn farms for other grains.

3. What's the main idea of the passage?

    (a) The state of the economy in Mexico

    (b) The link that continues to bind Mexico and the US

    (c) How NAFTA is helping the lack of corn in Mexico

    (d) The reasons for the rise in corn prices and its consequences

4. Choose the correct one from the following.

    (a) NAFTA ensured that Mexico had to pay a higher price for American corn than before.

    (b) The knock-on effect to livestock is grave, with farmers unable to afford to raise them.

    (c) Ethanol made from corn is totally replacing gasoline in America.

    (d) Bio-fuel demand is decreasing as people realize there isn't enough corn.

Words & Phrases

originate v. 비롯되다, 유래하다   tension n. 긴장감   tortilla n. 토르티야, 토틸라   shortage n. 부족   policy n. 정책
refining n. 정제   fermented a. 발효된   ethanol n. 에탄올   unstable a. 불안정한
State of the Union address 연두 교서   beneficiary n. 수혜자   renegotiation n. 재협상   livestock n. 가축
decline v. 감소하다   as a result 결과적으로   tofu n. 두부   natto n. (일본식 청국장) 나토   barley n. 보리
knock-on a. 연쇄적인

문장분석

■ In an effort to <u>meet the national demand</u>, the amount of corn exports has decreased greatly. ➡ meet demand (for)는 '요구를 충족시키다'는 뜻으로, 비슷한 표현으로는 meet/satisfy a need, meet/fulfill requirements 등이 있다.

Unit 60 That weather is a killer | 기상병 |

• 기상 •

"The temperature is expected to rise quickly in a short time today, so be careful if you are driving or quarreling with your spouse." You might be thinking, "What in the world is this?" However, it was the formal weather forecast made by the Japan Weather Association's Hokkaido branch in mid-April. The warning cautioned people to be aware of the Foehn Effect, in which a temperature rise from 3 to 5 degrees Celsius in an hour can have a bad effect on people's minds. There is no way to find out if the number of car accidents or fights between couples increased that day, but the idea of so-called meteorotropic diseases raised a sensation in Japan due to that forecast.

The term meteorotropic disease is used to describe various diseases caused by changes in the weather. Such diseases happen because the human body cannot adjust to an abrupt change of temperature or barometric pressure. Changes in the weather have subtle changes on the nervous system, shrinking or expanding the blood vessels. Another academic field called live meteorology is organized around predictions from old people, such as, "My shoulder hurts, so it might rain today."

The types of meteorotropic disease vary widely, and can cause neuralgia, cerebral hemorrhage, angina pectoris, heart attack and asthma. Some scholars pay careful attention to appendicitis. A professor from the Niigata hospital announced the research results after talking to hospital doctors on a sunny day, and noticed a higher number of patients coming in with acute appendicitis. When the barometric pressure rises, the percentage of granulocyte in the white blood cells increases and it is easier for inflammation to occur. The doctor's committee in Hiroshima reported that heart attacks and strokes have increased since 2004. The local dailies report the danger scale for meteorotropic diseases in three categories: warning, caution and normal.

Experts warn that the number of meteorotropic diseases will increase. Due to global warming, there are lots of unexpected weather changes and it is difficult for the human body to adjust. In the near future, watching the daily weather forecast next to the meteorotropic disease forecast might be routine. Today, be aware of this disease. It is not a fun thought to start a day with this forecast. Unlike the weather forecast, which gets widely criticized when the forecast is wrong, the more a meteorotropic disease forecast is wrong, the more welcome it will be.

1. What's the main idea of the passage?

    (a) How to avoid illnesses when the barometric pressure rises
    (b) The new direction of the Japan Weather Association
    (c) The competition between weather forecasters and meteorotropic disease forecasters
    (d) A report on new meteorotropic diseases and why they are being forecast alongside the weather

2. Which of the following is not an example of live meteorology?

    (a) I hear something strange a few hours before snow starts to fall.
    (b) I feel dizzy so there's going to be a thunderstorm.
    (c) My toes itch when rain is coming.
    (d) I hate the rain because it ruins my hair.

3. What can you infer about the weather forecast in Japan?

    (a) The Foehn Effect arose from trends that were spotted during the forecast.
    (b) They will become longer as people want to hear more meteorotropic disease forecasts.
    (c) The Japan Weather Association had many problems with listeners who did not accept the validity of the meteorotropic diseases.
    (d) It takes meteorotropic diseases seriously, understanding the link between illness and weather changes.

4. What's the difference between the weather forecast and the meteorotropic disease forecast?

    (a) The weather forecast is never criticized but the meteorotropic disease forecast is always blamed.
    (b) If the weather forecast is wrong, we are angry; when the meteorotropic disease forecast is wrong, we are happy.
    (c) One is based on science, the other one is based on divination.
    (d) The weather forecast is susceptible to last minute changes, the other forecast remains static.

Words & Phrases

quarrel *v.* 다투다   caution *v.* 주의를 주다   be aware of ~을 알아차리다   meteorotropic disease 기상병
abrupt *a.* 갑작스런   barometric pressure 기압   shrink *v.* 줄어들다, 줄어들게 하다   neuralgia *n.* 신경통
angina pectoris 협심증   asthma *n.* 천식   appendicitis *n.* 맹장염   granulocyte *n.* 과립성 백혈구
inflammation *n.* 염증   dizzy *a.* 어지러운   divination *n.* 점(미래의 예측)   susceptible *a.* 민감한   static *a.* 고정된

문장분석

- Such diseases happen because the human body cannot adjust to an abrupt change of temperature or barometric pressure. ➡ ⟨adjust to doing something⟩은 '~에 적응하다'는 뜻으로 to가 전치사이기 때문에 뒤에 명사나 동명사가 와야 한다. 비슷한 숙어로는 adapt to, get used to, become accustomed to 등이 있다.

Unit 61 Thunderstruck |벼락|

Ancient people in both the Western and Eastern worlds believed that meteorological phenomena were created by the gods. In particular, they feared thunder and lightning because they thought the gods created them to punish people who sinned. A thunderbolt looks frightening and yields enormous power, and was rightly feared. For a sinner, a thunderbolt was a punishment from above — but for an innocent person, it was a disaster out of the blue. Lightning has been observed for a very long time, but few scientific explanations were made for it until the modern age. In the Song Dynasty of China during the 11th century, a written record called lightning an electrical phenomenon. Only 700 years later, Benjamin Franklin verified the theory in an experiment. In 1752, Franklin conducted his famous kite experiment and discovered that lightning was static electricity, which was charged in the clouds and released to the ground.

A lightning bolt carries hundreds of thousands of amperes of electricity and travels 45 kilometers, or 28 miles, per second. The temperature in a lightning bolt is up to 3,000 degrees Celsius (5,432 F), five times higher than the temperature on the sun's surface. Thus, a large lightning bolt can cause serious damage to both people and property. Lightning hits frequently in places where climate conditions and topography are perfect to produce thunderheads, or cumulonimbus clouds. The area between the cities of Orlando and St. Petersburg, Florida in the United States, is called "Lightning Alley" because storms accompanied by thunder and lightning strike on an average of 120 days a year. Tall buildings have lightning rods to protect them, but still there are more chances to be hit by lightning there than in other areas. The Empire State Building is hit by lightning 23 times a year on average. Once, the building was hit by lightning eight times in 24 minutes.

1. What's the passage about?

   (a) Why lightning strikes some areas and not others

   (b) Ancient beliefs about extreme weather conditions

   (c) Where lightning comes from and where it is most likely to hit

   (d) The discovery of lightning

2. What can you infer about lightning?

   (a) Lightning is a fairly recent phenomenon that has arisen out of modern environmental damage.

   (b) A lightning bolt has the heat and power to seriously hurt and maybe kill a person.

   (c) Most American cities experience more lightning than any other country in the world.

   (d) Lightning Alley is a safe place to hide during a thundestorms.

3. Which of the following statistics is not mentioned in the passage?

   (a) The amount of damage done to the Empire State Building by lightning per year

   (b) The temperature of the lightning bolt compared to the temperature of the sun

   (c) How often lightning strikes the area known as Lightning Alley

   (d) How fast lightning travels on its way to the Earth

4. Why did ancient people fear lightning?

   (a) They had no means of protecting their homes and land from the destruction of lightning.

   (b) They believed it was a symbol of the dissatisfaction the gods felt for human behavior.

   (c) They had been told by their leaders that lightning could strike anyone, whether they were sinful or not.

   (d) They couldn't sleep during thunderstorms and feared having a sleepless night.

Words & Phrases

meteorological *a.* 기상의   phenomenon *n.* 현상 (*pl.* phenomena)   yield *v.* 생산하다   dynasty *n.* 왕조   verify *v.* 확인하다   theory *n.* 이론   conduct *v.* 실행하다   lightning *n.* 번개   static *a.* 정지 상태의   property *n.* 재산   frequently *ad.* 종종, 빈번히   topography *n.* 지형   thunderhead *n.* 적란운   cumulonimbus *n.* 적란운   alley *n.* 좁은 길, 뒷골목   accompany *v.* 동반하다   lightning rod 피뢰침   chance *n.* 가능성

문장분석

■ A lightning bolt carries <u>hundreds of thousands of</u> amperes of electricity and travels 45 kilometers, or 28 miles, per second. → hundreds of thousands of는 '수십만(명)의'라는 뜻이다. '수백(명)의'는 hundreds of이고, '수천(명)의'는 thousands of이고, '수백만(명)의'는 millions of이다. 이처럼 영어에서는 숫자 단위가 천 이상일 경우 0이 세 자리씩 늘어나기 때문에 중간의 '수만'이나 '수십만'은 tens of thousands of나 hundreds of thousands of로 표현한다.

Unit 62 Going ape |찜통더위|

•동물•

It is a well-known fact that chimpanzees are the closest animals to humans. It must be true, since 98.7 percent of our DNA organization is the same. However, due to the 1.3 percent difference, chimpanzees are inside cages and we human beings go and see them at the zoo. The main difference between the two is how well they adjust to the hot weather. Human beings endure well in hot weather. That is because we are able to sweat. Humans sweat a lot more than other animals in hot weather. By losing water, we are able to lower our temperature quickly. However, chimpanzees don't have this function. They aren't able to walk around under the hot sun like humans can. During hot humid weather, they hide in the shade under the trees and stay still. Chimpanzees do have perspiration glands. But they only sweat fat, not water. This fat makes their fur smooth and helps diffuse their body odor. Japan's famous professor of evolutionary biology, Hasegawa Mariko, writes in his book that human beings adjusted to hot weather when they started living outside of the tropical rainforest and in the plains where there was no shade to hide them. From this period on, humans lost much of their fur and started sweating a lot to survive in hot weather.

1. What's the main idea of the passage?

    (a) The difference between humans and chimpanzees in terms of sweating

    (b) The reasons why humans like to see chimpanzees in zoos

    (c) The similarities between humans and chimpanzees in terms of DNA

    (d) The disgust that other animals have for human sweat

2. How do humans endure hot weather that other animals cannot?

    (a) Humans are much more stubborn about weather than other animals.

    (b) Our ability to sweat means that we can lower our body temperature more quickly and stand hot weather for longer.

    (c) Humans cannot detect their own terrible body odor that comes with perspiration.

    (d) Humans do not have as much fur as other animals, thus, they feel cooler all the time.

3. Which of the following is true?

    (a) The most important difference between humans and chimpanzees is their smell and amount of hair.

    (b) The fat that chimpanzees perspire has a bad smell so chimpanzees want to be alone when they sweat.

    (c) Chimpanzees find shade when it's hot and remain there motionless until it's not so hot.

    (d) Chimpanzees sweat but not at the efficient rate that humans do.

4. Which of the following summarizes the beliefs of Hasegawa Mariko?

    (a) The evolution of humans began when they left the rainforest and found the plains.

    (b) Humans were forced to adjust to leave the rainforest as they started to lose fur.

    (c) Sweating in the rainforest was uncomfortable for humans so they sought out another place to inhabit.

    (d) The difficulties of living in the rainforest caused humans to seek out areas where they could live an easier life.

Words & Phrases

cage n. 우리   adjust to ~에 적응하다   endure v. 참다, 견디다   function n. 기능   shade n. 그늘   stay still 가만히 있다   perspiration n. 땀   gland n. 샘   diffuse v. 발산하다   odor n. 냄새   evolutionary a. 진화의   rainforest n. 열대우림   from this period on 이 시기 이후로 계속   fur n. 털   survive v. 살아남다, 생존하다

문장분석

■ From this period on, humans lost much of their fur and started sweating a lot to survive in hot weather.

→ From this period on은 '이 시기부터 (시작해서) 계속해서'라는 뜻이다. 전치사 on에는 '계속'이라는 의미가 있기 때문이다. 비슷한 표현으로 from now on은 '지금부터 계속'이란 뜻이고, from this moment on은 '이 순간부터 계속'의 뜻을 지닌다.

Unit 63 Percentage point
|1%의 힘|

A percentage is a way to express the proportion of something out of 100. It is an easy way to express a relative quantity in mathematics, science and daily life. The Ancient Greeks devised the concept of a percentage. A long time ago, the number 100 came to mean a flawless state for an entity. Therefore, a percentage using 100 as the standard has naturally become the most common way to describe proportion. When one says "I am 100 percent sure," he or she is completely sure. People also use "1 percent" to emphasize that the amount is minuscule. Thomas Edison said genius is 1 percent inspiration and 99 percent perspiration. By 1 percent, he really meant almost zero, a negligible amount.

But 1 percent is not always a small amount. Proportion is a tricky concept. A percentage is about proportion, so even when a percentage holds constant, if the entire amount increases, the absolute quantity of a certain percentage also increases. One percent of 200 trillion won is 2 trillion won, while 1 percent of 300 trillion won is 3 trillion won. The percentage is the same, but the end result varies a great deal. When handling a minute amount, 1 percent makes a huge difference. For precision machinery, an error of 1 percent is not tolerable. A change in the interest rate by 1 percent is powerful enough to shake the world's economy. The power of 1 percent goes even farther. Let's make a chain with 100 rings, each one with 1 percent chance of breaking. At that point, the possibility that the chain could break would be as high as 63 percent. If the danger of a 1 percent possibility is connected to bigger numbers, that can become destructive. Meanwhile, 1 percent of smart people can feed the remaining 99 percent of the population for the future. One percent might sound small but it can be very powerful.

1. What's the topic of the passage?

   (a) Making sure you are 100 percent sure of something

   (b) Understanding percentages by looking at the overall quantity

   (c) Reducing errors by checking their possibility

   (d) 1 percent is a very small amount

2. Which of the following is true?

   (a) It's unimportant if the interest rate changes by one percent.

   (b) The idea of percentage is a fairly recent idea.

   (c) Even if the percent remains the same, the amount can change.

   (d) Less than one percent of the world's people are smart.

3. What can you infer about percentage?

   (a) An error of one percent is unacceptable in many different things.

   (b) One percent and one hundred percent can sometimes mean the same thing.

   (c) Percentage will rise and fall depending on the full amount.

   (d) Edison realized the importance of one percent in everything he did.

4. What is the danger of disregarding one percent?

   (a) It can be very dangerous to ignore one percent of a large number because the difference will be very large.

   (b) There is no danger since one percent of anything is a very small amount.

   (c) If one percent is ignored it can have serious consequences on the world's economy and people might starve.

   (d) None of the above.

Words & Phrases

proportion *n.* 비율   quantity *n.* 양   devise *v.* 고안하다   concept *n.* 개념   flawless *a.* 흠이 없는, 오류가 없는
entity *n.* 독립체; 실체, 존재   emphasize *v.* 강조하다   minuscule *a.* 아주 작은   inspiration *n.* 영감   perspiration *n.* 땀
negligible *a.* 무시할 수 있는   tricky *a.* 까다로운   vary *v.* 변하다, 달라지다   destructive *a.* 파괴적인

문장분석

■ But 1 percent is <u>not always</u> a small amount. ➜ not always는 문법에서 '부분 부정'이라는 용어로 지칭하며 '항상 ~한 것은 아니다'는 뜻을 지닌다. '항상 ~은 아니다'는 100% 부정이 아니라는 사실에 주의한다. 비슷한 경우로 not과 all, both, every, necessarily 등이 결합해도 부분 부정이 된다. 예를 들어 'I don't know both of them.'은 '둘 다 아는 것은 아니다'는 뜻이고, 'I don't know either of them.'은 '둘 다 모른다'는 뜻이다.

Unit 64 A different side to drones
|드론|

・기술・

It seems like it is against the trend to oppose unmanned drones. You could look insensitive to technological advancement or you could be considered a skeptic. Holding a philosophical debate over drones is perhaps already meaningless. The market is already on the move, as regulations are expected to be lifted drastically. Drones are increasingly being used for positive purposes. Ambulance drones used in countries like the Netherlands arrive at the scene first and provide medical supplies. Compared to when their military uses were highlighted, people feel far less resistant to drones these days.

But the latest reports from the United States and Europe are casting concerns that we may be overly trusting the use of drones and the effectiveness of regulations on them. Reprieve UK claims that U.S. drone attacks on terrorist suspects in the Middle East have resulted in more than 1,000 civilian deaths. A U.S. drone struck a wedding in Yemen, killing 12 people including guests and the bride. A Federal Aviation Administration document reported by U.S. media is also noteworthy. In the last six months, there have been 25 cases of drones almost colliding with large aircraft. There have been 193 cases of passenger jet pilots spotting drones while flying and filing a report. And we need to think about terror threats as well as aviation safety.

The U.S. government's basic position is that meticulous regulation is possible. But optimism is not necessarily a good thing, as we have seen with gun control. Gun-related violence is practically impossible to prevent, so post-accident response capacity is improved as regulations are not effective when guns are already widely distributed. Drones are far more frightening than guns as weapons of destruction. In order not to follow the precedence of gun control, overly conservative reviews are necessary, which should not be swayed by economic theories or be swept up in optimism. The possibility of hacking and other technical discussions are also necessary. When the market moves first and regulations follow, it leads to a disaster. If the authorities are not confident in implementing perfect control, _____.

1. What is the overall tone of the passage?

   (a) Suspicion
   (b) Pessimism
   (c) Disappointment
   (d) Tension

2. What can you infer from the passage?

   (a) It is no longer worthwhile debating over the rights and wrongs of the existence of drones.
   (b) Drones are being increasingly used in terrorist attacks.
   (c) Staying out of the race to produce drones may be smarter than participating in the competition.
   (d) Drones are being used for more harm than good as regulations are being lifted.

3. Which of the following is true, according to the passage?

   (a) Drones are still viewed negatively even though they can be used in positive ways.
   (b) It has been proven impossible to hack into drone systems.
   (c) The last year has seen over two dozen collisions between drones and large aircraft.
   (d) Mistakes are sometimes made with drone use and innocent people are hurt.

4. Which of the following best completes the sentence?

   (a) tight restrictions could be a solution until thorough preparation is complete
   (b) the market will move on without the proper restrictions being put in place
   (c) no good can come of drone use in the long run
   (d) there will never be an appropriate time for implementing regulations

Words & Phrases

insensitive *a.* 둔감한   skeptic *n.* 회의주의자   unmanned *a.* 무인의   on the move 이동 중인, 전진 중인
highlight *v.* 강조하다   noteworthy *a.* 주목할 만한   meticulous *a.* 꼼꼼한, 정교한   sweep up 들어 올리다, 쓸어 담다
implement *v.* 실행하다

문장분석

■ <u>In order not to</u> follow the precedence of gun control, overly conservative reviews are necessary, which should not be swayed by economic theories or be swept up in optimism. ➡ 〈in order not to〉는 목적을 나타내는 in order to의 부정 표현으로 부사적으로 쓰였고, overly conservative reviews가 주어이다. which는 앞 문장을 받는다.

unit 64 드론

Unit 65 A depressing future
|우울증|

• 의학 •

When an artistic genius plagued by despair dies young, the depression is often viewed as a romantic rather than a psychological condition. Depression is sometimes referred to as the "cold of the mind," because people view it as something temporary and easily cured. "Against Depression" by psychiatrist Peter Cramer is critical of such attitudes. He rejects the notion that depression is a source of creativity and sensitivity. He explains that leftists regard depression as passive resistance to commercial capitalism, whereas rightists underscore the importance of mental strength and not turning to convenient solutions, such as medication. Both sides see the condition as a moral, ethical, aesthetic and intelligent trait rather than a disease.

But depression is not only a personal disease. It is also a social one, which frequently prevails in developed and capitalist nations because it is related to economic abundance and social frustration. It can be thought of as a mental emptiness that emerges after the necessities of life such as food, clothing, and shelter have been secured. In addition, depression is viewed as a psychiatric characteristic that is commonly found among people working in a cut-throat society.

The World Health Organization listed depression as a disease that will plague humankind in the 21st century. The organization has warned that depression will be the top-ranked disease of all age groups by 2020. Against Depression estimates that the cost to the United States of depression-related issues exceeds $40 billion, or 3 per cent of the gross national product. According to the book "Paradox of Progress," the number of patients plagued by monopolar depression in the U.S. and Europe increased tenfold in fifty years.

1. Which of the following is not a cause of depression according to the passage?

   (a) The lack of needing to continue to secure life's necessities
   (b) The social frustration created in a capitalist society
   (c) The lack of artistic ability in a young person
   (d) The type of work a person does in a certain type of society

2. What can be inferred from the passage?

   (a) As people in the world continue to acquire all their needs in life depression will increase.
   (b) Artists will become more and more depressed in order to become more creative.
   (c) All the capitalist nations will become medicated for depression by 2020.
   (d) People are meant to have all their needs met. Depression is a myth of modern society.

3. What will be the likely topic of the next paragraph?

   (a) The drugs that will be needed to prevent depression
   (b) How the U.S. and Europe will deal with the increase in depression
   (c) What you can do to prevent depression
   (d) Famous people who have had depression and done great things despite it

4. Which of the following would be a good title for the passage?

   (a) New diseases of the 21st century
   (b) The depression of capitalism
   (c) The common cold and how it causes depression
   (d) Depression in the 21st century

Words & Phrases

be plagued by ~으로 고통받다　depression n. 우울증　psychological a. 심리의　be referred to as ~로 지칭되다
temporary a. 일시적인　critical a. 비판적인　attitude n. 태도　reject v. 퇴짜놓다, 무시하다　notion n. 생각, 개념
leftist n. 좌파　rightist n. 우파　underscore v. 강조하다　medication n. 약품　moral a. 도의적인　ethical a. 윤리적인
aesthetic a. 심미적인　trait n. 특징　prevail v. 우세하다　abundance n. 과다, 풍부　frustration n. 좌절
emerge v. 나타나다　cut-throat a. 경쟁이 심한　monopolar a. 단극성의　tenfold a. 10배의

문장분석

■ It can <u>be thought of as</u> a mental emptiness that emerges after the necessities of life such as food, clothing, and shelter have been secured. → ⟨think of A as B⟩는 'A를 B로 생각하다'는 뜻으로, 수동태가 될 경우 ⟨A is thought of as B⟩ 형태로 바뀌게 되며, 'A가 B로 생각되다'는 뜻이 된다. 비슷한 표현으로 ⟨regard A as B⟩나 ⟨see A as B⟩가 있다.

Unit 66 An unnatural disaster
| 인공지진과 자연지진 |

• 환경 •

     In September, the news that stirred social media was earthquakes, both artificial and natural. On Sept. 9, 2016. North Korea conducted its fifth nuclear test, which caused a 5.0-magnitude artificial earthquake. Three days later, a 5.8-magnitude earthquake hit Gyeongju, North Gyeongsang, followed by a 4.5-magnitude earthquake exactly one week later. There were more than 430 aftershocks, leaving the Korean people shaken. An artificial earthquake and a natural earthquake are fundamentally different. A natural earthquake causes both vertical P waves and horizontal S waves, while S waves are hardly observed from an artificial one. The detection of sound waves resulting from an explosion is another trait that distinguishes the two. But regardless, both artificial and natural earthquakes lead to tremendous damage, and we need to be thoroughly prepared.

     The earthquakes revealed the poor state of Korea's disaster preparedness measures. It is especially serious that the natural earthquake turned into a man-made catastrophe. The Ministry of Public Safety and Security sent the first emergency disaster message nine minutes after the first earthquake. For the second earthquake, the message was not sent to the capital region. The prime minister gave his first directive two hours and 47 minutes later. With the slow and poor initial responses, the government wasted the "golden time" that has been emphasized over and over since the Sewol ferry tragedy in 2014.

     And what about the school that ordered its students to stay in school, saying the earthquake would subside soon? The response reminds me of the order "stay put" that resulted in the loss of so many lives two and a half years ago. What will young people learn from the older generation? The Korea Meteorological Administration's earthquake response manual was made public, and it says, "Do not wake up the minister at night." Just as the Coast Guard was dissolved in the aftermath of the Sewol ferry incident, will the government get rid of the weather authority? There are rumors that trout heading to sea from the Taehwa River and ants appearing on Gwangalli Beach in Busan were signs of coming earthquakes.

     When you lose your health, having the whole world is meaningless. Health is the basis of our lives. When the base is shaken, no tower can stand solid. No power, money or treasure is valuable when the ground is cracking and buildings are falling. Earthquakes affect everyone. Hannah Arendt wrote in "Eichmann in Jerusalem" that thoughtlessness created evil. It was a warning to a society that thoughtlessly repeated evil practices without giving thought to studying and repenting for the past and designing the future. A natural earthquake should have remained a natural earthquake. Man-made disasters are much more devastating. We must remember that when the thoughtlessness, irresponsibility and incompetence of humans are combined with an earthquake, _____ .

1. What is the main idea of the passage?

    (a) The need for further earthquake research and prevention.

    (b) Earthquakes do not discriminate and nobody can protect themselves.

    (c) The disappointing government response to the earthquakes.

    (d) Tragedies that could have been prevented.

2. Which of the following is false, according to the passage?

    (a) Korea was not prepared for the event of an earthquake.

    (b) The response of the government made things worse.

    (c) The government did nothing in the immediate aftermath of the earthquakes.

    (d) The earthquake response manual should have been followed to the letter.

3. What can the Korean government learn from Hannah Arendt?

    (a) To hold on to the things that have made you successful and not get swayed by others.

    (b) To learn from the past mistakes they have made instead of making them over and over again.

    (c) To pay attention to those who seek to convince you of another opinion and give them the respect they deserve.

    (d) To never give up or sway from what you believe is right even when it seems as if the whole world is against you.

4. Which best completes the sentence?

    (a) we must endeavor to be better than we have ever been before and help out our fellow men

    (b) a bigger disaster than anyone could even imagine is poised to be unleashed on the world

    (c) nobody knows just how bad the destruction will be when the dust finally settles

    (d) it becomes an artificial catastrophe, and we may end up with a catastrophe as bad as an earthquake

Words & Phrases

artificial *a.* 인공적인   nuclear *a.* 원자력의, 원자핵의   aftershock *n.* 여진, 여파   fundamentally *ad.* 근본적으로
catastrophe *n.* 큰 재해   initial *a.* 초기의   aftermath *n.* 여파, 영향   incompetence *n.* 무능   to the letter 정확히, 글자 그대로

문장분석

■ The detection of sound waves [resulting from an explosion] is another trait [that distinguishes the two]. → resulting from an explosion 분사구가 sound waves를 수식하며, 주어는 전치사구 of sound waves의 수식을 받는 The detection이다. another trait는 주격보어로 주격관계대명사 that distinguishes the two의 수식을 받는다.

Unit 67 Are electric cars eco-friendly?
|전기차가 친환경적이라고?|

• 환경 •

When electricity demand rises, supply should increase. But the problem is that power generating facilities cannot expand freely. Ninety percent of fuel used for power generation produces pollution. 30 percent is nuclear, 39.1 percent is coal, 21.4 percent is liquefied natural gas and petroleum is 1.5 percent. Technology development in renewable energy is slow, and the government predicts it would take up about 4.6 percent of total power generation. So increasing power generator facilities takes a long time, due to opposition of local residents. Therefore, the government focuses on controlling the demand rather than expanding the power supply.

However, the government is promoting electric vehicles as environmentally friendly. It is encouraging carmakers to develop related technologies and provide subsidies for electric car buyers. If you look at the electric car itself, it does not produce pollutants. However, to power these vehicles, power plants produce greenhouse gases and even radioactive materials. According to Danish scholar Bjorn Lomborg, author of *The Skeptical Environmentalist*," if the United States increases the number of gasoline cars 10 percent by 2020, 870 people would die from air pollution yearly. But the same increase in electric cars would lead to 1,617 deaths. Electric cars are less efficient than gasoline-powered cars, resulting in more pollution, he argues.

Korea is not ready to expand power generating facilities drastically. Concern about fine dust is growing and a high-level radioactive waste treatment site has not been chosen. Considering the current rate of increase, the government predicts that they won't considerably affect the electricity supply. However, demand for high-tech products grows exponentially. Then, we may be on the brink of a blackout. Unless we have a social consensus to expand power generation facilities, _____.

140

1. What is the passage mainly about?

    (a) Korea's contribution to the environmental movement that is trying to reduce pollution.

    (b) As more energy is required throughout Korea, the government is developing greater supplies.

    (c) Korea's increasing demand for electricity but current inability to meet that demand.

    (d) Korea has to focus on creating renewable energy stores if it is to reduce its pollution contribution.

2. Choose the false statement from the following.

    (a) The Korean government is trying to come up with ways to expand the power supply.

    (b) It is not an easy task to expand power generating facilities all of a sudden.

    (c) Those who live near the power generating facilities oppose any proposed expansion.

    (d) The government is relying on the fact that demand for energy won't rise too much too soon.

3. What is the opinion of Lomborg?

    (a) Those who change from gasoline cars to electric cars are helping the environment.

    (b) Gasoline and electric cars will both cause lots of pollution if used incorrectly.

    (c) Gasoline cars are certainly more dangerous than electric cars.

    (d) Electric cars may actually cause more pollution than gasoline cars.

4. Which best completes the sentence?

    (a) the demand is going to grow and grow

    (b) we cannot rule out a future electricity crisis

    (c) the government will start to do rolling blackouts

    (d) there soon won't be any electricity left

Words & Phrases

pollutant *n.* 오염 물질, 오염원   environmentalist *n.* 환경 운동가   skeptical *a.* 회의적인   drastically *ad.* 급격히
fine dust 미세 먼지   exponentially *ad.* 기하급수적으로   on the brink (멸망·죽음 따위)의 직전에
blackout *n.* 대규모 정전 사태

문장분석

■ Technology development in renewable energy is slow, and the government predicts it would take up about 4.6 percent of total power generation. ➔

in renewable energy는 주어 Technology development를 수식하는 형용사구이고, 등위 접속사 and가 절과 절을 연결하고 있다. 동사 predicts의 목적어자리에는 that 접속사가 생략된 명사절 it would take up about 4.6 percent of total power generation이 온다.

unit 67 전기차가 친환경적이라고?   141

Unit 68 UN tide turns against North
|지구촌|

• 환경 •

The Club of Rome drove the whole world into a shock through the 1972 book, "The Limits to Growth." It predicted that if economic growth is not restrained, natural resources would be drained, ruining earth for mankind in the latter part of the 21st century. Nevertheless, most every country has concentrated its efforts on competitive economic development. At the plenary session of the UN General Assembly and the G-20 Summit Meeting held last week — which respectively represent the "global village's" town hall meeting and a meeting of the village elders — the outdated war of nerves over finding solutions to global environmental problems were rekindled.

Developing countries put the blame on advanced countries, claiming that their overuse of resources has been the main culprit. On the other hand, advanced countries insist that developing countries that saw rapid growth recently should bear their share of responsibility. During the food crisis last year, the two sides traded childish accusations: "The crisis was due to overconsumption of meat and cheese by the middle-class people in India and China." "The starvation problem would be resolved if only obese Americans went on a diet."

The well-being of the global village gets even worse when there is such infighting. We must listen carefully to the World Wildlife Fund's warning that if all people in the world want to live as the Americans do, there would need to be two to three more earths. But since there is only one, all people, whether they are American, Indian, Chinese or Korean, should change their attitude. What's the use in rich and poor countries taking sides against each other? They are all residents of the same village, and this community shares a single fate.

1. What's the main topic of the passage?

    (a) The fighting of rich and poor countries over who is to blame for the economic problems

    (b) The encouragement of all countries around the world to make friends

    (c) The way "The Limits to Growth" affected average citizens around the world

    (d) Ways to improve the starvation problem in developing countries

2. How do developing countries think the food crisis problem could be solved?

    (a) Food needs to be made more expensive so that people eat less.

    (b) Fat people from developed countries should go on diets.

    (c) We need to create two or three more earths to get the land we need for farming.

    (d) People should stop eating so much meat and cheese and follow a more varied diet.

3. What can you infer from the passage?

    (a) The rich developed countries need to care more about the developing countries and help them to improve their situation.

    (b) We need to find other resources and change our eating habits if we are to survive.

    (c) Natural resources will never run out and world leaders are worrying for nothing.

    (d) If there is to be a change, countries should stop blaming each other and work on a solution together.

4. Which of the following is incorrect?

    (a) Developing countries blame developed countries and think they overuse natural resources.

    (b) Developed countries blame the new-found wealth of some developing countries for the food crisis.

    (c) The World Wildlife Fund says that it is possible for all countries to live like Americans if they grow carefully.

    (d) Competitive economic growth has continued despite the warnings laid out in the book "The Limits of Growth."

Words & Phrases

restrain v. 억제하다   drain v. 소모하다   ruin v. 망치다   plenary session 총회   summit meeting 정상회담
respectively ad. 각각   a war of nerves 신경전   rekindle v. (감정·생각 등을) 다시 불러일으키다, 불붙이다
culprit n. 범인, 주범   bear one's share of responsibility 자기 분량의 책임을 지다   trade v. 주고받다, 교환하다; 거래하다
accusation n. 혐의, 비난, 고발   obese a. 비만의   infighting n. 내분   take sides 편을 들다   fate n. 운명

문장분석

- <u>What's the use</u> in rich and poor countries taking sides against each other? → what's the use (of something)

구문은 '~해봐야 무슨 소용이 있느냐'의 의미로 '~하는 것이 시간낭비거나 쓸데없는 것'이란 뜻을 내포한다.

Unit 69 Dark clouds hang over the peninsula
|먹구름|

•기상•

A cloud consists of small water droplets or ice. When wavelengths of light pass through a cloud, the colors disperse. Among the substances that make up clouds, the smallest particles give off a blue light and the largest, red. When light passes through such particles in the clouds, all seven colors of visible rays are dispersed and then combine again to form a white color. This is why a cloud in the sky appears white.

A cumulonimbus, more commonly known as a storm cloud, creates a slightly different phenomenon. As this type of cloud is denser, less light passes through it and the amount of light that is dispersed is less, too. Thus, the underside of the cloud appears dark. This is why we also refer to cumulonimbus as "dark clouds."

A dark cloud is a natural phenomenon but it is often used as a metaphor for crisis, when a difficult situation looks likely to lead to a calamity. In fact, in many cultures and languages, a dark cloud is used to symbolize a looming crisis. Common examples in the media are: "The stock market is under a dark cloud" or "A dark cloud hangs over the Korean national team."

1. Which would be an example of why "A dark cloud hangs over the Korean national team"?

    (a) The team has just won their final match in a relegation round.

    (b) The team has been played almost an entire game but it is still tied.

    (c) The team has won their final game by 1 goal, needing 2 goals to advance.

    (d) The team has just put a new goal keeper in for the second half of the game.

2. Which of the following statements is true according to the passage?

    (a) Cumulonimbus clouds absorb less light than other clouds.

    (b) Dispersed light in clouds causes rainbows.

    (c) White light is made up of blue and red light.

    (d) Dark clouds can mean bad weather or misfortune.

3. What would be a good title for this passage?

    (a) The different aspects of light and dark clouds

    (b) Metaphorical clouds

    (c) How rainbows are formed in the clouds

    (d) The crisis facing the Korean national team

4. What can be inferred from this passage?

    (a) The Korean national team has a strong dislike of dark clouds due to their negative symbolism.

    (b) Dark clouds are heavier than light clouds due to the extra light absorbed into them.

    (c) There are dozens of different kinds of clouds which all have different colors based on their density.

    (d) Some elements of nature have both figurative and literal meanings.

Words & Phrases

consist of ~로 구성되다   droplet n. 작은 물방울   disperse v. 산란하다, 흩어지다   particle n. 분자
cumulonimbus n. 적란운   dense a. 빽빽한, 밀집한   metaphor n. 은유, 비유   calamity n. 재앙, 재난
symbolize v. 상징하다   looming a. 어렴풋이 보이는; 기분 나쁜

문장분석

- A cloud <u>consists of</u> small water droplets or ice. → be made up of, be composed of, comprise 등이 있다.
⟨A consist of B⟩는 'A가 B로 구성되다'는 의미로, 비슷한 표현으로는

Unit 70 Food for thought for a desolate land
|바오밥|

• 식물 •

On the tiny planet where the Little Prince came from, baobab trees were a bane and a menace. On a tiny planet where you can watch the sun set forty-three times, just by shifting your chair a little, one or two thick and tall baobab trees as big as castles would be disastrous. That's why weeding out the bad plants every morning before they spread is a discipline as important to this planet as doing one's ablutions when you wake up.

Baobab trees on planet Earth, however, are a precious source of food, water, shelter and medicine to the African people. The abundant green leaves provide valuable shade and the stems can be used for ropes and fishing lines. The huge trunks soak up and store water during the rainy season, serving as a water reservoir during the long dry season. The trees' most valuable assets are nutrient-rich leaves and fruit. The fruits, dried and made into white powder, can be used in soup and stored for many years, helping to keep many people alive in a land besieged by droughts and wars.

It has only been recently that scientists recognized the nutritional value of the tree. Its fruit contains six times more vitamin C than oranges and the calcium content is twice that of cow's milk. It is also rich in vitamin A, B and iron and its seeds are brimming with protein. Baobabs are truly a godsend in a land of desolation and dearth.

1. What is the main topic of this passage?

    (a) The life preserving plant of Africa

    (b) The plight of the Little Prince

    (c) The nutritional value of the baobab tree

    (d) How the baobab tree can be a troublesome thing

2. What is not a positive merit of a baobab tree?

    (a) It has six times the vitamin C of oranges.

    (b) It stores water in its trunk.

    (c) It blocks the sun from the little Prince.

    (d) It has a profusion of green leaves.

3. What cannot be inferred from the passage?

    (a) The little Prince is on a planet which is much smaller than Earth.

    (b) African people have been using the baobab tree for some time.

    (c) The baobab tree is possibly a central key to the survival of African people.

    (d) Weeding the baobab tree is an easy but necessary task in the morning.

Words & Phrases

tiny *a.* 작은   bane *n.* 골칫거리   menace *n.* 위협, 위협적인 존재   disastrous *a.* 재난의, 처참한, 형편없는
weed out (바람직하지 않은 것을) 제거하다, 잡초를 뽑다   discipline *n.* 규율   ablution *n.* 목욕   shelter *n.* 주거지, 피신
abundant *a.* 풍부한   shade *n.* 그늘   stem *n.* 줄기   trunk *n.* 나무의 몸통   soak up ~을 빨아들이다, 흡수하다
serve as ~의 역할을 하다   reservoir *n.* 저수지   asset *n.* 자산   nutrient *n.* 영양분   besiege *v.* 포위하다, 에워싸다
drought *n.* 가뭄   brim with ~으로 가득 차 넘치다   protein *n.* 단백질   godsend *n.* 뜻밖의[하늘이 준] 선물
desolation *n.* 황량함, 적막함   dearth *n.* 부족, 결핍   plight *n.* 역경, 곤경

문장분석

■ The huge trunks soak up and store water during the rainy season, serving as a water reservoir during the long dry season. ➡ 〈A serve as B〉는 'A가 B로 사용되다, A가 B의 역할을 하다'는 뜻이다. 비슷한 표현으로 〈A double as B〉가 있는데, 이 표현은 'A가 B로도 쓰인다'는 뜻으로, 예를 들면 'This company doubles as a hospital during the war.'라고 하면 '원래는 회사지만 전시에는 병원으로도 사용된다'는 뜻이 된다.

Unit 71 Wrangling with nuclear risk
|핵실험|

•환경•

The world's first atomic bomb was tested in Alamogordo, New Mexico, at 5 a.m. on July 16, 1945. The 20-kiloton device, code-named Trinity, left a large mushroom-shaped cloud over the desert. The explosive power of the bomb was confirmed in warfare within weeks of the test when Little Boy and the Fat Man were dropped on Hiroshima and Nagasaki, taking the lives of 200,000 people.

Tests of the United States' nuclear weapons technology peaked in the 1950s in the Cold War against the former Soviet Union. Tests were generally conducted in Nevada in the middle of the desert. It has been said that one of the nuclear tests caused the American movie star John Wayne to die. In 1954, Wayne was filming "The Conqueror," a movie about Genghis Khan, on the Utah plains. The location was 137 kilometers (85 miles) away from the nuclear test site. Over the next 30 years, 90 out of 220 of the film's cast and crew got cancer and 46 of them died, according to "Why John Wayne Died," a book by Japanese journalist Takashi Hirose. The figures are too high to deny the correlation with radioactivity. Wayne was diagnosed with lung cancer in 1964 but survived, before succumbing to stomach cancer in 1979. The film's director, Dick Powell, and its leading lady, Susan Hayward, also died of cancer.

America's first practical test of a thermonuclear hydrogen bomb was conducted on Bikini Atoll, part of the Marshall Islands, in 1954. The Japanese tuna fishing boat the Daigo Fukuryu Maru, or Lucky Dragon 5, was passing nearby when the bomb was detonated. It was exposed to the fallout, even though it was outside the safety line set by the U.S. Army. One sailor died and many complained of headaches and bleeding gums. After a series of accidents raised awareness of the danger of nuclear tests, countries signed an agreement to ban nuclear tests on the ground and in the water in 1963. But underground nuclear tests were excluded from the ban because they were thought to be unrelated to contamination of our air and oceans. But it is possible these tests contaminate our water and soil as well as cause earthquakes.

1. What is the main topic of the passage?

    (a) The effectiveness of nuclear weapons throughout the 1940's, 1950's and into the 1960's

    (b) The side effects of nuclear fallout from atomic bombs testing

    (c) The truth behind the death of John Wayne and other actors filming in the Utah plains

    (d) The history of the atomic bomb in America after the bombing of Hiroshima and Nagasaki

2. What can be inferred from the passage?

    (a) John Wayne's last movie as the lead actor was "The Conqueror".

    (b) Japan surrendered after Little Boy and Fat Man were dropped out of fear of further attacks.

    (c) Scientists were not fully aware of all the effects of radiation during this time.

    (d) The Utah plains are now the site for underground tests by the U.S. Army due to the ban on surface testing in the Marshall Islands.

3. Which of the following is false according to the passage?

    (a) Nuclear tests were usually conducted in unpopulated areas like the Utah plains or the Marshall Islands.

    (b) Scientists eventually became aware of the damaging effects of fallout from testing after side effects were noticed outside of safety lines.

    (c) Nuclear testing is now done underground, but there may still be unknown side effects such as seismic activity.

    (d) All the people exposed to radiation in the Utah Plains have died from cancer.

Words & Phrases

mushroom-shaped *a.* 버섯 모양의   correlation *n.* 상관관계   radioactivity *n.* 방사능
be diagnosed with ~로 진단받다   succumb to ~에 굴복하다   hydrogen *n.* 수소   detonate *v.* 폭파시키다
fallout *n.* 낙진   gum *n.* 잇몸   exclude *v.* 배제하다   contamination *n.* 오염

문장분석

■ The figures are <u>too high to deny</u> the correlation with radioactivity. → 〈too + 형용사 + to 부정사〉는 'to 이하 하기에는 너무(too) ~하다'는 뜻이다. 위의 예문을 보면 '그 수치는 방 사능과의 상관관계를 부인하기에는 너무 높다'라는 뜻이 되며, 달리 말 하면 '수치가 너무 높아 방사능과의 상관관계를 부인할 수 없다'는 부 정의 의미를 내포하게 된다.

Unit 72 A high-tech, brain-shrinking future
|진화하는 인간|

•기술•

Nowadays seeing a person walking down the street talking on a cell phone has become such a ubiquitous sight that a picture of modern man with one hand next to his ear should be painted next to the ape-like Cro-Magnon to depict the evolution of humans. According to recent press reports, American doctors are now warning of so-called "cell phone elbow" syndrome. It seems farcical that medical professionals are making such a fuss about this. Just like people who suffer daily from the constant pain of tennis elbow after playing tennis, cell phone gabbers complain of pain or numbness in the hand — especially the pinky and ring fingers.

We cannot avoid using cell phones, despite elbow pain and electromagnetic waves, as they empower humans to reach beyond geographical boundaries. In addition, human capabilities are much larger than a decade ago thanks to the emergence of laptop computers, wireless Internet and car navigation. Yet with all these portable digital devices, the memory devices they hold store much more information in a more precise manner than the human brain.

Recently, a new technology called brain-machine interface came into the spotlight. The technology is designed to control robots or machines by drawing on signals from the human brain. We cannot predict whether progress in genetic engineering, robotics engineering, information technology and nanotechnology will raise human capability to an even higher position. If such developments occur, we could live healthier and longer lives, and see huge progress in easily overcoming cultural and linguistic barriers. It is likely that a human with no need for sleep or food may emerge on earth.

However, it is a fact that we are deprived of true rest and spiritual freedom by cell phones ringing off the hook regardless of time or place. We have no need to use our brain due to calculators and dictionaries. Even the list of telephone numbers we remember is getting shorter. Research shows that as humans evolved from Australopithecus to Homo sapiens, the skull volume expanded. However, the size of the human brain has seen a 10 to 15 percent decrease over the past 30,000 years. While relying more on equipment or social systems, the role of the brain might be on the decrease.

Humans are slowly evolving toward becoming cyborgs. However, naturally born humans, the underprivileged who possess no cutting-edge portable digital devices, are unlikely to win in a battle of the species. We worry that the situation might be even worse than projections of the future.

1. What is the correct definition of "cell phone elbow"?

   (a) A pain in the upper arm because of the long periods of time holding the cell phone to the ear
   (b) Pain in all fingers of the hand that sends text messages
   (c) Pain in the elbow of the arm that lifts the cell phone to the ear
   (d) Some kind of pain in the hand that holds the cell phone after prolonged use of it

2. What can you infer from the passage?

   (a) The need for the human brain will become obsolete and information we need will be stored on a chip.
   (b) If a battle between naturally-born humans and cyborgs took place, humans would not see a favorable result.
   (c) Cell phones are enabling humans to advance in ways that were hitherto unseen, such as spiritually and socially.
   (d) Brain-machine interface makes the human brain unnecessary and relies on an electromagnetic brain.

3. What is the best title for this passage?

   (a) A high-tech, brain-shrinking future
   (b) The war between nature and technology
   (c) The reduced need for the human brain
   (d) How much memory can a human brain hold

4. What would be most appropriate for the next paragraph?

   (a) Ways in which we don't need to use our brains anymore
   (b) New technology that will open up possibilities about how our brain's abilities can be expanded
   (c) Common theories about our future society and existence
   (d) Some ailments that have arisen from using modern gadgets

Words & Phrases

ubiquitous *a.* 어디에나 있는, 아주 흔한   ape-like *a.* 유인원과 같은   depict *v.* 묘사하다   evolution *n.* 진화
farcical *a.* 웃음거리가 된   make a fuss 크게 떠들어대다, 소란 피우다   gabber *n.* 수다쟁이   pinky finger 새끼손가락
empower *v.* 권한을 주다   emergence *n.* 출현   portable *a.* 휴대[이동]가 쉬운, 휴대용의   draw on 이용하다
linguistic *a.* 언어의   barrier *n.* 장벽   be deprived of ~을 빼앗기다   ring off the hook 연속으로[쉴 새 없이] 울리다
regardless of ~와 관계없이   be on the decrease 줄어들다   underprivileged *a.* (사회·경제적으로) 혜택을 못 받는
cutting-edge *a.* 최첨단의   projection *n.* 예상, 추정   obsolete *a.* 더 이상 쓸모가 없는, 한물간, 구식의

문장분석

■ However, naturally born humans, the underprivileged who possess no cutting-edge portable digital devices, are unlikely to win in a battle of the species. ➔ 〈the + 형용사〉라는 형태로 사용되면 '~하는 사람들'을 의미한다. 예를 들어 the rich는 '부자들'을, the poor는 '가난한 사람들'을 의미하며, 예문과 같이 the underprivileged라고 하면 '경제적 혜택을 못 받는 사람들'이 된다. 주의할 것은 이때 의미가 복수형이기 때문에 동사의 수의 일치도 '복수'로 해야 한다는 점이다.

Unit 73 Helping turtles get back on their feet
|달려라 거북|

Turtles are one of the oldest reptile groups still in existence. The earliest known turtle appeared around 225 million years ago. Turtles witnessed both the disappearance of dinosaurs and evolution of humans. Their remarkable survival is thanks to their shells. The only drawback: They lack speed.

The characteristics of turtles were interpreted in different ways in different times and in different regions. Early Christians saw turtles as a symbol of evil and darkness, focusing on the trait of hiding inside their shells. Later, for Calvinist Christians, turtles symbolized the ideal married life. They saw turtles as similar to "decent" women who seldom left their homes. Those in western Africa think of turtles as sly, probably because they can hide their heads.

In modern society, people usually associate turtles or tortoises with slowness. That is thanks largely to "The Tortoise and the Hare," one of Aesop's fables. In the story, the tortoise is slow but as he never stops or rests he can defeat the speedy hare who takes a nap. The moral of the fable is that if one makes a persistent effort, one can achieve one's goal. But we feel nonetheless sorry for the tortoise that can win only when he struggles so hard, unlike the hare that has innate talent.

1. Which of the following proverbs can be used to describe the fable of "The Tortoise and the Hare"?

   (a) The best things come to those who wait.

   (b) Time waits for no man.

   (c) Slow and steady wins the race.

   (d) Time spent laughing is times spent with the gods.

2. Which of the following has not been an interpretation of turtles at one time?

   (a) Due to their wrinkly appearance, they are a symbol of the elderly and should be cared for as we care for the elderly.

   (b) They are similar to a good woman whose place is near the home.

   (c) Concealing themselves in their shells means they are evil and hiding from some kind of wrongdoing.

   (d) Since they cover their heads, turtles are devious and cunning.

3. Choose the correct one, according to the passage.

   (a) The hare has talent, whereas the tortoise has perseverance.

   (b) Turtles cannot walk very fast but they can crawl quite fast.

   (c) Turtles have had a rocky existence, their numbers rising and dropping with the changing climate.

   (d) Turtles and tortoises are popular pets these days because they cannot run away easily.

Words & Phrases

reptile *n.* 파충류   evolution *n.* 진화   drawback *n.* 단점   characteristic *n.* 특징   trait *n.* 특징   Calvinist *a.* 칼뱅파의   symbolize *v.* 상징하다   decent *a.* 점잖은   sly *a.* 교활한   associate A with B A와 B를 연관짓다   fable *n.* 우화   hare *n.* 토끼   nap *n.* 낮잠   the moral of the fable 우화의 교훈   persistent *a.* 끈질긴, 집요한   innate *a.* 타고난, 선천적인

문장분석

■ In modern society, people usually associate turtles or tortoises with slowness. That is <u>thanks largely to</u> "The Tortoise and the Hare," one of Aesop's fables.

→ thanks to는 '~덕분에'라는 뜻으로, because of, owing to, due to 등과 같은 의미를 지닌다. 이때 largely/entirely/partly/partially 등의 부사를 사용해 원인/이유의 '정도'를 나타낸다.

Unit 74 | All that glitters is not 'green' growth
| '그린 랜드'

• 환경 •

In the year 980, when the Vikings led by Erik the Red sailed to Greenland from Iceland, Greenland was a relatively warm place. In those days the land was covered with a considerable amount of wooded areas. Vikings cleared away swathes of forest for timber and to create pastures for their livestock to graze on. However, the disappearance of the woods soon caused soil erosion and led to a remarkable decrease in agricultural production. From 1300, the area we now know as Greenland became cold. Many people died of starvation. Until the Danes occupied the territory again in the 18th century, Greenland had been ruled by Inuit who hunted whales and seals.

Greenland became a colony of Denmark in 1775, and it was only last Sunday that Greenland's people gained self-rule over their territory. Global warming has contributed significantly to the end of the 230-year-long Danish occupation. Thanks to the melting of glaciers, valuable natural resources hidden below the permafrost have been discovered, allowing Greenland to achieve economic independence. The plot of land under cultivation is now four times larger than it once was, turning Greenland into a land befitting its name. That Greenland is now a green land is due to the greenhouse gases emitted by humans burning fossil fuels — hardly a matter deserving of congratulations.

If Greenland loses its ice, the melting of the ice sheet will cause sea levels to rise by about seven meters, or around 13 feet. Many of the world's coasts will be submerged. Countries such as Bangladesh will disappear from the map. In particular, Bangladesh highlights the plight of poor countries. In May of last year, more than 130,000 people died after a devastating tropical cyclone, leaving nearly 2 million homeless. Poor nations are especially vulnerable to natural disasters, while the world's largest greenhouse gas emitters have the resources to minimize the possibility of being victims of global warming by building dikes or improving the accuracy of weather forecasts.

1. What's the main topic of the passage?

   (a) Greenland's journey to becoming a self-governing nation

   (b) Greenland becomes a green land and farming flourishes.

   (c) Global warming helps one country and heeds another.

   (d) The effect of global warming in rich and poor countries.

2. "Bangladesh highlights the plight of poor countries". What is this plight?

   (a) Less developed countries are defenseless against the strength of natural disasters while rich countries are more able to protect themselves.

   (b) The crops of poor countries are more likely to fail with global warming and they have no other income to support themselves.

   (c) Poor countries are more likely to experience natural disasters due to their location.

   (d) Bangladesh and low-lying countries are slowly sinking into the sea and will soon be under water.

3. How has the landscape of Greenland changed?

   (a) Natural disasters and tempestuous weather have made the land of Greenland uninhabitable.

   (b) The glaciers are melting and transforming into huge lakes that cover vast areas of land.

   (c) The melting ice has revealed resources and land which can be cultivated for profit.

   (d) Land that was once used for grazing animals can now be used for crops.

4. All of the following are incorrect except _____.

   (a) The Inuit found Greenland inhospitable and couldn't live there, moving on to other lands.

   (b) Erik the Red raped the country of Greenland and left it barren, causing its journey into coldness.

   (c) Greenland is green due to the intent of the Danish government to clear the ice.

   (d) The Vikings cut down all of the trees to use the timber for housebuilding.

Words & Phrases

relatively *ad.* 상대적으로　considerable *a.* 상당한　swathe *n.* 풀, 농작물 등을 베어 낸 기다란 띠 모양 땅
timber *n.* 목재　pasture *n.* 목초지, 방목장　graze *v.* 풀을 뜯어 먹다　soil erosion 토양 침식　starvation *n.* 기아
seal *n.* 바다표범　colony *n.* 식민지　glacier *n.* 빙하　permafrost *n.* 영구 동토층　plot *n.* 작은 땅 조각, 터, 대지
befit *v.* 걸맞다　emit *v.* 방출하다　fossil fuel 화석연료　ice sheet 빙상　submerge *v.* 가라앉다　plight *n.* 곤경, 역경
devastating *a.* 대단히 파괴적인, 엄청난 손상을 가하는　vulnerable *a.* 취약한　dike *n.* 제방

문장분석

■ The plot of land under cultivation is now four times larger than it once was, turning Greenland into a land befitting its name. ➔ 〈turn A into B〉는 'A를 B로 바꾸다'는 뜻이며, 〈transform/change A into B〉도 같은 의미의 표현이다.

Unit 75 Painful patent protection
|특허의 역설|

The Rhine River, the longest river in Germany, was the most important waterway for European trade in the Middle Ages. Merchant ships paid tolls as they passed each state along the Rhine, in return for the Holy Roman Empire's protection. But in line with the decline of the empire in the 13th century, barons peppered the riverside with hundreds of castles to claim tolls from passing ships. Their toll demands became so audacious that merchants gave up ventures down the Rhine altogether. The trade business along the Rhine collapsed, bringing down the sponging barons along with it.

Such nibbling away at a public property or resource can in the end compromise its existence and make everyone worse off. Columbia Law School professor Michael Heller calls this effect the "tragedy of the anticommons." The waste of unclaimed property can be ruinous, but self-serving and expansive fights over a property can be equally disastrous, as seen in the Rhine River example. Heller, in his book "The Gridlock Economy: How Too Much Ownership Wrecks Markets, Stops Innovation, and Costs Lives" argued that overly fragmented property rights and broad ownership can eventually trap the industry and market in a dead end.

There is an overabundance of patents in the biotech industry right now. Patents licensed over the last 30 years associated with DNA alone top 40,000 cases. Pharmaceutical companies must go through numerous patent holders and negotiate terms before marketing a new drug. Many tests fail to go beyond the labs for fear of litigation backlashes from reclusive patent owners. The same problems interfered with the development of a vaccine against SARS during the outbreak.

The genetically engineered golden rice, developed to help millions of children in Africa and other impoverished areas suffering from vitamin A deficiency, also might have never seen daylight, if not for humanitarian relief efforts. Scientists who developed the miracle crop in 1999 were walled in by more than 70 patent rights. They were finally freed to hand out the grain after companies redefined the rice as having a "humanitarian use of license."

1. What can you infer from the passage?

    (a) Greed is at the root of all human problems.
    (b) Disputes over property are disadvantageous in the short run but have positive effects in the long run.
    (c) Patent issues are impeding the progress of science and medicine.
    (d) The SARS vaccine was delayed because of the inability of research scientists to deal with lawyers.

2. Which of the following is incorrect?

    (a) Loss of activity on the part of the merchants on the Rhine, damaged both themselves and the barons who controlled the waterway.
    (b) It is much easier to get a patent for a new product these days than 50 years ago because the process has been speeded up.
    (c) The biotech industry is suffering over a lack of knowledge about patents on the part of the scientists.
    (d) Genetically engineered rice was eventually given to African children after its use was renamed as humanitarian.

3. According to the passage, what is the problem with releasing a new drug on the market?

    (a) There are obstacles in the form of patent holders and terms must be agreed upon whereby all parties are satisfied.
    (b) About 40,000 patent holders are waiting to claim some money from profits of the new drug.
    (c) There is a struggle between those who wish to use new drugs for personal profit and those who have more humanitarian concerns.
    (d) Having to undergo numerous tests and trials to ensure the safety of the new drug.

4. What is the best title of the passage?

    (a) The economic downturn as a result of the overabundance of patents
    (b) Technological advances being hindered as a result of debate among scientists
    (c) Giving humanitarian aid through medical research
    (d) An economy and society at a standstill through extensive ownership

Words & Phrases

waterway n. 수로   in line with ~에 따라, ~와 함께   baron n. 남작   pepper v. 뿌려대다, 퍼붓다   audacious a. 대담한   collapse v. 붕괴하다   sponge v. 뜯어먹다, 빌붙다   nibble away 조금씩[야금야금] 먹다   compromise v. ~을 위태롭게 하다   worse off 더 가난한, 더 못한   unclaimed a. 주인이 나서지 않는   ruinous a. 파괴적인, 파멸을 가져올   self-serving a. 자기 잇속만 차리는   fragmented a. 분열된   dead end n. 난관   overabundance n. 과잉, 과다   patent n. 특허   top v. 능가하다, 더 높다   pharmaceutical a. 제약의   term n. 계약 조건   litigation n. 소송   backlash n. 반발   reclusive a. 은둔의   outbreak n. 발생   impoverished a. 빈곤한, 가난해진   deficiency n. 부족   humanitarian a. 인도주의적인   standstill n. 정지, 멈춤

문장분석

■ The genetically engineered golden rice, ... also might have never seen daylight, if not for humanitarian relief efforts. → 〈if it were not for something, if it had not been for something〉은 가정법으로 '~이 없었다면'의 뜻 이다. 예문에서는 이를 줄여서 if not for로 표현했으며, 예문 주절에 'might have never been'이라는 가정법 과거완료의 표현이 있으므로 if it had not been for something을 줄여서 만든 것이라는 사실을 알 수 있다.

Unit 76 Humility in the face of pandemics
|전염병|

•의학•

The number of Spanish troops that conquered the Aztec Empire when they invaded the New World in 1519 was only 600. Was it because the intrepid military skills of the conqueror Cortez were superior to those of the conquered? Or was it due to the overwhelming military might of the Spanish troops who were armed with rifles and other weapons that the Aztecs and other civilizations here did not possess? The truth is that the enigmatic "invisible hand" that helped the Spanish win was nothing else but smallpox. The wild spread of smallpox among the Aztecs was the source of the victory. While the Spanish soldiers were immune to the plague, the natives of the New World helplessly fell victim to the disease, which was newly introduced there.

In the eyes of the Aztecs, the Spanish soldiers' strength in the face of smallpox proved that they were none other than "the descendants of God." They decided to convert to Christianity, deserting their traditional gods. As smallpox, which was first introduced in Mexico, spread to South America, the Inca Empire lost two-thirds of its population to the epidemic. Like the Aztecs, the Inca Empire was weakened by smallpox and was forced to surrender to Spanish conqueror Francisco Pizarro's army in 1533.

Historically, the most severe damage mankind suffered from an epidemic was when the Black Death swept through Medieval Europe in the 14th century. The terrible disease, now thought to have been the bubonic plague, halved the population of Europe. Influenza, which is generally taken lightly today, can also be a deadly disease. The 1918 flu pandemic caused more casualties than those from World War I.

The history of human beings is the history of struggle against the spread of contagious diseases. The outbreak of new virus breeds has not only caused disastrous damage to mankind, but has also changed the course of history. Whenever such disasters took place, mankind managed to overcome them and continued to develop science and civilization. But viruses evolve too, and no matter how much we innovate, there will always be new diseases. Moreover, the outbreak of a new flu variety like the A(H1N1) virus should shake our modern complacency about disease. We must listen to nature's warning and be both vigilant against and humble in the face of the A(H1N1) virus and future pandemics.

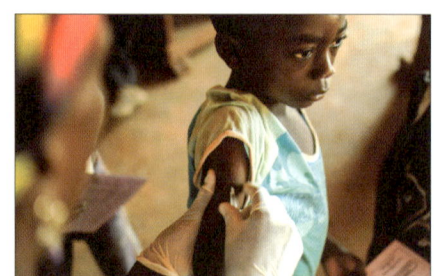

1. Why did the Aztecs think the Spanish invaders were "the descendants of God"?

   (a) As a result of the fervor of the Spanish soldiers, the Aztecs felt inferior.
   (b) Because of the color of their skin and their facial features which were so different.
   (c) Because they survived the outbreak of smallpox while the Aztecs were rapidly dying.
   (d) Due to their readings of the Bible, which told of a disease to come and kill the unbelieving.

2. What's the main purpose of the passage?

   (a) Encourage humans to look back at history and learn from mistakes
   (b) Smallpox vs. Black Death
   (c) The spread of Christianity throughout Europe and the New World
   (d) Humans should always be aware of their inferiority in the face of viruses.

3. According to the passage, which of the following is incorrect?

   (a) The A(H1N1) virus is an evolution of the bubonic plague of the 14th century.
   (b) Smallpox in the New World helped the spread and acceptance of Christianity.
   (c) Not only the Aztecs, but also the Incas suffered from smallpox outbreaks and were easily subdued by the Spanish.
   (d) As mankind evolves and develops new technologies, so viruses mutate and present new challenges to humans.

4. What can you infer from the passage?

   (a) A new virus that is stronger than any others before will soon arrive and seriously threaten humankind.
   (b) If it weren't for smallpox, the Aztecs would never have converted to Christianity.
   (c) The Aztecs might have put up more resistance to the Spanish but it is doubtful considering the weaponry of the Spanish.
   (d) The 1918 flu epidemic was the worst epidemic ever seen and killed more than 20 million men, women and children.

Words & Phrases

conquer v. 정복하다   intrepid a. 용감무쌍한, 두려움을 모르는   overwhelming a. 압도적인   might n. 힘   rifle n. 소총
enigmatic a. 수수께끼 같은, 불가사의한   nothing else but ~을 빼고는 다른 아무것도   smallpox n. 천연두
immune a. 면역이 된   plague n. 전염병   fall victim to ~의 희생(물)이 되다   none other than 다름 아닌
descendant n. 자손   convert v. 개종하다, 개종시키다   desert v. 버리다   epidemic n. 전염병   medieval a. 중세의
bubonic plague 흑사병, 선페스트   halve v. 절반으로 줄다[줄이다]   deadly a. 치명적인   pandemic n. 전염병
casualty n. 희생자   contagious a. 전염성이 있는   breed n. 품종, 유형   complacency n. 현 상태에 만족함, 안주
vigilant a. 바짝 경계하는   humble a. 겸손한   in the face of ~에 직면하여

문장분석

■ <u>The number of</u> Spanish troops that conquered the Aztec Empire when they invaded the New World in 1519 <u>was</u> only 600.   ➔ 〈the number of something〉은 '~의 수'를 의미하기 때문에 단수로 취급해야 한다. 반면 〈a number of something〉은 '~가 많은'이라는 뜻이므로 복수로 취급한다.

Unit 77 Modern-day Medusa stings
|해파리|

In Greek mythology, it was said that there were three sisters called the Gorgons among the monsters created by Gaia, the mother goddess who personified nature itself. The youngest of them, Medusa, was known for her beauty. She had a tryst with Poseidon, the god of the sea, inside the goddess Athena's temple of worship. As punishment from Athena, Medusa was given hair of living, venomous snakes and a visage so hideous that all who looked upon her were turned to stone. The hero Perseus, however, avoided this fate by only looking at Medusa's reflection in his highly polished shield, and then beheading her.

Jellyfish with wavy tentacles bear a resemblance to Medusa's head. Medusa, in fact, happens to be Latin for jellyfish. Jellyfish, corals and sea anemones are cnidarians, which have a single opening into the body which acts as both the mouth and anus. When their tentacles brush against their prey, thousands of tiny stinging cells explode and launch poisonous barbs into the victim. Jellyfish often sting people, resulting in sharp pain, and possibly leading to dyspnea, muscle paralysis or heart attack.

In the medieval era, cnidarians were considered plants. People thought that cnidarians existed at the boundary between animals and plants through the 18th century. It was not until the 19th century that they were started to be considered animals. The life cycle of jellyfish is diverse. Jellyfish progress through a number of forms, including a tiny free-swimming planula, a flower-shaped polyp that attaches itself to a solid surface, and a pelagic medusa. The segmented parts of the strobilating polyp, or strobila, develop into incipient medusae that eventually break loose and become free-swimming young jellyfish of their own.

Jellyfish have become a matter of concern on the south coast. The National Fisheries Research and Development Institute estimated that damage from jellyfish will exceed more than 300 billion won ($245 million) a year. They harm swimmers and cause substantial damage to fishing operations by ruining fishing nets. They also make it difficult to obtain cooling water for power plants. Jellyfish cause great distress in the Mediterranean, the North Sea, the Baltic Sea, the Caspian Sea and the Gulf of Mexico. The major culprits behind this phenomenon are a rise in seawater temperatures due to global warming, eutrophication due to land-based pollutants and the overfishing of natural predators of the jellyfish. This is a man-made disaster. Discharging filefish known to prey on jellyfish is not an adequate solution. However, it makes us feel sorry that we will not have a 21st-century Perseus to save the sea from its Medusa.

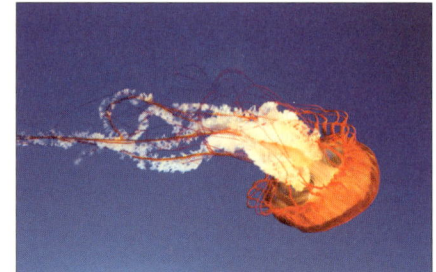

1. What's the passage mainly about?

    (a) What is a jellyfish and what is the curse of the jellyfish
    (b) The similarities of Medusa and jellyfish
    (c) The role that cnidarians play in aquatic life
    (d) The dangers of being stung by a jellyfish

2. What can't you infer from the passage?

    (a) The large presence of jellyfish is considered one of the many culprits, alongside global warming and eutrophication, of increasing sea temperatures.
    (b) A solution to the problem of jellyfish and the damage they cause has not yet been found.
    (c) Humans have had difficulty in the past correctly categorizing what jellyfish are.
    (d) Scientists have discovered that the introduction of filefish will control the population of jellyfish.

3. What does the underlined phrase "it makes us feel sorry that we will not have a 21st-century Perseus to save the sea from its Medusa" imply?

    (a) We should feel sorry for the humble jellyfish and the way it has been persecuted over time.
    (b) The jellyfish is in danger of extinction in the 21st century unless something is done to prevent it.
    (c) The need for someone to control the jellyfish population to prevent further harm coming to anyone or anything.
    (d) We need a hero to save us from this natural disaster that will cause irreparable damage to the world's oceans.

4. Choose the correct one from the following.

    (a) The jellyfish both ingests and excretes substances from one opening.
    (b) When jellyfish rub a victim, they eject an inky, viscous substance from their tentacles.
    (c) Jellyfish harm fishing by causing vast amounts of fish to migrate to different areas of the ocean.
    (d) When a jellyfish stings you, you feel nothing at first; the ache builds up gradually.

Words & Phrases

mythology n. 신화   personify v. 의인화하다   tryst n. 밀회   venomous a. 독이 있는   visage n. 얼굴, 용모
hideous a. 소름끼치는, 섬뜩한   reflection n. (거울에 비친) 모습   polished a. 윤이 나는   shield n. 방패   behead v. 목을 베다
tentacle n. 촉수   bear a resemblance 닮다   cnidarian n. 자포동물   planula n. 플라눌라   polyp n. 폴립
pelagic a. 원양의   incipient a. 막 시작된   substantial a. 막대한   culprit n. 주범, 범인
eutrophication n. (강·호수 등의) 부영양화   pollutant n. 오염 물질   predator n. 포식자   discharge v. 방출하다
filefish n. 쥐치   adequate a. 충분한

문장분석

■ It was not until the 19th century that they started to be considered animals. ➡ ⟨it was not until + 시점 + that ~⟩ 이란 구문에서 it은 가주어, that 이하가 진주어가 된다. 따라서 that 이 하의 내용은 특정 시점까지는 일어나지 않았다는 뜻이 된다. 다시 말하면, 특정 시점이 지나서야 that 이하의 내용이 일어났다는 뜻이다. 일종 의 'it is ~ that ~' 강조용법으로 생각할 수 있다.

Unit 78 Lawmakers eclipsed
|일식|

• 천문학 •

Let's say that the Earth is a ball the size of a grape. The Moon is then a crimson glory vine about 30 centimeters (11.8 inches) from the Earth. The Sun is as big as a person in diameter, 50 meters from the Earth. Around 200 meters from the Earth is Jupiter, the size of a melon. Uranus and Neptune are the size of lemons and they are 1 kilometer and 1.5 kilometers away from Earth, respectively.

The Sun is 400 times larger than the Moon and the distance between the Earth and the Sun is 400 times longer than the distance between the Earth and the Moon. This is why the Sun and the Moon appear the same size, more or less, from the Earth. The Earth revolves around the Sun, and the Moon orbits around the Earth. When the Sun, the Moon and the Earth lie on a line, an eclipse occurs; that is, the Moon covers part of or all of the Sun. Yesterday, the shadow of the Moon covering the Sun was cast on part of our planet and around 3 billion people on Earth could see a total eclipse.

The average distance between the Earth and the Moon is 380,000 kilometers. It is easy to imagine how far that is when considering that the average altitude of an international airplane is about 10 kilometers. Nonetheless, the Moon is still the closest celestial body to the Earth, and it has long been an object of study and observation. The Moon is the only body outside of Earth that humans have walked on. This year is the 40th anniversary of the United States' spaceship Apollo 11's moon landing.

1. What cannot be inferred from the passage?

   (a) All of the planets in the solar system orbit the Sun at different distances.

   (b) Venus would be the size of a cherry 20 meters from the Earth grape.

   (c) The Earth is closer to the Sun than Jupiter but further away than the Moon during an eclipse.

   (d) An eclipse can only be seen in the part of the world where the shadow is cast on the surface of the planet.

2. Which of the following is correct during an eclipse, according to the passage?

   (a) Sun – Earth – Moon – Jupiter – Neptune - Uranus

   (b) Human – grape – crimson glory – lemon – melon - lemon

   (c) Sun – Moon – Earth – Uranus – Jupiter - Neptune

   (d) Human – Crimson glory – grape – melon – lemon – lemon

3. What is the main topic of the passage?

   (a) Relationships of all the planets

   (b) The Moon and its importance to us

   (c) How to make a fruit model of the solar system

   (d) Why humans have only walked on the Moon

Words & Phrases

crimson glory vine *n.* 머루   respectively *ad.* 각각   revolve *v.* 돌다   orbit *v.* 궤도를 돌다   eclipse *n.* (일식·월식의) 식   altitude *n.* 고도   celestial *a.* 천체의

문장분석

■ Uranus and Neptune are the size of lemons and they are 1 kilometer and 1.5 kilometers away from Earth, respectively. → respectively는 '각각'이라는 뜻으로, 앞에서 등장한 순서대로란 의미로 보통 문장 맨 마지막에 쓰인다. 예문에서는 천왕성과 해왕성이 등장하고 있는데, 천왕성은 지구에서 1km 떨어져 있고, 해왕성은 지구에서 1.5km 떨어져 있는 것으로 각각 생각할 수 있다는 뜻이 된다.

Unit 79 Hats off to Naro's blastoff
|우주 개발|

The 19th-century Italian astronomer Giovanni Schiaparelli discovered a long line on the surface of Mars while observing the planet through a telescope. The long line he saw might have been the Mariner Valley that stretches some 6,000 kilometers (3,728 miles) across the Red Planet. The news caused huge amounts of excitement on Mars as rumors spread that the line was in fact an artificial canal. This lead to speculation that there was life on Mars. But it later turned out that the Italian word "canali," meaning "line," was mistranslated into English as "canal." Considering the speed of space science development today, the episode that took place in 1877 was nothing but an old folktale from a bygone era. Nevertheless, the existence of water on Mars, though short of the discovery of a canal, was later proved by a photo transmitted by a space probe sent to Mars 120 years later. The existence of water implies the possible existence of living organisms on the planet.

In space science, missions once considered preposterous are later achieved. Only a century after the publication of "From the Earth to the Moon" by Jules Verne, men took their first lunar steps. The longing for unknown worlds and to go to places that seem impossible to reach have been a source of imagination for much of recorded human history.

Of course, just satisfying people's curiosity wasn't the only reason that an enormous amount of money and energy was poured into space exploration during the Cold War era. The United States and the Soviet Union were engaged in a life-or-death grapple to win the space race. They did so because the technology for space development and that of military purposes were not mutually exclusive. The technologies developed for space exploration were diverted to more pragmatic ones in private sector industries. Satellite broadcasting technology, which was once called "space relay," and meteorological forecasts have developed on the back of research into space development. For instance, freeze-dried foodstuffs, CT scans used for diagnosing diseases and endoscopy technology are all connected to work carried out initially with space in mind.

1. What is the passage mainly about?

 (a) The discoveries of Giovanni Schiaparelli throughout his lifetime

 (b) The development of space science

 (c) The Cold War race to reach space

 (d) The benefits that have arisen from advances in space technology

2. Which of the following is correct, according to the passage?

 (a) Schiaparelli discovered that there was water on Mars, but nobody believed him at the time.

 (b) The United States and the Soviet Union were competing to reach space first not only for the accolade of doing so but also for the rewards it would bring militarily.

 (c) Space technologies were hoped to be used in other areas but, in the end, such a situation did not arise.

 (d) We are still waiting for the existence of water on Mars to be proven.

3. Why did people think there was a canal on Mars?

 (a) Schiaparelli thought he saw a canal, but it turned out to be something else.

 (b) The astronauts did not speak English well, and so there was confusion.

 (c) There was a misunderstanding in the translation of canali from Italian to English.

 (d) It was a widely-held belief at the time that there was a lake on Mars.

4. What can you infer from the passage?

 (a) Humans have always and continue to have an insatiable curiosity for the unknown.

 (b) Space development research is being scaled down due to its limitations in other areas.

 (c) Scientists predict that water will soon be found on Mars.

 (d) Jules Verne's book was not popular in his lifetime but became popular a century later when the era of space travel began.

Words & Phrases

stretch v. 뻗어 있다   artificial a. 인공의   canal n. 운하   speculation n. 추측, 짐작   turn out 밝혀지다   nothing but 오직, 단지 ~일 뿐인   folktale n. 민간설화   bygone era 지나간 시대   short of ~에는 미치지 못하는   transmit v. 전송하다   preposterous a. 말도 안 되는, 터무니없는, 가당찮은   longing n. 갈망, 열망   grapple n. 고투, 고심; 격투, 접전   mutually exclusive 상호 배타적인   divert v. 전환시키다, 우회시키다   pragmatic a. 실용적인   meteorological a. 기상의   endoscopy n. 내시경술   carry out 수행하다   initially ad. 처음에는   accolade n. 포상, 칭찬

문장분석

■ Nevertheless, the existence of water on Mars, though short of the discovery of a canal, was later proved by a photo transmitted by a space probe sent to Mars 120 years later. ➡ 〈be/fall short of something〉이란 표현은 '~에는 미치지 못하다'는 의미를 지닌다. 특정 대상에 이르기에는 좀 짧다(short)는 의미이다. short이 들어간 다른 표현으로, 〈stop short of doing something〉이라고 하면 '~까지 하는 것은 꺼리다'는 의미이며, 〈little/nothing short of something〉이라고 하면, '거의 ~이나 마찬가지인, ~이나 다름없는'이라는 뜻이 된다.

High hopes for hothouses
|비닐하우스|

• 환경 •

Almeria, in southern Spain, was virtually unknown to the world outside modern Spain until Italian film directors began shooting the so-called spaghetti westerns there during the 1960s. But it's now better known for its greenhouses. These huge artificial structures are identifiable from outer space, apparently, and, located in the western part of the city, they're about half the size of Seoul. In the eyes of scientists, they act like a huge mirror on the surface of the earth and provide a useful place to measure the effects of solar radiation.

The barren land in Almeria has been turned into a rich agricultural area that produces millions of tons of vegetables and fruits for export to the rest of Europe. But the Global Environment Outlook, published by the United Nations Environment Program, picked Almeria as one of the places where environmental changes have taken place most rapidly. As evidence, it presented comparisons between satellite photos taken in 1974 and 2004. There are also allegations that underground water supplies and the soil have been contaminated. And the disposal of agricultural garbage, which amounts to a million tons a year, is a headache.

But, interestingly, a research team from the University of Almeria has found a positive effect of the "sea of plastic," so-called because of the amount of man-made material used to make the greenhouses: The temperature there has apparently dropped 0.9 degree Celsius in the past 30 years, while other provinces of Spain rose 1 degree Celsius. The team claims that the hothouses reflect as much sunlight as glaciers, which have the highest reflective capability, and reduce radiant heat. They believe the greenhouses can actually help reduce global warming.

1. What's the main topic of the passage?

    (a) The destruction of Almeria by agricultural garbage

    (b) The cultural history of Almeria

    (c) The increase in global warming in Almeria

    (d) The environmental changes in Almeria

2. What does the "sea of plastic" refer to?

    (a) The appearance of the greenhouses which are made out of man-made materials, such as plastic, and are abundant in Almeria.

    (b) The material that was discarded after the greenhouses were built in Almeria.

    (c) The garbage that has accumulated over time due to the presence of environmental teams in Almeria.

    (d) The leftover equipment from the time when spaghetti westerns were shot in the area of Almeria.

3. All of the following are incorrect except _____.

    (a) Almeria used to be abundant in farming and crops, but has become infertile due to the effects of global warming.

    (b) The greenhouses in Almeria are larger than the area of Seoul and its suburbs.

    (c) Almeria has seen a drop in temperature compared to the rest of Spain which has seen a rise.

    (d) Due to the stark landscape and inhospitable climate, the area of Almeria has not changed much in the past 30 years.

Words & Phrases

virtually *ad.* 사실상   artificial *a.* 인공의   identifiable *a.* 인식할 수 있는   apparently *ad.* 외관상으로는, 언뜻 보기에
barren *a.* 척박한, 황량한   allegation *n.* 혐의, 주장   contaminate *v.* 오염시키다   disposal *n.* 처리, 처분
amount to ~에 달하다   hothouse *n.* 온실   glacier *n.* 빙하   reflective *a.* 반사하는   radiant *a.* 복사의

문장분석

■ And the disposal of agricultural garbage, which amounts to a million tons a year, is a headache. ➡   〈amount to something〉은 '합계가 ~에 이르다/달하다'라는 뜻이며, 〈~ is a headache〉라고 하면 '~ 문제가 골칫거리'라는 뜻이 된다.

Unit 81 X and Y |성별|

The sex of the baby depends on whether the sperm fertilizing the egg contains an X or a Y chromosome. If the Y-carrying sperm gets to the egg first, the baby will be a boy; if the first sperm has an X, you get a girl. But some experts insist that the egg chooses a sperm containing an X or Y chromosome under specific conditions. The general ratio of female to male births is 100 to 105. This can be explained by the fact that male birth rates see a huge increase during certain periods. A study on when we have a better chance of conceiving a boy is still under way.

In 2005, experts from the London School of Economics showed that accountants, mechanics, mathematicians and physicians have a higher chance of conceiving a son, while people engaged in jobs that involve taking care of people, such as nursing or education, are likely to give birth to a daughter. Other studies revealed that 51.5 percent of those couples who lived together during the pregnancy gave birth to a son, while only 49.9 percent of those who lived separately had a boy. In addition, researchers in New Zealand insisted that outgoing females conceived more boys than introverted, passive ones.

However, we have seen a consistent decline in male birth rates in developed countries in the past four decades. A variety of stress conditions and increased pollution hamper the vitality of the sperm that carry the Y chromosome, thus reducing male birth rates. Scientists from Columbia University reported that male children have a higher mortality rate than females when a young unmarried woman gives birth to a child.

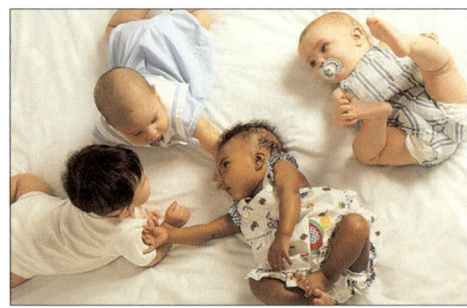

1. What's the main topic of the passage?

    (a) Different jobs produce different babies.

    (b) The ineffectiveness of the Y chromosome sperm

    (c) Environmental and social effects on birth

    (d) Birth patterns of developed countries

2. Which of the following is most likely to produce a male baby?

    (a) A mechanic father and an extrovert mother who live together.

    (b) Both parents are teachers who live in the city.

    (c) A doctor and a nurse who separated after the woman became pregnant.

    (d) An accountant father and a mathematician mother who feel strained at work.

3. Which of the following is incorrect?

    (a) Separated parents are less likely to have a boy.

    (b) People with jobs that require altruism are more likely to have a girl.

    (c) A single mother is more likely to give birth to a female child.

    (d) The Y chromosome can be affected by external factors more than the X chromosome.

4. What cannot be inferred from the passage?

    (a) The X chromosome is more resilient than the Y chromosome.

    (b) It is more difficult to conceive a male baby despite the higher birth rate.

    (c) The ratio of female to male births is gradually changing.

    (d) Gender selection, a viable possibility in the near future.

Words & Phrases

sperm *n.* 정자 fertilize *v.* 수정하다 egg *n.* 난자 chromosome *n.* 염색체 conceive *v.* 임신하다
be under way 진행 중이다 accountant *n.* 회계사 mechanic *n.* 기계공, 정비사 outgoing *a.* 외향적인, 사교적인
introverted *a.* 내성적인 consistent *a.* 일관된 hamper *v.* 방해하다 vitality *n.* 활력 mortality rate 사망률
resilient *a.* (충격·부상 등에 대해) 회복력 있는

문장분석

■ A study on when we have a better chance of conceiving a boy is still under way. ➔ be under way 라는 표현은 '~가 진행 중이다'라는 뜻으로, 비슷한 표현으로는 be in progress, be on the move, be going on 등이 있다.

Unit 82 Statistics use and misuse
|통계의 사용과 오용|

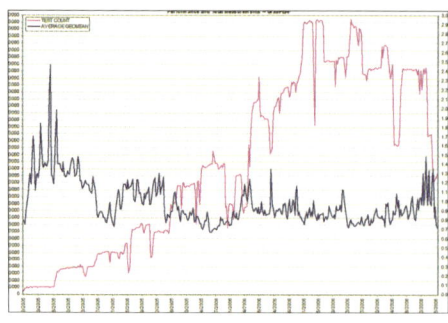

If Austrian priest Gregor Mendel (1822-1884) had stopped his preoccupation with garden peas at breeding and experimenting, his work [1] may not have had the same impact on the world of genetics. Mendel studied pea plants for 15 years to expand on his hypothesis that certain traits in these plants follow particular laws of inheritance. He recorded his findings of variations in numerical order for statistical analysis. His findings went largely unnoticed by his contemporaries [2] who were ignorant of statistics.

But scientists rediscovered his ideas at the turn of the 20th century, posthumously giving him the title "the father of modern genetics." The principle of heredity was not the only thing Mendel's followers uncovered from his studies. They discovered disparity in the result ratios, raising suspicion that Mendel may have censored his experiments to validate his hypothesis or excluded results that [3] will contradict his earlier belief.

English mathematician Charles Babbage in his 1830 book "Reflection on the Decline of Science in England," said there were three kinds of fraud scientists can commit: cooking, trimming and forging. In "cooking," scientists take in only the results that fit their theory, discarding others. "Trimming," which Babbage considered more evil, is an act of smoothing irregularities in order to make the data appear extremely accurate and precise. Such fabrication and rounding of numbers until they fit the desired result are rampant in social statistics.

Kevin Phillips, who served as an economic brain in the Richard Nixon administration, exposed the Nixon government for excluding food and energy prices in calculating the consumer price index in order to report a more positive economic indicator. Economist Steven Levitt in his best-selling nonfiction book "Freakonomics" cites a cheating incident in Chicago schools. Due to the city government's policy of punishing teachers with pay and promotion disadvantages based on school reports, the teachers [4] fabricated students' test results.

1. What's the main topic of the passage?

    (a) A discussion of scientific forgery and its effects
    (b) Mendel's breeding and experimentation of garden peas
    (c) Cooking, Trimming, Forging!
    (d) The study of Freakonomics

2. Which of the following is grammatically incorrect among [1] – [4]?

    (a) [1]
    (b) [2]
    (c) [3]
    (d) [4]

3. According to the passage, each of the following is true except _____.

    (a) Mendel was named as the father of modern genetics by other scientists.
    (b) Of cooking, trimming and forging, trimming and forging are the most alike.
    (c) Kevin Phillips became a whistleblower on the Nixon administration.
    (d) Chicago's education policy caused its teachers to forge students' test results.

4. Which of the following can be substituted for the underlined rampant?

    (a) extensive
    (b) exasperating
    (c) insane
    (d) shocking

Words & Phrases

priest n. 사제 preoccupation n. 몰두; 집착 genetics n. 유전학 hypothesis n. 가설 trait n. 특징
inheritance n. 유전, 상속 statistical a. 통계의 contemporary n. 동시대 사람 posthumously ad. 사후에
heredity n. 유전 disparity n. 차이 suspicion n. 의혹 censor v. 검열하다, 검열하여 삭제하다 validate v. 입증하다
contradict v. 모순되다; 부정하다, 반박하다 fraud n. 사기 trim v. 다듬다, 손질하다 forge v. 위조하다
irregularity n. 불규칙한 것, 고르지 못한 것 fabrication n. 위조, 꾸며낸 것 round v. 둥글게 하다; 반올림하다
rampant a. 만연하는, 걷잡을 수 없는 cite v. 예로 들다 promotion n. 승진 whistleblower n. 밀고자

문장분석

■ His findings <u>went</u> largely <u>unnoticed</u> by his contemporaries who were ignorant of statistics. → 〈go + 형용사〉는 '(시간이 감에 따라) ~이 되다'는 뜻을 지닌다. '가다'는 의미의 go가 아니라는 점에 주의한다. go bad는 '음식 등이 상하다'는 뜻이며, go bankrupt는 '파산하다'는 뜻이며, go wild는 '난폭해지다'는 뜻이다. 좀 덜 친숙한 표현들로는 go green, go nuclear, go public 등이 있는데, 각각 '친환경적으로 되다', '핵보유국이 되다', '상장 회사가 되다'는 뜻으로 사용된다. 위의 예문에서의 'went largely unnoticed'는 그가 발견한 것이 '대체로 (사람들의) 주목을 받지 못하게 됐다'는 뜻이다.

Unit 83 Reinventing the wheel
| 볼펜 · 아이팟 · 신문 |

• 발명 •

Working in a printing company, Yoshio Okada came to invent the snap-off blade in 1961, primarily out of necessity. At work, the major headache in his job of cutting paper corners was that the razor blade would become blunt too soon. One day he noticed a shoe repairman using a broken piece of glass as a cutter. The chocolate bars American soldiers broke off to hand out pieces to him and his friends in childhood days also fed his idea of designing a blade with a tip that could be snapped off [1] when worn to unused sections.

Hungarian journalist Ladislao Biro often got frustrated spilling ink over his finished articles. He tried using viscous oil-based ink, but it was too thick to come out of his fountain pen. With the help of his chemist brother, Biro unveiled in 1943 the first practical ballpoint pen [2] who uses a tiny metal ball bearing to push out ink. British air force pilots were the first to use them. Some even say that Allied forces won the Second World War because pilots were able to accurately indicate their targets in map coordinates using the ballpoint pens while flying.

These inventions helped to change the lives of mankind because their inventors saw and thought differently about the use of simple [3] item like a pen or a knife. Allowing people or users easier access and interaction with systems and machines is termed User Interface, or UI, in telecommunications terms. Revolutionary UI often can outpace progress in technology. The Wii game console [4] is marketing by Nintendo Inc. in 2006 added an entire new meaning to home video games. While its competitors were busy working on innovative game software and equipment, Nintendo came up with a wireless controller to allow a player to freely use the body to play the games. More than 50 million Wii consoles have been sold across the world.

The iPod is also a product of the UI concept. Apple Inc. discarded all the complicated functions of a digital music player to focus on the basics — sound and screen quality. The sleek, simple but bright-colored design that fits into a pocket soon became a major hit with young people throughout the world. Apple CEO Steve Jobs underscored that what's most important in making a new product was seeing through the user's eyes. Innovation is possible when the manufacturer stands in the user position.

1. According to the passage, why is the Wii so popular?

    (a) The Nintendo marketing company worked overtime.

    (b) It was different to all other game software of the time.

    (c) Nintendo targeted young people with money.

    (d) The sound and screen quality were better than had ever been seen before.

2. Which of the following is grammatically correct among [1] – [4]?

    (a) [1]

    (b) [2]

    (c) [3]

    (d) [4]

3. All of the following are true except ____.

    (a) The Wii and the iPod have both utilized the UI concept to great success.

    (b) Biro invented his ballpoint pen because he was frustrated with using his fountain pen.

    (c) Even though the iPod had a simple design, it sold enormously well.

    (d) Biro impeded the Allied forces in the Second World War.

4. What can be inferred from the passage?

    (a) Apple's designs will become even sleeker and simpler in the future to meet the wishes of consumers.

    (b) Nintendo copied what its competitors were doing but did it better.

    (c) With his invention of the snap-off blade, Okada made his work-life easier.

    (d) Ladislao Biro became an instant millionaire with his invention.

Words & Phrases

snap-off *a.* 찰칵 하고 여는, 찰칵 하고 끊는   out of necessity 필요에 의해서   blunt *a.* 무딘, 뭉툭한
frustrated *a.* 좌절감을 느끼는   viscous *a.* 끈적거리는, 점성이 있는   fountain pen *n.* 만년필
unveil *v.* 선보이다, 내놓다   coordinate *n.* 좌표   outpace *v.* 능가하다   come up with ~을 생각해 내다, 내놓다
discard *v.* 버리다   sleek *a.* 매끈한   underscore *v.* 강조하다

문장분석

■ While its competitors <u>were busy</u> working on innovative game software and equipment, Nintendo <u>came up with</u> a wireless controller to allow a player to freely use the body to play the games. ➔ 〈be busy -ing〉라는 표현은 '~하느라 바쁘다'는 뜻의 구문이며, 〈come up with + new ideas/methods〉는 '(새로운 것) 생각해내다'는 뜻의 숙어이다.

Unit 84 Sweetening up lethal diseases
|프랑스병|

• 의학 •

In 1530, Venetian poet Girolamo Fracastoro gave a new name in one of his poems to an ailment that was called "the French disease" during the 16th century. The sickness, which appeared to have originated from the New World recently "discovered" by Columbus, was called the French disease in Italy and Germany. However, the French called it the Italian disease. The same disease was also known as the Spanish disease in the Netherlands, the Polish disease in Russia, and the Christian disease in Turkey. Records show that it was called the British disease in Tahiti.

One can easily guess how the disease got so many names. Everybody wanted to hold their enemy countries "responsible for spreading the bad disease." If Fracastoro had not given the disease a new name, "syphilis," European countries might still be calling it by other countries' names and getting upset with each other. On April 30, the World Health Organization decided to use the name "type A influenza" or "H1N1" for the currently rampant flu now called swine influenza. The reason for changing the name swine flu, which is already widely used, is to prevent unnecessary misunderstandings.

The name of a disease spreads disgust and fear at the same time. Since the 20th century, people have come to the conclusion __(A)__ it is better to avoid disease names __(B)__ explain symptoms or causes explicitly for fear of upsetting too many people. That's why leprosy was changed to Hansen's disease, senile dementia was changed to Alzheimer's disease, and mad cow disease is now called new variant Creutzfeldt-Jakob disease. There is the claim that schizophrenia should be called "dopamine dysregulation disorder" to avoid social prejudice. The disease "hysteria," which was jiral in Korean — already a pejorative word — is now called "epilepsy," or ganjil, for the same reason.

1. What's the purpose of the passage?

   (a) To inform people about the work of Girolamo Fracastoro
   (b) To explain why diseases adopt neutral names
   (c) To persuade people not to encourage xenophobia with disease names
   (d) To clarify the symptoms of certain global diseases

2. Which of the following is false?

   (a) It was decided that disease names should avoid identifying the disease's symptoms.
   (b) Syphilis has been known by many names throughout the world, usually the country's name where it is believed to have originated.
   (c) The name syphilis was first used by Fracastoro.
   (d) The World Health Organization strongly argued against calling swine flu "H1N1".

3. Which of the following fits in both blanks (A) and (B)?

   (a) that
   (b) who
   (c) which
   (d) Nothing.

4. Why was syphilis originally known by so many different names?

   (a) Different countries had different variants of the same disease.
   (b) People wanted to keep the disease's existence a secret for as long as possible.
   (c) Each country wanted to blame its enemy country for spreading the disease.
   (d) Columbus didn't want the world to know what he had done to the New World.

Words & Phrases

ailment *n.* 병   originate *v.* 비롯되다, 유래하다   hold A responsible for B A를 B한 일에 대해 책임지게 하다   syphilis *n.* 매독
rampant *a.* 만연하는, 걷잡을 수 없는   swine influenza 돼지 독감   misunderstanding *n.* 오해   disgust *n.* 혐오감
symptom *n.* 증상   explicitly *ad.* 명백히   leprosy *n.* 나병, 문둥병   senile dementia *n.* 노인성 치매
mad cow disease 광우병   variant *n.* 변종   prejudice *n.* 편견   hysteria *n.* 히스테리, 병적 흥분
pejorative *a.* 경멸적인, 비난투의   epilepsy *n.* 간질

문장분석

■ Everybody wanted to <u>hold</u> their enemy countries "<u>responsible</u> for spreading the bad disease." ➡ 〈hold somebody responsible/accountable for something〉 또는 수동태로 사용해 〈somebody is held responsible/accountable for something〉 이란 표현은 '~를 …한 일에 대해 책임지게 하다'는 뜻을 지닌다. responsible 대신 accountable도 같은 의미를 지니므로 유의한다.

Unit 85 The life-saving act of washing
|팬데믹(pandemic)|

The year was 1346. The place was Caffa, a port city on the Cremian peninsula, the center of trade between the Eastern and Western worlds at that time. Jani Beg, the commander of the Mongol army who had surrounded the city for the past three years, left his farewell gift to the citizens there. He catapulted the bodies of his soldiers who had died suddenly from a mysterious disease over the fortress walls. The deadly germs infected the city this way. This was the moment when the Black Death, which broke out in Asia and spread rapidly through the Silk Road, reached Europe for the first time. The Genoese traders who took refuge inside the city walls became carriers of the disease. The next year, in every port that they dropped by on their way home, countless people were infected. The disease spread into every corner of Europe and within a year it reached Britain, the Arabian Peninsula and the Nile River Delta.

The Black Death swept ___(A)___ the globe except the New World, making it one of history's deadliest pandemics. In each country, one-third to half of the population succumbed to the disease. The number of fatalities reached 42 million, 25 million of them Europeans. The cause of the spread of the disease were the germ-laden fleas that feasted __(B)__ rats living close to humans in pursuit of food. However, as there was no concept of pandemics back then, people found a reason elsewhere. Instead of eradicating rats, tens of thousands of people whipped themselves, believing the plague was punishment from the gods who were enraged at the sins committed __(C)__ mankind. Witch hunts were common as well. A rumor spread that the Jews transmitted germs and some were burned alive.

The Jews fell victim to the rumor because for some reason, they were not infected. The Talmud explains that it was thanks to Jewish tradition, which emphasizes the importance of personal hygiene. Washing one's hands was regarded as a holy act of meeting with God and it was strictly abided by. Meanwhile, commoners in the Middle Ages didn't pay much attention to washing. There was even a joke that if money was hidden under the soap, they would still never find it.

1. What's the main idea of the passage?

   (a) The reasons why Jewish people escaped the Black Death
   (b) The effects of the Black Death on populations
   (c) The spread of the Black Death over the world
   (d) The importance of personal hygiene

2. What was Jani Beg's role on the spread of the Black Death?

   (a) He knowingly transmitted the disease to the merchants who traveled along the Silk Road.
   (b) He threw the infected bodies of his soldiers into the city of Caffa and infected the city.
   (c) He ordered the mass murder of the city of Caffa by siege.
   (d) He fed infected rats to his soldiers to prevent them from starvation during the war.

3. Which of the following best fits in the blanks (A), (B) and (C) respectively?

   (a) across – with – on
   (b) near – on – through
   (c) up – by – by
   (d) across – on – by

4. What can be inferred from the passage?

   (a) At that time, Jewish people were much more hygienic than others.
   (b) Jewish people knew where the disease had come from and protected themselves against it.
   (c) Poor people commonly ate rats as a source of nourishment when no other food could be found.
   (d) Traders were blamed for the spread of the disease and were publicly whipped as punishment.

Words & Phrases

port n. 항구   peninsula n. 반도   farewell n. 작별 인사   catapult v. (투석기로) 내던지다   fortress n. 요새, 성채
deadly a. 치명적인   germ n. 세균, 병균   break out 발생하다, 발발하다   refuge n. 피난, 피신   countless a. 셀 수 없는
pandemic n. 전국적인 유행병   succumb to ~에 굴복하다, 무릎을 꿇다   fatality n. 사망자, 치사율
germ-laden a. 세균을 잔뜩 실은   flea n. 벼룩   whip v. 회초리로 때리다   plague n. 전염병   enraged a. 분노한
witch hunt 마녀 사냥   hygiene n. 위생   abide by 준수하다, 지키다   commoner n. 평민, 서민

문장분석

■ This was <u>the moment when</u> the Black Death, which broke out in Asia and spread rapidly through the Silk Road, reached Europe for the first time. ➜ 〈the moment when + 주어 + 동사〉 구문에서 when을 '관계부사'라고 한다. 여기서 '관계'라는 말은 바로 앞의 선행사인 the moment와 when이 서로 관계가 있다는 뜻이고, '부사'라는 말은 when이 이 문장에서 부사(절)의 역할을 수행한다는 뜻이다. 관계부사에는 when 말고도, 이유를 나타내는 the reason why, 장소를 나타내는 the place where, 방법을 나타내는 the way (how), (the way) how 등 총 네 가지의 경우가 존재한다.

Unit 86 Seeking signs of aliens in universe
|외계인|

•우주•

A gilded record plate and a record player were loaded onto Voyager 1 and 2, which were launched in 1977 by the U.S. for the exploration of the outer solar system. Included were messages from Jimmy Carter, then president of the U.S., and Kurt Waldheim, then UN secretary general. It also included greetings in 55 languages, including Korean, and 27 pieces of music from the first movement of Beethoven's "Symphony No. 5" to a folk song from native Australian tribes. In one phrase, it was loaded with "the sounds of the Earth."

The main reason all this was loaded on the spaceships was the possibility that extraterrestrial life might one day find them. Voyager 1 and Voyager 2, which were launched 33 years ago, have flown about 115 and 93 astronomical units (a unit equivalent to the distance between the Earth and the Sun). And it is possible that they can reach an alien civilization, if they fly tens of thousands of years longer. The project may seem far-fetched. But Carl Sagan, an American astronomer who initiated the project, insisted that it was worth trying, like sending a letter in a bottle that drifts in the ocean.

Sagan, the author of "Cosmos," also initiated the Search for Extra-Terrestrial Intelligence (SETI) project, into which an enormous amount of government money was poured into to capture signals that might have been sent by aliens. The government no longer funds the effort. But even after the U.S. government concluded that the project was "useless" and decided not to support it in 1996, scientists from 125 countries continue to analyze signals with support from private institutions and donors.

1. What's the passage about?

   (a) The special feeling America holds for space projects

   (b) Attempting to make communication with extra-terrestrial life

   (c) The real missions of Voyager 1 and 2

   (d) Music that represents the human race on Earth

2. What can you infer about Sagan?

   (a) He is ridiculed by the U.S. government.

   (b) He is very interested in making contact with alien life forms.

   (c) He is disappointed that he has yet to make contact with other forms of life.

   (d) He has decided to give up his projects because they are useless.

3. What does the underlined 'the effort' refer to?

   (a) The Search for Extra-Terrestrial Intelligence (SETI)

   (b) The U.S. government

   (c) Carl Sagan's life work

   (d) The signals that have been received

4. Which of the following is incorrect?

   (a) Voyager 1 and 2 have already flown a long distance, equivalent to that from the Earth to the Sun.

   (b) Voyager 1 and 2 are still flying around in space.

   (c) Different kinds of music, including classical and folk, were loaded onto the spaceships.

   (d) Every country followed the U.S. decision to stop studying signals from space.

Words & Phrases

gilded *a.* 도금을 한   load *v.* 싣다   launch *v.* 발사하다   greeting *n.* 인사, 인사말   extraterrestrial *a.* 외계의
alien *a.* 외계의   civilization *n.* 문명   far-fetched *a.* 허황된, 믿기지 않는, 설득력 없는   initiate *v.* 시작하다, 주도하다
fund *v.* 자금을 지원하다   donor *n.* 기부자, 기증자

문장분석

■ But Carl Sagan, an American astronomer who initiated the project, insisted that it <u>was worth</u> trying, like <u>sending</u> a letter in a bottle that drifts in the ocean.

➡ 〈be worth -ing〉 구문은 '~할 가치가 있다'는 뜻으로, worth 뒤에는 명사나 동명사가 온다는 사실에 주의한다.

Unit 87 The high cost of the patent wars
|복제약|

• 발명 •

It was during the Renaissance that the importance of invention and innovation was recognized. Filippo Brunelleschi, who built the dome of the grand cathedral of Florence, acquired the first patent in history for a ship he designed to transport granite for the dome. But he did not make money on the ship. It sank on its maiden voyage with 50 tons of granite on board.

The patent system developed gradually. Today, people know that invention and innovation cannot flourish if there is no assurance of financial gain attached. Yet the counter-arguments are difficult to refute. Those who claim that the patent system should be abolished say that the desire to do good, not make money, can be the mother of invention. In the pharmaceutical industry, especially, the patent system is a punching bag. Patent rights are openly violated based on the claim that a patent is nothing compared to a human life. A typical example is the government of Thailand, which produced a generic drug for AIDS without permission in 2002. Although there was lots of protest in the international community, the Thai government responded that they were able to save a large number of lives because the price of the drug had plummeted to $30 from $500.

Pharmaceutical companies complain a lot when their patent rights are violated because of the time and money they invested in developing a new drug. When their patents expire, they direct their complaints against companies that produce cheap generic drugs. That is why the U.S. insisted, in Korea-U.S. free trade agreement negotiations, on delaying the sale of generic drugs in the market even after a patent expired. It is said that the suspension period was lengthened when the agreement was renegotiated.

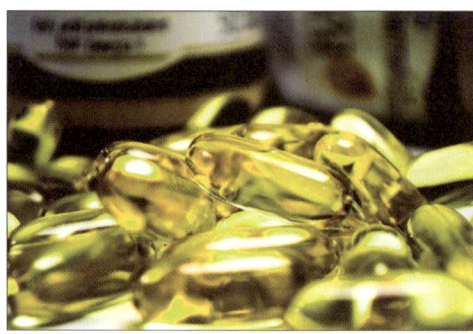

1. What's the topic of the passage?

    (a) The fight against AIDS

    (b) The Korea-U.S. free trade agreement

    (c) Medicines to fight diseases

    (d) Patent rights

2. Which of the following best paraphrases the underlined phrase?

    (a) Inventions and innovations do not come from the promise of financial gain these days.

    (b) Attaching the importance of financial gain to new inventions means they cannot flourish.

    (c) It is with the promise of financial gains that people pursue new inventions and innovations these days.

    (d) People do not invent new things to make money, but instead to enjoy the process of innovation.

3. What is the defense against violating a pharmaceutical patent?

    (a) Pharmaceutical patents have never been adhered to.

    (b) Without pharmaceutical patents, drugs will become cheaper.

    (c) There is no way to regulate pharmaceutical patents.

    (d) Human life is more important than a patent.

4. According to the passage, which of the following statements is correct?

    (a) Thailand is the center of new pharmaceutical innovations.

    (b) Generic drugs do not help against diseases.

    (c) New drugs take a lot of time and money to develop.

    (d) The first patent in history was for the design of the cathedral dome in Florence.

Words & Phrases

invention *n.* 발명   innovation *n.* 혁신   grand *a.* 웅장한   cathedral *n.* 성당   patent *n.* 특허   granite *n.* 대리석   gradually *ad.* 점차적으로   flourish *v.* 번창하다   counter-argument *n.* 반론   refute *v.* 반박하다   pharmaceutical *a.* 제약의   punching bag (권투 연습용) 샌드백, 동네북   generic drug 복제약품   plummet *v.* 곤두박질치다, 급락하다   expire *v.* 만기가 되다   direct *v.* ~로 향하다   free trade agreement 자유무역협정(FTA)   suspension *n.* 유예   lengthen *v.* 길어지다, 늘어나다

문장분석

■ **It is said that** the suspension period was lengthened when the agreement was renegotiated. ➔ ⟨it is said that ~⟩ 구문은 '~라고 (사람들이) 말하다'는 뜻으로, it은 가주어, that 절이 진주어가 된다. 원래 능동태로 ⟨they say that ~⟩의 표현이 수동태로 바뀌면서 변한 구문으로 생각할 수 있다. 비슷한 표현으로 it is reported that ~이라고 하면 '~라고 (기자들이) 보도하다'는 뜻이며, it is rumored that ~이라고 하면 '~라고 (사람들이) 소문으로 말하다'는 뜻이 된다.

Unit 88 The empty seat
|빈자리|

• 수학 •

Indian mathematician Brahmagupta called the number zero shunya in 600 A.D. Shunya is a Sanskrit word for emptiness and nothingness. He was the first to use zero as a number for absence of quantity based on a philosophical concept of void. Before Brahmagupta gave zero the characteristic of emptiness, zero was not considered a number on its own but a mere placeholder digit indicating a lack of quantity.

The significance of the emptiness is not limited to the world of mathematics. Absence is not just a physical void but can refer to the meaning of life and the rule of nature. In both Western and Eastern legends, the world always began from nothingness. In the beginning, there was no heaven, no earth, no water, no light, no darkness and no time. It all started from an empty space with no bottom and no ceiling. After all, the universe was just a dot the size of a "0" before the Big Bang 13.7 billion years ago, so we cannot blame the legends and myths for being outrageous.

Religions pursue the true self and mind of mankind, with emptiness also being a religious word. In Buddhism, your mind does not have a substance but is empty like the void. Emptiness is found everywhere. The endlessly wide empty space in the universe is what the Buddhists call "Sunyata." To the eyes of the awakened souls, whole things in the universe exist in the empty space.

Emptiness is also a rule of nature that helps you realize what you do not know and are not aware of. Professor Robert Root-Bernstein, the author of *"Sparks of Genius: The Thirteen Thinking Tools of the World's Most Creative People,"* uses the example of a jigsaw puzzle to explain what emptiness means. The unfilled space is as important as the completed picture because it shows what the missing piece is. It gives us a clue to what we do not know, and once we figure out what to look for, we are a step closer to finding the right piece for the empty spot.

1. What's the topic of the passage?

   (a) Meanings of emptiness

   (b) Buddhism

   (c) The value of 0

   (d) How the world was created

2. Which of the following is incorrect?

   (a) Absence always comes back to meaning the physical void.

   (b) Both Western and Eastern legends see the world created out of nothing.

   (c) Brahmagupta was first to give zero the meaning of a number.

   (d) A jigsaw puzzle shows us what we don't know as well as what we know.

3. What does the underlined 'it' refer to?

   (a) The completed area in a jigsaw puzzle

   (b) The uncompleted space in the middle of a jigsaw puzzle

   (c) A completed jigsaw puzzle

   (d) A jigsaw puzzle before starting to be completed

4. What can you infer from the passage?

   (a) Mathematics does not recognize the existence of nothing.

   (b) Buddhism is different to other religions.

   (c) Buddhism does not believe in the existence of emptiness in the world.

   (d) Studying emptiness is important in understanding human life.

Words & Phrases

Sanskrit *a.* 산스크리트어의   absence *n.* 부재   void *a.* 빈   characteristic *n.* 특징   placeholder *n.* 플레이스 홀더(빠져 있는 다른 것을 대신하는 기호나 텍스트의 일부)   digit *n.* 숫자   outrageous *a.* 터무니없는   substance *n.* 물질, 실체   jigsaw puzzle 조각 그림 맞추기

문장분석

■ Absence is <u>not just</u> a physical void <u>but</u> can refer to the meaning of life and the rule of nature. ➡ 〈not only/just A, but (also) B〉 구문은 'A일 뿐 아니라 B도'란 뜻이다. not only, not just, not merely, not simply 등이 같이 사용되며, 뒤에 오는 but also에서 also는 종종 생략된다. 그리고 의미상 A보다는 뒤에 오는 B를 강조한다는 점에 유의한다.

Unit 89 Scarier than genetic diseases
|유전질환보다 더 두려운 것|

• 건강 •

Lately, personal genetic testing is gaining popularity. Since the end of June, consumers can find out their genetic traits without going through a doctor. It is quite simple. You can swipe cells from inside the mouth and send it to the agency. For about 150,000 won ($132), you get a report of risks on 12 categories, blood sugar, aging of skin, hair loss and obesity. Due to the concerns for errors in analysis, it is prohibited by law to analyze genetic traits for severe illnesses such as cancer.

It is certainly useful to learn about your genetic information. But _____. For example, a pair of identical twins may have a different physique depending on how they are brought up. Obesity is also closely related to socioeconomic factors. We are familiar with studies that people with lower education and income are more prone to obesity. There are theories that environmental factors are also carried down to the next generation.

Koreans' alcohol and tobacco consumption is rapidly rising. According to the National Statistical Office's study on household spending in the first half of the year, the average consumption of alcoholic beverages and tobacco products increased by 7.1 percent compared to the same period last year, while spending on all other categories decreased. Global market research firm Euromonitor International's survey also shows similar results. Among 24 countries surveyed, Koreans drink the most alcohol, with an intake of 168 kcal from alcoholic drinks per day on average. This is disgraceful. We are worried that alcohol and tobacco consumption may be socially inherited to the next generation.

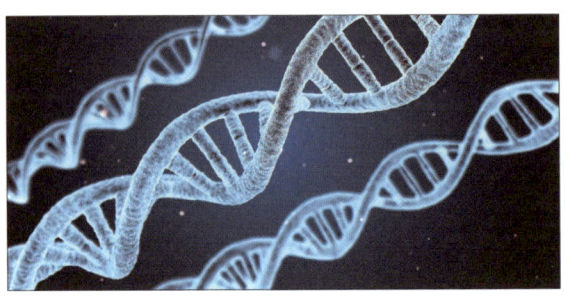

1. What's the purpose of the passage?

   (a) To understand why South Koreans drink and smoke to excess.

   (b) To discuss what South Koreans are passing down to the next generation.

   (c) To analyze how to prevent smoking and drinking from increasing.

   (d) To communicate ways to reduce bad habits among all generations of Koreans.

2. Why can't severe illnesses be included in genetic testing?

   (a) Mistakes might be made and recipients told erroneous life-threatening information.

   (b) People have a right to keep their illnesses private from family members.

   (c) It has not yet been confirmed whether being informed of this would be of any help.

   (d) Being told you have a serious illness in this way could be damaging to a person.

3. Which of the following statement is true, according to the passage?

   (a) While Koreans are smoking and drinking more, it looks to be slowing gradually.

   (b) If you are raised in a low-wealth environment, you are more likely to smoke and drink.

   (c) Spending is generally reducing in Korea, except on tobacco and alcohol, which is rising.

   (d) Socioeconomic factors are often ignored by scientists when testing for obesity causes.

4. Which of the following completes the passage?

   (a) some scientists are wary of genetic effects because of environmental variables

   (b) the real question should be why we want to know all this stuff

   (c) for most of us, this information serves no purpose at all

   (d) this data has made us all into a generation of searchers, always expecting answers

Words & Phrases

genetic *a.* 유전적인   blood sugar 혈당   obesity *n.* 과체중   prohibit *v.* 금지하다   identical twins 일란성 쌍둥이
physique *n.* 체격, 체형   be prone to ~하기 쉬운, 경향이 있는   consumption *n.* 소비   household *n.* 가족, 한 집안
beverage *n.* 마실 것, 음료   intake *n.* 섭취, 흡입

문장분석

■ Due to the concerns for errors in analysis, it is prohibited by law to analyze genetic traits for severe illnesses [such as] cancer. ➡ Due to는 이유 전치사, it은 가주어로 진주어는 to analyze genetic traits이다. 전치사 for severe illnesses는 genetic traits를 수식하며, such as는 A such as B의 형태로, B는 A에 대한 세부적인 예시를 제시한다. 즉, severe illnesses의 하나의 예로 cencer를 제시하고 있다.

unit 89 유전질환보다 더 두려운 것   185

Unit 90 Listeria hysteria |리스테리아|

•질병•

Listeria is often referred to as a "ubiquitous bacteria," owing to the fact that it seems to pop up everywhere. As listeria can be found in both soil and water, plants can easily become contaminated. Thus it can spread to grass-eating animals. The presence of Listeria is constantly tested for in some unpasteurized dairy products and some meat products. However, if a healthy human eats listeria-tainted food, it is not always such a huge problem. He may experience influenza-like symptoms or no symptom at all. In any case, the infection can easily be cured. Serious life-threatening side effects or death occur predominantly in the elderly or among pregnant women. These groups tend to exhibit weakened immune systems, which are more vulnerable to the listeria bacteria. Pregnant women, in particular, are about 20 times more likely than other healthy adults to get listeria, as their cell-mediated immunity naturally decreases during pregnancy so that their systems can embrace the unborn child. The United States Centers for Disease Control and Prevention deems listeria infections as serious, with an estimated 2,500 cases of infection and 500 deaths per year in the U.S.

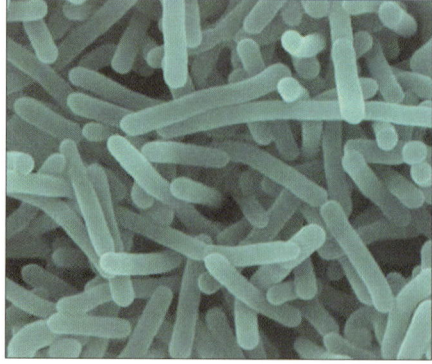

1. What can be inferred from the passage?

   (a) Listeria is a dangerous bacterium that all people should be very afraid of.
   (b) When you contract listeria you should go to the hospital immediately.
   (c) Even common bacteria can still be dangerous to us.
   (d) The CDC has little protection to offer people against listeria.

2. Which of the following is true according to the passage?

   (a) The CDC is unable to deal with listeria effectively.
   (b) The listeria bacterium is deadly to those who contract it.
   (c) A woman with a child is in danger if she comes in contact with listeria.
   (d) Listeria can be found in both soil and water as it is an air born bacteria.

Words & Phrases

listeria *n.* 리스테리아균   ubiquitous *a.* 어디에나 있는, 아주 흔한   pop up 불쑥 나타나다   soil *n.* 토양
contaminated *a.* 오염된   unpasteurized *a.* 저온 살균되어 있지 않은   dairy product *n.* 유제품
tainted *a.* 오염된   symptom *n.* 증상   infection *n.* 감염   predominantly *ad.* 대부분   immune system *n.* 면역체계
vulnerable *a.* 취약한   cell-mediated immunity 세포 (매개)성 면역 (세포막에 부착하는 항체의 증가에 의한 면역)
embrace *v.* 수용하다; 포옹하다   deem *v.* 여기다, 생각하다

문장분석

■ The presence of Listeria is constantly tested for in some unpasteurized dairy products and some meat products. → ⟨test/look/check/search/scrutinize (A) for B⟩ 구문에서, 전치사 for는 '~이 있는지 없는지'의 의미를 지닌다. 따라서 이 구문은 'B가 있는지 없는지 A를 검사하다/확인하다/체크하다/찾아보다/(면밀히) 조사하다'라는 의미를 각각 갖는다. 예문에 사용된 test의 경우 수동태로 사용되었으며, A에 해당하는 목적어는 생략되어 있고, B가 주어로 나와 있는 수동태 형태로 ⟨B is tested for in A⟩의 형태로 사용되었다. 따라서 전치사 for가 이 경우 꼭 필요하다.

Unit 91 The joy of leaving your car behind
|차 없는 날|

•발명•

In the spring of 2004, Italian scientists solved an old problem. They successfully created the automobile devised by Renaissance genius Leonardo da Vinci. The automobile was made out of wood according to a blueprint in Codex Atlanticus, da Vinci's bound set of drawings and writings. Although it is presumed that the vehicle was envisioned as an exhibit rather than to actually run on the road, the scientists finally got it up and running.

Automobiles started to run on the road around 120 years ago. In 1885, Karl Friedrich Benz developed a tricyclic automobile with a gasoline engine he created. In 1891, he created a four-wheeled automobile, too. American Henry Ford was the man who ushered in the era of the automobile. The Model T introduced by the Ford Motor Company in 1908 was sturdy, easy to drive and inexpensive enough so as to be affordable for the middle class. The company sold 16 million Model Ts before production was ceased in 1927.

In the 1920s U.S. motor companies started buying commuter trams in cities like Los Angeles. They reduced the number of times trams ran in a day to make tram use inconvenient, and ultimately stopped tram operations because of a supposed deficit. America's automobile culture was firmly established in the 1950s when highways were built throughout the nation.

1. What is the main topic of the passage?

    (a) Leonardo da Vinci

    (b) Cars

    (c) Motor companies

    (d) Automobile culture

2. How did companies encourage car use according to the passage?

    (a) They sold cars at low prices.

    (b) They lowered the price of gasoline.

    (c) They made public transit troublesome.

    (d) They produced many different models.

3. What can be inferred from the passage?

    (a) American car culture was created by the automobile industry.

    (b) Cars were not the best form of transportation available.

    (c) The invention of the car was taken from da Vinci.

    (d) There are more cars than trams on the road today.

4. What is the best title for the passage?

    (a) Trams and cars

    (b) Where to buy a good car

    (c) How cars were made

    (d) The introduction of the automobile

Words & Phrases

devise v. 고안하다   blueprint n. 청사진, 설계도   envision v. 상상하다, 구상하다   exhibit n. 전시품
up and running 작동 중인   tricyclic a. 삼륜의   usher in the era of ~한 시대를 열다   affordable a. (가격이) 알맞은
cease v. 중단하다   commuter tram 통근 전차   deficit n. 적자

문장분석

■ American Henry Ford was the man who ushered in the era of the automobile. ➡ 〈usher in the era of something, usher in a (new) era of something〉이란 표현은 '~한 (새로운) 시대를 열다'는 뜻이다. 예를 들어 'The discovery of the transistor ushered in a new era of microelectronics.'라고 하면 '트랜지스터의 발명이 초소형 전자공학의 새 시대를 열었다'는 뜻이 된다.

Unit 92 A critical look at global warming
|온난화 회의론|

• 환경 •

Europe in the summer of 2003 was hot like a frying pan. When the heat wave hit over 40 degrees Celsius (104 degrees Fahrenheit), nuclear power plants experienced difficulties in supplying cooling water. People suffered heat stroke and tens of thousands of deaths were reported. If global warming continues, it is inevitable that heat waves like this one will become more frequent. However, some people retort that cold periods would also be reduced. Bjørn Lomborg, a Danish professor of statistics, claimed in his 2007 book "Cool It" that a merit of global warming is the reduction of cold weather related casualties.

However, Lomborg — who first questioned global warming in his 2001 book "The Skeptical Environmentalist" — changed his position a little thereafter. Although he denied the scientific grounds for global warming, he _____(A)_____ global warming itself in 2007. But he argued that it would be more efficient to invest in fighting malaria and HIV/AIDS than pouring resources into cutting greenhouse gas emissions. In the background of the change was the 4th assessment report presented by the Intergovernmental Panel on Climate Change in February 2007. Rounding up the opinion of 2,500 specialists and experts, IPCC declared that there was no room for the argument that human beings caused global warming. To this, _____(B)_____ environmentalists had no choice but to retract some of their previous statements.

Nowadays, the skeptics are raising their voices again. The average temperature of the earth has not gone up since it recorded 14.5 degrees Celsius in 1998. Some time ago, about 4,000 e-mail messages and documents that well-known scholars in climatology exchanged were hacked and made public online. Among the e-mails exchanged were ones that raised suspicions that the scientists had been announcing research results that suited their own tastes and that only supported their theories on global warming.

1. What cannot be inferred from the passage?

    (a) Global warming may not be caused completely by man as previously thought.

    (b) There are no clear answers as to the true cause of global warming.

    (c) There are still viable alternate theories.

    (d) There is a new conscience on the issue of global warming.

2. Which of the following is the main topic of the passage?

    (a) Doubts about global warming

    (b) Where the warm weather comes from

    (c) Lomborg is correct.

    (d) The stabilization of global temperatures

3. Which of the following is incorrect according to the passage?

    (a) There is still debate on the issue.

    (b) Lomborg was proven to be correct.

    (c) There are major problems when heat waves strike.

    (d) Some feel differently about the use of funds for global warming prevention.

4. Which of the following best completes the passage?

    (a) (A) change   (B) climatology
    (b) (A) reduced   (B) declared
    (c) (A) degrees   (B) experienced
    (d) (A) recognized   (B) skeptical

Words & Phrases

heat wave 장기간의 혹서, 열파   heat stroke n. 열사병   retort v. 반박하다   casualty n. 사상자, 피해자
skeptical a. 회의적인   round up ~을 (찾아) 모으다   no room for the argument 논란의 여지가 없다
have no choice but to ~할 수밖에 없다   retract v. 철회하다   skeptic n. 회의론자   climatology n. 기후학
suspicion n. 의혹

문장분석

■ Rounding up the opinion of 2,500 specialists and experts, IPCC declared that there was <u>no room for</u> the argument that human beings caused global warming.

→ ⟨no/little room for something⟩에서 room은 가능성이나 여지를 뜻한다. 따라서 이 구문은 '~할 여지가 (거의) 없다'는 뜻이 된다. room for improvement는 '향상의 여지'를 뜻하며, room for doubt/argument는 '의심/논의의 여지'를 뜻한다. room for maneuver는 '운신의 여지'를 뜻한다. 참고로 room은 불가산 명사이므로 부정관사나 복수형이 올 수 없다.

Unit 93 Repent, ye carbon emitters
|환경 면죄부|

• 환경 •

An indulgence for the modern era has emerged, and this one ostensibly forgives the sin of carbon dioxide emission. The so-called carbon-offset system demands investment in environmentally friendly projects to compensate for the excessive emission of carbon dioxide. They are mainly bought by people who travel on airplanes, which emit more carbon gases than other forms of transportation. In addition to airfare, they pay $10 to $40 more for apparently contributing to planting trees in Africa and constructing hydroelectric power plants in Brazil. Thanks to the demand spurred by people's desire to rid themselves of a guilty conscience, the amount earned from the carbon-offset system worldwide has reached a couple million dollars.

But there are strong criticisms of the system, which is also known as carbon credit or cap and trade. As the indulgence in the Middle Ages allowed people to commit crimes and still have peace of mind, the carbon-offset system also encourages people to travel more frequently and consume more.

Environmental specialists point out that emissions trading, which has been partly regulated since 2005 by the Kyoto Protocol, simply exacerbates global warming. They say that the system, which allows countries that have exceeded their limit of greenhouse gas emissions to buy the right to emit from countries that have not crossed the limit, only results in indulging the countries that consume more and emit more, and that the effect of gas reduction is meager. James Hansen, a climatologist at NASA in the U.S., lamented to the Times of London, "They are selling indulgences there. The developed nations want to continue basically business as usual so they are expected to purchase indulgences to give some small amount of money to developing countries. They do that in the form of offsets and adaptation funds."

1. What is a true statement about the carbon credit system according to the passage?

    (a) It is an effective system for stopping greenhouse gases.

    (b) There are no other possible solutions.

    (c) It allows developed countries to maintain their current way of life.

    (d) In time all countries will produce less carbon emissions using this system.

2. What can be inferred from the passage?

    (a) The current carbon system needs to be replaced.

    (b) People don't really believe in the system.

    (c) No one ever gets the money that people pay into the system.

    (d) There are no winners in the carbon offset system.

3. Why do climatologists compare the carbon credit system to indulgences of the middle ages?

    (a) They can find no other way to explain it.

    (b) Because it has the same premise.

    (c) There are some who do, others disagree.

    (d) None of the above.

4. What is the best title for the passage?

    (a) Carbon offset system

    (b) The increase of transportation

    (c) The carbon savings program

    (d) The indulgence of carbon

Words & Phrases

indulgence *n.* 면죄부; 하고 싶은 대로 함[하게 함]   ostensibly *ad.* 외면상, 표면상   carbon-offset system 탄소 상쇄 제도
environmentally friendly 환경 친화적인   compensate *v.* 보상하다   emit *v.* 방출하다   hydroelectric *a.* 수력 전기의
carbon credit (= cap and trade) 탄소배출권   regulate *v.* 규제하다; 조절하다   exacerbate *v.* 악화하다   lament *v.* 한탄하다

문장분석

■ Thanks to the demand spurred by people's desire to rid themselves of a guilty conscience, the amount earned from the carbon-offset system worldwide has reached a couple million dollars.	→ 〈rid/clear/deprive/rob A of B〉 표현은 모두 기본적으로 'A에(게서) B를 제거하다/빼앗다' 는 뜻이다. A는 대상이 오고, B에 제거할 내용이 온다는 점에 유의한다.

Unit 94 Undersea calamity omen of greater ills
|온난화 부메랑|

• 환경 •

Coral reefs, inhabited by such a rich diversity of creatures that they might be called underwater rainforests, started to become more like deserts. Chlorosis caused seaweed to disappear, destroying the habitat of small organisms and depriving the sea of its beautiful color. Chlorosis has already caused 30 percent of the world's coral reefs to die, and is still spreading in the Great Barrier Reef near Australia.

Experts have been unable to agree on just why chlorosis, a condition in which leaves produce insufficient chlorophyll, is taking place in coral reefs. Some say dirt or pollution from land is the cause, while others blame a fungus in soil that blows in from the Sahara Desert in Africa.

But most experts say the biggest reason is probably the higher sea temperature due to global climate change. Carbon dioxide emitted by human activity may dissolve in the seawater and play a part in raising its acidity, too. In 2007, the United Nations Intergovernmental Panel on Climate Change predicted that more than 80 percent of the world's coral reefs would turn white if the average temperature of the planet rose just one degree Celsius (1.8 degree Fahrenheit). Scientists have also predicted that less than 10 percent of coral reefs will be left by 2050 if seawater continues to acidify.

Recently, scientists at the Hollings Marine Laboratory in South Carolina, the United States, revealed the mysterious cause of chlorosis. They blame a traitorous single-celled organism called Vibrio coralliilyticus. This microscopic flagellum causes no harm at low temperatures, but excretes a toxic chemical substance when the water temperature rises above 24 degrees, which puts stress on the coral. Global warming is not only harming the ecosystem, but is coming back like a boomerang to damage even the lives of human beings.

1. What would be the best title for the passage?

   (a) Life and death for coral reefs

   (b) Global warming

   (c) Where the best reefs are

   (d) Desert sand in the reefs

2. Which of the following is correct according to the passage?

   (a) No cause for the death of reefs can be identified.

   (b) Vibrio coralliilyticus emits toxins in warmer water.

   (c) All coral reefs are dead now because of the toxin.

   (d) Global warming is only damaging the ecosystem.

3. What can be inferred from the passage?

   (a) Something must be done quickly if coral reefs are to be saved.

   (b) People do not care about the fate of coral reefs.

   (c) There will be several solutions to the problem in the near future.

   (d) Coral reefs have no hope of survival.

4. What is another way of describing coral reefs according to the passage?

   (a) Seaweed covered rocks.

   (b) Homes for bacteria

   (c) Dead lumps of white

   (d) Underwater rainforests

Words & Phrases

coral reef n. 산호초   inhabit v. 거주하다   diversity n. 다양성   rainforest n. 열대우림   chlorosis n. 백화 현상
seaweed n. 해초   habitat n. 서식처   deprive A of B A에게서 B를 빼앗다
the Great Barrier Reef 그레이트 배리어 리프, 대보초(오스트레일리아 북동부에 위치한 세계 최대의 산호초 지대)   chlorophyll n. 엽록소
fungus n. 버섯, 균류   soil n. 토양   dissolve v. 녹다, 용해되다   acidity n. 산성   traitorous a. 배반하는, 반역적인
flagellum n. 편모   excrete v. 배설하다

문장분석

■ Carbon dioxide emitted by human activity may dissolve in the seawater and play a part in raising its acidity, too. → 〈play a (형용사) role/part in -ing〉 구문은 '~하는 데 있어서 … 역할을 하다'는 뜻을 지닌다. 앞에서도 한번 등장했던 구문이다. 특히 '중요한' 역할을 했다는 뜻을 덧붙이려면 role/part 앞에 key/vital/major/critical/leading 등의 다양한 형용사를 넣어 의미를 확장할 수 있다.

Unit 95 | Sky-high dreams |마천루|

Chapter 11 of the Book of Genesis relates the building and destruction of mankind's first high-rise — the Tower of Babel. The people of Babel, the Hebrew name for the ancient city of Babylon where people spoke a single language, started to build a tower out of bricks so high it would reach the heavens. God, disapproving of the motive behind the building, which was to depict the glory of man and not for God's worship, created confusion by giving each person a different dialect that quickly brought construction to a halt.

The Bible does not tell exactly how tall the tower was but scholars estimate the height to be as much as 6,000 meters (19,685 feet). Skyscrapers in the modern sense appeared with the 10-story Home Insurance Building in Chicago in the 1880s. The tallest building was displaced by New York's iconic 449-meter Empire State Building in 1931.

Today's modern high-rises fear the force of gravity more than God's fury. In order to withstand the enormous G-forces, they need a reinforced concrete and steel skeleton. Without the advent of super-strong steel, today's skylines would not have been the same. Bricks and stones theoretically could go as high as 1,600 meters, but in reality they cannot sustain more than 12 stories.

Environmental factors like high winds and earthquakes also pose serious challenges to tall buildings. Wind is four times more powerful on the 100th floor than on the 50th. A building may withstand a few slight shakes, but it is a different story if the building is inhabited. A skyscraper should house speedy elevators and massive tanks and storage to maintain water pressure for use by the thousands of people working in or occupying the building.

1. What statement in the passage can be found to be false?

    (a) Environmental factors influence how high a building can be.
    (b) There are many factors to consider when building tall buildings.
    (c) That the tower of Babel was as tall as scholars think it was.
    (d) The Empire State building is taller than the Home Insurance building.

2. What can be inferred from the passage?

    (a) New Yorkers are very proud of having such a tall building.
    (b) In Babel God's fury was most likely the effect of environmental factors.
    (c) God's fury will be unleashed on New York if they build higher.
    (d) No one really believes it was God's fury that ruined the tower of Babel.

3. What is the main topic of the passage?

    (a) The book of Genesis
    (b) The fury of God
    (c) The competition to have the highest building
    (d) People trying to build higher and higher

4. What is not the meaning of the underlined word?

    (a) Parlance
    (b) Vernacular
    (c) Parlay
    (d) Language

Words & Phrases

Genesis n. [성경] 창세기   relate v. 이야기하다, 들려주다   destruction n. 파괴   high-rise n. 고층건물   brick n. 벽돌   disapprove v. 탐탁찮애[못마땅해] 하다   depict v. 묘사하다   confusion n. 혼란   dialect n. 방언   bring ~ to a halt ~을 멈추게 하다   estimate v. 추산하다   skyscraper n. 마천루, 고층건물   iconic a. 상징적인   gravity n. 중력   fury n. 분노   withstand v. 견디다   reinforced a. 보강된   skeleton n. 뼈대, 골격   advent n. 도래   theoretically ad. 이론상으로   sustain v. 지탱하다   factor n. 요인   pose challenges to ~에 도전을 가하다   inhabit v. 거주하다   parlance n. (특정 집단 등의) 말투/어법/용어)   vernacular n. (특정 지역·집단이 쓰는) 말, 토착어, 방언   parlay n. 원금과 그 상금을 다시 다른 말에 걸기

문장분석

■ Without the advent of super-strong steel, today's skylines would not have been the same. ➡ without 뒤에 가정법 구문이 오는 경우가 있는데, 이때 without은 if it were not for나 if it had not been for로 대체할 수 있다. 위의 예문에서는 주절에 가정법 과거완료 표현이 왔으므로 without이 'if it had not been for'의 의미 (과거에 ~가 없었더라면)로 사용됐다고 생각할 수 있다.

Unit 96 Turn off the lights |빛 공해|

• 조명 •

In July 1938, physiologist Nathaniel Kleitman of The University of Chicago emerged from a cave with an overgrown beard, after having spent 32 calendar days underground. During this time he tried living on a 28-hour cycle but failed to adapt himself to the new biorhythm, indicating that the human body contains a powerful clock clinging to the 24-hour cycle.

Plants and animals, as well as humans, are strongly influenced by sunlight. Paddy rice, perilla and cosmos require daily exposure to sunlight to bloom and bear fruit during autumn. Last March, teams from the Roslin Institute in Britain and Japan's Nagoya University found that birds begin to sing more often to attract potential ___(A)___ partners in the spring, when they receive more light. Some birds, such as quails, burst into song in the spring, because cells on the surface of the brain trigger hormones when the days get longer, expanding male testes as a result.

The average temperature of the Earth's surface is around 15 degrees, and plants go through the process of photosynthesis, thanks to light ___(B)___ from the sun. However, night is also important to living organisms. In the dark, male fireflies expose themselves to females. Small and weak animals hunt at night to hide from their predators.

Human-made light sources also impact the order of the night. As seen from a satellite, the strong light from the Earth's night dazzles our eyes. Living organisms are used to day and night, and seasonal ___(C)___ throughout the long history of the Earth, but if they receive more light at a strange season or time, they will naturally fall into confusion.

Artificial light is a murky subject for humans as well. Perhaps two-thirds of the world's population can no longer see the Milky Way at night. Australia is losing sight of the Southern Cross. The stars depicted on its flag are no longer visible to the naked eye. Last February, a new study by Israeli researchers revealed that females exposed to artificial lighting such as lamps or television screens at night have a 37 percent higher risk of breast cancer than females living in the dark with no lamps.

1. What can be inferred from the passage?

    (a) Exposure to light effects most life on Earth.

    (b) People can change their internal clock.

    (c) Light is the only factor to consider when studying behavior.

    (d) The Earth is moving further away from the Milky Way and other stars.

2. Which of the following is incorrect according to the passage?

    (a) Many plants require sunlight for blooming.

    (b) Animals react to exposure to light levels.

    (c) Artificial light can affect human life.

    (d) Exposure to light has no effect on health.

3. What does the underlined phrase mean?

    (a) Shoot drugs in the body

    (b) Produce chemicals in the body

    (c) Start using drugs to feel better

    (d) The brain creates new signals

4. Which words best complete the passage?

    (a) (A) mating   (B) energy   (C) change
    (b) (A) energy   (B) night   (C) visible
    (c) (A) visible   (B) change   (C) mating
    (d) (A) mating   (B) energy   (C) important

Words & Phrases

emerge v. 나타나다   overgrown a. 다 자란   beard n. 수염   adapt oneself to ~에 스스로 적응하다
cling to ~을 고수하다, ~에 매달리다   paddy rice n. 벼   perilla n. 들깨   exposure n. 노출   bloom v. 꽃이 피다
quail n. 메추라기   trigger v. 작동시키다, 촉발시키다   photosynthesis n. 광합성   firefly n. 개똥벌레, 반딧불
predator n. 포식자   dazzle v. 눈이 부시게 하다   confusion n. 혼란   artificial a. 인공적인   murky a. 흐린, 탁한
lose sight of ~이 더 이상 안 보이게 되다   depict v. 묘사하다   naked eye 육안

문장분석

- Living organisms are used to day and night. → 〈be 이다. 이때 to가 전치사이기 때문에 뒤에는 명사나 동명사가 와야 한다.
used/accustomed to -ing〉라는 표현은 '~(하는 것)에 익숙하다'는 뜻

Unit 97 Political deja vu
|기시감|

• 신경 •

You sometimes have a feeling that you've seen before the events that you are seeing now: in your dreams or your previous incarnation, perhaps. There are memories that give you uncanny feelings, as though you've experienced them before. This is the feeling of "already seen," or déjà vu in French.

Such uncanny feelings due to déjà vu date back to ideas of reincarnation and karma. For instance, the story develops when a newly born Western baby surprises his parents by making a Buddhist bow never taught him, and then he bows likewise naturally to a Tibetan monk he runs into on the street. Nevertheless, one cannot conclusively say that Oriental thought on reincarnation and karma is the origin of déjà vu. The Western bedrock of déjà vu was laid when the German philosopher Friedrich Nietzsche said, explaining his thought of eternal recurrence, that the world has repeated itself eternally and all we experience is the eternal recurrence of its plays.

The situation of déjà vu was first identified by French medical researcher Florence Arno, and the term déjà vu was established as a medical appellation by a French psychic researcher, Emile Boirac. Recently neurologists at the Massachusetts Institute of Technology set about removing the mystery of déjà vu. Conjectures have long existed that déjà vu must be a function of brain, but this time they pinpointed the specific part of brain that might have produced the déjà vu effect and concluded that déjà vu must be the result of an abnormality in the body.

1. What can be inferred about the passage?

   (a) There will continue to be a serious debate over déjà vu.

   (b) There is no conclusive explanation why déjà vu occurs.

   (c) The French disagree greatly with the conclusions made by MIT neurologists.

   (d) Tibetan monks believe in reincarnation more than the French.

2. What is the meaning of déjà vu according to the passage?

   (a) Seeing something that you think you've seen before

   (b) Being reincarnated

   (c) The act of seeing the future moments before it happens

   (d) Reliving your past life through the eyes of another

3. Which of the following is correct according to the passage?

   (a) French people were the first to notice the phenomena known as déjà vu.

   (b) The neurologists at MIT proved that déjà vu doesn't really exist.

   (c) Children often experience a sense of déjà vu.

   (d) Oriental thought might be the basis of déjà vu.

4. Which of the following is the best title for the passage?

   (a) Déjà vu fraud

   (b) French philosophy

   (c) This life connected to the last

   (d) Where we come from

Words & Phrases

previous *a.* 이전의   incarnation *n.* 생애; 화신   uncanny *a.* 이상한, 묘한   déjà vu *n.* 기시감 (일종의 착각)
date back to 시기가 ~로 거슬러 올라가다   karma *n.* 카르마, 업보   bow *v.* 절하다   monk *n.* 수도자, 수도승
conclusively *ad.* 결정적으로   bedrock *n.* 기반   eternal *a.* 영원한   recurrence *n.* 되풀이, 반복   term *n.* 용어
appellation *n.* 명칭, 호칭   conjecture *n.* 추측   pinpoint *v.* 정확히 집어내다   abnormality *n.* 기형, 이상

문장분석

■ There are memories that give you uncanny feelings, <u>as though</u> you've experienced them before. ➜ as though, as if는 '마치 ~인 것처럼'이란 뜻의 접속사로 실제로는 그렇지 않은데 마치 그러한 것처럼 보인다고 할 때 사용한다.

Unit 98 Planet's apes in peril
|고릴라|

There are two species of gorilla: The western gorilla and the eastern gorilla. The dark-colored eastern gorilla is found in the Democratic Republic of Congo in central Africa. About 380 mountain gorillas live in the Virunga National Park, one of Africa's oldest national parks. It represents almost half of the total population of the mountain gorillas in the world, which is estimated to be around 700. The rest live on the borders of Rwanda and Uganda.

Gorillas in the Virunga National Park suffer from continued instability in the surrounding human societies, and have faced a grave internal war over the past decade. A genocide of more than half a million people was carried out by Hutu extremists against Tutsi and moderate Hutus in Rwanda in 1994. While the civil war raged between the Hutu tribe and the government army, gorillas also died in great numbers. The rebels kill the mountain gorillas whenever they feel hungry, and threaten to annihilate the whole population of gorillas if the government carries out a military offensive to root out insurgents.

Another major culprit in this sordid affair is coltan, a dull black mineral that is refined into a powder called tantalum, and then used to make cell phones, laptops and jet engines. With unprecedented demand, it is worth hundreds of thousands of Korean won per kilogram. The rebels sell coltan on the black market to finance their wars.

Western lowland gorillas, one of the two subspecies of western gorillas, live in Cameroon, Gabon and the Congo in midwestern Africa. They are also severely threatened by hunting, internal wars, the Ebola virus and destruction of habitats caused by the building of palm oil plantations. Experts estimate that there are fewer than 100,000 western lowland gorillas. A survey, conducted across the Congo's sweeping forests and swampy wilderness, has shown that the population of western lowland gorillas there is around 125,000.

1. What can be inferred from the passage?

    (a) Gorillas may become extinct in the future if things stay the same.

    (b) The rebels will win against the government forces.

    (c) The gorillas will eventually leave the area to find safer places to live.

    (d) Countries will stop buying coltan to force the rebels to surrender.

2. What are the reasons for people killing the gorillas?

    (a) For food, and for protection

    (b) For profit, and sport

    (c) For hunting and war

    (d) For food, and as a threat

3. Which of the following is not true according to the passage?

    (a) Rebels kill gorillas for food whenever they want to eat.

    (b) The gorilla fights are becoming worse with time.

    (c) There are lower and lower numbers of gorillas.

    (d) There are many factors shrinking the gorilla population.

4. What is the main purpose of the passage?

    (a) To inform people of the serious nature of the plight of the gorilla

    (b) To explain where the rebels gain their money

    (c) To tell the world where to find gorillas

    (d) To offer an explanation of why rebels are killing gorillas

Words & Phrases

represent v. 해당하다, 상당하다; 대변하다   estimate v. 추정하다   grave a. 중대한, 예사롭지 않은   decade n. 10년
genocide n. 대량 학살   extremist n. 극단주의자   moderate a. 온건한, 중도의   civil war 내전
rage v. 맹위를 떨치다, 급속히 번지다   tribe n. 부족   rebel n. 반군   annihilate v. 전멸시키다   carry out 수행하다
root out 뿌리 뽑다   insurgent n. 반군   culprit n. 주범, 범인   sordid a. 추악한, 몹시 지저분한
unprecedented a. 유례가 없는   finance v. 자금을 지원하다   habitat n. 서식처   sweeping a. 휩쓰는   swampy a. 늪의
wilderness n. 황야, 황무지

문장분석

■ Gorillas in the Virunga National Park suffer from continued instability in the surrounding human societies, and have <u>faced</u> a grave internal war over the past decade. → ⟨face something⟩에서 face가 동사로 사용되면 '마주하다, 직면하다'의 뜻을 지닌다. 비슷한 의미로 be faced with something의 형태로도 사용되지만, face with something 형태로는 사용되지 않는다는 점에 주의한다.

Unit 99 Kimchi in space
|우주식품|

• 우주 •

John Glenn, the first American to orbit the Earth, carried semi-fluid applesauce aboard Friendship 7 in 1962. In space, people eat three balanced meals a day. A daily diet totaling between 2,000 and 2,200 calories is given to male and female astronauts, respectively. The taste falls below most standards. The first requirement in the manufacturing of space food is that it be light in weight. Dragging 1 kilogram of food to outer space costs 50 million won ($51,250). Freeze-drying and pulverization of the space food are mandatory to reduce the production costs. Additionally, it is of great importance to give sanitation due consideration in the production of space foods. Since Columbus (the International Space Station module) is not equipped with a refrigerator, it is too difficult to store up large stocks of food for a long period. The Hazard Analysis and Critical Control Point is an internationally recognized system to ensure food safety and protect consumers. Its origin is deeply rooted in the beginnings of space exploration, to manage the preparation of food for manned space flights. The lack of a refrigerator on the ISS module is mainly due to a lack of electricity.

The United States and Russia share the responsibility of providing astronauts with space food. Records show that the United States and Russia listed 200 and 130 food and beverage items, respectively, as of January 2008. Even though there are no differences in their menus, they differ in packaging materials and container openings. The Americans use light disposable packaging materials, such as aluminum foil, while the Russians use transparent packaging. The dispensers for American products remind us of gas valves on LPG vehicles, while Russian products resemble the valves of gasoline-powered vehicles. The American space foods are better equipped with airtight containers than the Russians'. As shown in these cases, the preparation of space foods has greatly contributed to improving the container and packaging technologies of foods on Earth.

1. What is the best title for the passage?

    (a) Dining in space

    (b) Food restrictions

    (c) Space food

    (d) Eating in space

2. What can be inferred from the passage?

    (a) U.S. space food will probably be used more than Russian space food.

    (b) Russian research is slower than the U.S.

    (c) No other countries have the technology to produce space food.

    (d) Refrigerators will soon be on the space station.

3. What is not a difference between the U.S. and Russian foods according to the passage?

    (a) Packaging

    (b) Valves

    (c) Number of items available

    (d) Preparation standards

4. How has space exploration helped improve things on Earth according to the passage?

    (a) New foods are being developed.

    (b) Container and packaging technology

    (c) Gas technology for cars

    (d) Food safety standards

Words & Phrases

semi-fluid *a.* 반 액체의   astronaut *n.* 우주비행사   respectively *ad.* 각각   outer space 우주
pulverization *n.* 가루로 만듦, 분쇄   mandatory *a.* 의무적인   sanitation *n.* 위생   due consideration 충분한 고려
ensure *v.* 보장하다, 확실히 하다   exploration *n.* 탐험   disposable *a.* 사용 후 버리게 되어 있는, 일회용의
transparent *a.* 투명한   dispenser *n.* 용기

문장분석

■ The first <u>requirement</u> in the manufacturing of space food is that it <u>be</u> light in weight. → 〈insist/demand/require/recommend that 주어 + (should) 동사원형〉 구문을 설명한 바 있다. 동사뿐만 아니라 requirement와 같은 명사의 경우에도 뒤의 that 절에 should가 들어오거나 생략된다는 것을 예문을 통해 알 수 있다.

Unit 100 A cry for the wolf | 늑대의 죽음 |

There are many stories about wolves in the book "Wild Animals I Have Known," a classic collection of animal stories by Ernest Thompson Seton. One tells the tale of a wolf with black fur on its neck named "Badlands Billy" who weighed more than 63 kilograms (139 pounds) and had a 14-centimeter (5.5-inch) footprint. Billy evaded his enemies and often preyed on domestic animals. One day, he happened to be chased by a pack of persistent hunting dogs. Billy tricked the 15 hounds into following him down a narrow path leading to a cliff and then shoved them over, one after the other.

Last February, researchers at Stanford University in the United States presented their findings in Science magazine that the black fur of some North American wolves, like Billy, is the result of interbreeding with domestic dogs in the distant past, perhaps 15,000 years ago. This tells us something about the genetic and biological relationship between dogs and wolves.

Wolves rarely attack humans. Half-bred or tamed wolves sometimes attack children, but wild wolves are afraid of humans. A skilled hunter featured in Seton's book also said he has never seen a fatal attack on a human by a wolf. Even today, though rarely discussed, some wolves freely roam around cities in the U.S. and Russia. Wolves and humans coexist in peace.

However, people justify killing wolves, insisting that they cause substantial damage to domestic animals. Canadian conservationist and author Farley Mowat has criticized human cruelty toward animals and needless animal suffering in his book "Never Cry Wolf," insisting that a considerable decrease in the number of reindeer in the North Pole is not caused by wolves, but mainly due to reckless hunting by furriers for thousands of species per year. Wolves, which appeared 800,000 years ago, spread out across Europe, Asia and North America. However, only about 100,000 remain worldwide due to habitat destruction and excessive killing.

J KOREA JOONGANG DAILY

NEW READING Spectrum 자연과학편

| 원문해석 · 문제해설 · 정답 |

Jonghap Books

KOREA JOONGANG DAILY

NEW
READING
Spectrum

| 자연과학편 |

READING Spectrum

자연과학편

Jonghap Books

Unit 1 | A dark omen settles over Korea
일조량 천재지변

하루 햇빛이 오뉴월에는 큰 차이를 가져온다. 이때는 모내기가 끝나고 벼가 쑥쑥 자라는 시기다. 이 무렵엔 식물에게는 땅에서 얻는 영양분 못지않게 햇빛의 양 또한 중요하다. 그렇지만 햇빛이 부족하면 벼의 잎사귀가 길고 얇아져 단위면적당 엽록소와 세포 수가 감소한다. 따라서 광합성 능력도 떨어진다. 결과는 쭉정이들만 거둔 별 수 없는 수확이다. 식물의 생장에서 일조량(日照量)은 하루의 차이가 이처럼 크다.

일조량 변화는 공룡 멸종의 직접 원인으로 지목된다. 지질학자와 고생물학자 41명으로 구성된 국제 전문가단의 연구 결과에 따르면, 6,500만 년 전 직경 10km짜리 소행성이 멕시코의 유카탄 반도에 충돌하면서 공룡시대가 끝났다고 한다. 당시 엄청난 지진과 쓰나미로 반경 1,500km 내 모든 생물이 사멸했지만, 무엇보다 충돌로 생긴 먼지와 유황 성분이 햇빛을 가려 지구가 기나긴 겨울에 들어갔다는 것이다. 결국 극심한 일조량 부족이 지구상 동식물의 3분의 2를 사라지게 한 것이다. 지난 3월 과학 저널 '사이언스'에 이 연구가 실린 바 있다.

필리핀의 활화산인 피나투보 화산이 1991년 분출했을 때도 2,000만 톤의 이산화황이 지상 40km 성층권까지 솟아올랐다. 이 연무질(煙霧質) 미세입자가 지구를 감싸 태양광을 차단하여 이후 1년간 평균 기온이 이전 10년에 비해 섭씨 0.58도 낮아졌다. 이 역시 일조량 감소가 빚은 결과다.

문제해설

1. 본문은 일조량에 관한 글이다. 일조량을 설명하기 위해 식물의 광합성, 소행성 충돌과 공룡의 멸종, 필리핀 화산 등을 차례로 언급했다. 따라서 정답은 (b)가 된다.

2. 유카탄 반도에 충돌한 소행성은 공룡이 죽은 직접적인 원인은 아니라는 사실을 두 번째 문단에서 추론할 수 있다. 지진과 쓰나미가 뒤이어 일어났고, 소행성 충돌로 인한 먼지와 유황 성분이 햇빛을 가려 일조량이 줄어들어서 지구 상의 동식물이 감소했다고 했기 때문에 (b)보다는 (a)가 더 적합하다.

3. 피나투보 화산의 영향으로 사람들과 식물들이 죽었다는 내용은 등장하지 않기 때문에 (a)와 (b)는 정답이 될 수 없다. (c)의 경우 피나투보 화산이 빈번히 폭발했다는 내용이 아닌 1991년 폭발로 인한 온도 하락만을 언급하고 있으므로 정답으로 부적절하다. 정답은 (d)로 일조량 감소에 따른 온도 하락을 언급하고 있다.

4. 첫 번째 문단을 통해 일조량이 충분하지 않을 경우 광합성과 물질 생산 능력이 떨어진다고 했으므로 정답은 (d)가 적합하다.

정답 1(b) 2(a) 3(d) 4(d)

Unit 2 | Turning yellow dust into gold
'녹색 계열'

'모래바람이 해를 가렸다(沙塵朝蔽日)'라는 얘기가 당(唐)대의 한 시인의 시구에 나온다. 중국으로부터 불어와 매년 아시아 전역을 뒤덮는 황사에 대한 이야기는 그 역사가 장구하다. 요즘에는, 황사 영향권이라는 것도 모호해졌다. 황사로부터 안전하다고 생각했던 홍콩마저도 최근에 황사로 뒤덮였다. 백악질 파편(주: 황사를 지칭)이 한반도를 넘어 대한해협을 건너 일본까지 날아간다. 베이징 국영 기상당국의 예보에 따르면, 올해 황사로 인한 피해는 역대 최악이 될 거라고 한다.

황사 발원지는 신장(新疆) 남부, 간쑤(甘肅) 지방, 네이멍구(內蒙古)(내몽골) 남부 등 중국의 3곳이다. 전체 27개 성(省)·자치구 가운데 21개 성이 모래 구름이 휩쓰는 피해권이다. 국토의 5분의 1이 사막 지대고, 인구의 5분의 1이 황사에 시달린다. 황사가 이처럼 악화한 데는 마오쩌둥(毛澤東) 탓이 크다. 그는 무기를 얻고자 무차별 벌목으로 쇠를 녹이고, 산을 밀어 계단밭을 만들고, 목초지를 걷어내고 곡식을 심었다.

황사는 중국에서 진행되고 있는 환경 파괴의 한 단면에 불과하다. 중국은 전역이 오염된 물과 쓰레기로 넘쳐난다. 중국 초원들의 사막화를 막고 황사의 진행을 둔화시키기 위해, 원자바오(溫家寶) 총리는 최근 당 기관지(誌)에 '녹색 계열'을 발표했다. 모든 산업에 적용되는 가이드라인으로, 임산자원, 수자원 보호를 '100년 국가 과제'로 선언했다. 중국 정부는 또 방풍림 조성계획을 발표했고, 재생에너지 개발, 기후변화 대비를 위한 특별 대책반도 꾸렸다.

문제해설

1. 본문은 중국의 황사(yellow dust)에 대한 내용이며, (c)에 언급된 사막화(desertification)는 황사의 원인으로 언급되고 있으므로 지엽적인 내용이다. 따라서 정답은 (b)가 된다.

2. (a)의 경우 마지막 문단에서 원자바오 총리가 녹색 계열(Green Policy Guidelines)을 발표했다는 내용과 동일하므로 정답이 된다. (b)는 본문과 무관하고, (c)는 (a)와 배치되는 주장이 되므로 적합하지 않다. (d)의 경우 첫 번째 문단에서 당나라 시대에도 황사가 나오며, 연원이 장구하다고 했으므로 이 또한 본문의 내용과 맞지 않다.

3. 황사는 위생(hygiene)의 결과가 아닌 벌목 등으로 인한 자연훼손이다. 중국은 황사의 발원국인 동시에 최대 피해국으로 5분의 1이 피해 지역이라고 했으므로 (b)의 내용은 사실이 아니며, (c)는 본문과 무관하다. 정답은 (d)로 첫 번째 문단에서 황사가 이전에 비해 경계마저 사라지며 피해 지역이 늘어나는 등 악화되었다는 내용을 통해 짐작할 수 있다.

4. 두 번째 문단에서 황사를 악화시킨 인물을 마오쩌둥으로 돌리고 있으므로(The person credited for exacerbating the dust problem should be Mao Zedong) 정답은 (c)가 된다.

정답 1(b)　2(a)　3(d)　4(c)

Unit 3 | Racing toward a dissonant drive
전기자동차와 소음

　모터사이클 '할리 데이비슨'의 특징은 무엇보다 우렁찬 배기음이다. 엔진의 연소 주기를 사람의 심장 박동수와 연계시켰다고 한다. 시동을 거는 순간 사랑에 빠진 젊은이의 심장이 고동치는 것처럼 둥둥거린다. 할리는 특유의 배기음에 대해 1944년 특허를 출원하기도 했지만, 복잡한 서류 절차에 결국 포기했다. 한국에 수입되는 할리는 현지 법규에 따라 배기음이 80데시벨(db) 이하로 조정돼 있다. 그래서, 따로 조작하지 않는 한 원래의 우렁찬 배기음을 감상하기 어렵다. 스포츠카의 대명사 페라리도 마무리에서 가장 신경 쓰는 것이 엔진 배기음이라고 한다. 낮은 금속성 박동 소리는 이탈리아 명차에 대한 스포츠카 마니아들의 탄성을 자아낸다. 자동차 경주 팬들에 따르면 F1의 묘미도 레이싱카가 내뱉는 찢어지는 듯한 굉음이라고 한다.

　물론 엔진 소음은 로맨틱한 매력 말고도 실용적인 목적이 있다. 고급 세단은 너무 조용해서 시동이 꺼진 줄 알고 다시 키를 돌리는 경우가 있다. 그래서 재규어는 시동이 켜질 때 '테너 C' 높이로 조절된 엔진음을 차내로 흘려보낸다고 한다. 이에 반해 전기자동차는 연소기관이 아닌 전기 모터로 움직이니 소음이 없다. 시속 40km 이하로 달리면 바퀴와 노면 사이에 마찰음도 없다. 이렇게 소음이 너무 없으니 탑승자와 보행자의 안전에 적신호가 켜진 것이다. 다른 차들이나 도로를 건너는 사람들이 차가 다가오는 소리를 듣지 못하기 때문에, 사고의 가능성도 크게 증가한다. 한때는 고급차 제조사들의 자부심이었던 이 무소음이 안전상의 문제로 대두된 것이다. 현재 미국 의회는 전기자동차에 안전 차원의 최소 소음을 강제하는 방안을 검토 중이다.

문제해설

1. 본문은 소음으로 치부될 수 있는 소리의 중요성에 관한 글이다. 할리 데이비슨의 심장이 고동치는 소리에서부터 페라리의 엔진 배기음, 재규어의 테너 C로 맞춰진 엔진음, 소리가 나지 않아 문제인 전기자동차에 최소 소음을 강제하려고 하는 움직임까지. 이 모두를 아우르는 것이 (a)이다.
2. (a)의 경우 재규어는 음악을 내보내는 것이 아니라 엔진음을 테너 C로 내보낸다고 했으며, (c)의 경우 전기자동차가 사고의 가능성이 큰 이유는 주행(driving)의 문제가 아니라 무소음이라고 했다. (d)의 경우 우렁찬 엔진 배기음을 강조한 것이므로 본문과 다르다. 정답은 (b)로 두 번째 문단의 'They do not even make noise from the friction ... at speeds less than 40 kilometers per hour' 부분을 다시 설명하고 있다.
3. 마지막 부분은 전기자동차에 최소 소음을 강제하는 방안을 검토하고 있다는 내용으로 끝나므로, 이와 이어지는 내용이 와야 한다. 따라서 정답은 새로운 법안에 관한 내용인 (d)가 정답이 된다.
4. 자동차 소음의 정도(level)가 중요하다는 내용은 할리 데이비슨, 페라리, 재규어 등에 해당하고 자동차 소음의 부족(lack)은 전기자동차에 해당하므로 정답은 (b)가 적합하다.

정답 1(a)　2(b)　3(d)　4(b)

Unit 4 | The weird thing about warming
글로벌 위어딩

　"지구에서 열이 난다." '환경 전도사'로 변신한 앨 고어 전 미국 부통령이 즐겨 쓰는 말이다. 그가 말하는 열은 '지구 온난화'(global warming)를 뜻한다. 그러나 지구 온난화에 대해 회의론이 만만치 않다. 특히 지난겨울 북반구에 이상 한파와 폭설이 몰아치자 회의론자들은 "온난화라기보다는 지구 한랭화"라는 냉소가 쏟아졌다. 짐 인호프 상원의원(오클라호마 주)은 기후 변화에 대한 경각심을 높인 공로로 고어가 받은 노벨평화상을 반납하라고 목소리를 높였다. 워싱턴 국회의사당 근처 내셔널 몰에 이글루를 만든 뒤 '고어의 새 집'이란 표지를 붙여 조롱하기까지 했다.

　그럼에도 한파와 폭설 역시 온난화와 무관치 않다는 게 많은 전문가의 지적이다. 북극이 따뜻해지자 한기(寒氣)를 감싸고돌던 제트기류가 약화해 (그 틈새로) 찬 공기가 남하하며 아시아와 유럽, 북미가 큰 추위를 겪었다는 것이다. 그러는 한편, 태평양 해수 온도가 높아져 생긴 수증기가 한파와 부딪쳐 큰 눈을 퍼붓게 된 것이다. 당시 남반구가 폭염과 폭우에 시달린 걸 고려하면 '온난화는 사기극'이란 주장은 섣부르다.

　(계절이 뒤바뀐) 요즘 지구촌의 남과 북은 정반대의 시련을 겪고 있다. 여름을 맞은 북반구는 살인적인 무더위로 사망자가 속출하는 중이다. 반면 겨울철인 남반구에선 혹독한 추위로 고통 받고 있다. 온난화를 '길고 더운 여름과 짧고 따뜻한 겨울'이라 여긴 건 오해였던 셈이다. 폭설과 폭우, 극심한 가뭄이 이쪽저쪽에서 동시에 일어난다. 홍수, 폭풍, 산불도 더 빈번하고 더 세졌다.

　지구 온난화란 한마디로 이런 총체적 기상이변을 일컫기엔 무리가 있는 게 사실이다. 그래서 사람들은 '글로벌 위어딩(global weirding)'이란 신조어를 사용하기 시작했다. 우리가 뭐라 부르건 간에 원인은 매한가지다. 급증하는 에너지 소비가 문제다. 2050년까지 전 세계 에너지 소비량이 최소 두 배로 늘 거라는데, 나는 그새 기후는 얼마나 비정상적이 되고 피해는 어떠할지 짐작조차 안 간다. 올여름 남아공과 브라질에서 펭귄들이 수백 마리씩 떼죽음한 걸 의미심장한 경고로 받아들여야 한다. 현 추세가 지속된다면 30년 내에 지구상 생물체의 5분의 1은 사라질 거란 전망이다. '비정상'의 원인을 모두 설명하고도 우리만 피해 없이 살아남을 것이라고 생각하는가? 그렇다면 정말 비정상일 것이다.

문제해설

1. 본문은 물론 지구 온난화인 global warming에 대한 글이다. 하지만 지구가 그저 따뜻해지는 것으로 끝나지 않는다는 것을 강조하고 있다. 한파와 폭설 역시 지구 온난화와 관련이 있으며, 북반구와 남반구가 각각 정반대의 시련을 겪고 있는 것도 강조되고 있다. 따라서 본문의 필자가 진정으로 주장하고 싶었던 것은 마지막 문장에 나온 global weirding이라고 해야 적합하다.

2. 세 번째 문단과 마지막 문단에 각각 지구 온난화로 인한 피해가 설명되어 있다. 이를 종합해보면 이미 기상 이변으로 인간과 동물들이 모두 피해를 보고 있으며, 미래에 받게 될 피해는 더욱 엄청날 것이란 것을 추론할 수 있으므로 정답은 (d)가 된다. 동물이 에너지를 소비하고 있는 것은 아니므로 (a)는 정답으로 적합하지 않다.

3. 인호프 상원의원은 미국 국회의사당 앞에 이글루를 만들었고, 앨 고어 전 부통령을 기념하기 위한 것이 아니라 조롱하기 위해서였으므로 정답은 (a)가 된다. 나머지 보기는 모두 본문에 등장한다.

4. 환경 전도사로 변신한 앨 고어 전 부통령에 대한 비판자들의 생각을 읽을 수 있는 곳은 첫 번째 문단이다. 대표적인 예가 인호프 상원의원이라고 나온다. 지구 온난화라고 하지만, 온난화 대신 한랭화를 겪고 있는 것을 어떻게 설명할 것이냐는 의문을 제기하고 있으므로 이에 대한 정답으로는 (c)가 적합하다.

정답 1(d) 2(d) 3(a) 4(c)

Unit 5 | Calming the fires on our planet
지구가 뿔났다

　지금 지구는 도처에서 곪은 상처를 터뜨리며 신음하고 있다. 무차별적 화석연료 사용과 온실가스 배출로 인간이 이런 비참한 상황을 몰고 왔다는 설(說) 외에는 달리 설명할 방도가 없다. 앨 고어 전 미국 부통령은 2006년 제작한 다큐멘터리 '불편한 진실'에서 화석연료 사용을 당장 줄이지 않으면 지구는 회생 불가능하다고 역설했다. 우리는 석유와 가스, 합성품과 플라스틱을 대체할 것이 필요하다. 좋은 생각이긴 하지만, 마틴 루터가 말했다고 전해지는 "내일 지구의 종말이 와도 오늘 한 그루의 사과나무를 심겠다"는 숭고한 다짐만으로 해결될 단계는 이미 넘어선 듯하다.

　과학자들은 지구 온난화의 영향을 완화시키기 위한 조작 방법으로 지구공학(geo-engineering)에 눈을 돌리고 있다. 그들은 1991년 필리핀 루존 섬의 피나투보 화산 폭발 때 단초를 찾은 것이다. 즉 엄청난 양의 화산재에서 희부연 황산 입자가 생성되는 바람에 결과적으로 그 지역의 일조량이 떨어졌다고 보고 이 때문에 지구가 냉각됐다는 사실을 알아냈다. 이를 실용화하기 위해 세계적인 '특허 산업체'로 불리는 미국의 인텔렉추얼 벤처스(IV)는 '하늘에 닿는 정원용 호스(Garden hose to the sky)'라는 프로젝트를 구상 중이라고 한다. 지상에서 성층권까지 이어지는 길이 29km의 호스를 통해 헬륨 가스 풍선으로 고정된 기지국에서 액화 이산화황을 뿌리자는 발상이다. 대략 3년이면 완공이 가능하고, 초기 설치비용 1억 5,000만 달러에 연간 운영비 1억 달러 정도면 된다고 IV는 추산한다. 환경론자들은 이러한 프로젝트가 실행되는 것을 반대하지만, 그래도 지구를 위해 노력하는 사람들이 있다는 사실은 위안이 된다.

문제해설

1. 본문은 온실가스 배출로 촉발된 지구 온난화 및 이로 인한 환경 파괴에 관한 글이다. 그리고 두 번째 문단에서는 이를 위해 한 회사에서 추진하고 있는 프로젝트에 관해 설명하고 있다. 하지만 이 프로젝트로 인해 모든 문제가 해결될 수 있다는 것은 지나친 억측이며, 반대론자들로 인해 무산될 수도 있다고 했으므로 (c)는 정답이 될 수 없다. 정답은 (b)로 지구 온난화를 되돌리기 위한 작업들이 진행 중(under way)이라는 내용은 본문 마지막의 'But it's nice to know that people are still trying' 내용과 잘 연결된다.

2. (a)에 대한 내용은 두 번째 문단 첫줄에 나온다. 지구공학(geo-engineering)을 통해 기후를 조작해 지구 온난화의 영향을 줄이려는 것이 목적이므로 지구를 구하기 위한 한 방편으로 생각할 수 있다. 그리고 (b)는 피나투보 화산 폭발로 인한 지구 냉각에서 힌트를 얻어 IV사가 프로젝트를 진행하고 있는 부분을 설명하는 내용이다. (c)에 대해서는 첫 번째 문단에 나와 있다. 마지막 보기를 보면, 화산 분출을 인위적으로 한다는 것도 의문의 여지가 있으며, 이를 통해 지구 냉각이 될지는 더 의문이다. 본문과 무관하므로 정답은 (d)가 된다.

3. 이 문제는 이산화황과 지구 온난화의 관계를 묻고 있다. 피나투보 화산 폭발로 인해 이산화황이 분출되고, 이 입자 때문에 일조량이 떨어져 지구가 냉각되었다고 나오므로 정답은 (a)가 된다.

4. 이산화황은 하나의 예로 나온 것이므로 제목으로 적절하지 않다. 그리고 화석연료 사용을 언제쯤 중단할 수 있을지에 관한 글도 아니다. 지구공학을 통해 지구를 회복할 수 있는 방안에 대한 설명인 (d)가 제목으로 적합하다.

정답 1(b) 2(d) 3(a) 4(d)

Unit 6 | The unwinnable war on germs
슈퍼박테리아

　1942년 11월 19일 미국 보스턴의 한 나이트클럽에서 대형 화재가 발생했다. 큰 화상을 입은 수백 명의 운명은 처음에는 암울한 상태였다. 당시까지만 해도 세균에 대한 치료제가 개발되지 않아서, 화상 때문에 포도상구균이란 박테리아에 감염된 환자는 대부분 숨졌기 때문이다. 이때 정제되지도 않은 검증이 덜 된 '페니실린'이 사용돼 200여 명의 목숨을 구하는 기적을 만들어 냈다. 페니실린이 감염된 환자들에게 처음 사용된 역사적인 순간이었다.

인류의 역사는 세균과의 끊임없는 전쟁으로 점철돼 있다. 인간의 몸에만 600조 가지 이상의 세균과 미생물이 더불어 사니 그럴 만도 하다. 세균과의 전쟁에서 첫 대승을 거둔 것이 바로 페니실린이다. 페니실린이 등장한 건 고작 70년 전 일이다. 그전의 인류는 세균의 위협에 속수무책(束手無策)이었다. 14세기 유럽 인구의 4분의 1을 죽음으로 몰아넣은 전염병 또한 세균 감염의 결과이다.

그러나 '기적의 약'으로 불렸던 페니실린의 효과는 그리 오래가지 못했다. 페니실린의 분자 구조를 파괴해 무력화해 버리는 신종 세균이 나타나서다. 의학 전문가들에 의하면, 40년대에 이미 포도상구균의 50%가 페니실린에 내성(耐性)이 생겼다고 한다. 이는 곧 페니실린이 채 10년도 못 버티고 세균의 반격에 손을 들어 버린 것을 의미한다. 인류는 2세대, 3세대 항생제를 계속 개발해 대응하긴 하지만, 세균과의 전쟁은 끝내기는 어렵다. 그 이유는 세균도 계속해서 최신 약품에 내성을 지닌 세균으로 돌연변이가 하기 때문이다.

슈퍼박테리아는 에이즈(AIDS·후천성면역결핍증)보다 더 무서운 적이다. 미국의 2005년 에이즈 관련 사망자는 1만 2,500명이었지만 슈퍼박테리아의 일종인 '메티실린 내성 포도상구균' 감염 사망자는 1만 8,650명에 이른다. 슈퍼박테리아와 관련한 사망자 소식이 대대적으로 보도되고 있다. 며칠 전 일본에선 슈퍼박테리아인 '아시네토박터균(MRAB)' 감염으로 9명이 사망한 소식이 전해졌다. 한국에서도 2년 전 4명이 이 균 때문에 사망한 것으로 보고된다. 지난달엔 세계 보건 관계자들이 신종 박테리아 'NDM-1'의 확산에 대한 경고를 하기도 했다.

슈퍼박테리아의 출현은 부분적으로는 항생제 남용의 결과이기도 하다. 세균과의 전쟁에서 새로운 항생제를 내놓기 전에 항생제 남용 방지가 우선돼야 하는 이유다. 과유불급(過猶不及)이라고 했다. 인류가 페니실린 이전 시대로 돌아가지 않으려면 이 말부터 새길 일이다.

문제해설

1. 박테리아로 대표되는 세균과의 전쟁에서 인간은 항생제인 페니실린을 개발했다. 하지만 세균도 진화를 거듭해 항생제에 내성을 지닌 세균이 계속해서 등장했고, 현재는 치명적인 슈퍼박테리아까지 출현한 상태이다. 따라서 치료제가 없거나(c), 적시에 박테리아가 발견되지 않아서(d)라기보다는 마지막 문단에서 강조한 것과 같이 항생제의 남용으로 인한 박테리아의 내성으로 보는 것이 합리적이다. 따라서 정답은 (b)가 된다.

2. 약을 사용하는 것이 적절하지 못하다는 내용은 없으므로 (a)는 부적절하며, 항생제를 개발하는 것과 박테리아의 진화 사이에는 격차가 크지 않다고 해야 하므로 (b)는 반대의 내용이 되어야 한다. 그리고 (c)에 대한 내용은 지나친 추측이며 본문과는 무관하다. 정답은 (d)로 내성을 가진 새로운 박테리아의 출현으로 자칫 위험에 처할 수 있는 상황을 묘사하고 있다.

3. 슈퍼박테리아는 나와 있는 항생제에 모두 내성을 지닌 박테리아를 의미하므로 정답은 (c)가 적합하다.

4. 향후 이어질 내용은 슈퍼박테리아에 대한 내용, 특히 이를 예방하기 위한 내용이 적합하므로 정답은 (b)가 된다. (d)는 일반인들의 대처에 관한 내용이므로 어색하다.

정답 1(b) 2(d) 3(c) 4(b)

Unit 7 | The benefits of bug science
곤충 테크놀로지

보풀처럼 가벼우면서도 강철만큼 단단하고 나일론만큼 질긴 소재가 있다면? 정답은 거미줄이다. 굵기가 머리카락의 10분의 1 정도인 거미줄을 뭉치면 그 강도가 같은 굵기의 강철보다 다섯 배 강하다. 하지만 5,200년 전부터 실크를 만드는 데 사용된 누에와 달리 거미는 인류에게 도움을 주지 못했다. 거미 한 마리가 평생 뽑아내는 거미줄의 양도 한정되어 있거니와, 함께 있으면 서로 잡아먹는 습성이 있어 사육이 불가능하기 때문이다. 대신 인공 거미줄이 머잖아 상용화될 가능성이 점쳐진다. 몇 해 전 캐나다의 한 벤처기업은 거미줄에 관련된 유전자를 염소의 젖샘에 이식한 뒤 염소젖에서 거미줄 원료를 추출하는 데 성공했다.

100여 가지 병균을 옮기는 바퀴벌레는 가정에선 박멸의 대상이다. 하지만 로봇 공학자들에겐 배우고 따라야 할 본보기다. 그들이 바퀴벌레를 연구하는 것은 여섯 개의 다리로 안정적이면서도 빠르게 달리는 능력을 구현하기 위해서다. 미국 연구진이 바퀴벌레의 해부학적 구조를 응용해 만든 로봇은 무척 짧은 시간에 몸길이의 50배에 해당하는 거리를 이동할 수 있다. 이 소형 다족(多足) 로봇에 원격제어 침을 탑재하면 사람이 들어가기 힘든 공간에 투입할 수 있고, 군사용 정찰용으로 쓸 수도 있다.

곤충의 능력을 활용하거나 모방하는 것을 '곤충 테크놀로지'라고 부른다. 곤충은 인공적으로 합성할 수 없는 물질을 만들거나, 인간이 흉내 낼 수 없는 탁월한 감각과 기능을 갖고 있다. 지구상에 100만 종 이상 존재하는 곤충 이야말로 최고의 자원이라고 과학자들은 주장한다.

지난주 외신 보도에 따르면 미국의 국립 연구소가 후각이 발달한 꿀벌을 훈련시켜 폭발물 탐지에 활용하는 연구를 진행 중이라고 한다. 미군은 이미 실제 이라크 전에서 꿀벌을 이용해 지뢰나 폭탄을 찾아내기도 했다. 곤충 산업에 일찍 눈을 뜬 일본은 금색, 녹색 등 일곱 가지 화려한 빛을 내는 비단벌레의 발색(發色)구조를 자동차와 기타 금속 표면에 재현하는 기술을 개발했다. 이것이야말로 환경 친화적 착색 기술이다.

문제해설

1. insect technology는 본문 세 번째 문단에서 볼 수 있듯이, 곤충의 능력을 활용하거나 모방하는 것을 의미하므로 정답은 (d)가 된다.

2. 바퀴벌레는 몸집에 비해 매우 빠른 속도로 안정적으로 이동하며, 사람이 들어가기 힘든 공간에도 들어갈 수 있다고 서술하고 있다. 정답은 (b)로 두 번째 문단 서두에 'the stable and speedy movement of its six legs' 부분이 힌트가 된다. 즉 바퀴벌레를 연구하는 목적은 수명이 긴 것이 아닌 빠르고 안정적인 바퀴벌레의 속도 때문임을 알 수 있다.

3. 거미줄의 우수한 성질은 본문 첫 번째 문단에 등장하며, 머잖아 상용화될 가능성이 있다고 했으므로 (b)가 정답임을 알 수 있다. (c)의 경우 서로 잡아먹는 거미의 습성으로 사육이 불가능하다고 나오므로 사육하기 비싸다는 것은 적절하지 않다. (d)는 본문과 무관해서 부적절하다.

4. 바퀴벌레의 예는 두 번째 문단에 나오며, (c)와 (d)는 마지막 문단에 등장한다. 정답은 (b)로 염소젖에서 거미줄 원료를 추출한다고 했으므로 염소가 젖을 만들어내듯 거미줄을 만든다는 (b)는 부적합하다.

정답 1(d) 2(b) 3(b) 4(b)

Unit 8 | Patriotism perverts science
과학과 우상

원자탄의 원리는 히틀러 지배하의 독일에서 처음 발견됐다. 화학자 오토 한은 우라늄에 중성자를 느리게 충돌시키면 핵분열과 함께 엄청난 에너지가 발생한다는 사실을 보고했다. 그러나 그는 원자탄을 만들라는 나치의 지시는 거부했다. 평화적인 원자로 개발에만 힘을 쏟았다. 독일의 패전 이후 한은 연합군 포로수용소에 유폐돼 있었다. 포로수용소장은 원자탄이 투하됐다는 소식에 그가 자살하지 않을까 전전긍긍했다.

헝가리 출신의 레오 질라드는 고향 사랑이 유별난 과학자였다. 그는 히틀러가 조국 헝가리를 침공하자 자진해 맨해튼 프로젝트에 참가했다. 1945년 7월 16일, 미국 네바다주 사막을 지나던 트럭 운전수는 "갑자기 지평선 위로 천 개의 태양이 떠오르더니 사라졌다"고 신고했다. 원자탄의 위력을 실감한 질라드는 이때부터 원폭 투하에 반대했다. 그는 동료인 페르미에게 "오늘은 인류 역사에 가장 불행한 날로 기록될 것"이라고 말했다.

"과학은 인류의 친구인가 적인가?" 영국의 화학자 막스 페루츠가 던진 질문이다. 질소에서 암모니아를 합성한 프리츠 하버는 질소 비료를 만들어 인류를 기아의 공포에서 해방시킨 인물이다. 그러나 1차 대전 때 연합군을 공포의 도가니에 몰아넣은 독가스 개발자도 하버였다. 패전 후에는 전쟁 배상금에 시달리는 조국을 위해 바닷물에서 금을 추출해내는 엉뚱한 연구에 매달렸다. 그런 하버도 결국 나치에 의해 '유대인 과학자'로 몰려 비참한 최후를 맞았다.

일본 히로시마 사립 여자고등학교에는 세 소녀의 상이 서 있다. 원폭 위령비다. 소녀 중 한 명의 가슴에는 아인슈타인의 'E=mc²' 공식이 새겨져 있다. 인류가 과학에 어떻게 접근해야 할지 말없이 경고하고 있다. 이제 줄기세포 논쟁이 (과학의 영역을 넘어) 사회 문제가 됐다. 흥분부터 가라앉혀야 한다. 과학이 우상이 되면 언제든 흉기로 돌변할 수 있다.

문제해설

1. 본문의 목적은 마지막 문단을 통해 알 수 있다. 인류가 과학을 어떻게 접근할 것인가에 대한 물음을 던지고 있기 때문이다. 인류에게 혜택을 줄 수 있는 과학이 무서운 무기로도 돌변할 수 있다는 말로 마무리하고 있다. 따라서 정답은 과학 발전의 이면을 설명하고 있다는 (d)가 된다.

2. 핵분열이 가장 우수한 발명이라는 말은 등장하지 않으며, 일본의 핵공격에 대한 책임이 아인슈타인에게 있다는 내용 또한 사실과 다르다. 마지막 보기로 나온 원자폭탄 없이도 연합군이 빠르게 승리할 수 있었을 것이란 내용 또한 본문과 무관하다. 정답은 (b)로 과학과 기술의 발전이 항상 긍정적인 것만은 아니라는 것을 설명하고 있다.

3. 과학을 경계(wary)해야 하는 이유는 과학이 가져올 수 있는 부정적인 측면이기 때문에 정답은 (c)가 적합하다.

4. 본문의 제목으로 가장 적합한 것은 앞의 문제들과 같은 의미에서 (a)가 된다.

정답 1(d) 2(b) 3(c) 4(a)

Unit 9 | Hackers and crackers
해커와 크래커

흔히 1946년 미국에서 개발된 에니악(ENIAC)을 세계 최초의 컴퓨터로 알고 있지만 사실 그게 아니다. 디지털 사회를 가져온 선각자의 영예는 영국 수학자 알렝 튜링에게 돌아가야 옳다. 그는 2차 대전 중 독일의 무선통신 암호 '에니그마'를 해독하는 영국 첩보조직 '울트라 프로젝트' 팀의 일원이었다.

그는 암호화된 에니그마 메시지를 읽을 수 있는 콜로서스(Colossus)라는 전자 계산기를 개발했는데, 처음에는 에니그마를 기계적 방식으로 해독할 수 있었지만 이후에는 정교해져 기계 장치로는 해독에 너무도 오랜 시간이 소요됐다. 콜로서스는 어찌나 빠르고 정확했던지 연합군은 독일의 군 통신을 해독하고 있다는 걸 숨기느라 진땀을 뺐고, 나치의 폭격 계획을 알고도 지켜봐야 하는 경우마저 있었다.

종전 후 울트라팀은 해체됐고 (콜로서스를 비롯한) 모든 기계와 설계도가 파기됐다. 튜링은 그가 이룬 공적도 인정받지 못한 채 콜로서스보다 2년도 더 늦게 나온 에니악이 영광을 누리는 것을 지켜볼 수밖에 없었다.

튜링이 '세계 최초의 해커'로 인정받는 것을 알았다면 그에게 조그만 위로가 될 수 있겠다. 튜링의 발명 이후 컴퓨터는 전 세계의 창의적 두뇌들을 매료시켰다. 몇몇 프로그래머들은 순전히 재미로 소프트웨어를 만들고 즐겼다. 이들에게 해커란 이름이 붙은 것은 미국 매사추세츠 공대(MIT)가 2세대 컴퓨터 PDP-1을 구입한 1961년이다. MIT의 철도 시스템 연구 동아리인 테크모델 철도클럽 학생들은 밤마다 몰래 학교 컴퓨터를 가지고 놀았다. 그들은 놀이 삼아 오늘날 우리가 쓰고 있는 프로그래밍 툴과 환경, 관련 은어들을 만들어내고 즐겼다.

문제해설

1. 두 번째 문단에서 튜링이 발명한 암호 해독기인 콜로서스로 독일의 군사 계획을 알아내어 결과적으로 종전을 앞당겼다고 볼 수 있으므로 (a)도 부분적으로는 바른 설명이다. 하지만 (b)가 더 적합한 추론이기 때문에 정답은 (b)가 된다. 발명의 영예가 항상 그 발명가에게 돌아가는 것은 아니라는 것을 튜링의 예를 통해 보여주고 있기 때문이다.

2. jargon은 특정 영역의 전문가 집단이 자기들끼리 사용하는 전문용어를 지칭하므로 정답은 (a)가 된다.

3. (a)의 경우 독일군을 속이기 위해 콜로서스로 해독을 해서 폭격계획을 알고 있으면서도 이를 그냥 지켜봤다는 내용을 통해 독일군이 콜로서스에 대한 존재를 알지 못했음을 알 수 있다. (b)의 MIT 학생들이 많은 돈을 벌었다는 내용은 본문에 등장하지 않으므로 (b)가 정답이 된다. (c)는 첫 번째 문단의 암호 해독을 통해 알 수 있고, (d)는 마지막 문단의 내용을 통해 해커라는 이름이 어떻게 유래했는지 알 수 있다.

정답 1(b) 2(a) 3(b)

Unit 10 | Gender and the courts
성전환증

성전환증(Transsexualism)에 대해 의학계가 학문적 관심을 갖게 된 것은 1950년대 이후다. 덴마크 코펜하겐에서 성 정체성 장애를 겪던 조지 조르겐슨이라는 26살의 젊은 이가 1952년 처음으로 성 전환 수술을 받으면서다. 엘라가발루스라는 로마 황제가 남성 절개수술을 받고 여성이 됐다는 얘기도 있지만 확인되지 않은 이야기이다. 존스홉킨스 대학에 성적 장애 클리닉센터가 만들어진 것을 시작으로, 1960년대 들어 세계 각국에선 성전환 수술이 이뤄지기 시작했다. 국제보건기구(WHO)는 1994년에 '자신과 반대되는 성으로 살며 인정받고 싶은 욕망이 있고, 자신의 해부학적 성에 대해 불편해 하며, 자신이 바라는 성에 일치되도록 호르몬 치료와 수술을 받으려는 욕구가 있을 경우' 성전환자라고 규정했다.

우리의 경우 뿌리 깊은 유교적 관습 때문에 성전환자들을 비판적인 시각으로 바라보았다. 자신의 성을 바꿔달라는 성전환자들의 소송도 재판부 성향에 따라 판결이 엇갈렸다. 대법원이 마침내 자신의 성을 바꾼 50대에게 "인간다운 생활을 한 권리가 있다"며 호적상의 성별을 바꿔주라는 판결을 내렸다. 하지만 종교계와 법조계 일각에서는 "법원이 인간의 성까지 정해주는 전지전능한 신이 된 것 같다"는 비판도 있다.

문제해설

1. 본문 첫 번째 문단에서는 성전환의 대략적인 역사 및 정의에 대해 말하고 있으며, 두 번째 문단에서는 우리나라의 경우 최근 성전환자에 대해 달라진 환경에 대해 말하고 있다. 따라서 과거에 비해 보다 더 인정하는 분위기가 되었다는 (a)가 정답이 된다.

2. 정답은 (c)로 성전환증이 신에 대한 혐오라는 내용은 본문에 등장하지 않는다.

3. 마지막 문단에서 성전환의 호적상 성별을 바꿔주라는 판결에 대해 일부 반대자들의 목소리로 끝났기 때문에 이들의 주장이 이어지는 것이 자연스럽다. 따라서 정답은 (c)가 된다.

정답 1(a) 2(c) 3(c)

Unit 11 | The footprint of food
로컬 푸드

300년 전 7%에 불과하던 열대우림의 농경지, 목초지화 비율이 최근 몇 년 사이 40% 이상 엄청나게 늘어났다. 이미 지구 열대우림의 40% 이상이 파괴되면서 온실가스 흡수도 줄고 있다. 수백에서 수천㎞씩 먹을거리를 실어 나를 때 온실가스가 배출되는 것도 환경에 심각한 위험이 되고 있다. 노르웨이에서 잡힌 대구가 중국으로 운송되어 저민 생선으로 다듬어진 뒤 다시 판매 목적으로 노르웨이로 실려 간다. 유럽에서 대구를 다듬으면 kg당 2.99달러가 들지만, 중국에서 작업하면 0.5달러면 충분하기 때문이다.

이때 배출되는 온실가스에는 구속력 있는 규제가 없다. 1944년 체결된 국제민간항공협약 즉 시카고 조약에 따라, 항공기나 배로 다양한 국제 노선을 통해 상업 화물을 운송할 때 소비되는 연료에 대해 세금을 부과하는 게 간단치가 않다. 환경론자들은 각국 정부에서 연료에 관련 세금을 매기거나 온실가스 배출을 규제해야 한다고 주장한다. 유럽 연합(EU)은 유럽을 오가는 모든 화물운송 항공기에 대해 자기가 내뿜는 만큼의 온실가스 배출권을 사도록 할 계획이다.

어떤 이들은 규제보다는 소비자에게 맡겨야 한다고 주장한다. 온실가스 발자국, 즉 상품을 생산하고 수송하는 과정에서 배출한 온실가스의 양을 상품에 표시하자는 얘기다. 실제로 자기 지역에서 생산된 먹을거리를 먹게 함께

9

노력하자는 '로컬 푸드' 운동이 소비자들 사이에 나타나고 있으며, 소비자들에게 대중적 인기를 끌고 있다. 예를 들면, 미국 뉴욕 주에서는 '100마일 다이어트 운동'이 빠르게 확산되고 있다. 이는 수확철만이라도 100마일(161㎞) 이내에서 생산된 것만 소비하자는 운동이다.

문제해설

1. 본문은 온실가스로 인한 지구 온난화에 관해 서술하고 있다. 이 중에서도 수송(transport)에 의해 발생하는 온실가스에 관해 집중적으로 다루고 있으므로 정답은 (b)가 적합하다.

2. 수송에서 발생하는 온실가스를 규제만 할 것이 아니라 소비자들에게 맡겨야 한다는 주장의 예로, 뉴욕 주에서 번지고 있는 100마일 운동이 나오고 있다. 따라서 이에 대한 설명인 (a)는 올바른 서술이다. (b)는 이 운동이 전국으로 퍼진다고 했으므로 올바르지 않으며, (c)의 경우 환경론자들이 연료에 세금을 매기거나 배출을 규제해야 한다고는 했지만 모든 항공기가 비행해서는 안 된다는(be grounded) 내용은 없다. (d)의 경우 EU에서 계획하고 있는 내용이므로 아직 성공한 것은 아니며, (e)의 경우 본문과 반대로 설명하고 있으므로 적합하지 않다.

3. 첫 번째 문단에 나온 노르웨이의 대구는 맛이나 가격, 신선함을 말하고 있지 않다. 가격은 오히려 더 싸기 때문에 중국에서 작업되어 다시 재수입된다고 나왔다. 가격은 더 싸지만 대구를 중국에 보낸 후 다시 가져오는 수송의 문제로 환경오염이 발생한다는 (a)가 정답이 된다.

4. 사람이 걸어가면 발자국(footprint)이 남는 것과 같이 greenhouse footprint는 한 물건이 생산되기 위해 온실가스가 어느 정도 발생하는지를 나타낸 것이므로 정답은 (e)가 된다.

정답 1(b)   2(a)   3(a)   4(e)

Unit 12 | A cure for obsessions
강박장애

어떤 행동을 하지 않고는 도무지 안심할 수 없을 때 뇌에서는 무슨 일이 일어나고 있을까? 학자들은 강박장애 환자들은 뇌에서 비정상적으로 빠른 신진대사가 이뤄지고 있다고 주장한다. 즉 뇌에서 과도한 비율로 에너지가 급격히 소모되고 있다는 것이다. 이 이론에 따르면 "강박장애 환자들은 다른 통제 집단의 사람들에 비해 뇌의 크기가 다소 작다"는 것이다.

미국 국립정신보건연구원의 라포폴트 박사는 '강박장애는 특정한 행동을 끊임없이 반복함으로써 안정감을 느끼는 상태'라고 정의했다. 강박적인 행동은 크게 세 가지 유형이 있다. 확인형(Checkers), 정확형(Exacters), 청결형(Washers) 등이다. 확인형은 뭔가를 확인하려고 똑같은 행동을 끊임없이 반복하는 데 반해, 정확형은 대칭적인 방식에 따라 사물을 배열하는 데 모든 시간을 보내는 것이다.

청결형은 자신의 몸을 반복적으로 씻고, 주변의 물건들을 계속 닦아야 한다고 믿는 경우이다. 라포폴트는 "강박증은 현실에 대한 지각을 왜곡하는 쪽으로 이끌며, 거의 마술에 가깝다"고 말했다.

이런 상황으로 인해 방해를 받으면, 뇌는 길을 잃고 헤매게 된다. 뇌가 이상한 방식으로 작용하게 되면 괴상한 행동들이 나타나는 경우가 생긴다. 뇌의 잘못된 작동 때문에 개인은 물론 주변 사람들, 나아가 조직에도 나쁜 결과를 가져올 수도 있다.

문제는 중증의 강박장애를 치유하기 위해서는 장기간 치료가 필요하다는 것이다. 특히 환자들이 완전히 절망감에 빠질 수 있다는 위험도 있다. 다른 사람들은 손쉽게 해결할 수 있는 일들을 자신의 정신 상태 때문에 이루지 못할 때 받는 좌절감은 실로 엄청나다. 여기다 사회적 비난이나 조롱 등이 뒤따르게 되면 정신적 황폐함마저 느끼게 된다. 집착의 대상을 놓아버리고 이해와 관용, 연민과 용서를 좀 더 키워나가는 것이 강박장애의 적합한 치료책이다. 하지만 강박장애로 줄어들 대로 줄어든 뇌를 원상 복구하는 것이 만만치 않은데다, 이를 패배나 굴복으로 인식하게 된다는 점이 문제이다.

문제해설

1. 강박장애에 대한 치료법이나 새로운 연구 결과에 대한 내용이 아니므로 (a)와 (b)는 정답으로 적합하지 않다. 또한 강박장애를 어떻게 완치할 것인가를 두고 서술한 글이라고는 할 수 없다. 물론 부분적으로 마지막 문단에서 다루고 있지만 주제가 되기에는 지엽적인 내용이다. 본문에서는 강박장애를 겪는 이들은 누구이고, 어떤 유형이 있으며, 왜 그런 질병을 겪고 해결책은 무엇인지를 종합적으로 말하고 있으므로 정답은 (c)가 가장 적절하다.

2. 강박장애는 장기적 치료가 필요하다고 했으므로 치료책이 없거나, 기적과도 같은 치료법이 나오지 않으면 불가능하다는 내용은 사실과 다르다. (c)는 강박장애를 가진 이들을 조롱하는 말이므로 정답이 될 수 없다. 정답은 (d)로 뇌의 잘못된 작동으로 인해 길을 잃고 헤매게 된다는 내용을 재서술한 것이다.

3. 마지막 문단의 "Combined with social criticism and derision, they can even feel psychological devastation." 부분을 재서술한 (a)가 정답이 된다. 나머지 보기는 모두 본문에 등장하지 않는다.

4. 강박장애는 3가지 유형으로 구분된다고 나오며, 같은 행동을 반복하는 확인형(checkers), 좌우대칭에 집착하는 정확형(exacters), 끊임없이 주변 물건을 닦는 청결형(washers)으로 나눌 수 있다. 이런 맥락에서 (a)는 청결형의 특징이고, (b)는 확인형의 특징이라고 할 수 있다. 하지만 문제에서는 증상(symptom)을 묻고 있으므로 (a)가 더 적합해서 정답은 (a)가 된다.

정답 1(c)   2(d)   3(a)   4(a)

Unit 13   Out for blood
헌혈

　윌리엄 하비는 혈액 순환의 실체를 밝혀낸 영국 외과 의사다. 그는 또 심장이 펌프와 같은 역할을 한다는 사실도 발견했다. 1628년에는 피가 인간 몸속을 순환한다는 사실도 발견했다. 하비는 그동안 의학 이론에서 우위를 차지하고 있던 갈레누스의 이론을 1,500년 만에 뒤집었다. 갈레누스는 로마의 아우렐리우스 황제의 주치의였다. 그는 '간에서 만들어진 피는 살을 만들기 위해 몸의 외부로 보내지며, 또한 피는 오줌과 땀과 같은 노폐물의 형태로 몸에서 빠져 나간다'고 주장했다.

　하비의 '혈액순환론'은 간신히 정설로 인정받았으나 수혈이 이뤄지기에는 190년의 시간이 필요했다. 영국의 산과 전문의였던 제임스 블런델이 1818년 사람의 혈액 400cc를 수혈해서 출혈로 죽어가는 환자를 살리는 데 처음 성공한 것이다. 당시에는 피의 응고를 막기 위해 헌혈자의 동맥과 환자의 정맥을 직접 연결하는 수혈 방법이 동원됐다.

　인공 심장까지 개발한 현대 의학도 완벽한 인공 혈액을 만들어내는 데까지는 성공하지 못했다. 산소를 실어 나르는 대체 혈액은 고혈압 등 부작용이 심각하다. 노폐물을 운반하고 면역까지 맡는 인공 혈액은 아직 엄두조차 못 내고 있다. 수혈이 필요한 환자들은 여전히 보존기간이 평균 3주, 길어도 35일을 넘기지 못하는 헌혈을 기증받기를 간절히 기다리고 있다.

문제해설

1. 본문은 과거 갈레누스의 이론에서 혈액 순환론이 확립되는 과정을 다루고 있으며, 이후 실제 응용에 관한 내용으로 이어지고 있다. 따라서 정답은 (b)가 된다. 영국 의사인 제임스 블런델과 로마 황제 주치의인 갈레누스는 예시로 나오고 있으므로 주제로 적절하지 않으며, 수혈의 위험성도 지엽적인 내용이므로 적절하지 않다.

2. 하비의 이론이 가까스로 정론으로 인정받았다고 했으므로 (a)는 사실과 다르며, 수혈은 그 이후 200년 가까이 기다려야 했다고 나오므로 (b) 또한 사실과 다르다. (c)의 경우 죽기 전에 발견했다는 내용은 본문에 등장하지 않는다. 정답은 (d)로 1,500년 동안 정설로 받아들여진 갈레누스의 이론에 반하는 내용을 주장했으므로 (d)와 같이 주장하는 것은 무리가 아니다.

3. 갈레누스의 이론이 대체되었다고 나오므로 정답은 바로 (a)가 된다. 그리고 하비의 이론은 가까스로(by a close shave) 정론으로 인정받았다고 했으므로 즉시 인정받았다는 (b)는 맞지 않다. 블런델은 자신에게 한 것이 아니라 죽어가는 환자에게 수혈을 한 것이므로 (c)도 아니며, (d)는 최초 수혈에 관한 내용이므로 사실이 아니다.

4. 이 문제는 현대의학으로 불가능한 것을 묻고 있다. 수혈은 당연히 오래 전에 발견되었으므로 가능하지만 인공 심장과 같이 인공 혈액은 아직도 해결할 문제가 많다고 했으므로 (b)가 정답이 된다.

정답 1(b) 2(d) 3(a) 4(b)

Unit 14   The year of the Earth
지구의 해

　이 행성을 지구가 아니라 수구(水球)라 불러야 한다는 주장도 있다. 바다의 넓이는 3억6,000만㎢로 지구 표면의 3분의 2를 차지하고, 평균 수심도 3,800m에 이른다. 최근까지도 사람들은 바다를 제대로 알지 못했다. 1872년에서 1875년 사이에 대양의 깊이 측정에 나선 영국 해양탐사선인 챌린저호 대원들은 태평양에서 줄을 내려서 해저 8㎞ 이상 들어간다는 사실에 놀랐다. 이처럼 넓고 깊은 바다도 여러 위험을 받고 있다. 특히 육지로 둘러싸인 내해(內海)와 만(灣)은 극심한 환경오염으로 산소가 없는 죽은 바다가 되고 있는 경우가 많다.

　하늘은 바다보다 더 넓고 높다. 지구에서 가장 낮은 대기층이며 날씨를 좌우하는 대류권의 두께는 위도와 계절에 따라 팽창하거나 줄어들지만 대체로 10㎞에서 15㎞에 이른다. 대류권 위에는 성층권도 있다. 그러나 인간 앞에서는 그 넓은 하늘도 좁다. 성층권에 생긴 구멍은 인류가 프레온 가스 사용을 줄였음에도 앞으로 50년은 더 있어야 메워질 전망이다. 지구 공기에서 온실가스인 이산화탄소가 차지하는 비율이 과거 200년 동안 0.028%에서 0.038%로 늘어 지구를 따뜻하게 하는 온실 효과를 낼 정도가 되었다.

　2008년은 유엔이 정한 '행성 지구의 해'다. 2004년 12월 동남아를 강타한 쓰나미를 지켜보았던 지구촌은 자연재해를 예방하고 지구과학자들의 연구 성과를 정책에 반영하자는 뜻에서 이렇게 정했다. 하지만 아무리 지구를 연구한들 하늘보다 높고 바다보다 넓은 인류의 욕심을 먼저 조절하지 않는다면 과연 지구의 건강이 유지될까. 지난해 11월 유엔개발계획(UNDP)이 경고한 것처럼 65억 인류 모두가 선진국들 마냥 에너지를 쓰고 온실가스를 배출한다면 지구가 아홉 개로도 부족할 것이기 때문이다.

문제해설

1. 본문의 전체 내용을 보면, 첫 번째 문단에서 바다가 거대하며, 이 바다에 환경오염이 발생하는 내용을 담고 있으며, 다음 문단에서는 하늘은 바다보다 더 거대하며, 하늘에서도 환경오염이 발생해 오존층이 파괴되고 있다는 내용을 담고 있다. 그리고 마지막 문단에서는 이 글이 쓰인 해는 UN이 정한 '행성 지구의 해'로 인류가 욕심을 조절하지 않는다면 환경오염 해결은 요원할 것이라고 말하고 있다. 따라서 이 글은 해양 오염에 대한 글도 아니고, 해양과 대기 양측의 과학자들 간의 라이벌 관계에 대한 글도 아니다. 또한 과학자들이 문제 해결에 얼마만큼의 진척을 보이고 있는지의 글도 아니며, 인간의 욕심에 대한 글도 아니다. 정답은 (d)로 해양과 상공에서 진행되는 오염과 이를 위해 우리가 명심해야 하는 상황에 대해 서술하고 있다.

2. 이 문제는 본문 마지막 구절을 통해 짐작할 수 있다. 마지막 줄에서 65억 인구가 선진국처럼 에너지를 사용하고 온실가스를 배출한다면

11

절대 안 된다고 말하고 있으므로 지금의 환경오염은 대부분 선진국에서 발생하고 있다고 생각할 수 있다. 따라서 정답은 (b)가 된다.

3. 대기 중의 이산화탄소 비율이 증가했다는 내용(a)이 있으며, (b)는 첫 번째 문단을 통해 유추할 수 있다. 하지만 본문에 직접 명시되어 있지는 않다. (c)의 경우 인간의 욕심이 하늘보다 혹은 바다보다 더 넓고 깊어 문제라고 했으므로 (c)가 정답이 된다. (d)는 2번 문제에서 나왔던 내용이며, (e)는 첫 번째 문단을 통해 이제 해양의 규모와 지구 생태계에 미치는 영향을 이미 알고 있다는 내용을 추론할 수 있다.

4. 마지막 문단에 환경오염에 대한 해결책으로 제시한 부분을 통해 정답은 (a)라는 것을 알 수 있다. 과학만이 아니라 우리 스스로 변화해야 한다는 내용이다.

정답 1(d) 2(b) 3(c) 4(a)

Unit 15 | Medicine and poison
탈리도마이드

1960년대 탈리도마이드를 복용한 임산부들에게서 선천적 결손증을 가진 아이들이 태어나자 끔찍한 부작용 때문에 이 약은 영원히 사라질 것으로 보였다. 하지만 이 약은 무덤에서 깨어났다. 뉴잉글랜드 의학 저널 최근호엔 탈리도마이드가 만성 림프구성 백혈병 치료에 놀라운 효과를 보인다는 연구 결과가 실렸다. 약은 독이 될 수 있고, 독은 약이 될 수도 있다는 얘기다.

탈리도마이드는 독일에서 1958년에 첫선을 보였는데, 처음에는 신경안정제로 팔렸다. 그러나 곧 임신부의 입덧을 완화하는 제제로 더 널리 쓰였다. 1961년까지 48개국 임산부가 이 약을 복용했다. 그러나 임신 초기에 약을 복용한 여성이 낳은 아기 10명 중 두세 명은 팔다리가 없는 등의 심각한 결함을 안고 태어났다. 이들 '탈리도마이드 아기'는 1만여 명에 달했다.

1962년 7월 15일자 워싱턴 포스트의 1면 헤드라인은 '나쁜 약의 출시를 막은 미 식품의약국(FDA)의 영웅'이었다. 영웅은 FDA에 고용된 지 2년밖에 안 된 여의사 프랜시스 켈시 박사였다. 그는 서류 미비 등을 이유로 탈리도마이드의 시판 허가를 내주지 않았다. 결과적으로 미국에서 그 약으로 인한 피해 사례는 극도로 적었고, 이 일이 FDA가 세계인의 신뢰를 받는 계기가 되었다.

문제해설

1. 주제문에 대한 질문이다. 본문에서는 탈리도마이드라는 약품에 관해 서술하고 있다. 처음에는 신경안정제로 임산부에 사용되었지만 이후 심각한 부작용으로 사용이 전면 중단되었다가 향후 이 약이 림프구성 백혈병 치료에 효과가 있다는 연구 결과가 나와 다시 사용될 수도 있을 것 같다는 내용을 담고 있다. 따라서 이에 대한 내용을 담고 있는 (d)가 정답이 된다.

2. 1번의 설명과 같이 '약품이 독약으로 밝혀지기도 하고, 다시 그 독약이 약품이 될 수 있다'는 것이 2번 문제의 내용이므로 이에 대해 서술한 (b)가 정답이 된다. 약품의 특성이 바뀐다는 내용은 아니므로 (a)는 적절하지 않고, 어떤 사람에게는 좋은데 다른 사람에게는 치명적이라는 뜻의 (c) 또한 바르지 못한 설명이다. 또한 복용법(dosage)을 잘 몰라 그럴 수 있다는 (d)도 사실과 다르다.

3. '탈리도마이드 아기'는 임신 초기에 탈리도마이드를 복용한 여성이 낳은 아이 중 기형을 가진 아이를 말하므로 (a)가 정답이 된다. 다른 이유가 아닌 어머니가 그 약을 복용해서 기형이 발생했다고 설명하고 있기 때문이다. 본문에 이런 아기들에 대한 보상(compensation)에 대한 내용은 등장하지 않으며 (c)도 역시 추측은 가능하지만 본문을 근거로 판단하기는 어렵다.

정답 1(d) 2(b) 3(a)

Unit 16 | Fish story
참치

참치는 대략 20여 종이 있으며, 참다랑어·눈다랑어·황다랑어 등이 참치에 포함된다. 참다랑어도 사는 곳에 따라 북반구의 북방 참다랑어와 남반구의 남방 참다랑어로 나뉜다. 북대서양 참다랑어는 길이가 3m에 이르고, 몸무게도 560kg까지 자란다. 전 세계 바다에서 잡아 올리는 참치는 연간 400만이 넘고, 전 세계에서 참치 소비량이 제일 많은 일본이 전체 어획량의 4분의 1을 소비한다. 한국도 연간 25만에서 30만을 먹는다. 일본은 참다랑어·눈다랑어만 해도 연간 48만을, 미국은 3만에서 5만을 소비한다.

참치는 오메가-3 지방산과 셀레늄이 풍부한 음식으로, 심장병과 대장암을 예방해준다. 웰빙 바람을 타고 참치 수요가 늘어나고 있다. 전 세계에서 가장 활발한 국제환경단체인 그린피스는 5년 내에 참다랑어가 멸종할 것이라고 주장한다. 자원이 고갈되면서 일본에서는 참다랑어 한 마리 값이 소형차 한 대 값까지 치솟았다. 일본은 초밥 재료를 다른 것으로 대체하느라 고심하고 있다.

최근 뉴욕타임스(NYT)는 미국 뉴욕 맨해튼의 음식점 등에서 판매되는 참치 초밥에서 수은이 다량 검출됐다고 보도했다. 참다랑어 초밥 대부분은 1주일에 여섯 조각만 먹어도 혈중 수은 수치가 미 정부에서 정한 안전 기준을 초과한다는 것이다. 영국 식품표준국에서는 이미 임신 여성에 대해 참치를 피하라고 권고하고 있다. 맛있다고 너무 많이 먹는다면 생태계는 물론 건강에도 좋지 않다고 참치가 인류에게 경고하는 것만 같다.

문제해설

1. 본문은 참치에 관한 내용으로 첫 번째 문단은 참치의 종류와 특징, 어획량 등을 서술하고 있다. 두 번째 문단에서는 참치가 건강에 좋은 점과 그로 인해 참치 자원이 고갈되면서 발생하는 문제점에 대해 서술되어 있다. 마지막 문단은 참치에 수은이 다량으로 검출된 점 등장한다. 따라서 본문은 수산시장이나 초밥에 대한 내용이라고 볼 수 없으며, 참치의 종류도 부분적인 설명일 뿐이다. 본문의 전체적 내용을 모두 담고 있는 참치의 장·단점에 대한 내용이라는 (d)가 정답으로 적합하다.

2. 마지막 문단에서 참치를 많이 먹을 경우 참치에 포함된 중금속인 수은을 다량으로 먹는 것일 수 있기 때문에 특히 임산부는 조심해야 한다는 내용이 있다. 이를 통해 정답이 (a)라는 것을 알 수 있다.

3. 장·단점이 있다는 내용의 (a)는 틀린 설명이 아니며, 웰빙 바람을 타고 참치 수요가 더 늘고 있다고 했으므로 (b)가 본문과 반대되는 내용이 되어 정답이 된다. (c)의 경우 두 번째 문단에서 유추가 가능하며, (d)의 경우 마지막 문단에서 수은 중독으로 임산부는 피하는 것이 좋다는 내용을 재서술한 것이므로 올바른 설명이다.

4. 두 번째 문단에 참다랑어가 고갈되면서 한 마리 값이 소형차 한 대 값 정도까지 치솟았다는 내용을 통해 비싸도 계속 소비하는 것을 알 수 있으므로 정답이 (b)가 된다.

정답 1(d) 2(a) 3(b) 4(b)

Unit 17 Chips on shoulders, too?
생체 칩

무선주파수 인식 기술(Radio Frequency Identification)이 보편화되면 이러한 일들이 실제로 일어날 수 있다. 위치 추적의 원리는 간단하다. 전자 칩에 각종 정보를 담고 송수신 안테나를 붙인 것이다. 칩의 정보를 송출하거나, 기종에 따라서는 새로운 정보를 칩에 담을 수도 있다. 전자 칩을 사람 몸속에도 심을 수도 있다.

2004년 7월 AP통신 보도에 따르면, 멕시코 정부가 법무부 장관을 비롯한 검사와 수사관 160여 명의 몸에 전자태그 칩을 이식한 것으로 드러났다. 중요 정보기관에 출입할 때 보안 및 신원 확인을 위한 것이라고 한다. 사용된 칩은 미국 '베리칩(VeriChip)' 사의 제품으로, 길이 12mm, 폭 2.1mm로 주사기를 사용해 피부 밑에 이식했다.

영국 인디펜던트지는 정부가 가석방 범죄자를 감시하는 수단으로 전자 칩을 이용하는 것을 고려하고 있다고 보도했다. 칩을 몸에 이식하고 위성을 통해 이동 상황을 감시하겠다는 계획이다.

2006년 미국에서는 베리칩 사의 스콧 실버만 회장이 국내 거주 이주민의 몸에 전자태그 칩을 넣자고 주장한 바 있다. 조지 W 부시 대통령이 국가안보상의 이유를 들어 관리들이 "미국에 누가 살고 있고, 어디에 살고 있는지 알아야 한다"고 강조한 데 따른 안이다.

전자태그 칩이 발전하면 생체 칩(bionic microchip)이 된다. 미국 버클리 캘리포니아 대학의 한 연구진은 2002년 2월 인체 세포를 전자 칩 회로와 결합한 생체 칩을 개발했다고 발표했다. 미국 정보기관의 연구에 따르면 피부의 온도 변화에 따라 재충전되는 배터리를 내장한 반도체를 이식하기 적당한 위치는 이마와 손등이라고 한다. 성경의 요한 계시록은 말세의 우상 숭배를 예언하면서 "그들의 오른손이나 이마에 표를 받게 한다."고 적고 있다. 전자태그에 반대하는 음모론이 나오는 배경이다.

문제해설

1. 본문은 전자 칩에 대한 설명으로 보안이나 감시를 위해 멕시코, 영국, 미국에서 실제로 보안 칩을 사용하고 있는 예들을 나열하고 있다. 따라서 정답은 (a) 혹은 (c)이며, 전자 칩을 반대하는 내용이나, 왜 전자 칩을 사용해야 하는지에 대한 내용은 아니다. 전자 칩의 용도가 감시와 보안, 모두 등장하는데 보안을 위해 감시를 하는 것이므로 감시가 좀 더 포괄적인 개념이 되어 (a)가 정답이 된다.

2. 멕시코에서 보안 및 신원 확인 목적으로 사용한다고 두 번째 문단에 나와 있으므로 정답은 (a)가 된다. (b)의 경우 모든 국민이 아닌 미국에 거주하는 이주민을 대상으로 한다고 했으며, 생체 칩은 피부의 온도 변화에 따라 재충전되는 배터리를 내장하고 있다고 했으므로 충전을 위해 제거할 필요가 없다. 영국의 경우 가석방 대상자들을 대상으로 전자 칩 사용을 고려하고 있다고 했으며, 미국의 상황을 예의주시하고 있다는 내용은 본문과 무관하다.

3. 마지막 문단을 보면 바코드에 이어 생체 칩에 반대하는 음모론이 나오고 있다고 했으므로 이것이 옳지 않다고 주장하는 세력이 있다는 것을 추론할 수 있다. 따라서 정답은 (c)가 된다.

4. 정답을 부시 대통령의 설명에서 추론할 수 있는데, 누가 살고 있고 어디에 사는지(who lives in the United States, and where)를 알기 위해서라고 했으므로 정답은 (d)가 된다.

정답 1(a) 2(a) 3(c) 4(d)

Unit 18 Bogus complaints
가짜약

치료 효과가 전혀 없는 가짜약도 네 가지 부류가 있다. 출현한 지 오래된 것부터 보면 첫 번째는 플라시보(placebo)다. 정상적인 약처럼 보이지만 의학적 효과가 전혀 없다. 의사가 처방을 그렇게 해주어서인지 효과는 심리적인 면이 더 크다. 두 번째는, 약효는 전혀 없지만 엄청난 효과가 있는 것으로 홍보되는 치료제이다. 세 번째는 진짜를 흉내 낸 짝퉁약이다. 최근 국내에서 유통 직전에 적발된 가짜 아모디핀(혈압약)이 여기 속한다. WHO(세계보건기구)는 전 세계 유통 약의 10%, 개발도상국에서 팔리는 4알 중 1알은 짝퉁이라고 발표했다. 가짜 비아그라 적발 소식이 끊이지 않는 데서 짐작되듯이, 짝퉁 대상 약은 노바스크·디오반·시알리스·프로페시아 등 잘 팔리는 브랜드 약들이다. 네 번째는 유해 성분이 든 불량약이다. 최근 미국에서 19명의 사망자를 낸 헤파린(피를 묽게 하는 약), 파나마·아이티에서 약 200명을 숨지게 한 감기약이 좋은 예다. 헤파린엔 불순물, 감기약엔 공업용 글리세린이 들어 있었다. 두 사건의 공통점은 허가된 제약회사에서 생산됐으나 중국에서 들어온 불량 약품 원료를 사용했다는 것이다. 넷 중에서 플라시보는 먹어도 해가 없다. 유당(알약)·증류수(물약)·생리 식염수(주사약) 등 무해한 물질이기 때문이다. 나머지 셋은 생명을 위협한다. 짝퉁 유통률이 53%에 달하는 말라리아약 아르테수네이트는 가짜 약 생산의 위험성·비윤리성을 잘 보여준다. 말라리아로 연간 100만 명이 숨지는데 진짜 약이 사용됐다면 20만 명은 구했을 것으로 WHO는 추산한다.

문제해설

1. (a)의 경우 세계보건기구에서는 특정 정보를 발표하고는 있지만 특정 제약회사를 상대로 조치를 취하겠다는 내용은 등장하지 않는다. 제약회사들이 행동에 책임을 지고 있다는 내용인 (b)도 본문에는 등장하지 않는다. 가짜 약 중에서도 몇몇 가짜 약은 사람을 숨지게 할 수 있다고 했으므로 치명적인 영향을 미친다는 것을 알 수 있으므로 정답은 (c)가 된다. (d)의 경우 중국에서 들여온 원료에서 불량 약품 원료가 섞여있어서 문제가 됐다는 내용은 있지만 중국의 제품 모두 신뢰할 수 없다는 것은 지나친 비약이다.

2. 4가지 약 모두 가짜(bogus)이기 때문에 의약적 효과가 없다. 따라서 medical, remedy, genuine, safe 등의 단어가 들어갈 수 없다. 정답은 (d)로 psychological에 해당하는 것이 위약(placebo)이며, non-medical에 해당하는 것이 사기약에 해당한다. duplicate에 해당하는 것이 진짜를 흉내 낸 짝퉁 약에 대한 설명이며, toxin에 해당하는 것이 마지막에 나온 가짜 성분이 든 불량약이다.

3. 이런 짝퉁 약이나 불량 약이 시중에 유통되는 이유는 위약 효과나 직원의 실수라기보다는 이익(profit)을 위해 인위적으로 만들어진 것으로 보는 것이 합당하므로 정답은 (a)가 된다.

4. 위약은 환자에게 해가 가는 것은 아니라고 했으므로 정답은 위약이 환자에게 위험하다고 설명한 (b)가 된다.

정답 1(c) 2(d) 3(a) 4(b)

Unit 19 | UN World Water Day
물의 날

사람의 몸무게가 70kg이라면 그중 거의 절반은 물이다. 그중에서 1%만 모자라도 갈증을, 5%만 부족해도 현기증을 느낀다. 또 10%가 부족하면 걷기조차 힘들고, 12%가 모자라면 생명까지도 위태로워진다. 물을 마시지 않고 수일을 버티기가 불가능하다.

한국 가정에서는 한 사람이 매일 178L의 물을 사용하지만, 사하라 사막 남쪽 지역이나 몽골 일부 지역에서는 하루 5L로 모든 것을 해결해야 한다. 유엔은 1992년 "한 사람이 하루에 물 40L를 공급받아야 한다"고 선언했지만 지구상에서 11억 명은 여전히 물 때문에 고통을 받고 있다. 이들은 깨끗한 물을 얻기 위해 1km 이상을 걸어가야 하거나, 가까운 곳에 있더라도 심하게 오염된 물을 마셔야 한다. 가뭄에 시달리는 아프리카 소말리아 같은 곳에서는 물을 차지하기 위해 부족 간에 살육전도 벌어진다.

3월 22일은 유엔이 정한 세계 물의 날이다. 매년 이 무렵이면 한국이 물 부족 국가냐, 아니냐를 놓고 논란이 벌어지곤 한다. 스웨덴의 말린 폴켄마르크라는 학자는 한

사람이 1년에 사용할 수 있는 물이 $1700m^3$보다 적은 나라를 물 부족 국가로 분류했고, 이 기준이 국제적으로도 널리 사용된다. 한국인 한 사람이 연간 사용할 수 있는 물의 양은 $1488m^3$이므로 이 기준으로는 물 부족 국가다. 하지만 봄철 갈수기 일부 지방을 제외하면 부족함을 못 느끼는 것도 사실이다.

이런 차이는 한국이 부족한 물을 수입해 보충하기 때문에 나타난다. 물론 실제 물이 아니라 식량이라는 형태를 통해 '가상의 물(Virtual Water)'을 수입하는 것이다. 밀 1t을 생산하는 데는 $1300m^3$, 쇠고기 1t을 생산하는 데는 1만 $5000m^3$의 물이 필요하다. 식량을 수입하면 그만큼의 농업 용수를 절약하는 것이다. 유네스코에 따르면 한국은 1997~2001년 5년 동안 390억m^3에 이르는 '가상의 물'을 수입하고 70억m^3을 수출, 순 수입량이 320억m^3에 이르는 것으로 분석됐다. 한국은 일본·이탈리아·영국·독일에 이어 세계 5위의 물 수입국이다.

문제해설

1. (a)는 마지막 문단에 대한 설명이므로 정답이 된다. (b)도 정답으로 생각할 수 있지만 마지막 줄에서 일본이 한국보다 더 많은 물을 수입하는 국가인 것은 맞지만 실제 소비할 수 있는 양의 절대적 기준으로 따졌을 때 반드시 한국보다 더 적다고 할 수 없다. 본문에 명시되어 있지는 않지만 일본의 인구 규모가 한국에 비해 두 배 이상이기 때문에 절대 수치는 일본이 많을 것으로 예상할 수 있다. 그리고 (c)의 경우 명확하게 입증되어 있지 않다. 그래서 세계 물의 날이 되면 한국이 물 부족 국가인지를 두고 논쟁이 벌어진다고 했다. (d)는 본문에 나와 있지 않기 때문에 추론이 불가능하다.

2. virtual water는 마지막 문단에서 설명하고 있는 것과 같이 실제 물이 아닌 곡물 등 다른 형태로 들어오는 물을 말한다. 이에 대한 설명으로 (c)가 정답이 된다.

3. 물을 이용할 수 있는 수준이 나라마다 매우 다르다는 설명인 (d)가 정답이다.

4. 마지막 문단 서두에 왜 한국이 물 부족 국가이면서도 실제 물 부족 현상을 느낄 수 없는지 이유가 나온다. 바로 부족한 물을 '가상의 물' 형태로 수입하기 때문이라는 것이다. 따라서 이에 대한 설명인 (d)가 정답이 된다.

정답 1(a) 2(c) 3(d) 4(d)

Unit 20 | Potent pill
비아그라

1990년대 후반 다국적 제약사 화이자(Pfizer)의 연구팀은 새로 개발하던 심장병 치료제의 임상 실험을 중단했다. 협심증 약인 실데나필이 기대만큼 효과가 없었기 때문이다. 그런데 실험 중단 통고 받은 남성 환자들이 "왜 그만두느냐"고 불만을 표시했다. 이들은 먹다 남은 약의 반납

도 거부했다. 연구팀이 실험 대상자들을 조사한 결과 뜻밖의 부작용이 밝혀졌다. 협심증에는 그다지 효과가 없었지만 발기부전에는 효과가 있었던 것이다.

대박을 예감한 화이자는 이 약의 부작용에 초점을 맞췄고, 그 결과 최초의 발기부전 치료제인 비아그라(Viagra)를 내놓기에 이른다. 활력(Vigor)을 나이아가라(Niagara) 폭포처럼 넘치게 해준다는 의미다.

1998년 3월 27일 미 식품의약국(FDA)에서 판매 승인을 받았다. 비아그라는 의약품 시장에서 전례를 찾기 힘든 히트를 기록하며 화이자를 세계 최대의 제약회사로 성장시켰다. 지난 10년간 18억 정이 소비되었으며, 공식적으로 세계 3,500만 명의 남성이 복용했다. 지금도 1초에 6알이 소비되고 있다고 한다.

비아그라는 20세기 성(性)혁명을 마무리 짓는 약으로 꼽힌다. 1차 혁명을 이끈 것은 1950년대에 나온 피임약이다. 단순히 '피임약'으로만 알려진 이 약은 여성에게 임신에 대한 불안을 씻어주었다. 2차 혁명의 주역은 비아그라다. 고령화 사회의 도래와 함께 특히 노인들의 삶 개선에 결정적인 도움을 주었다. 영국 일간 인디펜던트는 비아그라의 등장을 약 색깔에 빗대 '푸른 기적'이라고 표현한 바 있다.

비아그라는 또 심부전증, 당뇨, 기억력 감퇴, 뇌졸중(뇌졸중) 등에도 효과가 있다고 한다. 보편적으로 '만병통치약'이라 불리는 아스피린에 필적한다는 평가가 나오기도 한다. 문제는 부작용도 만만치 않다는 점이다. 재채기나 두통, 소화 불량, 심장 떨림, 빛 공포증, 지속 발기증, 저혈압, 심근경색 등 다양하다. 실명(失明)과 사망이라는 치명적 사례도 보고돼 있다. 그렇다고 복용을 꺼리는 사람은 드물다.

문제해설

1. 비아그라는 특히 노인들에게 큰 도움을 주었다고 나온다. 또한 비아그라의 전신인 실데나필을 실험하던 화이자는 뜻밖의 부작용 발견이 대박임을 예감하며 발기부전에 초점을 맞춰 개발했다는 내용이 나온다. 많이 팔리는 약이므로 소수의 사람들만이 복용할 리 없다. 정답은 (b)로 20세기 발기부전 치료에 2차 혁명이었다는 내용이 네 번째 문단에 등장한다.

2. 비아그라는 개인 성생활에 도움을 주며, 마지막 문단에서 밝히고 있는 것처럼 다른 증상에도 효과가 있다고 했으므로 여러 목적으로 사용될 것임을 추론할 수 있다. 비아그라의 히트로 화이자가 세계 최대의 제약회사가 되었다고 했으므로 많은 돈을 벌었음을 알 수 있고, 노인들에게 특히 도움이 된다는 내용도 등장한다. 부작용이 일부 있지만 그렇다고 치명적인 것은 아니므로 (d)가 정답이 된다.

3. 본문은 비아그라가 탄생한 과정을 서술하고 있으므로 정답은 (a)가 적합하다. (d)는 일반적인 의학 기술들을 지칭하고 있으므로 어색하다.

4. 비아그라를 blue miracle이라고 부른 이유는 비아그라 색상이 파란색이며, 발기부전에 기적과도 같은 효력을 보였기 때문이다. 보기 (a)도 일부 맞는 설명이지만 갑자기 나타났다는 뜻의 'from nowhere'라는 설명이 부적절하다. 하늘에서 떨어진 것이 아니고 목적은 달랐지만 다른 임상 실험 중에 발견된 것이기 때문이다. 정답은 (d)로 이전에는 치료제가 없었던 문제를 해결해 주었고, 일부 사람들(발기부전 환자들)에게 기적과도 같았기 때문이다.

정답 1(b) 2(d) 3(a) 4(d)

Unit 21 | The captive mammoth 매머드

지난해 5월 러시아 시베리아 북서쪽 영구 동토층에서는 어린 매머드 사체가 발견됐다. 지나가던 목동의 발에 채이면서 1만 년 동안 얼음 속에 갇혀있던 매머드가 세상에 모습을 드러낸 것이다. 태어난 지 6개월 정도 된 암컷 매머드의 사체는 이제껏 발견된 동물 중 가장 잘 보존돼 마치 살아있는 것처럼 생생했다.

러시아와 일본의 전문가들은 이 사체에서 얻은 세포와 코끼리 난자를 합치면 매머드를 복제할 수 있을 것이라는 꿈에 부풀어 있다. 이 꿈이 이뤄진다면 1993년 스티븐 스필버그 감독이 만든 공상과학영화 '쥬라기 공원'에서 나온 것처럼 공룡 복제가 조만간 현실이 되는 셈이다.

매머드는 거대함의 상징이다. 살아있으면 어깨까지 높이가 5m, 몸무게 12t의 아주 큰 것도 화석으로 발견되기도 한다. 매머드는 약 160만 년 전 아프리카에서 처음 나타나 홍적세 말기인 5만 년 전 번성했다. 대략 1만 년 전까지 아프리카와 유럽, 아시아, 북미 대륙에 살았다. 일부는 3,600년 전까지 살아남았지만, 결국 멸종되고 말았다.

최근 스페인 학자들이 기후, 매머드의 종과 숫자를 모델 분석한 결과, 8,000~6,000년 전 기후 변화로 매머드의 숫자가 급격히 줄었다. 그렇지만 결국 매머드의 마지막 숨통을 끊은 것이 인류의 사냥이었음을 밝혀냈다. 하지만 매머드와 인류의 악연은 지금도 반복되고 있고, 인간에 의해 멸종으로 간다.

지구 온난화의 영향으로 영구 동토층이 빠르게 녹아내리면서 매머드 화석 찾기 열풍이 벌어지고 있다. 상아 전문 사냥꾼은 말할 것도 없고 순록 사냥꾼이나 유전·가스전 노동자까지 가세했다. 매머드 화석은 러시아의 주요 수출 상품으로 떠올라 세계 곳곳으로 팔려나간다. 1989년 연간 2t에 불과하던 매머드 상아 수출이 지난해에는 40t에 이르렀다. 길이 3m에 이르는 엄니가 온전한 매머드 머리 화석은 우리 돈 2,000만 원 수준이고, 완전한 형태로 복원된 매머드 화석은 1억 5,000만~2억 5,000만 원을 호가한다.

문제해설

1. 매머드의 복원도 가능하겠다고 희망하는 이들이 있지만 실현될지는 미지수이다. 그리고 매머드의 '화석' 상아를 찾기 위해서 많은 이가 뛰어들고 있다고 했지 실제로 매머드를 복제해 상아를 얻으려는 것은 아니다. 지구 온난화나 다른 요인으로 모든 종이 멸종할 것이라는 내

용은 극단적이다. 정답은 (b)로 지구 온난화로 영구 동토층이 녹으면서 매머드의 화석을 찾으려고 하는 이들이 더 많아졌다는 내용이 마지막 문단에 등장한다.
2. 매머드가 복제에 성공한 것도 아닌데 다시 멸종할지도 모른다는 (d)는 본문과 부합하지 않기 때문에 정답이 된다.
3. 마지막 부분의 내용은 인류와 매머드 간의 악연이 현재도 반복되고 있다면서, 매머드 상아 찾기의 열풍과 수출되는 상아의 가격과 양의 증가에 대해 다루고 있다. 이런 맥락에서 봤을 때, 어디에서 매머드를 발견하기 좋은지, 또는 어떻게 얼음에서 매머드 화석을 추출하는지 등은 흐름과 맞지 않다. 마치 이런 상아 찾기를 상세히 설명하는 것으로 흐르기 때문이다. 대신 이렇게 발견된 상아가 어디로 팔리고 어떤 용도에서 이들을 사들이는 것인지를 설명하는 (b)가 자연스러운 흐름이 된다.
4. (a), (b), (d) 모두 부분적 설명이 되지만 전반적 설명은 되지 못한다. 따라서 정답은 (c)이다.

정답 1(b)　2(d)　3(b)　4(c)

Unit 22 | Up to the challenge
파란 장미

이집트의 절세미인이었던 클레오파트라는 장미광(狂)이었다. 그녀는 남성들이 자신을 오랫동안 기억할 수 있도록 장미를 사용했다. 장미 냄새를 맡을 때마다 자기를 떠오르게 하기 위해서였다. 로마 제국의 통치자인 안토니우스를 유혹할 때도 방에 처음 효과가 있는 장미 향수를 잔뜩 뿌렸다. 그 냄새를 잊지 못한 안토니우스는 시저의 군대에 패해 죽으면서 자신의 무덤에 장미꽃을 뿌려달라고 했을 정도다. 빨간 장미였다. 그래서 빨간 장미의 '꽃말'은 욕망, 사랑 그리고 열정을 뜻한다.

백장미를 문장(紋章)으로 하는 영국의 봉건귀족 요크가(家)와 빨간 장미를 문장으로 한 랭커스터가 사이의 30년 전쟁은 장미전쟁으로 불린다. 헨리 7세가 '튜더 왕조'를 열며 장미전쟁은 끝났다. 빨간 장미와 백장미를 합친 튜더 왕조의 왕기(王旗)는 오늘날 영국 왕실의 문장으로 이어졌다. 그래서 '튜더 장미'의 꽃말은 물과 불의 결합, 즉 통일과 평화를 의미한다.

2만 5,000종에 달하는 장미에는 3,000개 정도의 색깔이 있다. 장미의 꽃말도 영어와 불어를 합해 60가지 이상이다. '파란 장미(Blue rose)'는 영어사전에 '불가능한', '있을 수 없는 것(일)'으로 나온다. 장미에는 원래 파란 색소가 없어 아무리 품종 개량을 해도 '파란 장미'가 나올 수 없음을 빗댄 것이다. 12세기부터 전 세계에서 온갖 교배를 시도했지만 소용이 없었다. '파란 장미'는 꿈의 영역이었던 셈이다.

일본의 주류 업체 산토리가 지난주 파란 장미의 판매를 정부로부터 승인받아 내년부터 시판에 들어간다고 발표했다. 장미에 델피니딘 청색 색소를 지닌 팬지의 유전자를 이식, '있을 수 없는' 파란 장미를 세상에 탄생시킨 것이다. 연구 시작으로부터 14년의 세월이 걸렸다. 산토리 창업자 도리이 신지로(鳥井信治郎)의 평생 입버릇이었던 "도전하라"가 마침내 결실을 맺은 것이다. 2,600억 엔 규모의 장미 시장에서 20%(520억 엔)는 파란 장미의 몫이 될 전망이다. 그런데 산토리가 지난 14년간 투입한 비용은 '불과' 30억 엔이다. 무엇보다 술만 만드는 줄 알았던 산토리가 이런 연구에 나섰고, 또 성공했다는 것이 놀랍고 흥미롭다. 술도 장미도 인간을 취하게 하는 점에서 통했던 것일까.

문제해설
1. (a), (c), (d)는 지엽적인 내용이므로 주제로 적합하지 않다. 각 시대에 걸쳐 장미는 어떤 역할을 했었는지를 설명하는 (b)가 전체 내용을 담을 수 있는 포괄적인 내용이다.
2. 클레오파트라는 장미의 효용을 잘 알고 이를 남성들을 유혹할 때 사용했다고 했으므로 정답은 (c)가 된다. 나머지 보기는 모두 본문과 무관한 내용이다.
3. 세 번째 문단에서 온갖 교배를 통해서도 파란 장미는 만들 수 없었다고 했으므로 파란 장미는 원래부터 존재하는 것이 아님을 알 수 있다. 그리고 (a)는 본문에 등장하지 않는다. 따라서 정답은 (d)가 된다.
4. 일본의 주류업체인 산토리가 유전자 조작을 통해 파란 장미를 만들었으므로 인공적으로 조작하지 않았다(not artificially tampered with)는 내용은 올바르지 않으므로 정답은 (c)가 된다.

정답 1(b)　2(c)　3(d)　4(c)

Unit 23 | Written in wrinkles
보톡스

요즘 주름을 펴 주는 대표적인 약은 바로 보톡스(Botox)다. 보톡스는 상품명이지만 보툴리눔 독소를 이용한 여러 주름 개선제를 사실상 통칭한다. 이 약은 약효의 지속기간이 3~6개월에 그치고, 자연스러운 얼굴 표정을 짓기가 어렵다는 것이 약점이다. 그러나 주름 제거 수술에 비해 비용 부담이 적다는 점과 사람들이 실제 나이보다 젊어 보이고 싶어하기 때문에 인기가 있다. 보톡스는 의약품 분야에서 비아그라에 이어 No. 2의 브랜드 파워를 갖고 있다.

약 이름 끝에 붙은 'tox'는 '독소'(toxin)에서 딴 것이다. 보툴리눔 독소는 자연 발생하며, 식중독을 일으킨다. 인공 유해물질 중 독성이 최고라는 다이옥신보다 최소 100배는 더 유독하다. 그래서 설사·복통에 그치는 일반 식중독과는 달리 보툴리눔 식중독의 치사율은 50%에 달한다. 한마디로 보툴리눔은 가장 치명적인 독소이다.

지난달 미국 식품의약청(FDA)이 보톡스의 안전성에 우려를 표명했다. 보톡스 시판 뒤 16명이 보톡스 치료를 받고 부작용으로 숨졌다고 지난달 말 미국의 시민단체인 '퍼블릭 시티즌'이 발표한 것이 계기였다. 우리 식약청도 조치를 취했다. 보톡스를 과량 주사하면 숨쉬기와 음식을 씹어 넘기기가 힘들어져 생명이 위태로워질 수 있다고 봐서다. 여기서도 문제는 용량 과다이다. 희생자는 대부분 근육 경련을 보톡스로 일시 해소하려 했던 뇌성마비 환자였다. 이들에겐 주름을 펼 때 쓰는 양의 28배가 주입됐다.

주름은 그 사람의 인생을 보여주는 자취이다. 20대 후반에 눈가부터 생기기 시작해 30대 후반엔 이마, 40대 후반엔 입가로 옮겨가면서 세월의 궤적(軌跡)을 남긴다. "눈가 주름은 이성(理性), 이마 주름은 인생, 입가 주름은 천리(天理)를 알만한 나이에 생긴다"는 속담이 있다.

문제해설

1. (a)는 마지막 문단만 설명할 수 있고, (b)는 첫 번째 문단에만 해당되므로 전체 주제가 되지 못한다. 본문에서는 보톡스의 독성과 위험성을 설명하고 있으므로 정답은 (c)가 된다. 마지막으로 (d)는 본문과 무관해서 답이 될 수 없다.

2. 보톡스를 맞고 사망한 이들은 대부분 근육 경련을 보톡스로 치료하려고 했던 뇌성마비 환자라고 세 번째 문단에서 설명하고 있다. 주름 개선을 위한 양보다 28배가 더 많았다고 한 부분을 통해 과다 주입(overdose)이 있었음을 알 수 있으므로 정답은 (a)가 된다. 식약청이 관심을 보이고 있기 때문에 (b)는 적절하지 않으며, 취급 주의로 보톡스의 독성이 줄어드는 것이 아니므로 (c)도 적절하지 않다. 보톡스의 위험을 모르고 구입한 사람들이 사망한 것도 있겠지만, 치료 중 목숨을 잃었다고 나오기 때문에 (d)는 이 전체를 설명하지 못한다.

3. 보톡스는 부작용이 있다고 했으며, 보톡스를 맞으면 표정 짓기가 어렵다고는 했지만 아픔을 참고 지내야 한다는 내용은 등장하지 않는다. 그리고 약효가 떨어질 때쯤 주름이 더 많아진다는 내용도 본문과는 무관하다. 정답은 (d)로 보톡스를 맞는 주요 목적은 주름 개선과 젊어 보이려는 갈망이라고 첫 번째 문단에서 설명하고 있다.

4. 보톡스를 맞는다고 대부분 사망하는 것은 아니므로 (a)는 어색하며, 얼굴 주름을 일시적이 아닌 영구적으로 제거해준다는 것은 본문과 다르므로 (c)도 답이 될 수 없다. 정답은 (b)로 일시적으로 주름이 사라진다는 점과 얼굴 표정을 짓기 어렵다는 점을 설명하고 있다.

정답 1(c) 2(a) 3(d) 4(b)

Unit 24 | Astro trash
케슬러 신드롬

지난해 1월 11일 중국은 미사일을 발사, 863km 상공에 떠 있던 자국의 기상위성 평원(風雲)-1C를 격추했다. 이 위성은 1999년 발사됐으며, 용도 폐기된 채 우주공간을 떠돌고 있었다. 위성의 격추 이후 중국은 미국과 러시아에 이어 탄도 미사일 기술을 보유한 세 번째 국가가 됐다. 문제는 파괴된 위성의 잔해가 우주 쓰레기가 되고 있는 것이다. 파편은 대개 초속 5~7km의 속도로 궤도를 돌기 때문에 그 자체로 총알이나 폭탄과 다를 바 없다.

지난 수십 년간 인간이 쏘아 올린 우주선과 위성에서 빈 연료탱크와 공구, 금속 파편에 이르는 쓰레기를 우주공간에 남기거나 떨어뜨리면서 우주 쓰레기가 증가하고 있다. NASA는 47개국에서 쏘아 올린 3,100개의 인공위성 외에도 직경 5cm가 넘는 우주 쓰레기 9,300여 개를 감시하고 있다. 파편 중에서 2,600개는 작년 파괴된 중국 위성의 파편이라고 한다. 1cm 짜리 쓰레기는 수십만 개에 이르지만 추적이나 감시가 불가능하다. 이 정도 크기라도 인공위성에 충돌해 기능을 마비시킬 수 있다.

'케슬러 신드롬'이 떠오르는 이유다. 우주의 쓰레기 파편이 다른 파편이나 인공위성과 부딪쳐 기하급수적으로 숫자가 늘어나면서 지구 궤도 전체를 뒤덮는다는 시나리오다. 그렇게 되면 우주선이나 위성 발사가 아예 불가능해질 수도 있다는 말이다. 그럼에도, 2월 13일 AP 보도에 따르면, 미 국방부는 이번 주 고장 난 첩보 위성을 격추할 계획이라고 한다. 만일 위성을 그대로 두면 다음 달이면 지구로 추락해 연료의 유독성 물질이 사람들에게 해를 줄 수 있다는 이유에서다.

문제해설

1. 우주 쓰레기가 문제가 되고 있다는 것이 본문의 주제이므로 정답은 (b)가 적합하다.

2. 향후 우주 파편이 문제가 될 수 있으며, 이를 해결할 방안을 찾아야 한다는 내용도 그럴 것으로 응당 생각해 볼 수 있다. 그리고 중국이 위성을 요격할 수 있는 기술을 가진 3번째 나라라고 했기 때문에 아직 요격 기술을 가진 나라는 얼마 되지 않는다는 것도 추론할 수 있다. 정답은 (c)로 모든 위성을 없애자는 말이 아니기 때문에 이 보기가 정답이 된다.

3. (d)에 나와 있는 내용은 '케슬러 신드롬'이라는 가상 시나리오이기 때문에 이를 사실로 보기에는 무리가 있다. 따라서 가능성이나 추측의 측면이 몇 년 후면 그런 일이 벌어질 것이라는 식으로 서술했기 때문에 본문의 내용과 달라 정답이 된다.

4. 일단 (b)와 (d)는 정답으로 적절하지 않다는 것이 명백하다. 그리고 (a)는 본문 마지막에 나오는 미국 국방부의 설명으로 적당하며, (c)는 본문에는 등장하지 않지만 중국이 미사일로 위성을 격추한 것에 대한 이유일 수 있다. 중국 또한 (a)의 이유로 위성을 격추했다고 보기에는 본문에 나와 있는 내용만으로는 근거가 빈약하지만 (c)는 그 자체로 본문에서 추론할 수 있는 내용이 아니기 때문에 정답은 (a)가 적합하다.

정답 1(b) 2(c) 3(d) 4(a)

Unit 25 | Food for thought
GMO(유전자변형)

식량의 혁명적 발달 가운데, 사용한 내역을 밝혀야만 하는 것이 두 가지 있다. 방사선조사식품과 GMO(유전자변형)식품이다. 정부가 안전성을 딱 부러지게 검증할 능력이 없어 국민에게 결정권을 남겨 둔 것이다. GMO는 과거엔

'녹색혁명'의 총아였다. 이러한 열기는 유전공학·생명공학을 1970~80년대 최고의 인기 학문으로 부상시키는 데 기여했다. '인류는 기하급수적으로 늘어나지만 식량은 산술급수적으로 늘어난다'는 맬더스의 『인구론』을 용도 폐기시키고 인류를 기아에서 해방시킬 것으로 기대를 모았다. 그러나 미국의 칼젠사가 최초의 GMO 작물인 잘 물러지지 않은 토마토(상품명, Flavr Savr)를 선보인 1994년 이후 여론이 반전됐다. 시민 단체와 일부 미디어가 새로운 토마토를 잠재적인 안전성을 담보할 수 없는 '프랑켄 푸드'(Franken food)로 낙인찍었기 때문이다. 이후 'GMO는 해롭다'는 막연한 인식이 사람들에게 뿌리내렸다. 현 시점에서 GMO의 안전성에 대한 판정은 아직 기대하긴 이르다 'GMO로 피해를 본 것이 있으면 신고하라'고 채근하는 GMO 지지자와 '피해 사실을 입증할 순 없지만 무해하다는 것을 증명해보라'는 반대자 사이의 논쟁은 늘 결론을 내릴 수 없다.

문제해설

1. (a)의 경우, GMO와 같은 식품을 미디어에서는 절대 허용하지 않을 것이란 주장은 극단적이다. 과학적으로 검증이 된다면 굳이 언론에서 반대할 필요가 없기 때문이다. 그리고 (b)의 경우와 같이, 칼젠사가 성공했다고 GMO 시장이 성공이란 보장은 없다. 물론 그럴 가능성은 있지만 칼젠사의 성공이 GMO의 성공을 보장해주지 않기 때문에 적절한 추론이 될 수 없다. 예를 들어 칼젠사가 성공한 후에라도 GMO의 식품 건강에 논란을 가져올 제2, 제3의 칼젠사가 등장한다면 상황은 달라질 수 있기 때문이다. 정답은 (c)로 만일 GMO의 안전성이 판명되었다면 기아의 종식(the end of hunger)을 가져올 수 있을 것이라고 본문 중반에 서술하고 있다. 마지막으로 GMO를 입증하지 못하고 있는 것은 사실이지만 해로울 가능성이 매우 크다는 것을 추론할 내용은 본문에 등장하지 않는다.
2. GMO 토마토는 잘 물러지지 않는다고 했으므로 정답은 (d)가 된다.
3. GMO 식품을 "Franken-food"라고 묘사한 것은 괴물이 등장하는 소설에 빗댄 표현이기 때문에 정답은 (a)가 된다. 유전자 조작을 죽은 시신을 조작해 괴물을 만든 프랑켄슈타인 소설에 비유하고 있다.
4. 이 글은 (a)의 주장처럼 GMO를 만드는 프로세스에 대한 글이 아니다. 그리고 언론이 어떤 식으로 사람들의 인식을 바꿔 놓았는가에 관한 글도 아니기 때문에 (c)는 적절하지 않다. 그리고 이 글은 기아를 없앨 수 있는 방법을 찾기 위해 서술된 글도 아니다. 따라서 이 글은 식품공학으로 탄생한 GMO와 이것이 사회에 미친 영향이라는 (b)가 주제문으로 가장 적합하다.

정답 1(c) 2(d) 3(a) 4(b)

Unit 26 | Temperamental children
라니냐

1989년 3월 24일 알래스카 연안에 유조선 엑슨 발데즈 호가 좌초돼 엄청난 양의 원유를 바다에 쏟아냈다. 빙산을 피하기 위해 항로를 이탈한 게 원인이었다. 빙산은 해류의 방향이 바뀐 때문이었고 그 뒤에는 라니냐(La Niña)가 버티고 있었다. 엘니뇨와 라니냐는 반대 현상이지만, 대부분의 경우 엘니뇨 이후에 라니냐가 따라온다. 적도 부근 동태평양 바닷물이 평상시보다 0.5℃ 이상 더워져 5개월 이상 지속되면 엘니뇨이고, 0.5℃ 이상 더 낮아지면 라니냐다. '니뇨'는 스페인어로 남자 아이, 즉 아기 예수를 뜻하고, '니냐'는 여자 아이를 뜻한다. 엘니뇨는 19세기 페루 연안 어민들도 알고 있었다. 수온이 올라가면 생선이 제대로 잡히지 않았다.

엘니뇨를 처음 과학적으로 규명한 것은 1923년 영국 수학자 길버트 토마스 워커였다. 그는 40년 치 기상 자료를 수집해 분석했다. 그 결과 타히티 동쪽 남태평양 해역과 호주 다윈 서쪽의 인도양 해역 사이에서 해수면 기압이 시소처럼 오르내리는 것을 발견했다. 한쪽 기압이 올라가면 다른 쪽은 내려갔다. 워커는 이를 남방진동이라 불렀다. 남방진동과 엘니뇨·라니냐는 동전의 양면이다. 남방진동이 기압 시소라면 엘니뇨·라니냐는 바닷물 온도의 시소다. 인도양쪽 기압이 올라가면 엘니뇨가 시작된다. 무역풍이 강해지면 찬 바닷물이 솟아나고 수온은 낮아져 라니냐가 나타난다. 엘니뇨 때엔 페루·에콰도르에 홍수가, 동남아·호주에 가뭄이 든다. 라니냐 때엔 동남아에 장마가 지고, 남미엔 가뭄이 든다.

문제해설

1. 특정 기상 현상인 엘니뇨와 라니냐에 관한 설명이므로 정답은 (b)가 된다.
2. (c)와 (d)는 특정 현상만을 지칭하는 것이다. (c)는 엘니뇨에 대한 설명이고, (d)는 라니냐에 대한 설명이다. 그리고 이 두 현상은 남자 아이와 여자 아이에서 명명되었지만 어린 아이들을 지칭하는 것은 아니므로 (b)는 답이 될 수 없다. 정답은 (a)로 남방진동이라고 불린다는 것과 두 현상이 서로 반대되는 기상 조건을 일으킨다는 것을 알 수 있으므로 정답이 된다.
3. 첫 번째 문단 후반부에 보면 엘니뇨는 이미 19세기에 페루 연안 어민들에게도 알려져 있었다고 나오므로 이들이 이런 현상에 이름을 붙여놓았다는 것을 알 수 있다. 따라서 정답은 (d)가 된다.
4. 엘니뇨와 라니냐는 동전의 양면과 같다고 했으므로 (a)는 올바르며, 두 번째 문단의 마지막 부분을 통해 이 둘이 서로 다른 기상 조건을 일으킴을 알 수 있으므로 (b) 또한 올바르다. 엘니뇨와 라니냐는 홍수나 가뭄을 동반하기 때문에 심각한 경제적 피해를 줄 수 있음을 유추할 수 있으므로(어획량에 대한 부분도 설명되어 있음) (d)도 올바르다. 정답은 (c)로 특정 현상이 5개월 이상 지속되어야 한다거나 40년간의 기상자료를 분석해 이들 현상을 밝혀냈다는 것 등을 토대로 추론했을 때 아주 빠른 속도로 일어나는 현상은 아님을 알 수 있다.

정답 1(b) 2(a) 3(d) 4(c)

Unit 27 | New materials, old weapons
다마스쿠스 검

　다마스쿠스 검(劍)은 세계에서 가장 신비한 무기 중 하나로 여겨진다. 인도산 철강을 수입해 시리아 지역에서 만든 역사상 최강의 칼로 추정된다. 다마스쿠스 검(劍)의 명성 때문에 로마군은 감히 사산조 페르시아를 넘보지 못했다. 유럽 십자군도 예루살렘에서 살라딘이 이끄는 이슬람군에게 밀려났다. 대조적으로, 이 시기의 육중하고 투박한 유럽의 칼은 가볍고 예리한 다마스쿠스 검에 상대가 되지 않았다. 상대방의 칼을 두 동강 내고 갑옷을 뚫었다는 기록도 남아있다.

　다마스쿠스 검(劍)은 표면에 '무함마드의 사다리'라고 하는 무늬가 새겨져 있다. 이 칼은 아름답지만 제조 방법은 끔찍했다. 기록된 연대기에는 "왕의 옷과 같은 자홍색이 날 때까지 쇠를 달군 뒤 튼튼한 노예의 근육에 찔러 넣어 식힌다"고 했다. 그래야 "노예의 힘과 영혼이 옮겨가 날카롭고 단단한 칼을 얻는다"는 것이다.

　이 칼은 지금은 희귀해서 자취를 찾기 어려운 보물이다. 1750년 무렵, 인도의 철강이 고갈되면서 흥미와 호기심을 더한다. 현대 금속학계는 이 칼을 극소량의 바나듐과 몰리브덴이 포함된 탄소 합금으로 분류한다. 이 불순물들이 탄소와 결합해 강도를 크게 높였다는 것이다.

　그러나 2년 전 과학 잡지『네이처』지에 실린 발견 내용은 세상을 놀라게 했다. 독일 드레스덴 대학 연구팀이 전자현미경을 이용해 이 검의 분자 구성에서 탄소 나노선과 나노튜브를 발견한 것이다. 최첨단 신소재가 800년 된 수수께끼의 칼에도 숨어있는 셈이다.

문제해설

1. 다마스쿠스 검은 시리아 지역에서 생산된 검으로 로마군이나 십자군의 갑옷도 뚫었다는 내용이 나오지만 (b)의 내용은 등장하지 않는다. 검이 가벼웠다고 했으며, 표면에 새겨진 무늬가 아름답다는 내용은 나오지만 적들이 이런 문양에 홀려 패했다는 내용은 등장하지 않는다. 또한 이 검이 무거웠다는 내용은 찾아볼 수 없다. 따라서 정답은 이 검이 가볍고 날카로웠다고 설명하는 (a)가 된다.

2. 두 번째 문단에 다마스쿠스 검의 제조법이 나온다. "왕의 옷과 같은 자홍색이 날 때까지 쇠를 달군 뒤 튼튼한 노예의 근육에 찔러넣어 식힌다"는 것이다. 이에 대해 서술한 (d)가 정답이 된다.

3. 현대에 발견된 나노 기술이 이미 당시에 사용되었다는 말이므로, 당시 기술이 매우 진보한 것임을 알 수 있다. 따라서 정답은 (d)가 된다.

4. 무함마드의 사다리는 칼의 양면에 새겨진 문양이지 칼날의 모양을 의미하지 않는다. 그리고 세 번째 문단에서 인도 철강이 고갈되면서 이제는 이 검을 찾기 어렵다고 했다. 따라서 (a)와 (b) 모두 정답이 아니다. (d)의 경우 2번째로 강한 검이라고 했으므로 틀렸다. 정답은 (c)로 첫 번째 문단의 "Owing to the Damascus swords' reputation, the Roman army didn't dare attack the Sassanid Empire." 부분을 통해 알 수 있는데, 심지어 그 명성만으로도 감히 전쟁을 벌일 생각조차 하지 못했을 것이며, 그 명성만으로도 시리아군을 두렵게 만들 수 있다는 추론이 가능하다.

정답 1(a)　2(d)　3(d)　4(c)

Unit 28 | Shame on Volkswagen
폭스바겐의 사기극을 보며

　'우리는 몰라서 속았던 걸까?' 폭스바겐의 배기가스 실험 조작 사기극의 내막이 밝혀지면서 처음 든 생각은 이거였다. 우리는 폭스바겐을 비롯한 독일계 자동차 회사들이 2000년대 중반 '클린 디젤' 기술 홍보에 열을 올리던 장면을 기억한다. 유럽 승용차 업체들은 디젤 승용차를 한국에 도입하며 공격적으로 마케팅을 펼쳤다.

　당시 디젤차의 이미지는 나빴다. 한국에서 디젤차는 시커먼 매연가스를 풍풍 풍겼던 매연 버스로 기억되고 있었다. 한데 클린 디젤이라니. 디젤이 가솔린에 비해 연비와 힘이 좋고 이산화탄소 배출은 적지만, 세계보건기구(WHO)도 일급 발암물질로 지정한 산화질소와 미세먼지를 배출한다는 건 상식에 속한다. 한데 "이런 디젤이 어떻게 청정이냐"고 의문을 제기하면 이들 자동차 업계 관계자는 디젤 엔진의 청정성을 증명하는 각종 실험 자료들을 들이밀면서 반박했다. 그들은 세계 최고 수준의 독일 자동차 기술로 연료를 완전연소시키고 매연을 잡는 기술을 실현했으며, 유럽이 지금 디젤차 중심으로 가고 있는 게 청정 디젤 기술의 신뢰성을 보여주는 것이라고 외쳤다.

　실제로 1990년대 중반부터 유럽연합(EU) 회원국들은 디젤 엔진 사용을 촉진하는 다양한 정책을 내놨다. 더 낮은 세율이나 장기적인 세금 혜택 등의 정책들이다. 90년대 초반까지 유럽에서 낮은 비중을 차지했던 디젤 차량이었는데, 현재는 35%에 이르는 차량이 디젤 엔진을 사용한다. 어쩌면 우리는 독일 자동차 기술과 친환경 유럽의 명성이라는 허구에 눈이 가려져 상식을 내다버렸는지도 모른다.

　일각에선 현대자동차의 반사이익을 운운한다. 하지만 주식시장의 냉담한 반응만이 아니더라도 이번 사태에서 공격적으로 디젤을 도입했던 국산차들이 무슨 반사이익을 얻겠는가. 만약 디젤 진영이 이대로 주저앉는다면 한국의 자동차 업계는 손실을 볼 수도 있다. 폭스바겐 디젤차가 '실험실에선 청정, 실제 주행에선 오염원 배출' 사실이 들통나고 각국의 조사가 전 디젤차로 확산되면서 일각에선 벌써 진정한 청정차로 '전기차' 대안론이 나온다. 어떤 연구자들은 전기 생산 과정의 대기오염을 생각한다면 전기차의 대기 질 개선 효과가 거의 없다고 말한다. 또 전기차는 대용량 배터리를 장착해야 하는데 배터리는 일정 충전 주기가 되면 성능이 떨어져 교체해야 한다. 이런 배터리는 리튬을 포함한 각종 광물질로 구성된다. 전기차의 대중화는 배터리 폐기물로 인한 오염을 가져올 것이다.

결국 완벽한 청정차는 없다. 미국의 한 자동차 잡지는 "합리적 가격의 클린 디젤은 말이 안 되는 목표였다"는 전직 폴크스바겐 임원의 고백을 실었다. 연료를 태우며 움직이는 차량이 환경에 이로울 방법은 애초에 없는데, 기술로 극복할 수 있는 것처럼 위장해 환경에 대한 죄책감을 덜어보자는 속셈이 소비자와 기업 사이에 맞아떨어져 청정차 신화를 퍼뜨리고 있는 것일 뿐이다. 어쩌면 우리도 청정 디젤이 허구임을 이성적으로 알고 있었을지도 모른다. 하지만 힘 좋고 연비 좋고 명망 높은 독일차를 타면서 환경도 위한다는 명분까지 세우고 싶었던 소비자 이기심이 발동해 모른 척 눈감았을 수도 있다. 폴크스바겐의 부정직성을 질타하는 것뿐만 아니라 소비자로서 나의 정직성에 대해서도 돌아봐야 하는 것은 아닐까.

문제해설

1. 이 글은 소비자들을 대상으로 과연 그들이 정말 배기가스의 해로움에 관해 몰랐는지 혹은 알면서도 모르는 척했던 것은 아닌지 지적하는 것이 목적이지 자동차 생산자들을 질타하려는 것은 아니다. 이를 가장 잘 보여주는 것은 본문의 첫 문장이다. 그러므로 혹 독자들이 '깨끗한 디젤'이라는 사기에 가담한 것은 아닌지를 본인 스스로에게 질문하는 (c)가 정답이다. (b)가 답이 아닌 이유는 단순히 왜 사람들이 명백한 사실을 부정하고 잘못된 것을 믿는지를 이야기하는 것과는 달리 본문에선 구체적으로 배기가스 실험 조작에 초점을 두고 있기 때문이다. 만일 (b)가 답이 되려면 배기가스뿐만 아니라 다른 사례들도 함께 제시되어야 할 것이다.

2. 두 번째 단락의 "If anyone raises a question how diesel can be clean, automakers refuted by presenting various test results proving how clean diesel engines can be" 문장에서 디젤이 과연 깨끗한지에 관해 의문을 갖는다면 자동차 업계 관계자는 다양한 실험 결과를 보여주며 이를 반박했다는 점에서 (d)는 올바른 내용임을 알 수 있다.

3. 마지막 단락의 문장 "But we may have turned blind eye to drive a powerful, efficient and brand-name German car and claim to be environmentally at the same time"을 통해 우리는 자동차 업계의 잘못된 주장들을 믿고 싶어 했다는 점을 알 수 있다.

4. 첫 문장에서 "우리는 과연 몰랐던 것일까?"라는 질문을 시작으로, 이 글은 그저 브랜드의 명성에 기대는 소비자를 지적하고 폴크스바겐의 사기극을 보며 소비자의 무거운 의무에 대해 숙고해봐야 한다고 주장한다. 그러므로 오로지 폴크스바겐의 정직성을 질타하기보다는 소비자들도 자신이 과연 그것을 알면서도 모른 척했던 것은 아닌지 돌아봐야 한다고 하는 것이 맞다.

정답 1(c) 2(d) 3(d) 4(a)

Unit 29 | Surveillance has a role
CCTV

세계적인 사생활 보호 NGO단체인 GILC(Global Internet Liberty Campaign)는 사생활을 네 가지 범주로 나눈다. 정보·신체·통신·공간 프라이버시다. 공간 프라이버시를 침해하는 대표선수는 주거지, 작업장, 공공장소에 설치되는 CCTV다. 외부침입, 도난방지 등을 내세운 감시 시스템이다. 세계적으로 CCTV가 많은 나라 중 하나가 영국이다. 420만 개에 이른다. 전 세계적으로 2,000만 개의 CCTV가 있는 것으로 추정되니, 세계 인구의 1%밖에 안 되는 나라에 전 세계 CCTV의 20%가 있는 셈이다. 통상적인 공공장소, 주요 건물뿐 아니라 길거리 곳곳에 설치돼 있다. CCTV 중심지답게 기술도 계속 발전한다. 영국 경찰은 하늘을 나는 CCTV를 도입했다. 군사용으로 제작된 초소형 무인 정찰기에 최첨단 CCTV를 장착해, 500m 상공에서 고해상도 영상을 촬영할 수 있다. 범죄를 저지를 것 같은 사람을 미리 판별해내는 지능형 CCTV 기술도 시험 중이다. 카메라 8대를 배치해 사람들을 관찰하면서 수상한 행동패턴을 보이는 이를 짚어내는 소프트웨어가 깔려 있다. 범죄를 저지르거나 나쁜 행동을 하면 말로 꾸짖는 CCTV도 있다. 실제는 카메라에 달린 스피커를 통해 감시원이 경고하는 것이다. 사생활 침해 논란이 끊이지 않지만 CCTV에 대한 국민감정도 부정적이지만은 않다. 2005년 7월 런던 버스·지하철 폭탄테러 용의자를 잡는 데 CCTV가 결정적 역할을 했다. 그 이후에는 기술이 발달하면서 범죄가 발생하면 당일 저녁 BBC 뉴스에 CCTV 화면이 공개될 정도다. CCTV 1대가 경찰 10명에 준한다는 말도 나온다. 공교롭게도, 소설 『1984』를 통해 '빅 브라더'라는 감시 시스템에 대해 경고했던 조지 오웰은 영국인이다.

문제해설

1. '빅 브라더'는 행동 하나하나를 감시하는 거대 독재 권력을 지칭한다. 따라서 어린 동생들을 감시하는 맏형과도 같이 시민들을 감시하는 정부라는 의미의 (b)가 정답이 된다. 컴퓨터나 카메라를 의미하지 않고, 남을 못살게 구는 bully도 거리가 멀다.

2. 영국의 거리 곳곳에 CCTV가 설치되어 있고, 하늘을 나는 CCTV까지 도입한 것으로 봐서 영국 정부는 감시 카메라가 범죄 예방에 도움이 된다고 생각하는 것을 알 수 있다. 감시카메라 1대가 경찰 10명에 맞먹는다는 내용이 있지만 향후에는 정규군을 대체할 것이라는 것은 지나친 추론이며, (c)와 (d)는 본문과 무관하다.

3. CCTV의 광범위한 사용과 긍정적 측면에서 기술하면서 마지막에는 개인의 사생활을 침해받는 '빅 브라더' 얘기를 한 것으로 봐서 두 가지 관점을 모두 포함하고 있는 것을 알 수 있다. 따라서 개인의 사생활을 감수하면서까지 광범위하게 사용되는 CCTV가 과연 가치가 있는지를 묻고 있다는 (c)가 정답이 된다.

4. 본문 중반의 "As a CCTV stronghold, the United Kingdom is

continuously developing its technology." 부분을 통해 (a)를 추론할 수 있다.

정답 1 (b) 2 (a) 3 (c) 4 (a)

Unit 30 | Joining the space club
우주인

냉전 시대 미국과의 경쟁에서 유일하게 옛 소련이 앞섰던 분야는 우주 개발이었다. 1957년 인공위성 스푸트니크를 쏘아 올린 소련은 4년 뒤엔 최초의 우주비행사 유리 가가린을 탑승시킨 우주선 보스토크 1호를 대기권 밖으로 올려 보냈다. 유리 가가린 중위는 육안으로 확인한 사실을 인류에게 전했다. "지구는 푸른색이다." 더불어 "열심히 찾아보았지만 우주에 신은 없었다"는 말도 남겼다. 변증법적 유물론을 신봉하는 소련 군인에게는 당연한 얘기였다.

미국의 코는 납작해졌다. "보드카 제조와 발레 빼고는 잘하는 게 없는 줄 알았던" 소련에게 우주에 나아갈 첫 번째 나라가 될 선수를 빼앗긴 것은 일본군에 의한 '진주만 기습' 이래 가장 큰 충격이었다. 가가린의 위업을 가능하게 한 우주 개발 책임자는 세르게이 코롤료프 박사였다. 하지만 그는 말 그대로 '이름 없는 영웅'이었다. 코롤료프가 암살당할 것을 두려워한 소련 당국은 1966년 숨질 때까지 그의 이름을 1급 기밀에 부쳤다. 최초의 유인 우주비행을 성공시킨 사람에게 노벨상을 주겠다는 제의도 물리쳤다.

당시에 우주 개발은 이처럼 강대국들이 국운을 걸고 달려든 프로젝트였다. 그 속성상 군사 기술과 불가분의 관계이기 때문이다. 2003년 중국이 세계 3번째로 유인 우주선 발사에 성공한 것도 오랜 기간 축적한 군사력 덕분이었다. 민간 경제 부문으로의 기술 파급효과 또한 막대하며, 그러기에 강대국들은 우주 기술 공유에 인색하다.

문제해설

1. "우주에 가서 열심히 찾아 봤지만 신을 찾을 수 없었다"는 유리 가가린의 말이므로, (a)와 같이 원래부터 무신론자였고, 신의 존재는 없다는 것을 널리 알리고 싶었다는 내용이 정답으로 적당하다. 신자가 아니어서 볼 수 없었다는 말은 신의 존재를 믿는 사람들이 할법한 말이고, 시간이 없었다거나 아니면 신이 우주의 다른 곳에 있었기 때문이라는 것은 적절한 설명이 될 수 없다.

2. 우주 개발은 군사 기술과 불가분의 관계라고 마지막 문단에서 거론하고 있으므로, 정답은 (a)임을 알 수 있다. 중국이 군사 기밀을 훔친 것이라는 내용은 등장하지 않으며, 미국의 경우 소련의 우주 비행으로 코가 납작해졌다고 했으므로 도전으로 받아들였다고 할 수 없다. (d) 또한 미국이 그럴 의도가 있었는지는 전혀 알 수 없다.

3. (a)와 (b)도 일부 수긍이 가는 부분이 있지만 (c)에서와 같이 자국의 군사력(military might)과 경제력을 과시(demonstration)하는 것이라는 설명이 더 적절하다.

4. 본문은 우주 개발에 초점을 두고 있지 노벨상에 대한 서술은 아니다.

또한 소련과 중국의 예가 모두 등장하고 있으므로 어떤 방식으로 소련이 미국을 앞질렀는가에 대한 내용도 아니다. 과정도 소상히 나와 있지 않다. 그리고 중국의 부상만을 다루고 있지 않기 때문에 (d)도 적절하지 않다. 정답은 20세기의 우주 개발 경쟁이라고 보는 것이 타당하다.

정답 1 (a) 2 (a) 3 (c) 4 (c)

Unit 31 | Flying pandemics
조류 인플루엔자

1918년 3월 11일에 미국 캔자스 주 포트 라일리의 캠프 펀스턴 내 군병원은 하루 종일 비슷한 증상을 보이는 유난히 많은 군인들을 치료하느라 분주했다. '감기에 걸린 것 같다'는 병사가 수백 명 넘게 몰려왔기 때문이다. 이들 중 일부는 며칠 뒤 1차 대전에 참전하기 위해 유럽으로 향했다. 그해 5월 프랑스군의 참호에서 '감기'가 돌았다. 6월엔 스페인에서만 800만여 명의 '감기' 환자가 발생했다. 이 역병을 프랑스인은 '스페인 감기', 스페인인은 '프랑스 감기'라 불렀다. 인플루엔자는 프랑스군이 독일군을 향해 쏘아 올린 포탄보다 더 위력적이었다. 그해 여름이 끝날 무렵 인플루엔자는 독일군 막사를 덮쳤고 독일에서만 40만 명이 생명을 잃었다. 재앙은 아시아로 건너가 인도·중국을 휩쓸었다. 1918년 전 세계적으로 퍼진 유행성 전염병(pandemic)은 이듬해까지 지속되었고, 세계는 패닉 상태에 빠졌다. 더 놀라운 사실은 대재앙이 너무 빨리 잊혔다는 것이다. 지금도 가장 치명적인 유행병이었던 중세의 흑사병(黑死病)은 알아도 20세기의 '스페인 감기'는 모르는 사람이 더 많다. 그 대재앙의 주 원인은 감기 바이러스가 아니고, 인플루엔자(독감) 바이러스였다. 2005년 미 군사병리연구소 제프리 타우벤버거 박사는 1918년 발생한 유행성 전염병의 바이러스 유전자 물질을 밝혀내는 데 성공한다. 그는 보존 조직에서 1918년의 바이러스 샘플을 추출해서 게놈 배열을 한 업적으로 잘 알려졌다. 그는 조류독감이 발생했던 해인 1918년에 사망한 후 80년 동안 알래스카의 얼음 속에 묻혀있던 원주민 남성의 사체에 대한 심층적인 연구를 수행했다. 그도 처음엔 '범인'이 돼지일 것으로 봤다. 돼지인플루엔자는 인수공통 전염병으로 사람에게 전염 가능하다. 그러나 시신에서 얻은 바이러스 유전자를 면밀히 검토한 뒤 조류에서 유래했다는 결론을 내린다.

문제해설

1. 1차 대전 당시 독감 바이러스는 유행성 전염병을 일으켰으므로 엄청난 파괴력을 지녔음을 짐작할 수 있다. 그리고 독감에 걸린 미군들이 유럽에 참전하러 가면서 프랑스와 스페인, 독일에서 바이러스가 퍼졌으므로 전쟁이 없었다면 그렇게까지 심각한 지경에 이르지 않았을지 모른다는 (c)는 일리가 있다. 중세의 흑사병은 알아도 당시의 독감은 금세 잊혔다고 했으므로 (d)도 바른 추론이다. 정답은 (b)로 치료약을

과학자들이 개발했다는 내용은 등장하지 않는다.
2. 스페인과 프랑스에서 서로 상대 국가의 독감이라고 부른 것은 바이러스 유입에 대한 책임을 떠넘기려 한 것이므로, 그리고 실제로 어디에서 유입됐는지 알지 못한 것이므로 정답은 (c)가 적합하다.
3. 처음에는 돼지일 것으로 의심됐지만 알고 보니 조류에서 넘어온 것이라고 마지막 부분에 설명되어 있다.
4. 유행병이 있던 해 숨져 80년간 알래스카의 얼음 속에 묻혀 있던 원주민의 시신에서 바이러스 샘플을 추출한 것이므로 (a)와 (b)는 적합하지 않다. 그리고 프랑스에 바이러스를 옮긴 나라는 미국이었다. 정답은 (d)로 원래는 돼지에서 유래했을 것으로 생각했지만 사실은 조류에서 넘어온 것이었다고 나온다.

정답 1(b) 2(c) 3(a) 4(d)

Unit 32 | Mobile gold rush
도시광업

골드러시가 성행하던 19세기 중반 호주 빅토리아 주 벤디고의 한 호텔 바에는 인근에서 금을 찾은 후 이를 축하하기 위해 몰려든 광부들로 항상 북적였다. 바닥 청소를 담당하던 이들은 처음엔 청소할 일이 많아 투덜거렸지만 이내 불평을 멈추었다. 청소를 하면서 광부들 장화에서 떨어진 금가루를 긁어모을 수 있었기 때문이다. 그 당시에는 전 세계 노동자들이 몰려들어 세계 금 생산량의 40%를 채굴하였다. 오지를 마다않고 노다지를 캐러 몰려들던 사람들은 이젠 찰리 채플린의 영화에서나 볼 수 있을 뿐이다. 사람의 손길이 닿지 않은 전인미답의 금광이 급격히 줄었기 때문이다.

대신에 21세기에는 도시에서 광업이 행해지고 있다. 선진국에서는 폐전자제품 등 각종 산업 폐기물에서 유용한 광물을 찾아내는 이른바 도시 광업(urban mining)이 주목을 받고 있다. 휴대전화 한 대에는 평균 6.8mg의 금이 들어있다. 1,000대면 금 6.8g이 들어있다는 것이다. 작고 가벼운 것이 첨단 전자 기기에 들어가는 금의 표준이 되고 있다. 대부분 휴대전화의 회로판에는 금이 사용되는데 전도성이 뛰어나기 때문이다. 그 양도 절대 무시할 수 없다. 금광에서 채굴하는 원광 1t에서 얻을 수 있는 금의 양이 겨우 5g에 불과한데 비해, 못쓰게 된 휴대폰 1t을 분해하면 그 30배에 달하는 150g 이상의 금을 얻을 수 있다. 뿐만 아니라 폐휴대폰 1t에서는 구리 100kg과 은 3kg, 그밖에 이리듐 등 각종 희소 금속을 캐낼 수 있다.

문제해설
1. 선진국에서는 각종 폐기물에서 유용한 광물을 찾아내는 도시 광업(urban mining)이 주목을 받고 있다고 말하면서 사용하지 않는 휴대폰에서 희귀 금속을 추출할 수 있다고 했으므로 귀금속을 얻을 수 있는 새로운 원천이 생겼다는 (c)가 정답이 된다.
2. 불평을 했던 이들은 호텔 바에서 바닥을 청소하던 이들로 몰려드는 광부들로 인해 할 일이 많아서였다. 따라서 (c)가 본문과 상이한 내용이다.
3. 이 글은 사람들에게 투자를 권유하거나 폐가전에서 희소 금속을 찾는 데 동참하도록 권유하는 내용은 아니다. 이전에는 광산 등지에서 금을 채굴했지만 이제는 새로운 곳에서 원하는 금속을 얻을 수 있다는 내용이므로 정답은 (c)가 적합하다.
4. 주제문이 후반에 등장하기 때문에, 제목은 도시 광업(urban mining)이 적절하다.

정답 1(c) 2(c) 3(c) 4(a)

Unit 33 | Risk management
위험사회

1986년 4월 구소련(현 우크라이나)의 체르노빌 원자력 발전소에서 사상 최대의 원전사고가 일어났다. 4호기의 폭발로 약 10톤가량의 방사성 물질이 방출됐다. 히로시마에 투하된 원자폭탄보다 훨씬 더 많은 양이 방출됐다. 기밀 누설과 주민 불안 등을 이유로 소련 정부가 사건을 은폐하는 동안 피해는 커졌다. 인근 국가들까지 공포에 떨었다.

체르노빌 원전 사고의 충격을 목도한 독일의 사회학자 울리히 벡은 『위험사회』를 발표했다. 산업화·근대화가 기술 발달과 물질적 풍요를 가져오지만 그만큼 내재된 위험도 커진다는 '위험사회론'이다. 벡의 위험사회론은 그저 재앙이 많을 뿐 아니라 재앙이 현대 사회의 한 구조적 요소가 됐다는 뜻이다. 재난과 관련된 파국성을 일상생활 안에 안고 살아가는 사회라는 뜻이다.

위험에는 생태학적 재앙, 핵 관련 사고, 실업과 금융대란, 환경파괴, 지구 온난화 등이 포함된다. 이처럼 위험이 반복 재생산되는 가운데, 위험에 대한 자각은 무뎌지며 통제 역시 불가능해진다. 위험이 세계화됨에 따라 모든 사람이 영향을 받는다. 기름유출 사고에서 보듯 정밀한 피해 계산도 책임 배상도 쉽지 않다. 벡은 "국민이 대처할 수 있는 위험에는 어떤 것이 있으며, 국가가 우선 관리할 위험은 어떤 것인가에 관해 국가와 국민이 신중하게 논의하고 그에 관한 합의를 도출해내는 것이 중요하다"고 말했다.

문제해설
1. 예전에는 대참사가 발생하려면 자연 재해나 전쟁 등 평소에는 볼 수 없는 것들이었지만, 시대가 바뀌면서 일상생활에서도 대형 참사를 겪을 수 있는 그런 사회가 되었다는 내용이다. 따라서 엄청난 재난을 가져올 수 있는 일을 평소에도 하고 있다는 내용인 (c)가 정답이 된다.
2. 마지막 문단에서 "Thus risks are repeatedly produced and our awareness of the dangers become muted"라고 했으므로 위험이 매번 반복돼서 이에 무덤덤해지고 결국에는 위험에 대한 인식(awareness)조차 잘 하지 못한다고 서술되어 있다. 따라서 (d)에서처럼 너무 흔해서 이런 위험에 대해 주목(notice)하지 않는다고 볼 수 있다.

3. 두 번째 문단의 "industrialization and modernization brings technological development and material prosperity, but also greater risk" 부분을 통해 현대 사회가 안고 있는 내재된 위험을 알 수 있으며, 세 번째 문단의 "Thus risks are repeatedly produced and our awareness of the dangers become muted, as does their control." 부분을 통해 이런 위험에서 사람들의 자각이 무뎌진 것을 알 수 있으므로 (a)가 적합하다.

4. 마지막 문장에서 독일의 사회학자 울리히 벡의 발언을 통해 짐작할 수 있다. "It is important ... what risks they can handle and what risks it would first manage ..."라는 부분을 통해 사람들이 직면하는 위험에 대한 평가와 이를 국가가 어떻게 대응할 것인지에 관한 행동 계획이 올 것으로 추론할 수 있다.

정답 1(c) 2(d) 3(a) 4(c)

가물가물할 줄 미처 예상하지 못했다(I didn't expect it would be so hard to recall what my day was like just two days ago – not one month ago.)"라고 나와 있다.

2. 기억의 미로를 헤맨다는 것은 바로 기억을 떠올리기 위해 안간힘을 쓰며 기억을 재생시키려고 애쓰는 것을 의미한다. 그러므로 (c)가 정답이다.

3. 처음부터 난관에 부딪쳤다(I struggled from the beginning)고 하였으므로 정답은 (a)이다.

4. 우리의 기억이란 것도 왜곡·소실·변형·주입되기 쉬우므로 주의할 필요가 있다는 것이다.

정답 1(d) 2(c) 3(a) 4(b)

Unit 34 | Remembering the day before yesterday
기억력

사람의 뇌는 나이가 들수록 단기 기억을 장기 기억으로 바꿔 저장하는 능력이 떨어진다. 기억력 약화를 늦추는 방법으로 일본의 시라사와 다쿠지 박사가 권한 것은 이틀 전 일을 기억해 일기를 쓰는 것이었다. 나는 6월 초 일기를 쓰기 시작했다.

처음부터 난관투성이였다. 한 달도 아니고 바로 이틀 전의 내 하루가 이렇게 가물가물할 줄 미처 예상하지 못했다. 점심을 누구와 먹었는지, 저녁은 어떻게 보냈는지 떠오르지 않는 경우가 많았다. 직장 동료 네 명이 외부 인사와 함께 점심 먹은 것까지는 기억났지만, 그중 세 명밖에 기억나지 않았다.

한 시간 이상 기억의 미로를 헤매다 그 외부 인사가 우리 동료 한 명에게 책자를 한 뭉치 준 것을 그가 사무실로 챙겨왔다는 사실이 머리를 스쳤다. 그 순간의 대화와 장면을 되살리자 비로소 얼굴·이름이 선명하게 떠올랐다. 시험에서 100점이라도 받은 양 기뻤고, 한편으론 나의 나빠진 기억력이 슬펐다. 고백하자면 내 일기 내용 중 3분의 1 정도는 일정을 따로 기록해 둔 수첩을 참고하며 적어야 했다.

동물학자들에 따르면 침팬지·오랑우탄도 3년 전 일을 기억하는 능력이 있다고 한다. 덴마크 과학자들이 침팬지 15마리, 오랑우탄 4마리를 대상으로 먹이를 구하는 데 필요한 도구를 어디서 찾는지 보여주고 나서, 3년 뒤 그 영장류들을 같은 환경에 놓이게 했더니 도구가 있던 장소를 금세 기억하더라는 것이다. 과연 조상을 인간과 공유하는 유인원답다. 사람의 기억력이 지구 생물 중에서는 가장 뛰어나기는 하지만, 그 기억력이란 것도 왜곡·소실·변형·주입되기 쉬워 마냥 자신할 것만은 아니다.

문제해설

1. 필자는 이틀 전 일기를 쓰려고 했을 때 생각처럼 쉽지 않음을 알게 되었다. 본문에도 "한 달도 아니고 바로 이틀 전의 내 하루가 이렇게

Unit 35 | Life on Mars
화성

외계 생명체가 존재하느냐는 의문은 오래 전부터 인류의 상상력을 자극했다. 인류는 우주탐사선을 직접 띄워 우주를 탐험하기 시작했다. 특히 지구에서 7,800만km 떨어진 화성에 생명체가 존재하느냐를 밝히기 위해 1975년과 1976년에 미 항공우주국(NASA)의 바이킹 프로그램의 일환으로 각각 바이킹 1호와 2호를 발사했고, 이후 지구로 많은 자료를 보내왔다. 현재는 NASA의 탐사로봇 피닉스가 화성 북극에 착륙해 임무를 수행하며 계속 사진을 보내오고 있다. 과학자들은 화성에 물이 얼어붙은 대형 호수가 존재하고 있어 생명체가 존재할 가능성이 있다고 판단한다. 하지만 화성이 태양과의 거리, 공전주기 등에서 지구와 비슷하다고는 해도 기후가 너무도 가혹하기 때문에 생명체가 살 수 없다. 화성 지표면 부근의 평균 기온이 지구의 영상 13도보다 크게 낮은 영하 53도나 된다. 제임스 러브록의 '가이아(Gaia) 이론'에 따르면, 공기나 땅, 물 등과 같은 우리 세계의 여러 요소들이 합쳐져 복잡한 시스템을 구성하고 있다는 것이다. 러브록은 시스템이 생명체를 지탱할 수 있는 것은 기후와 기타 조건들이 각기 다른 구성 요소들의 상호작용을 통해 균형을 유지하고 있기 때문이란다. 이 이론의 근본에는 지구가 단일한 유기체이며, 그 위의 모든 것은 전체의 일부라는 생각이 자리 잡고 있다. 많은 이들이 지구 생태계가 온난화로 인해 심각한 상황에 처했다고 우려하고 있다.

문제해설

1. 화성에 탐사선을 보낸 이유는 본문 첫 문장에 나온 것과 같이 외계 생명체의 존재 유무를 확인하기 위해서였으므로 정답은 (d)가 된다.

2. 마지막 부분을 보면 '가이아의 이론'이 등장하면서 지구가 복잡한 시스템으로 다른 여러 요소들이 맞물려 균형을 유지하고 있다고 설명하고 있다. 즉 지구가 단일 유기체라는 설명인데, 현재 지구 생태계가 온난화 문제로 위기에 처했다고 말하고 있으므로 (b)와 같이 지구 온난화가 생태계에 어떤 영향을 미칠 것인지에 대한 내용이 다음 문장

23

에 나오는 것이 적절하다.
3. 바이킹 1호와 2호는 각각 1975년과 1976년에 화성으로 발사되었지 그 해에 착륙한 것은 확실하지 않기 때문에 정답은 (c)가 된다.
4. 본문 중간에서 "it cannot sustain life due to its brutal climate" 부분을 통해 화성에 생명체가 살기에는 기후가 적절하지 않다는 것을 알 수 있다. 따라서 정답은 (a)가 된다.

정답 1(d) 2(b) 3(c) 4(a)

Unit 36 | Unfounded fears
공포의 문화

1982년 4월 19일, 미국 NBC 방송은 'DPT: 백신 룰렛'이라는 한 시간짜리 프로그램을 방영했다. 백일해 백신 성분이 신경에 끔찍한 손상을 일으켜 죽음을 초래할 수 있다는 내용이었다. 심한 장애를 앓는 어린이의 영상과 가슴 저미는 부모들의 증언을 내보냈다. 이 내용은 그 후 몇 주에 걸쳐 NBC의 '투데이 쇼'와 여러 신문에서 다시 보도됐다. 그러자 전국의 모든 소아과 의사들에게 전화가 쇄도했다. (예방접종을 받은) 자기 자녀들이 곧 죽게 되느냐고 부모들이 문의했기 때문이다.

이에 대해 FDA(식품의약국)는 즉시 45쪽에 달하는 백신이 사망이나 심각한 합병증을 유발할 가능성은 극히 희박하다는 반박 자료를 배포했다. 그러나 대부분의 언론은 이 같은 해명을 축소 보도했다. 몇 주 만에 백신 피해자 단체가 결성돼 조직적으로 모금과 홍보 활동을 시작했다. 1984년에 이르자 항의 집회, 피해자 단체의 청문회 증언, 수많은 소송에 시달리다 못해 DPT 백신 제조업체 세 곳 가운데 두 곳이 문을 닫았다. 몇 년 후 100만 명에 가까운 어린이를 대상으로 한 조사연구 결과 백신의 위험은 터무니없이 과장된 것으로 밝혀졌다.

그렇다면 피해는 어떠했을까? 미국에선 부모들이 백신 접종을 꺼린 탓으로 백일해에 걸리는 아이들이 늘어났다. 백신이든 아니든 실질적인 위험이 그토록 작은데도 대중이 우려하는 이유는 무엇일까? 『공포의 문화(The Culture of Fear)』를 쓴 미국 사회학자 배리 글래스너는 '공포의 상인'들을 지목한다. 신문 판매 부수나 시청률을 높이기 위해 공포를 선전하는 언론매체, 공포 분위기를 조장해 표를 얻고 정작 중요한 사회 이슈들로부터 국민의 이목을 돌려놓는 정치인들, 사회의 공포를 자신의 마케팅에 동원하는 각종 단체들 모두가 주된 책임이 있다는 것이다.

문제해설

1. 세 번째 문단에서 말하는 '공포의 문화'가 무엇인지는 그 문단의 마지막 줄에 잘 나타나 있다. 한마디로 언론이나 정치인, 각종 단체 등이 공포를 이용해 자신들에게 유리한 방향으로 이용한다는 것이다. 그리고 본문 전체로 보면 나중에 그다지 위험하지 않다고 판명된 DPT의 위험성에 대한 공포로 인해 일반인들이 오히려 피해를 보았다는 것이 본문의 요지이다. 따라서 (b)와 (c)보다 더 근원적 내용인 (d)가 정답이 된다.

2. 본문은 백신이나 백일해가 위험하거나 심각한 질병이라는 것을 말하고 있는 것이 아니다. 오히려 공포심에 질려 사람들이 사실이 아닌 것을 사실로 받아들일 수 있다는 내용이므로 (b)가 정답으로 적합하다.

3. 결국 DPT가 그다지 위험하지 않은 것으로 두 번째 문단의 마지막 줄에 나온다. 따라서 실상은 DPT가 위험하다고 했던 것만큼 실제로는 위험하지 않다는 내용의 (a)가 정답이 된다.

4. 다시 말하지만 이 글은 백신이나 백일해에 대한 내용이 아니다. 따라서 (a)와 (d)는 제목으로 적합하지 않다. 세 번째 문단의 내용이 글의 저자가 지적하고 싶은 본질적 내용으로, 공포를 하나의 도구로 사용한다는 (b)가 제목으로 가장 적합하다.

정답 1(d) 2(b) 3(a) 4(b)

Unit 37 | Bad branding
낙인

1960년대에 미군은 야전에서 더 오래 식품을 보관할 수 있는 새로운 방식을 찾아냈다. 약한 감마선을 쏘아보니 야전식품 보관 기간이 늘어나고 신선도를 훨씬 오래 유지할 수 있었다. 새로 개발된 '방사선 조사(照射)'는 식품을 포장하기 전 멸균할 수 있고, 초기의 화학 처리와 달리 유해물질도 잔류하지 않았다. 세계보건기구(WHO)는 그런 공정 처리를 거친 식품을 인체에 해가 없는 것으로 분류했고, 미 식품의약국(FDA)은 학교 급식에까지 허용했다.

그렇지만 환경 단체들은 여전히 방사선 조사를 금지해야 한다고 주장한다. 이에 따라 포장지에 5cm 크기의 '방사선조사식품'이란 심벌을 붙이도록 의무 규정이 마련됐다. 소비자에게 이 마크는 피해야 하는 음식이라는 인상을 준다. 방사선 하면 2차 대전 당시 원자폭탄의 재앙부터 떠오르기 때문이다.

정작 감마선은 병원에서 일반인들이 알고 있는 것보다 훨씬 많이 이용한다. 1회용 주사기나 화상용 거즈는 감마선으로 멸균한다. 콘택트렌즈 세척용 생리식염수도 방사선을 쏘아 미생물을 죽이는 경우가 적지 않다. 감마선을 발사해 뇌종양과 암세포를 없애는 감마나이프는 인기를 얻고 있다.

문제해설

1. 본문은 감마선이 식품의 멸균 처리에 사용된 역사와 향후 검증 및 사용 인증까지 받았음에도 환경 단체들의 반발로 소비자들에게 기피 대상이 된 사연, 그리고 오히려 일상보다는 병원에서 더 멸균 등에 중요한 역할을 하고 있는 사례를 소개하고 있다. 따라서 식품 저장과 의료 분야에서의 방사선(감마선) 사용이라는 (d)가 주요 내용이라고 할 수 있다.

2. 병원에서 주로 사용되므로 병원에 가면 일정 형태의 방사선을 접하

게 된다는 (a)는 사실이다. (b)와 (c)는 본문에서 전혀 언급된 적이 없으며, (d)는 본문의 앞뒤 내용을 부적절한 방식으로 합성해 놓은 것이므로 올바르지 않다.

3. 방사선 처리 식품에 대해 부정적인 인식을 갖고 있는 것은 본문에서 "radiation reminds us of the damage caused by World War II atomic bombs"라고 말한 부분을 통해 알 수 있으므로 정답은 (c)가 된다. 나머지 보기는 모두 본문과 무관하다.

4. 미군에서 감마선을 사용한 이유는 본문 서두에 나온다. 바로 야전식품의 보관 기간을 늘리고 신선도를 오래 유지하기 위해서라는 것이다. 따라서 정답은 (d)가 된다.

정답 1(d) 2(a) 3(c) 4(d)

Unit 38 | Chain reactions
연쇄 반응

1996년 세계적인 제약회사 애보트사는 HIV 및 AIDS 치료제로 항레트로바이러스 약물인 리토나비어의 시판을 시작했다. 2억여 달러를 들여 신약을 개발한 애보트사는 2년 후 당혹스런 사태에 직면했다. 일리노이 주의 제약회사에서 그때까지 알려지지 않은 리토나비어의 다형체(흑연과 다이아몬드가 그렇듯, 화학적 성분은 같지만 물리적 구조가 다른 결정)가 나타났던 것이다. 그러자 주변에 있던 약의 기존 구조가 잇따라 신형 다형체로 바뀌었다. 문제는 신형이 에이즈 바이러스의 단백질 결합을 방해하는 치료 효과를 발휘하지 못한다는 점이었다.

다행히도, 이탈리아 공장에서는 신형이 발견되지 않았지만 일리노이의 과학자들이 방문하고 얼마 지나지 않아 같은 현상이 일어났다. 방문자들의 옷에 붙어 있던 미세한 다형체가 씨앗이 됐다.

회사는 이 기간 중 만들어진 모든 제품을 시장에서 회수해야 했다. 새로운 씨가 뿌려져서 기존의 구조를 바꾸는 연쇄반응은 이처럼 엄청난 파급력을 가진다. 광우병의 원인 물질인 변형 프리온 단백질도 그런 예다. 정상 프리온과 성분은 같지만 아미노산 결정 구조가 달라 인체 내에서 원래의 기능을 수행하지 못한다. 이것이 뇌에 들어가 주변의 정상 프리온을 자신과 같은 구조로 계속 바꿔나가는 것이 (인간) 광우병의 발병 메커니즘이다.

문제해설

1. 본문은 다른 물질로 쉽게 변할 수 있는 2개의 물질, 즉 에이즈 치료제인 리토나비어와 광우병의 원인 물질인 변형 프리온 단백질에 대해 설명하고 있다. 리토나비어의 구조가 변경된 이유가 방문자들의 옷에 있던 미세한 물질로 인해서라고 했으므로, 제약회사들은 자사의 제품이 오염되지 않도록 조심해야 한다는 (b)가 정답이 된다. 나머지 보기는 모두 본문과 무관하다.

2. (a)의 경우 흑연과 다이아몬드는 성분(element)은 동일하지만 구조(structure)는 다르다고 했으므로 사실이 아니다. (b)는 본문에서 설명

한 다형체의 특징에 관한 사항이므로 올바른 내용이다. (c)의 경우 변형 프리온 단백질이 광우병을 일으킨다고 했으므로 모든(all) 프리온 단백질이 해당하는 것은 아니며, (d)의 경우는 본문에 나와 있지 않기 때문에 사실 여부를 판단할 수 없다.

3. 본문은 다형체의 문제점을 설명한 내용이지, 이를 생성하거나 문제를 방지하는 내용에 관한 것은 아니므로 정답은 (a)가 적합하다.

4. 이 글을 쓴 이유는 다형체를 다루는 데 있어서 발생할 수 있는 문제를 설명해 주고 있으므로 (c)가 적합하다.

정답 1(b) 2(b) 3(a) 4(c)

Unit 39 | Power paralyzed
뇌졸중

1945년 2월 제2차 세계대전의 세 주역인 미국의 루스벨트 대통령, 영국의 처칠 수상, 소련의 스탈린 최고인민위원이 전시 중 얄타회담에 모였다. 그런데 이들은 모두 뇌졸중으로 생을 마감했다. 루스벨트는 1945년 얄타회담 두 달 뒤에 세상을 떴다. 숨지기 1년 전부터 그는 자주 숨이 차서 괴로워했다. 고혈압으로 심장이 현저히 약해진 탓이었다. 병마 탓인지 회담에서 루스벨트는 스탈린에게 너무나 많이 양보했다. 건강이 좋지 못하다는 이유로 중대사를 처리하는 데 있어 그는 자신도 수치스러울 정도로 어설픈 일처리를 해버렸고, 이 회담으로 그는 미국 역사와 외교사에서 오점을 남기게 된다.

스탈린은 회담 8년 후에 죽었다. 사망하기 1년 전 165cm 키의 스탈린은 몸무게가 많이 늘어났다. 주치의가 '의사의 음모'에 가담한 혐의로 체포된 뒤 의사를 믿지 않았던 그는 1953년 3월 자신의 별장에서 밤샘 파티가 끝난 뒤 쓰러져 침상에서 일어나지 못했다. 부분 마비가 온 그는 혼수상태에 빠져서 사흘 후 사망했다. 역사에 가정이란 없지만, 만일 스탈린이 제대로 된 약으로 치료를 받았다면 1963년 쿠바 미사일 위기가 전면적인 핵전쟁으로 비화했을 수 있다.

처칠은 비만·고혈압으로 오랫동안 고통 받고 있었고, 산소 호흡기를 쓴 채 얄타회담에 참석했다. 그렇지만 처칠은 그로부터 21년을 더 살았다. 처칠은 골초로 항상 파이프를 물고 다녔다. 뇌졸중 발생 소인도 다분히 많았다. 그러나 1960대에 개발된 (고혈압) 약과 낙천적인 성품 덕분에 81세까지 현직 정치인으로 활동했고 91세까지 장수했다. 하지만 그도 3번째 뇌졸중엔 굴복하고 말았다.

문제해설

1. 본문의 내용은 얄타회담의 주역 3명이 결국은 뇌졸중으로 생을 마감했다는 내용이다. 따라서 주제는 이들의 사망과 관련한 (b)가 된다.

2. 처칠의 경우 세 번째 문단에 잘 나타나 있다. 얄타회담 참석자 중에서 가장 오랫동안 살아남았던 인물이지만 비만과 고혈압에 장기간의 흡연으로 인해 건강이 좋지는 않았을 것이라고 나오므로 건강한 삶을

영위했다는 (a)는 부적절하다.

3. 루스벨트는 첫 번째 문단에 나와 있는데, 건강 탓인지 회담에서 스탈린에게 지나치게 많이 양보한 측면이 있다고 했으므로, (d)에서처럼 건강이 좋았다면 회담 결과가 다른 양상을 보였을 것으로 충분히 추론할 수 있다. (a)처럼 회담에서 그의 행동이 우려를 나타냈다는 말은 본문에 등장하지 않으며, 사망하기 1년 전부터 자주 숨이 차서 괴로워했다고 했으므로 (b)에서처럼 그의 사망이 충격으로 다가오지는 않았을 것으로 생각된다. (c) 부분은 앞서 말한 회담에서의 양보 문제를 생각해보면 사실일 수 없음을 알 수 있다.

정답 1(b) 2(a) 3(d)

Unit 40 | Gold rush
우주의 금

    금과 백금 같은 무거운 금속의 천체 물리학적 기원은 오랫동안 수수께끼였다. 상황은 이렇다. 우주는 약 140억 년 전 빅뱅, 즉 대폭발을 통해 탄생했다. 보통은 별이 단순한 핵반응을 통해 수소를 헬륨으로 변형시키며, 별들의 수명 주기에 따른 핵융합이나 핵분열을 통해 탄소, 산소, 마그네슘, 규소, 황, 니켈, 철 등의 무거운 원소 등이 만들어진다. 이 과정에서 별 중의 일부는 초신성으로 폭발하고 그 잔해가 흩어져 또 다른 별의 재료가 된다. 문제는 초신성 정도의 에너지로는 금이나 백금 같은 무거운 금속을 제대로 융합해내기 어렵다는 점이다. 영국과 스위스의 공동연구팀은 이에 대한 새로운 해답으로 중성자별의 충돌이라는 새로운 이론을 제시했다. 중성자별의 물질은 질량이 태양의 1.6배 정도로 아주 밀도가 높다. 연구팀은 쌍을 이루고 있던 두 개의 중성자별이 서로 충돌해 폭발한 뒤 블랙홀을 만드는 과정을 슈퍼컴퓨터로 계산해냈다. 이때 10억 도의 온도와 엄청난 밀도 덕분에 철과 니켈이 중성자를 흡수해 금과 백금으로 변하면서 우주에 폭발의 파편으로 흩뿌려진다는 것이다. 다만 이런 현상은 우주에서 10만 년에 한 번 정도밖에 일어나지 않는다고 한다. 이렇게 보면 지구에서 금이 희귀한 것은 당연하다. 금이 지각에서 차지하는 비율은 10억분의 5에 불과하고 채굴할 수 있는 양은 더욱 적다. 세계금평의회(WGC)에 따르면, 지난 6,000년 동안 지구상에서 채굴된 금의 총량은 약 12만 5,000t에 지나지 않는다고 한다.

문제해설

1. 본문은 우주의 기원에 초점을 맞추고 있는 글이 아니라 우주의 기원으로부터 금은 어떻게 생겨나게 되었는가에 초점을 맞추고 있다. 따라서 글의 주제는 (a)가 적합하다.

2. 금과 같은 무거운 금속은 초신성 정도의 에너지로도 융합해내기 어렵다고 나오므로 (a)는 적합하지 않으며, 10만 년에 한 번 정도로 중성자별이 충돌해 금과 백금이 생성된다고 했으므로 (b)의 설명은 적합하다. (c)와 (d)는 본문과 무관하므로 정답이 될 수 없다.

3. 금이 생성되려면 중성자별이 충돌해 10억 도의 온도와 엄청난 밀도를 생성하고, 이 환경에서 철과 니켈이 중성자를 흡수해 금과 백금으로 변한다고 했으므로, 이때 필요하지 않은 것은 초신성(supernova)이 해당된다.

4. 본문에 두 중성자별이 서로 충돌해 블랙홀을 만든다고 했으므로 정답은 (a)가 된다. (b)에서는 과학자들이 금을 제조하는 법을 알고 있다고 설명하고 있지만, 이는 제조법이 아닌 금의 생성에 대한 과학적 추론을 슈퍼컴퓨터를 사용해 수행한 것이므로 이는 증명할 방법이 없다는 것은 자명하므로 (b)와 같이 말할 수는 없다. (c)의 경우 초신성이 아닌 중성자별이라고 했으며, (d)의 경우 100년(century)이 아닌 10만 년이라고 했으므로 모두 적합하지 않다.

정답 1(a) 2(b) 3(d) 4(a)

Unit 41 | Breast is best
모유

    모유는 엄마가 아기에게 줄 수 있는 가장 큰 선물이다. 하지만, 이러한 장점을 입증한 연구에도 불구하고, 최근 국내 모유 수유율은 37.4%에 그치고 있다. 그나마 2002년 6.5%까지 떨어졌다가 요즘은 꾸준히 느는 추세이다. 논란이 있긴 하지만 모유를 먹은 아이가 분유를 먹고 자란 아이보다 더 똑똑하다는 연구 결과도 많다.
    임신 7개월부터 분만 후 처음 며칠 동안 나오는 초유에는 단백질과 유체가 풍부하게 들어있다. 수유할 때 처음 나오는 초유에는 뇌세포 발달에 영향을 미치는 비타민 A나 DHA 등이 들어있다고 한다. 2005년 호주에서는 모유 수유로 인한 경제적 효과가 연간 22억 호주 달러(원화로 2조원)에 이른다는 분석을 내놓기도 했다.
    모유 수유에 따르는 불편함이 적지 않지만 엄마에게도 좋은 점이 많다. 모유 수유를 하면 하루 평균 500kcal의 에너지가 더 소모돼 산후 체중 감량에 도움이 된다고 한다. 또 모유 수유는 난소암과 유방암, 당뇨병, 류머티즘성 관절염 위험을 낮춰주어 엄마의 건강에도 좋다는 최근 연구 결과도 있다.
    지난해, 덴마크 코펜하겐 대학의 연구팀은 엄마가 무엇을 먹느냐에 따라 모유의 맛이 달라진다는 연구 결과를 내놓았다. 엄마가 바나나 같은 특정 과일을 먹으면 아기에게 수유를 하기 전 한 시간 안에 모유에서 그 맛이 나타난다는 것이다. 뒤집어 생각하면 이것은 엄마가 건강에 해로운 것을 먹으면 그대로 아기에게 전해질 수도 있다는 말이다.

문제해설

1. 본문은 모유 수유와 그 장점에 관해 설명한 글이므로 정답은 (a)가 된다.

2. (a)의 경우 마지막 문단에서 해로운 것을 먹는 경우 그것이 아이에게 전해질 수 있다고 했으므로 영양소가 전해진다는 것은 장점이지만 독소가 전해진다는 것은 단점으로 볼 수 있다. (b)는 본문에서 언

급되지도 않았지만 문제에서 물어본 모유 수유의 장점이라고도 할 수 없으며, (c)도 본문의 문제에서 벗어난 답이다. 정답은 (d)로 산모가 하루 평균 500kcal가 더 소모돼 산후 체중 감량에 도움이 된다고 설명하고 있다.

3. (a)의 경우 수유 전에 산모가 특정 음식을 먹어서 아이들의 기호(좋고 싫음)에 영향을 준다는 것이므로, (a) 자체로 말이 되지 않는다. (b)에 나온 내용은 국내 모유 수유율이 6.5%까지 떨어졌다가 최근 37.4%라는 첫 번째 문단의 내용을 통해 알 수 있으므로 정답이 된다. (c)의 경우 초유는 아기들이 먹으면 좋지만 반드시(must) 먹어야 하는 것은 아니므로 부적절하며, (d)의 경우는 본문과 무관하다.

4. 필자는 산모에게 모유 수유를 권장하고 있으므로 (c)가 필자의 주장으로 적합하다. 참고로 (a)의 'mixed feeling'은 '찬반'의 생각을 동시에 가지고 있다는 뜻이 되므로 부적절하다.

정답 1(a) 2(d) 3(b) 4(c)

Unit 42 | Refugee plants
난민 식물

　미국의 공식 통계에 따르면, 세계 인구의 1%인 6,700만 명이 고향에서 쫓겨나 살아가는 난민으로 분류된다. 난민은 고국을 떠나 계속적인 긴장과 불안, 두려움 속에 살아가는 사람들로, 정치적 원인도 있지만 지진·사이클론 같은 자연재해 때문에도 발생한다.

　기후 변화도 사람이 아닌 동·식물이 고향을 떠나는 원인이 되고 있다. 유럽에서는 지난 20년 간 산새의 숫자가 20% 가까이 줄었다고 한다. 영국에서는 산새 숫자가 4분의 3이나 줄었다. 기온이 올라가면서 적당한 자연 서식지가 줄어든 탓이다.

　식물도 예외는 아니다. 미국에서는 식목 지대를 구분하는 경계선 일부가 과거에 비해 북쪽으로 300km 정도 이동했다고 한다. 따뜻한 곳에 살던 종류가 더 북쪽에서도 살아가게 됐음을 의미한다.

　유럽 포도주 업체들은 서늘한 곳을 찾아 산으로 올라가고 있다. 따뜻해진 기온 탓에 전통적인 재배지에서 포도농사가 어려워지게 되어서이다. 프랑스 전문가들이 서유럽 산악지대에서 171개 식물종의 생장 고도를 비교한 결과, 지구 온난화로 10년에 평균 29m씩 높은 곳으로 이동한 것을 확인했다.

문제해설

1. 본문의 시작을 난민 이야기로 하고 있지만 사실은 기후 변화로 인한 동·식물의 이동을 다루고 있는 글이다. (a)가 정답이 되려면 각국의 난민들에 대해 자세히 나와야 하지만 첫 문단에만 간략히 나와 있어서 정답이 될 수 없다. (b)는 본문과 무관하고, (d)는 지엽적인 내용이다. 따라서 정답은 (c)가 된다.

2. 포도주 재배와 관련해서는 마지막 문단에 나와 있다. "European winemakers have been scouring mountains in search of cool places." 부분을 통해 (c)를 추론할 수 있다.

3. 난민들이 생기는 원인은 정치적 원인과 자연재해 때문이라고 했으며, 난민의 수가 늘어나고 있는 내용은 나와 있지 않으므로 (a)는 올바른 내용이 아니다. (b)는 정치적 원인에 해당하므로 맞는 내용이며, (c)는 두 번째 문단에 나와 있다. (d)는 세 번째와 네 번째 문단에서 설명되어 있다.

4. 동·식물의 이동으로 많은 부분에서 변화가 오고 있다는 것을 추론할 수 있으므로 (c)가 정답이다. (a)의 경우 인간의 이동은 나와 있지 않기 때문에 정답이 될 수 없으며, (b)는 본문과 무관해서 답이 될 수 없다. (d)는 본문과 정반대로 설명했기 때문에 답이 될 수 없다.

정답 1(c) 2(c) 3(a) 4(c)

Unit 43 | Insane or sane?
정신분석 요법의 귀환

　정신과 의사들은 어떤 사람이 정신질환자인지 아닌지 제대로 가려낼 수 있을까? 1970년대 초반 미국의 무명 심리학자였던 데이비드 로젠한은 이를 시험해보는 실험을 진행했다. 로젠한과 그의 친구 7명은 전국의 정신 병원으로 흩어져 거짓 증상을 호소했다. "목소리가 들립니다. '쿵' 소리요". 이 증상을 말한 것만으로 모두 정신 병원에 입원이 되었다. 하지만 입원 후에는 정상인과 똑같이 행동했다. 그들은 의사에게 일상생활의 만족과 불만족에 관해 있는 그대로 털어놓았다. 실험이 끝날 무렵, 7명은 정신분열증, 1명은 조울증 진단을 받았다. 평균 19일 입원 치료 후 모두 '일시적 증세 회복'으로 퇴원했다. 실험 결과를 기초로 로젠한은 '정신 병원에서 제정신으로 지내기'란 논문을 발표했다. 부정적인 여론이 일자 한 정신 병원에서 "우리에게 앞으로 3개월간 가짜 환자를 보내보라. 찾아내겠다"라고 주장했다. 3개월 뒤 병원 측은 가짜 환자 41명을 찾아냈다고 발표했다. 그렇지만 실제로는 가짜 환자는 단 한 명도 보내지 않았었다.

　그런데 이런 치료법이 다시 유행인 듯하다. 미국의 뉴욕타임스 10월 1일자 인터넷판은 '정신분석 요법, 지지를 얻다'란 새로운 소식을 전했다. "프로이트 이론에 바탕을 둔 집중적인 정신분석학적 '상담 치료'(talking cure)는 투약 처방과 관리 요법에 밀려 존재가 희미해졌다. 그러나 불안 장애와 경계선 인격장애(감정을 조절하지 못하는 병) 같은 만성 정신질환 등에는 효과가 큰 것으로 드러났다"는 것이다. 1,000여 명 이상의 환자가 관련된 이 연구는 금요일 미국의 학협회지에 실렸다. 정신분석 요법의 귀환은 정신 의학이 로젠한의 공격을 계기로 더욱 실질적이고 효과적인 방향으로 발전했다는 증거로 보아야 할 것이다. 문명과 마찬가지로 학문도 도전을 통해서 발전하는 것이 아니겠는가?

문제해설

1. 첫 번째 문단에 등장하는 로젠한 실험에서는 기존의 상담 치료에 문제가 상당하다는 내용을 내포하고 있다. 실제 정신병 환자를 제대로

가려내지 못한다는 것을 무명의 심리학자가 실험을 통해 제시했기 때문이다. 따라서 (a)와 반대의 내용인 (c)가 정답이 된다.

2. 병원 측에서는 (d)처럼 41명의 환자를 찾아냈다고 했지만 실제로는 한 명도 가짜 환자를 보내지 않았기 때문에 한 명도 제대로 찾아내지 못한 것이 되어서 (c)가 정답이 된다.

3. 두 번째 문단의 "Intensive psychoanalytic therapy, the 'talking cure' … has all but disappeared in the age of drug treatments and managed care." 부분을 통해 상담 치료가 사라진 이유는 투약 처방과 관리 요법 때문이라는 것을 알 수 있다. 따라서 정답은 (d)가 된다.

4. 1970년대에는 상담 치료에 문제가 있다는 공격을 받았지만 최근에는 다시 각광을 받고 있다는 내용이므로 (a)가 정답이 된다.

정답 1(c) 2(c) 3(d) 4(a)

Unit 44 | Hearing voices
목소리 무늬

1970년 미국에서 구소련 지도자였던 흐루쇼프의 회고록, 『흐루쇼프는 기억한다』가 출간되었다. 그러나 출간 직후 회고록의 테이프 녹음 진위 논란이 일었는데, 그 가운데에는 미 중앙정보국(CIA)의 조작설까지 나왔다. 출판사의 얘기에 따르면, 흐루쇼프가 1964년 (소련 공산당 제1서기에서) 실각한 뒤 은밀히 녹음했던 테이프를 입수했다고 한다. 그러나 가택연금 상태에서 감시를 받던 그의 육성 테이프가 어떻게 철의 장막을 뚫고 유출될 수 있었겠느냐는 의문이 끊이지 않았다. 논란은 목소리의 무늬, 즉 성문(聲紋)을 분석함으로써 종식됐다. 해당 테이프의 음성과 1960년 흐루쇼프의 유엔총회 연설 녹음을 비교한 결과, 성문이 일치한 것이다.

성문이란 목소리의 고저와 음량, 공명을 나타내는 주파수를 시각적으로 표시한 것을 말한다. 지문처럼 사람마다 독특한 목소리 특징이 있다. 성문 분석 장치는 1963년 벨 연구소의 로렌스 커스타에 의해 처음 개발됐다. 그는 5만 명의 목소리를 녹음·분석해 사람마다 성문에 뚜렷한 차이가 있다는 점을 입증했다. 오늘날 성문 분석은 개인 식별에 결정적 역할을 하는 도구로 자리 잡았다. 2001년 오사마 빈 라덴의 메시지를 담은 육성테이프가 방영됐을 때도, 2003년 사담 후세인의 육성테이프가 방영됐을 때도, CIA는 성문 분석을 통해 본인임을 확인할 수 있었다.

문제해설

1. (a)는 성문이 정확하기는 하지만 한계성이 있다고 했는데, 본문에는 성문이 지문과 같이 사람마다 뚜렷한 차이가 있기 때문에 개인 식별이 가능하다고 했다. (b)의 경우 육성테이프의 주인공이 사담 후세인임을 밝혔다는 내용이지 이를 통해 후세인을 체포했다는 내용은 아니다. (c)의 경우 성문을 통해 정확히 범인을 찾아내는 데 사용될 수 있다는 내용이므로 본문에서 추론 가능하지만, (d)의 경우는 100% 성문을 신뢰할 수 있다는 내용이 본문에 나오지 않고 극단적인 내용이

므로 정답에서는 배제하는 것이 적절하다.

2. (a)는 지엽적인 내용으로 주제가 될 수 없으며, (b)와 (c)는 본문과 무관한 내용으로 정답이 될 수 없다. 녹음된 음성의 진위 여부와 이를 통해 녹음한 사람이 누구인지를 밝힌다는 내용인 (d)가 정답이 된다.

3. (a)의 경우 벨 연구소의 로렌스 커스타에 의해 개발됐다고 했으므로, (a)와 (c)는 올바르지 않다. 흐루쇼프의 경우 본인이 인정해서가 아니라 그의 육성 테이프의 성문 분석을 통해 밝혀진 것이므로 (d) 또한 올바르지 않다. 정답은 (b)로, 첫 번째 문단에 나온 왜 녹음테이프가 논란이 되었던 것인지와 일치한다.

정답 1(c) 2(d) 3(b)

Unit 45 | The silent organ
간

과학 전문지 『사이언스』 276호엔 프로메테우스 신화는 간은 일부를 절제하거나 손상돼도 바로 재생된다는 사실을 고대 그리스인도 알고 있었다는 것을 보여주는 것이라는 논문이 실렸다. 이처럼 간은 손상된 조직을 자연스럽게 재생할 수 있는 몇 안 되는 장기 중 하나이다. 15% 정도의 크기로도 두세 달 뒤면 원래 크기로 자란다. 과음이나 간염으로 손상돼도 며칠 술을 끊거나 간염이 완치되면 곧 원상회복된다.

성인의 간은 보통 1.5kg이 나가며, 인체의 장기 중 가장 크고, 몇몇 중요한 기능을 수행한다. 알다시피 간은 알코올을 대사시키거나 분해하는 주요 장기다. 알코올 같은 독성 물질을 덜 위험한 형태로 변환해 몸 밖으로 배출한다. 하지만 간이라고 해서 모든 독성 물질을 해독하거나 제거할 수 있는 것은 아니다. 중성화시킬 수 없는 유독성 물질은 그대로 통과시킨다.

인체 내 간의 역할을 축구 포지션으로 비유하자면 링크맨(미드필더) 같은 존재다. 우리가 먹는 음식은 포도당, 아미노산, 지방산 등 기본 성분으로 분해된 뒤 몸 안에서 완전히 소화가 된다. 이 물질들은 모두 (장과 간을 잇는) 간문맥을 거쳐 간에 들어와 각각 필요한 세포로 '볼 배합'이 된다. 음식의 양이 적어 식욕을 채워주지 못할 때 "간에 기별도 안 간다"고 하는 것은 과학적인 근거가 있는 말이다.

바로바로 고장 신호를 보내는 다른 장기와는 달리 70%가 파괴될 때까지도 묵묵히 일만 하기 때문에 간은 '침묵의 장기'다. 따라서 간이 '신음 소리'를 내면 이미 돌이킬 수 없는 상황이기 십상이다. 경고 신호를 보내기 전에 간에 신경 쓸 필요가 있는 것이다.

문제해설

1. 본문은 간의 특징에 관한 대략적인 설명이므로 주제로는 (d)가 적합하다.

2. '침묵의 장기'라고 간이 불리는 것은 손상을 입어도 별다른 신호를 보내지 않기 때문이다. 따라서 정답은 (a)가 적합하다.

3. (a)의 경우 마지막 문단을 통해 추론이 가능하다. 간은 다른 장기와는 달리 70%가 파괴될 때까지도 묵묵히 일만 한다고 했기 때문이다. (b) 또한 마지막 문단의 '침묵의 장기'라는 부분을 통해 추론 가능하며, (d)는 첫 번째 문단에 나온 간의 재생력을 통해 추론할 수 있다. 정답은 (c)로 두 번째 문단에 보면 모든 독성 물질을 해독할 수 있는 것은 아니라고 했으므로 사실과 다르다.

4. 두 번째 문단에서 간은 몇몇 중요한 기능을 수행한다고 했으므로 하나의 기능만을 수행한다는 (a)는 올바르지 않다. (b)는 세 번째 문단에 "간에 기별도 안 간다"는 부분을 참고하면 되고, (c)는 첫 번째 문단에서 간이 최고의 재생력을 지녔다는 것을 통해 유추할 수 있다. 그리고 마지막 문단을 통해 간은 '침묵의 장기'라는 설명에서 (d)를 추론할 수 있다.

정답 1(d)　2(a)　3(c)　4(a)

Unit 46　Countering counterfeits
위조지폐 방지책

　현대의 위조지폐 중 가장 악명 높은 것은 '슈퍼노트'(supernote)이다. 슈퍼라는 이름이 붙은 것은 위조에 사용된 화폐 제작 기술 수준이 원본보다 더 높기 때문이라고 한다. 달러화에 사용된 모든 위조방지 기술을 돌파한 까닭에 전문가조차도 진짜와 구별하기 어려울 정도다. 현재 유통되는 달러화 1만 장당 한 장은 슈퍼노트일 것으로 추정되고 있다. 제조원은 미스터리로 남아있다. 북한이 범인이라는 미국 정부의 주장이 유력하지만 이란, 시리아뿐 아니라 미국 CIA까지 의심을 받고 있다. 슈퍼노트를 예외로 하면 판별이 사실상 불가능한 위조지폐는 없다. 하지만 최첨단 컬러복사기, 스캐너와 컴퓨터가 널리 보급되면서 외면상 진짜와 유사한 위조지폐를 만드는 게 가능해지고 있다. 범죄집단이나 고도의 전문성을 갖춘 이들이 아니어도 되는 것이다.

　각국 정부는 이런 위조를 막기 위해 첨단 기술을 총동원하고 있다. 대표적인 것이 복사 자체를 불가능하게 만드는 소위 '유라이온(EURION)' 마크다. 우리의 1만 원권 화폐 앞뒷면에 있는 오리온 별자리 모양들이 그 예다. 신형 컬러복사기는 이런 표시가 있는 화폐는 복사 자체가 안 되도록 프로그램되어있다. 대부분의 국가에서 이 마크를 채택하고 있다. 두 번째는 컴퓨터의 포토샵 같은 이미지 처리 소프트웨어를 대상으로 하는 '위조방지시스템(CDS)' 기술이다. 화폐에 투명 인쇄된 특정한 디지털 표식을 인식하면 컴퓨터에서 해당 이미지를 스캔해 불러오거나 수정하는 작업을 차단한다. 이 기술은 서방세계 주요국의 중앙은행 30곳이 참여한 '중앙은행 위조방지 그룹'에서 회원국에 보급했다. 문제는 한국은행은 여기서 빠져 있다는 점이다. 한국은행권은 컴퓨터를 이용한 위조지폐 방지책이 허약하다.

문제해설

1. (a)의 경우 북한뿐 아니라 이란, 시리아, CIA 등 위폐 제조원으로 의심되는 곳은 많이 존재한다. (b)의 경우 마지막 문장에서 한국이 '중앙은행 위조방지 그룹'의 회원국이 아니기 때문에 위폐 방지책이 허약하다고 했으므로 한국에서 위폐가 만들어지기 더 쉬운 상황이라는 것을 알 수 있으므로 (b)가 정답이 된다. (c)의 경우 전문가들조차 슈퍼노트를 찾아내기 어렵다고 했으므로 사실이 아니며, (d)의 경우 슈퍼노트의 제조원이 어디인지는 미스터리로 남아있다고 했으므로 사실이 아니다.

2. 본문은 슈퍼노트와 이런 위조지폐를 방지하기 위한 기술들에 관해 서술되어 있으므로 정답은 (b)가 된다.

3. 본문 초반에 보면, 슈퍼노트에 '슈퍼'라는 이름이 붙은 것은 위조에 사용된 기술이 원본보다 더 높기 때문이라고 나온다. 그리고 슈퍼노트는 전문가조차도 판별하기 어렵다고 했으므로, 사실상(virtually) 위폐임을 알기 불가능하다고 말한 (c)가 정답이 된다. 완전히 불가능한 것은 아니기 때문에 virtually란 단어를 같이 사용했다.

4. 본문 마지막 부분에 한국은행는 '중앙은행 위조방지 그룹' 회원국이 아니라고 했으며, 내년에 가입한다는 내용은 등장하지 않는다.

정답 1(b)　2(b)　3(c)　4(b)

Unit 47　History in color
피부색

　인간의 피부색에 대한 과학적 설명은 멜라닌, 헤모글로빈, 카로틴 등 주로 세 성분에 의해 결정된다는 것이다. 이중 카로틴은 당근, 귤 등 카로틴이 풍부한 식품을 과다 섭취했을 때 피부색을 노랗게 바꾸는 등 일시적인 영향을 미친다. 헤모글로빈은 피부 표면에 많으면 피부가 불그스름해지는 정도다. 하지만 인종과 피부색을 가르는 핵심은 피부의 진갈색 멜라닌 색소의 양이다. 인종에 따라 멜라닌 세포의 수가 달라지는 것은 아니며 멜라닌 세포 속에 멜라닌 소체가 얼마나 조밀하게 들어있느냐에 따라 피부색이 결정된다.

　피부색은 태양의 자외선에 대한 적응의 산물이란 이론도 설득력이 있다. 대부분 아프리카 적도 부근에서 살았던 현대 인류의 조상은 검은 피부였다. 열을 반사하고, (땀을 빨리 발산시켜) 체온을 낮추며, '유해한' 자외선을 막는 데 검은 피부가 더 효과적이어서이다. 같은 양의 햇볕을 받았을 때 백인이 흑인보다 피부암에 걸릴 위험은 10배나 높다. 그런데 신체가 자외선을 너무 적게 받아들이면 '선샤인 비타민'으로 통하는 비타민 D가 결핍된다. 흑인이 백인에 비해 비타민 D의 부족에 의한 구루병, 류머티즘 관절염, 심혈관 질환, 대장암, 폐암, 전립선암에 걸릴 위험이 높은 것은 이래서다.

　인류가 아프리카를 떠나 유럽, 아시아 등에 정착한 뒤엔 비타민 D를 더 많이 받을 필요가 있었을 것이다. 이들은 생존을 위해 노랗거나 흰 피부를 갖게 됐다. 예외적으로 알래스카 원주민들은 햇볕 보기가 힘든 극 지역에 살면서도 피부가 검다. 전문가들은 이들이 평소 비타민 D가 풍부한 생선을 많이 먹어 굳이 피부가 밝을 필요가 없었을 것이라고 풀이한다.

문제해설

1. 햇볕과 비타민 D가 관련 있기 때문에 이를 충분히 받지 않으면 여러 질병에 걸릴 가능성이 커진다고 했다. 그리고 두 번째 문단에서 피부색은 자연의 적응에 의한 산물이라고 말하고 있다. (c)는 본문의 서두에 나오는 내용이다. 정답은 (d)로, 인종이 피부색에 미치는 영향이 아닌 환경이 피부색에 미치는 영향에 대해 진화론적 관점에서 설명하고 있다.

2. (a)는 알라스카 사람들의 예에서 알 수 있으며, (c)는 "Africa had darker skin because it was more effective at reflecting heat"에서 확인할 수 있다. (d)는 본문 초반의 "Excessive consumption of foods high in carotene … may turn one's skin yellow for a short time" 부분을 통해 알 수 있다. 정답은 (b)로 흑인이 백인에 비해 상대적으로 비타민 D 결핍과 관련된 질병에 더 많이 걸린다는 것이지, 백인은 이런 질병을 겪지 않는다는 뜻은 아니다.

3. 이 글은 피부색에 관한 내용이다. 따라서 아프리카인들의 이주나 식단의 중요성은 관련이 없으며, 건강에 관한 내용도 아니다. 정답은 (c)로 피부색은 태양의 자외선에 대한 적응의 산물이라고 설명하고 있다.

4. 본문 후반부에 알라스카에 살고 있는 원주민들은 햇볕을 보기 힘든 극 지역에 살지만 피부가 검다고 나온다. 평소 비타민 D가 풍부한 생선을 많이 먹어서라고 했으므로 정답은 (a)가 된다. 피부암에 대한 내용은 두 번째 문단 중반에 나오는데 백인이 흑인보다 피부암에 걸릴 위험이 10배라고 했으므로 피부색과 관련이 있다는 것을 알 수 있다. (c)의 경우 적도에 가까울수록 피부색이 검은데, 예외적으로 알래스카 사람들을 들고 있다. (d)의 경우 첫 번째 문단 후반에 인종에 따라 멜라닌 세포 수가 달라지는 것은 아니라고 했다.

정답 1(d) 2(b) 3(c) 4(a)

Unit 48 | Addicted to speed
속도

세계에서 가장 빠른 여객 철도편인 알스톰사의 고속 열차 TGV는 파리~스트라스부르 사이를 최대 시속 575km로 달린다. 2007년 4월 성공적인 데뷔를 치른 업그레이드된 이 프랑스의 총알 열차는 경쟁 관계인 독일의 ICE나 일본 신칸센을 능가한다. 속도 면에서, 신칸센이 2003년 시속 581km로 달린 기록이 있으나 당시에는 자기부상 방식이었다. 이 방식은 엔진 과열과 무게 문제로 상용화되기 어렵다. 평상시 TGV는 시속 300km 남짓으로 유럽을 관통한다.

세계에서 가장 빠른 차로 통하는 GTBO는 영국의 아카비온에서 디자인 제작되었다. 이 콘셉트 카는 올 2월 최고 시속 547km로 달리는 모습을 선보였다. 360kg의 무게가 나가는 돌고래 모양의 이 2인용 자동차는 불과 30초 만에 시속 480km까지 도달할 수 있다. 물론 가격이 2백만 달러를 호가해서 일반인들이 넘보기는 어렵다. 하늘에서는, 록히드사의 SR-71 블랙버드 정찰기가 단연 발군이다. 이 장거리 전략정찰기는 시속 4,000km에 이르는 마하 3.3의 속도로, 한때 마하 2.23 속도를 자랑하던 콩코드기보다 훨씬 빠르다.

21세기는 '속도의 시대'다. 역사는 속도는 곧 힘이란 사실을 실증적으로 보여준다. 징기스칸은 기마군의 도움으로 몽골 제국을 세웠고, 독일의 영웅 롬멜 장군은 2차 세계대전 동안 북아프리카 사막에서 아프리카 콥스 탱크로 승리를 이끌었다. 속도를 높이면 더 높고, 먼 곳까지 갈 수 있고, 더 빠른 시간에 더 많은 정보를 얻을 수 있고, 더 많은 일을 할 수 있다. 속도는 성장을 부추기고, 성장이 다시 속도를 내도록 재촉한다. 어떤 이들은 '속도 바이러스'를 얘기한다. 현대 사회의 빠른 속도에 보조를 맞추지 못하는 사람은 도태되고 소외될 수밖에 없다며 비판한다. 인간의 더 빠른 속도에 대한 갈증으로 자연과 자원이 희생양이 된다. 인류가 일 년 동안 소모하는 에너지의 양은 거의 100만 년 동안 축적된 화석 연료의 양에 해당한다. 석유, 석탄 같은 화석 연료의 과소비는 지구 온난화를 더욱 부추기고 있다.

문제해설

1. '속도 바이러스'가 무엇을 지칭하는지는 바로 앞부분(Speed can accelerate growth while growth presses on for more speed.)에 나온다. 빠르게 일을 처리해서 성장이 이뤄졌는데, 오히려 그 성장이 더 빠른 일처리를 요구하고 있는 상황이다. 마치 끊임없이 더 빠른 속도를 원하는 속도 바이러스가 사람들을 감염시키는 것 같다는 것이다. 그리고 이런 속도에 적응하지 못하는 사람들은 뒤처지고 소외된다는 것이다. 따라서 이 바이러스는 실제 바이러스가 아닌 비유적인 표현인데, 마치 이를 실제 바이러스처럼 묘사한 (a)는 적절하지 않다.

2. (a)는 본문 마지막 부분을 통해 알 수 있으며, (b)와 (d)는 1번 문제에서도 다루었던 부분이다. 정답은 (c)로 이는 본문을 통해서는 알 수 없는 내용이다.

3. 영국에서 제작된 '아카비온 GTBO'는 최고 시속 547km까지 달려 가장 빠른 자동차 자리에 올랐지만, 가격이 비싸 일반인들이 넘보기 어렵다고 했으므로 이를 승용차(passenger vehicle)라고 할 수 없으므로 (d)가 정답이 된다.

4. 마지막 부분이 화석 연료의 대량 소비와 지구 온난화로 끝났으므로 이에 대한 대체에너지가 나올 수 있을 것으로 예상할 수 있다.

정답 1(a) 2(c) 3(d) 4(c)

Unit 49 | Man's best friend
사람과 개

폼페이는 서기 79년 베수비오 화산이 폭발하면서 (화산재에) 완전히 덮였다. 1,700년의 세월 동안 모습을 보이지 않다가 1748년 우연히 재발견되었다. 그때 이후 발굴된 폼페이는 고대 로마제국 절정기의 모습을 있는 그대로 보여줬다. 특히 흥미로운 것은 거리로 향해있는 집들의 현관바닥에 많은 고대의 개의 모자이크 무늬에 '개조심'이라 쓰인 경고문이다.

길들여진 개가 사람과 함께 살기 시작한 것은 이보다 훨씬 전이다. 길들여진 최초의 개로 여겨지는 개의 화석 가운데 가장 오래된 것은 1만 4,000년 전 중동 지역의 한 동굴에서 인간의 유해와 함께 발견된 것이다. 하지만 최근, 개와 사람이 함께 생활한 역사가 3만 년도 넘을 것이라는 주장도 나왔다. 최근 벨기에의 한 동굴에서 3만 1,700년 전의 개 화석이 발견됐기 때문이다.

전 세계 500종이 넘는 견종(犬種)의 DNA를 분석한 학자들은 이들 견종들이 1만 5,000년 전 동아시아에 살았던 조상인 늑대 시절부터 길들여진 것으로 추정한다. 모든 동물 가운데 맨 처음 가축화된 동물은 개일 것이다. 사람에게 털가죽이나 고기를 제공했고, 사냥감을 추적하거나 짐을 나르는 일을 맡게 됐다. 진화라는 관점에서 볼 때 개는 엄청난 성공을 거뒀다. 늑대는 전 세계 10만 마리 수준으로 줄어들어 멸종 위기에 처했다.

개는 인간과 함께 살게 될 만큼 영리했고, 무엇이 옳고 그른지 알 만큼 똑똑했다. 얼마 전 오스트리아 학자들은 개들이 불공평한 상황을 인식하면 질투심을 나타내기도 한다는 연구 결과를 내놓았다. 같은 재주를 똑같이 부렸는데 옆의 다른 개는 대가로 뭔가를 받지만 자신은 못 받았을 때 스트레스와 불만을 보인다는 것이다. 최근 칠레에서는 목숨을 걸고 동료 개를 살렸던 떠돌이 개 한 마리가 새로운 영웅으로 떠올랐다. 산티아고에서 자동차가 질주하는 고속도로에 뛰어들어 차에 치인 동료를 갓길로 끌어낸 개가 CCTV 영상에 포착된 것이다.

문제해설

1. 본문은 화산재로 덮였던 폼페이에서 발견된 '개 조심'이라는 장식에서 알 수 있듯이 당시에도 개를 키웠다는 내용으로 시작한다. 그러면서 언제, 그리고 어느 동물로부터 개가 유래했는지에 관해 설명하고 있다. 따라서 인간과 개가 서로 어울리게 된 '역사'가 주제라고 보는 것이 맞다.

2. 마지막 문단에서 개도 질투심을 느낀다는 내용이 나온다. 두 번째 문단에서는 3만 년 전 개의 화석이 발견되었다는 내용을 통해 (b)를 추론할 수 있다. 또한 세 번째 문단에서 개는 늑대로부터 진화했으며, 늑대의 개체 수가 줄어들어 얼마 남지 않은 상황과 개의 개체 수는 대조적이라는 내용이 등장한다. (d)는 본문을 통해 알 길이 없으므로 정답이 된다.

3. (a)와 (b)는 본문에 나오지 않으며, 개가 영리하다는 내용이 마지막 문단에 나오므로 (c)도 맞지 않다. 마지막 부분에서 개들이 사람들처럼 불공평한 상황을 인식하고 질투의 감정까지 느낀다는 연구 결과를 (d)에서와 같이 '인간과 같은 감성이 더 발견될 수도 있을 것 같다'라고 추론한 것이므로 정답이 된다.

4. 세 번째 문단에서 개가 인간에게 제공한 것이 나온다. 털가죽과 고기를 제공했고, 사냥감을 추적하고 짐을 날랐다는 내용을 통해 (a), (b), (c) 모두 해당한다는 것을 알 수 있다.

정답 1 (b)   2 (d)   3 (d)   4 (d)

Unit 50 | The capitalist line
포드주의

포드주의는 포드 자동차의 창업자인 헨리 포드가 개발한 대량 생산 시 사용되는 현대적 생산 라인이다. 차 한 대의 조립 과정을 단순 노동으로 세분화하고, 컨베이어 시스템으로 가동되는 자동차 조립 라인에서 부품을 조립하는 노동자 한 명에게 머무는 시간을 최소화했다. 생산 효율화, 고임금, 업무시간 단축 등 획기적인 변화를 가져왔다.

좌파 경제학자들은 노동자의 소외를 우려했지만, 대량 생산이 대량 소비로 이어지면서 서구 사회에서 경제적 풍요를 창출하는 데 중추적 역할을 했다. 1970~1980년대 경제 위기 이후에는 지구화·정보기술의 빠른 발달·탈산업화·탈국가화를 반영하는 '포스트 포디즘'이 등장했다.

포드와 같은 미국의 거대 자동차 회사들이 금융 위기 가운데 큰 타격을 입고 휘청거리고 있다. 그러면서 무한 경쟁이 바람직하지 않다는 얘기가 설득력 있게 나오고 있다. 1936년 찰리 채플린 주연의 코미디 영화에서 그는 포드주의에 대한 극도의 냉소를 표출했다. 찰리 채플린이 '현대적인' 사료 공급기에 빨려 들어가는 장면은 현실을 과장한 것이라 하더라도, 우리는 마음속에 자본주의의 시대에도 가장 중요한 것은 인간의 모습을 지니는 것이라는 것을 새겨두어야 한다.

문제해설

1. (a)에서는 포드주의가 처음 도입되었을 때 상당한 반대에 직면했다고 말한다. 본문에서는 좌파 경제학자들이 노동자의 소외를 우려했다고 밝히고 있으므로 이를 '상당한 반대'라고 하기는 무리다. (b)는 본문과 무관하며, (d)는 이미 1970~1980년대에 포스트 포디즘이 등장했고, 지구화가 아닌 금융 위기 속에서 거대 자동차 회사들이 어려움을 겪고 있기 때문에, 이를 지구화의 영향으로 미래에 자동차 산업이 몰락할 것이라고 추론하는 것은 무리다. 정답은 (c)로 포디즘으로 대변되는 산업화에는 두 얼굴이 존재한다고 보는 것이 전체 흐름과 부합한다.

2. 본문에서는 포드사에서 시행한 대량 생산의 과정(process)은 밝히고 있지는 않다. 대신 첫 번째 문단에서 대략적인 내용이 나온다. 따라서 정답은 (c)가 된다.

3. 대량 생산을 위한 기계화나 신자유주의에서 그칠 것이 아니라 이 모든 것이 누구를 위한 것인지에 대한 물음, 즉 인본주의가 필요하다고 했으므로 이어질 내용은 이 인본주의에 관한 내용이어야 한다. 혹은 이렇게 방향이 선회하게 된 배경이 적합하다. 찰리 채플린이 스타덤에 오른 것은 이런 상황과 관계없으므로 정답은 (b)가 된다.

정답 1(c)   2(c)   3(b)

Unit 51 | Under the microscope
다이옥신

　극미의 세계를 향한 인간의 지적 호기심은 끝이 없다. 과학의 발달이 탐구욕을 채워준다. 바이러스나 프리온은 전자현미경으로, 극소량의 화학 물질은 GC-MS나 HPLC-MS같은 분석 장비로 탐색한다. 현재 40대 이상은 '마이크로(micro, 100만분의 1)'라는 개념을 보고 신기해했다. 1990년대엔 나노(nano, 10억분의 1)라는 용어가 유행했다. 지금은 과학용어 앞에 붙는 피코(pico, 1조분의 1)까지 낯설지 않게 되었다.

　요즘은 식품업계가 현미경하에 놓여있다. 과거엔 너무 작아 측정이 불가능해 보이지 않던 vCJD(변종크로이츠펠트야콥병)나 노로바이러스, 다이옥신, PCB 등까지 신경 써야 하기 때문이다. 이러한 맥락에서 "식품에서 발암 물질이 일체 검출돼선 안 된다"는 1958년의 '딜레이니 조항'(Delaney clause)을 미 식품의약국(FDA)이 슬그머니 없앤 것이다.

　분석 화학의 발달로 검사 과정에서 실체가 드러난 대표 유해 물질은 최근 아일랜드산 돼지고기 파문의 주범인 다이옥신(dioxin)이다. 다이옥신 등 유해 물질은 먹이 사슬의 위쪽(최종 소비자 방향)으로 갈수록 누적된다. 그래서 최종 소비자의 다이옥신 수치가 1차 소비자의 수치보다 훨씬 높다. 이런 유독성 물질은 물보다는 플랑크톤과 같은 미생물에 더 고농도로 축적된다. 물고기가 플랑크톤을 먹게 되면 더 고농도로 물고기 몸에 쌓이게 되는 것이다.

　사람 중에서도 엄마 젖을 먹는 아기가 먹이 사슬의 최정점에 있다. 1999년 벨기에서 있었던 다이옥신 오염사고 같은 인재(人災)가 아니라면 우유보다 모유에서 다이옥신이 더 많이 검출되는 것은 당연한 일이다. 그럼에도 모유 먹이기를 권장하는 것은 전반적인 아기의 건강과 성장에 모유의 득이 훨씬 크다는 신빙성 있는 증거 때문이다.

문제해설

1. 이 글은 기술을 이용해 먹거리에서 유독성 물질을 제거한다는 내용이 아니며, 또한 모유 수유를 권장하는 글도 아니다. 그리고 기술의 발달이 지금의 먹거리가 내포한 문제를 해결해 줄 수 있을 것이라 낙관한다는 내용도 아니다. 기술의 발달로 이전에는 알려지지 않았던 유독 물질들을 검출할 수 있게 되었으며, 그런 물질 중에서 다이옥신에 대해 상세한 설명을 하고 있으므로 정답으로는 (a)가 적합하다.

2. 본문 마지막 줄에서 모유 수유가 더 많은 다이옥신에 노출될 수 있지만 장점이 단점보다 많기 때문이라고 말한 것으로 봐서 저자가 모유 수유를 반대하는 것이 아니라는 사실을 알 수 있다. 따라서 정답은 (d)가 된다.

3. 첫 번째와 두 번째 문단을 통해 측정 및 분석 기술의 발달로 이전에는 발견할 수 없었던, 그래서 신경 쓰지 않아도 됐던 vCJD, 노로바이러스, 다이옥신 등까지 이제는 신경 써야 한다고 했으므로 정답은 (a)가 된다.

4. (a)에 대한 내용은 세 번째 문단에 등장하지만 아일랜드산 돼지고기의 판매량 여부는 본문에 등장하지 않는다. 그리고 다이옥신은 먹이 사슬 상단에 있는 생명체에 더 많이 검출된다고 했으므로 먹이 사슬의 가장 꼭대기에 있는 인간에게 가장 많은 다이옥신이 검출되는 것은 당연하다. 이런 내용을 통해 어느 정도의 다이옥신은 몸에 쌓이는 것은 어쩔 수 없는 사실이란 것을 알 수 있으므로 (b)는 올바른 추론이 된다. (c)의 경우 물보다는 플랑크톤에 다이옥신과 같은 유독성 물질이 더 고농도로 축적된다는 내용이므로 (c)와는 무관하며, (d)의 경우 개연성은 있지만 본문에는 명시적으로 등장하지 않는다. 측정 및 분석 기술의 발달로 보다 다양한 미세 물질을 구별할 수는 있겠지만 현재도 잘 먹고 있는 음식에서 미래에 더 많은 위험 물질을 발견한다면 지금 당장 그 음식을 먹지 말아야 하기 때문에 논리적으로 맞지 않게 된다.

정답 1(a)   2(d)   3(a)   4(b)

Unit 52 | Carbon not always to blame
탄소를 위한 변명

　탄소 나노튜브는 '21세기 꿈의 신소재'로 칭송받는다. 일본 NEC의 이지마 스미오가 1991년 흑연 탄소 실험 도중 이 소재를 발견했을 때만 해도 그 무궁무진한 가능성을 가늠하지 못했을 것이다. 이는 이후 반도체와 평면 TV, 초강력 섬유, 생체 센서 같은 차세대 첨단 장치들의 토대가 됐다. '산업의 쌀'로 군림한 반도체의 위광을 빼앗을지 모른다. 탄소 나노튜브를 발견한 이지마 스미오 박사는 노벨상 단골 후보로 오르내린다.

　탄소(炭素)는 원소기호 C, 원자번호 6인 화학 원소이다. 숯을 뜻하는 라틴어인 carbo라는 어원만큼이나 칙칙한 이미지가 떠오른다. 하지만 화학자들 사이에 탄소는 '밝은 성격의 사교적인' 존재로 통한다. 우선 다른 원소와 쉽사리 반응한다. 사슬·고리형을 가리지 않고 무수히 많은 화합물을 만들어 낸다. 탄소끼리 뭉치는 데도 능하다. 다이아몬드가 바로 탄소의 결정체다. 탄소를 사람으로 치면 가정·사회생활을 두루 잘 하는 모범생이다. 이게 다가 아니다. 단백질·탄수화물 같은 탄소 화합물을 빼고 생명의 신비를 다루는 생화학이나 유기화학을 논할 수 없다. 나일론·아스피린·페놀처럼 인류의 경제생활을 뒤바꾼 혁명적 물질도 대개 탄소 화합물이다.

　뭐니 뭐니 해도 탄소의 가장 큰 소임의 하나는 광합성을 통한 지구 생태계 순환일 것이다. 이산화탄소(CO_2)가 물과 공기를 만나 포도당과 산소를 만들고 동식물의 생로병사를 통해 탄소 성분이 대지로 되돌아오는 과정이다. 문제는 온실가스의 일종인 이산화탄소가 과다할 때 생기는 지구 온난화 현상이다. 지난해 영국 정부는 '탄소 카드'라는 이색 구상을 내놨다. 휘발유를 넣을 때마다 카드에 판독이 되도록 해서 탄소 과소비자에 불이익을 주자는 것이다. 환경론자들은 화석연료 위주의 '탄소경제' 시대를 보내고 청정에너지 위주의 '수소경제' 시대를 앞당겨야 한다고 재촉한다. 탄소 나노튜브 연구자들이 머쓱해질지 모르겠다.

문제해설

1. 이 글은 꿈의 신소재 탄소 나노튜브로 시작을 하지만 결국은 탄소에 대한 여러 특성과 이 탄소가 어떤 역할을 하는지에 관해 서술하고 있다. 그리고 마지막에 가서는 환경 문제 중 하나인 지구 온난화 현상이 탄소와 어떤 관계가 있는지에 관해 설명하고 있다. 이런 맥락에서 (a), (b), (c) 모두 부분적으로 등장하는 내용이지만 주제는 (d)가 된다는 것을 알 수 있다.

2. 이 문제의 힌트는 두 번째 문단 도입부에 나온다. 탄소라고 하면 석탄이 떠올라 보통의 경우 칙칙한 이미지를 떠올리기 쉽지만 탄소는 다른 원소와 잘 반응하고 무수히 많은 화합물을 만드는 팔방미인이라는 설명이다. 따라서 정답은 (a)가 적합하다.

3. 탄소 카드(carbon credit card)에 대한 설명은 세 번째 문단 후반부에 등장한다. 한마디로 "휘발유를 넣을 때마다 카드에 판독이 되도록 해서 탄소 과소비자에 불이익을 주는 것"이 핵심이므로 정답은 (a)가 적합하다. 이에 적당한 보기는 (c)가 된다.

4. (a)는 2번 문제에서 나왔던 내용이며, (c)의 경우 본문 후반에 나오는 지구 온난화 현상의 주범이 과다한 이산화탄소란 설명에서 확인할 수 있는 내용이다. (d)의 경우 두 번째 문단 후반부 "it would be impossible to discuss biochemistry or organic chemistry ... without mentioning carbon compounds" 부분을 통해 확인할 수 있다. 정답은 (b)로 사람들의 탄소 소비를 줄이는 정책이나 운동이 실제로 실효성이 있을지는 본문에 명시되어 있지 않다.

정답 1(d) 2(a) 3(a) 4(b)

Unit 53 | Government stuck in a rut
경로 의존성

모든 물체는 자신의 운동 상태를 그대로 유지하려는 성질이 있다. 정지한 물체는 계속 정지하려 하고, 움직이는 물체는 원래의 속력과 방향으로 계속 가려고 한다. 갈릴레오가 발견하고, 뉴턴이 '운동의 제1법칙'으로 체계화한 이른바 '관성(慣性, inertia)의 법칙'이다. 자연계의 물체는 스스로 멈추거나 방향을 바꿀 수 없다. 관성을 제어하는 것은 외부의 힘이다. 날아가는 야구공은 자신의 의지가 아니라 공기의 저항과 중력이라는 외부의 힘에 의해 땅에 떨어진다.

관성이 인간의 삶에 투영되면 늘 하던 방식을 답습하고 웬만해선 바꾸려 하지 않는 경향을 뜻한다. 물체의 관성은 질량이 클수록 커지는데 비해, 인간의 타성은 시간이 오래될수록 벗어나기 어렵다. 그래서 제 버릇 남 못주고, 세살 버릇이 여든까지 간다는 속담이 있는 것이다. 관성은 사회의 제도와 조직에서도 발견된다. 어떤 제도나 조직도 일단 생기고 나면 여간해선 없애거나 바꾸기 어렵다. 규모가 커지고 역사가 쌓이면 운영 방식이 관행으로 고착되고, 스스로 확대 재생산하려는 경향마저 생긴다.

사회과학에선 이를 '경로 의존성(Path Dependency)'이라고 부른다. 일련의 사건들이 최초에 특정한 방향으로 진행되면 그 뒤에는 제도와 조직을 변경 불가능할 정도로 경직되게 만드는 현상을 말한다. 과거에 지나온 경로에 의해 미래의 진행 방향이 결정된다는 것이다. 영연방 국가에서 차량의 좌측통행 관행은 이제는 바꿀 수 없는 제도가 됐다. 운전대의 위치와 교통 체계가 그에 맞춰졌기 때문이다. 1868년 크리스토퍼 숄즈가 창안한 QWERTY 자판 배열 방식이 자판의 표준이 된 것은 단지 그것이 처음 나왔기 때문이다. 아무리 좋은 대안이 새로 나와도 이미 제도로 굳어진 자판 배열을 바꾸지 못했다.

문제해설

1. 본문에서는 '관성'이라는 물리적 법칙을 개인에게 적용해 '타성'이라고 부르고 있으며, 이를 다시 제도나 조직에도 적용하고 있다. 더 나아가 사회과학에서는 이런 현상을 '경로 의존성'이라고 부른다고 설명하면서 이에 해당하는 사례들, 예를 들어 운전대의 위치나, 자판 배열방식 등을 소개하고 있다. 따라서 정답은 관성의 법칙을 실재 물체나 추상적 개념에도 적용할 수 있다는 (c)가 된다.

2. '요람에서 배운 것이 무덤까지 간다는 것'은 개인의 타성에 대한 설명이다. 이는 절대 (d)와 같은 긍정적 어감을 내포하지 않는다. 따라서 정답은 어떤 것을 처리하는 방식이 나중에도 변하지 않는다는 내용의 (a)가 정답이 된다.

3. 첫 번째 문단에서 관성은 현재의 운동 상태를 그대로 유지하려는 성질이라고 말하면서, 외부의 힘이 없이는 스스로 멈추거나 방향을 바꿀 수 없다고 설명하고 있다. 따라서 책이 선반에서 떨어졌다는 것은 중력과 같은 외부의 힘이 작용했음을 의미한다. 따라서 정답은 (a)가 된다.

4. QWERTY(쿼티) 자판 배열이 더 나은 대안이 나와도 계속해서 사용되는 이유는 쿼티 자판이 맨 처음 나온 것이기 때문이라고 본문 마지막 문단에서 설명하고 있다. 따라서 처음은 아닐 수 있지만 그럼에도 널리 쓰인다는 내용의 (d)는 사실과 다르다.

정답 1(c) 2(a) 3(a) 4(d)

Unit 54 | Silence leads to true inspiration
미래를 여는 힘, '깊은 침묵'

1847년 2월 11일 한 아이가 태어났다. 그는 자라면서 학교에 다닐 때 주목받지 못했다. 선생님한테 "멍청

하다"는 막말을 들을 정도였고 학교를 반년도 채 못 다녔다. 게다가 청소년기에 청력도 상당 부분 잃었다. 하지만 그런데도 전구는 물론이고 축음기까지 발명했다. 그가 죽을 때까지 그의 이름으로 출원된 발명특허만 자그마치 1,093건이나 되었다. 그의 이름은 토머스 에디슨이다.

19세기에 나온 그의 발명품들은 20세기에 더 나은 삶을 창조하고 새로운 미래를 열었다. 그런데 그로 하여금 미래를 열게 만든 힘의 근원은 과연 무엇이었을까? 그것은 스스로를 가둔 채 실험에 몰두했던 그의 '길고도 깊은 침묵'이었다.

에디슨 하면 떠오르는 말이 있다. "천재는 1%의 영감(靈感)과 99% 노력의 산물"이 그것이다. 물론 그에겐 창조성을 격발시키는 1%의 영감도 있었고, 백열전구의 필라멘트 재료를 확보하기 위해 300여 가지가 넘는 재료로 줄기차게 실험하는 99%의 노력도 있었다.

하지만 절대 간과해선 안 될 것은 그 창조적 영감도, 부단한 노력도 모두 그의 '깊은 침묵' 없이는 불가능했다는 사실이다. 에디슨은 혼자만의 시간을 가지면서 영감을 발견했다. 실험실 문에 스스로 자물쇠를 걸어놓았기에 그 많은 발명을 해낼 수 있었다. 그 덕분에 19세기와는 전혀 다른 20세기가 열릴 수 있었다. 에디슨이 외부 세계로부터의 소음과 복잡한 문제들을 차단한 것이 창조적 발상과 발명을 가능케 한 것이다.

미래는 오는 것이 아니다. 우리가 가는 것이다. 미래는 기다림의 대상이 아니라 오늘 나의 의지와 노력으로 만들어지는 대상이다. 나의 시선과 발걸음이 어디를 향하고 있느냐에 따라 미래는 달라진다. 하지만 더 나은 미래를 여는 진짜 밑동아리 힘은 다름 아닌 '깊은 침묵'에서 나온 영감에 있음을 잊지 말자.

문제해설

1. 에디슨은 주목받지 못한 아이였고, 선생님한테 막말을 들을 정도였고, 학교를 반년도 채 다니지 못했다고 나온다. 하지만 다른 학생들의 무자비한 괴롭힘이라는 내용은 등장하지 않는다. 그리고 그가 가진 질병은 잘 듣지 못하는 것이었다. 그렇다고 해서 어린 시절을 친구들과 놀거나 말하지 못하고 고립되어 살았다는 내용은 없다. 대신 발명을 위해 실험실에서 홀로 '깊은 침묵'으로 몰두했다는 내용은 등장한다. 이상으로 (a), (b), (d)는 본문과 다름을 알 수 있다. 정답은 (c)로 다른 사람들로부터 그다지 총명하다고 생각되지 않은 아이였다는 내용이 적절하다.

2. 먼저 이 글은 에디슨에 관한 것으로, 에디슨이 이룩한 업적들도 포함되어 있다. 하지만 이 글은 어떻게 그가 그런 대단한 업적들을 이끌어낼 수 있었는지에 초점을 맞추고 있다. 에디슨의 천재적 영감과 줄기찬 노력이 있었던 것은 두말하면 잔소리로, 이 모든 것 이전에 에디슨의 '깊은 침묵'이 더 근본적인 요인이었다는 세 번째 문단이 이 글의 주제를 잘 요약하고 있다. 따라서 정답은 (c)가 아니라 (d)가 된다.

3. 에디슨의 죽음이나 죽었을 당시의 상황은 본문에 나타나있지 않으므로 정답은 (a)가 된다.

4. (a)와 (c)는 내용이 지나치게 극단적이며, (d)는 마지막 문단을 나타낸 것은 사실이나 에디슨의 사상을 반영하고 있지 못한다. 정답은 (b)로 "천재는 1%의 영감과 99% 노력의 산물"이라는 내용을 재진술하고 있다.

정답 1(c)　2(d)　3(a)　4(b)

Unit 55 | Weather not an exact science
수치예보

날씨 예측의 정확성을 높이는 일은 그리 간단치 않다. 기상 예보가 근본적으로 자주 틀릴 수밖에 없는 숙명을 안고 있기 때문이다. 사실 날씨를 과학적으로 예측하기 시작한 것은 비교적 최근의 일이다. 정확한 기상 관측기구가 없었던 시절에는 감각기관이나 경험에 의존해 날씨를 점칠 수밖에 없었다. 갈릴레오 갈릴레이가 온도계를 발명한 것이 1660년대 초였고, 벤자민 프랭클린이 기상현상이 지역별로 움직인다는 사실을 발견한 때가 1773년이었다. 무선전신이 발명된 19세기에 이르러서야 광범위한 지역의 날씨를 보여주는 일기도가 일기예보에 활용되기 시작했다. 20세기 중반에는 인공위성과 기상레이더 등 첨단 기상 관측 장비가 발명되고, 대규모 기상정보를 처리할 수 있는 슈퍼 컴퓨터가 등장했다. 현재의 날씨에 관한 정보를 바탕으로 미래의 날씨 정보를 수치로 계산해 내는 이른바 '수치예보'의 시대가 열린 것이다.

문제는 날씨에 영향을 미치는 엄청난 양의 정보를 슈퍼 컴퓨터를 사용해 분석해도 예보의 정확성을 높이는 데는 한계가 있다는 점이다. 1961년 미국의 기상학자 에드워드 로렌츠가 만든 용어인 이른바 '나비효과' 때문이다. '브라질에 있는 나비의 날갯짓이 텍사스에 토네이도를 불러올 수 있다'는 말처럼, 사소한 초기의 기상 현상이 엄청난 차이를 만들어낸다는 이론이다. 아무리 정교한 기상예측 모델을 만들어도 처음에 입력한 정보가 조금만 잘못되면 예측 결과가 판이하게 달라진다. 날씨에 대한 정보가 많아지고, 예측모델이 정교해진다고 해서 예보가 더 정확해진다는 보장은 없다. 숫자가 정확하다고 예보가 정확한 것은 아니란 얘기다. 컴퓨터가 계산해낸 수치를 분석해 날씨를 예보하는 것은 결국 사람의 몫이다.

문제해설

1. 나비효과는 두 번째 문단에 정의가 나오는데, "The flap of a butterfly's wing in Brazil can set off a tornado in Texas." 부분을 보면 알 수 있다. 한 곳에서 발생한 아주 사소한 현상이라도 다른 곳에서는 큰 영

향을 미칠 수 있다는 말로, 기상현상이 초기 조건에 매우 민감해서 그만큼 예측이 어렵다는 것을 설명하고 있다. 따라서 정답은 (b)가 된다.

2. 첫 번째 문단 마지막 부분에 수치예보의 시대가 열린 것은 대규모 기상정보를 처리할 수 있는 슈퍼 컴퓨터가 등장한 이후라고 했으므로 정답은 (a)가 된다.

3. 슈퍼 컴퓨터는 두 번째 문단에 나오는 내용으로, (a)의 내용은 등장하지 않는다. (b)의 경우 정확한 예보를 하는 것은 '나비효과' 등의 이유로 어렵다고 했으므로 정확히 사용된다고 해서 나올 수 있는 결과는 아니다. (c)의 경우 수치는 컴퓨터가 해석하지만 결국 날씨를 예보하는 것은 사람이라고 마지막 줄에서 설명하고 있으므로 사람은 아무런 인풋도 제공하지 않는다는 내용은 본문과 일치하지 않는다. 정답은 (d)로 모든 데이터를 사용한다고 하더라도 정확한 날씨 예측은 예기치 않은 변수가 많아 어렵다는 것이므로 내용과 부합한다.

정답 1(b)   2(a)   3(d)

Unit 56 | A rose by any other name
구인배율

수량을 비교할 때 흔히 비율(比率)과 배율(倍率)을 쓴다. 비율이든 배율이든 비교 수량을 비교되는 수량으로 나눈 숫자라는 점에서는 매한가지다. 두 가지 모두 어떤 것이 다른 것에 비해 얼마나 큰지, 또는 얼마나 작은지를 한눈에 보여준다.

비율과 배율은 계산하는 방법은 같지만 실제 쓰임새에선 미묘한 차이가 있다. 우선 비율(rate)에는 기준량이 있다. 비율은 비교하려는 수량이 기준 수량에서 얼마만큼을 차지하고 있는지를 본다. 예컨대, 실업률은 경제활동인구 중에서 실업자가 차지하는 비율이다. 비교하는 수량이 기준량보다 큰 경우는 별로 없기 때문에 비율은 대개 1보다 작다. 특히 어떤 것의 구성 비율은 항상 1 이하일 수밖에 없다. 다만 증가율의 경우 간혹 증가분이 기준량보다 커서 예외적으로 1을 넘기는 사례가 있다.

이에 비해 배율(ratio)은 딱히 기준량이 없이 한 가지 수량이 다른 것의 몇 배나 되는지를 따진다. 현미경이나 망원경의 확대배율은 실제 크기보다 몇 배나 크게 보이는지를 나타낸다. 그래서 배율은 대개 1보다 크고, 곱절을 뜻하는 '배(倍)'를 단위로 쓴다. 복사기의 축소배율처럼 1보다 작은 경우도 더러 있지만, 대부분 비교하는 수량이 비교되는 수량보다 상당히 클 경우에 주로 쓰인다.

문제해설

1. 본문은 비율(rate)과 배율(ratio)의 차이에 대해 설명하고 있다. 따라서 정답은 (b)가 적합하다.

2. (a)는 첫 번째 문단에 대한 설명이며, (b)는 나머지 문단에서 각각 설명하고 있는 내용이다. (c)의 경우 두 번째 문단에서 비율(rate)에는 기준량이 있다고 한 내용을 서술한 것이다. 정답은 (d)로 어떤 것이 증가하는 비율은 거리로 따지자면 속도와 같은 개념으로 본문에서 설명

하고 있는 비율과 배율에는 적합하지 않는 내용이다.

3. 본문에서는 비율과 배율의 유사한 점을 서두에 설명해 두었기 때문에 정답을 (a)라고 생각할 수 있지만, 사실 유사성에 대해 언급한 것은 이 둘이 얼핏 보기에는 비슷해 보이지만 실은 아래와 같은 차이가 있다는 점을 더 강조하기 위해서 사용한 것이므로 (a)보다는 (b)가 제목으로 적절하다.

4. 일단 (c)와 (d)의 설명은 배율과 비율을 각각 본문에 맞게 잘 설명하고 있다. 배율의 경우 몇 배(times)인가가 중요했고, 비율의 경우 기준 값이 중요했다. (a)의 설명도 첫 번째 문단의 내용과 일치한다고 볼 수 있다. 정답은 (b)로, 본문에서 비율이란 기준 값의 비(the ratio of the standard)가 아닌 기준 값과 상대 값의 비율(proportion)이라고 했으므로 (b)는 적절한 설명이 되지 못한다.

정답 1(b)   2(d)   3(b)   4(b)

Unit 57 | Dangers of tunnel vision
터널시야

엄청난 중력으로 인하여 전투기 조종사나 곡예 비행사가 이른바 터널시야(Tunnel Vision) 현상을 겪게 되는 경우가 있는데, 이는 앞쪽 가운데 부분을 제외한 주변부가 시야에서 사라지는 현상이다. 어두운 터널을 빠른 속도로 달리면 터널의 출구만 동그랗게 밝게 보이고 주변은 온통 깜깜해지는 시각효과를 말한다. 이는 망원경을 통해 볼 때 세상이 원통의 동그라미 영역으로 한정되는 것과 유사한 현상이다. 동그라미 밖의 상황을 인지하지 못하니 당연히 판단력이 떨어질 수밖에 없다.

의학적으로 터널시야 현상은 여러 가지 원인에 의해 일어날 수 있다. 안질환에 의한 각막 착색이나 손상으로 시야가 축소될 수도 있고, 뇌출혈이나 중추신경계의 산소 중독도 터널시야를 불러올 위험이 있다. 고산증이나 저산소증, 편두통이 터널시야 현상을 일으킨다는 보고도 있다.

흔히 경험하는 터널시야는 음주에 의한 것이다. 과도하게 알코올을 섭취하면 눈 근육이 이완되면서 초점을 잘 잡지 못한다. 급기야는 대상이 흐려지거나 이중으로 보이며 시야가 좁아진다. 터널시야 현상이 나타나면 사고의 위험이 커진다. 비행기 조종이나 자동차 운전, 중장비 조작, 도로 횡단 중에 터널시야 현상을 겪으면 치명적인 사고를 당할 수 있다.

문제해설

1. 본문의 마지막 부분에서 터널시야를 겪는 사람은 특정 행위 중 치명적인 사고를 당할 수 있다고 했으므로 (b)에서와 같이 자신이나 남을 위험에 처하게 할 수 있는 어떤 일도 해서는 안 된다는 설명이 적합하다.

2. 터널시야를 유발하는 요인이 아닌 것은 (a)의 숙취(hangover)로, 음주와 관련이 있다고 세 번째 문단에서 설명하고 있지만 음주한 다음 날까지 이어지는 취기인 숙취와는 무관하다.

3. 본문 마지막 부분에서 터널시야를 겪는 경우 위험한 대상에 대해 설명하고 있는데, 반드시 위험한 직업을 가진 사람이 아닐지라도, 예를 들어 도로를 횡단하고 있는 평범한 사람이라도 터널시야를 겪게 되면 치명적일 수 있기 때문에 정답은 (c)가 된다.

4. 본문은 터널시야를 겪게 되는 의학적 원인과 그에 따른 영향에 대해 설명하고 있으므로 정답은 (c)가 적합하다. (a)는 본문에 언급되어 있지 않으며, (b)는 사고를 당할 수 있다고 설명은 하고 있지만 발생할 수 있는 사고에 대해 설명하거나 나열하고 있지는 않다. (d) 또한 본문과 무관하므로 정답에서 제외된다.

정답 1(b) 2(a) 3(c) 4(c)

Unit 58 | Joining in the game
지구 온난화

지구 온난화는 인류에 축복인가? 화석연료가 요즘만큼 대량 소비되지 않던 100년 전만 해도 유럽의 세계적 과학자들의 이런 주장은 받아들여졌다. 이온 물질 연구로 1903년 노벨상까지 받은 화학자 아레니우스는 이산화탄소의 증가가 대기를 덥게 한다는 사실을 1890년대에 알아냈지만 문제의 심각성까지 깨닫지는 못했다. 그가 『완성 중인 세계』라는 저서에서 제시한 미래상은 목가적이었다. '이산화탄소 증가로 온난화가 진행되면 추운 지역이 따뜻해지고, 지구 전체로 곡물의 수확이 늘어 급증하는 인구 부양에 큰 도움이 된다'는 것이었다.

이제 온실가스가 해롭다는 건 모두가 다 안다. 유엔의 정부 간 기후변화위원회(IPCC)는 최근 이런 논의에 종지부를 찍었다. 이산화탄소의 과도 배출이 지구를 망가뜨리는 주범이며, 인류를 살리려면 이산화탄소 증가세를 8년 안에 반드시 잡아야 한다는 것이다.

명쾌한 총론에 비해 각론은 복잡하다. 지구 온난화 현상은 특히 중위·고위도 지방에서 심하게 나타난다. '온난화'라는 용어 때문에 으레 폭염과 가뭄을 연상하지만 재앙의 형태는 홍수와 해일·태풍 등 다양하다. 이런 현상에 대처하는 능력은 부국과 빈국 사이의 메우기 힘든 간극이다.

남극 빙하가 녹으면서 해수면이 상승해 바다 속으로 가라앉을 위기에 처한 남태평양 폴리네시아의 섬나라 투발루, 국토의 90%가 사막이 될지 모르는 몽골. 이처럼 온난화가 초래한 위험에 속수무책인 나라가 수두룩하다. 그런데 선진국들은 탄소거래소·녹색기술 같은 자금력과 첨단 기술로 파고를 넘고 있다.

문제해설

1. 지구 온난화의 결과로 우려되는 점을 찾는 문제인데, 본문 후반부에 보면 빈국과 부국이 이를 대처하는 데 큰 차이를 보인다고 설명하고 있다. 그러면서 지구 온난화에 속수무책인 빈국과 첨단 기술 등에 힘을 쏟고 있는 부국의 모습을 대조해서 설명하고 있다. 따라서 이런 모습을 지적한 (a)가 정답으로 적합하다.

2. 본문의 서두에 보면 100여 년 전만 해도 세계적 과학자인 아레니우스는 이산화탄소의 증가가 대기를 덥게 한다는 사실을 1890년대에 알아냈지만 문제의 심각성까지 깨닫지는 못했으며, 다소 낭만적인 생각을 했다고 설명하고 있다. 즉 보기 (d)에서와 같이 지구 온난화로 인해 추운 지역이 따뜻해지고, 곡물의 수확이 늘어 인구 부양에 도움을 줄 것으로 예상한 것이다.

3. (a)의 경우, 부국보다는 빈국이 걱정이라고 했으므로 (a)는 적절하지 못하다. (b)의 경우 본문과 비슷해 보이지만 조금 차이가 있다. 본문에서 말한 8년은 문제를 해결하기 위해 필요한 최대 허용 가능한 시간을 의미하며, 보기에서 말한 8년은 문제가 일어나기까지 버틸 수 있는 시간을 말해서 차이가 있다. (c)의 경우 투발루는 물에 잠길 가능성이 있다고 했지만, 몽골의 경우 사막화의 위험에 처해있다고 했으므로 올바른 내용이 아니다. 정답은 (d)로, 과거 100년 동안 과학자들의 인식 변화가 컸다는 것을 첫 번째와 두 번째 문단을 통해 확인할 수 있다.

4. 이 글은 문제의 심각성에 대해 경고하고 있는 글이므로 (b)가 적합하다. (a)가 답이 되려면 본문에서 지구 온난화 논쟁에 대한 찬반이 나와야 하는데 지구 온난화가 문제라고 생각하는 측의 내용만 담겨있다. (c)와 (d)는 부분적인 지적에 그치고 있다.

정답 1(a) 2(d) 3(d) 4(b)

Unit 59 | Corny economics
옥수수 쟁탈전

옥수수의 원산지인 멕시코가 옥수수 값 폭등으로 힘겹다는 소식이다. 지난봄에는 수도 멕시코시티의 한복판에 12만 명이 모여서 항의 집회를 열어 정부 당국을 긴장시킨 일도 있었다. 최근 1년 새 토티야 값이 세 배로 뛰었다. 1994년 북미자유무역협정(NAFTA) 발효 이래 싼 값에 들여오던 미국산 옥수수 물량이 확보되지 않아서다. 옥수수 흉작 때문이 아니다. 부시 행정부가 추진 중인 바이오연료 정책의 여파다.

옥수수를 발효시킨 뒤 정제하면 에탄올이 나온다. 이를 휘발유와 혼합해 만든 바이오 에탄올은 자동차 연료로 쓸 수 있다. 최근의 기록적인 고유가와 중동 정세 불안 등으로 미국은 어느 때보다 바이오연료 생산에 적극적이다. 조지 W 부시 대통령은 올해 연두 교서에서 바이오연료 소비를 늘려 향후 10년간 휘발유 소비를 20% 줄이겠다고 발표했다. 바이오연료 공장과 주유소가 우후죽순처럼 생겨나면서 옥수수 가격 곡선도 가파른 상승 커브를 그렸다. 미국 내 수요를 충당하느라 수출 물량은 크게 줄었다. 10여 년간 NAFTA의 덕을 톡톡히 봐 온 멕시코 인들이 'NAFTA 재협상'을 시위구호로 내건 연유다.

멕시코인들만 괴롭게 된 게 아니다. 바다 건너 일본인들에게도 바이오연료 붐의 여파가 밀어닥치고 있다. (옥수수가 주재료인) 사료값 폭등을 견디지 못한 일본의 양계업자나 축산농가가 폐업하는 사례가 잇달아 나타났다. 고기

값과 햄 가격이 뛴 것은 불문가지다. 옥수수뿐 아니라 다른 곡물의 가격도 덩달아 뛰었다. 농민들이 너도 나도 '돈이 되는' 옥수수로 재배 품종을 전환하면서 다른 곡물의 생산량이 줄어든 탓이다. 그 결과 미국산 콩으로 두부나 낫토(納豆)를 만드는 일본 업체들이 콩의 양을 줄이는 사실상의 가격 인상 조치를 단행했다. 독일에선 맥주 값이 올랐다. 이 역시 보리 농가가 옥수수로 전업한 까닭이다.

문제해설

1. 갑자기 옥수수 가격이 상승한 원인은 다름 아닌 부시 행정부(이 글은 2007년에 작성된 것이다)가 추진 중인 바이오연료 정책의 여파라고 첫 번째 문단의 후반부에 설명되어 있다. 따라서 정답은 이로 인한 옥수수의 부족이라는 (c)가 정답이 된다.

2. 이전에는 싼 가격으로 멕시코에 공급되던 옥수수가 이제는 자국의 바이오연료로 사용되면서 수출이 되지 않고 국내에 머무르고 있다. 따라서 정답은 (a)라는 것을 알 수 있다. (b)의 경우 낫토나 두부를 만드는 데 사용되는 것은 옥수수가 아닌 미국산 콩이다. (c)의 경우 NAFTA로 가격이 낮췄던 것이 바이오연료로 인해 가격이 오른 것이므로 사실이 아니다. (d)의 경우 반대로 설명해야 올바르다. 다른 작물을 재배하던 농민들이 점점 더 옥수수를 재배하고 있다고 해야 한다.

3. 이 글에서 말하고자 하는 것은 바이오연료 산업으로 인해 옥수수 가격이 상승하게 되었고, 그 여파로 각국에 부정적인 영향이 발생했다는 것이므로 정답은 (d)가 적합하다.

4. (a)는 실제 상황과 반대되는 설명이다. NAFTA로 인해 미국 옥수수는 싼 값에 멕시코에 수입됐다. (b)의 내용은 세 번째 문단에 나와 있기 때문에 사실이다. (c)의 경우 휘발유와 혼합해 바이오 에탄올을 만들 수 있다고 했으므로 사실이 아니며, (d)의 경우는 반대로 고유가나 중동 정세 불안 등에 힘입어 바이오연료 수요가 늘었다고 나와 있다.

정답 1(c)　2(a)　3(d)　4(b)

Unit 60 | That weather is a killer
기상병

"오늘은 짧은 시간에 급격하게 기온이 올라갈 것으로 예상되므로 자동차 운전이나 부부싸움에 주의하시기 바랍니다." 웬 뚱딴지같은 소리냐고 반문할지 모르지만 지난 4월 중순 일본 기상협회 홋카이도 지사가 내린 정식 일기예보다. 한 시간에 3~5℃씩 급격히 온도가 올라가는 '푄 현상'이 사람의 심신에 악영향을 미칠 수 있음을 경고한 것이다. 실제로 예보 당일 교통사고나 부부싸움이 증가했는지는 알 길이 없지만, 이 예보를 계기로 일본에서 큰 화제를 모은 것이 이른바 '기상병'(meteorotropic disease)이란 용어다.

기상병은 날씨 변화로 인해 생기는 각종 질병을 통틀어 일컫는 말이다. 인체의 조절 능력이 기온이나 기압의 갑작스런 변화를 따라가지 못해 생기는 현상이다. 날씨의 변화는 혈관 확장·수축 등 신경계에 미묘한 영향을 미친다. "어깨가 욱신거리는 걸 보니 곧 비가 올 모양이구먼." 노인들의 이런 입버릇을 체계화하는 것이 '생기상학'(生氣象學)이란 학문 분야다.

신경통뿐 아니라 뇌출혈, 협심증, 심근 경색, 천식 등 기상병의 종류는 다양하다. 심지어는 맹장염에 주목한 학자도 있다. 니가타 의대의 한 교수는 날씨가 좋은 날에는 급성 맹장염으로 구급차에 실려 오는 환자가 늘어난다는 의사들의 경험담에 착안한 연구결과를 발표했다. 고기압일수록 백혈구에서 과립구가 차지하는 비율이 증가하여 화농성 염증을 일으키기 쉽다는 것이다. 히로시마현 의사회는 2004년부터 심근 경색·뇌졸중 증상이 늘었다고 보고했다. 지역 신문은 날씨와 기온에 따른 발병 위험도를 '경계' '주의' '보통'의 세 단계로 나눠 싣는다.

전문가들은 날이 갈수록 기상병이 증가할 것이라고 경고한다. 지구 온난화의 영향으로 기상 이변이 빈발하는 반면 인체의 적응력은 한계가 있기 때문이란다. 머잖아 일기예보와 동시에 기상병 예보가 일상화되는 날이 올지도 모르겠다. "오늘은 이런 저런 병에 주의하십시오." 이 같은 예보를 들으며 하루 일과를 시작한다고 생각하니 상상만으로도 별로 달갑지 않다. 틀리면 큰 비난을 받는 일기예보와 달리 기상병 예보는 빗나가면 빗나갈수록 환영받는 예보가 될 듯하다.

문제해설

1. 본문은 일기예보와 함께 날씨가 신체에 영향을 미칠 수 있는 것을 경고하는 기상병 예보가 일본에서 인기를 모으고 있다는 내용을 소개하고 있다. 어떻게 질병을 예방할지 혹은 날씨 변화에 따른 질병에는 어떤 것들이 있는지는 본문에 일부 등장하기도 하지만 이는 부분적 요소라고 생각할 수 있다. 따라서 정답은 이런 내용의 기사가 있었다고 말한 (d)가 적합하다.

2. 두 번째 문단에서 날씨의 변화는 혈관 확장·수축 등 신경계에 미묘한 영향을 미치며, 그렇기에 날씨 변화가 있을 때 이를 사람들이 감지한다고 말하고 있다. 그리고 그런 현상을 생기상학(live meteorology)이라고 부르고 있다고 나온다. 보기 중 (d)는 이런 날씨의 변화로 발생하는 신체의 이상이 아닌 개인의 감정이나 기호이기 때문에 부적합하다.

3. 일본에서는 일기예보와 함께 기상병 예보를 한다고 했으므로 날씨 변화와 관련한 기상병을 가볍게 생각하지 않는다는 것을 보여주며, 날씨 변화와 질병 사이의 관계에 대해서도 중요하게 생각한다고 볼 수 있으므로 정답은 (d)가 된다.

4. 본문 마지막 부분에서 "Unlike the weather forecast, which gets widely criticized when the forecast is wrong, the more a meteorotropic disease forecast is wrong, the more welcome it will be."라고 한 부분을 통해 (b)를 추론할 수 있다.

정답 1(d)　2(d)　3(d)　4(b)

Unit 61 | Thunderstruck
벼락

　동서양을 막론하고 고대인들은 기상 현상을 신의 조화라고 생각했다. 특히 천둥과 번개는 죄 지은 인간에 대해 신이 내리는 천벌이라고 여겨 두려워했다. 벼락 또는 낙뢰(落雷)는 그 섬뜩한 광경과 엄청난 위력 때문에 큰 두려움의 대상이었다. 죄 지은 사람에게 떨어진 벼락은 천벌이지만 죄 없이 맞는 벼락은 날벼락이었다. 벼락은 오랜 기상 현상임에도 그에 대한 과학적 규명은 근대에 이르기까지 거의 이루어지지 않았다. 11세기 중국 송(宋)대에 벼락이 일종의 전기적 현상이라는 기록이 있지만, 이를 실험으로 입증한 것은 그로부터 700년이 지난 후였다. 벤자민 프랭클린은 1752년 그 유명한 연(鳶)을 이용한 실험을 통해 벼락이 구름에 모인 정전기가 지면으로 방전되는 현상이라는 것을 밝혀냈다.

　벼락은 최고 수십만 암페어에 이르는 전기를 수반하며, 초속 45km로 이동할 수 있고, 온도도 태양표면 온도의 5배인 3,000℃에 이른다. 이 때문에 큰 벼락이 떨어지면 심각한 인명과 재산 피해를 입을 수 있다. 벼락이 많이 떨어지는 곳은 기상 조건과 지형이 적란운을 만들어내기 쉬운 곳들이다. 미국 플로리다 주의 올랜도와 세인트 피터스버그 사이의 지역은 천둥과 번개를 동반한 폭우가 내리는 날이 연평균 120일에 달해 '번개 통로'라고 불린다. 높은 건물은 피뢰침을 세워 낙뢰 피해를 예방하지만 아무래도 다른 곳보다는 벼락을 맞을 확률이 높다. 엠파이어스테이트 빌딩은 매년 평균 23회 벼락을 맞는데, 한번은 24분 동안 8번이나 떨어진 적도 있다고 한다.

문제해설

1. 첫 번째 문단은 번개의 과학적으로 알게 된 기원과 역사를 다루고 있고, 두 번째 문단은 번개와 천둥에 대한 기타 특징이나 자주 발생하는 곳 등에 대해 서술하고 있다. (a)와 (b)는 특정 부분만 다룬 단편적 내용이므로 적절하지 않고, (d)의 경우 번개는 고대부터 알고 있었던 것이므로 이를 발견이라고 하면 어색해진다.

2. (a)와는 달리 번개는 고대에도 잘 알려진 현상이며, 미국의 특정 지역에서 천둥과 번개를 동반한 현상이 자주 발생한다고 했으므로 (c) 또한 올바르지 않다. 그리고 (d)에 나온 '번개 통로'는 천둥과 번개가 자주 발생하는 곳을 의미하므로 안전한 장소와는 거리가 멀다. 정답은 (b)로 벼락은 엄청난 위력 때문에 큰 두려움의 대상이라고 했으므로 보기와 일치한다.

3. 본문의 후반부에 보면, 엠파이어스테이트 빌딩에 벼락이 몇 번 치는지는 나오지만 얼마만큼의 피해(damage)를 입었는지는 등장하지 않는다. 따라서 (a)가 정답이 된다.

4. 엄청난 위력으로 두려워했다는 내용은 나오지만 (a)나 (c)와 같은 내용은 등장하지 않는다. 그리고 (d)는 본문과 무관하다. 정답은 (b)로 본문 초반의 "they feared thunder and lightning because they thought the gods created them to punish people who sinned" 부분을 통해 신의 벌로 두려워했다는 것을 알 수 있다.

정답　1(c)　2(b)　3(a)　4(b)

Unit 62 | Going ape
침팬지더위

　인간과 가장 가까운 동물은 침팬지라는 건 널리 알려진 이야기다. DNA 구조의 98.7%가 동일하다 하니 그럴 만하다. 그러나 거꾸로 이 1.3%의 차이 때문에 인간은 동물원 우리 밖에서 구경하고, 침팬지는 우리 안에 갇히는 신세가 됐다. 둘 사이의 주된 차이점은 '더위'에의 적응 능력이라 한다. 인간은 더위에 강하다. 땀을 흘리는 '발한(發汗) 기능' 때문이다. 더우면 땀샘에서 다른 동물에 비해 훨씬 많은 수분을 발산한다. 그리고 수분을 증발시켜 빠르게 체온을 내리는 효과를 얻는다. 침팬지에는 이런 기능이 없다. 사람처럼 땡볕 속을 걸어 다니는 일은 거의 없다. 더울 때는 꿈적 않고 나무 그늘에서 더위를 피한다. 침팬지도 물론 땀샘은 있다. 그러나 나오는 것은 수분이 아니라 지방(脂肪)이다. 이 지방은 체모를 매끄럽게 하거나 체취를 발산하는 역할에 그친다. 일본 굴지의 생태학자인 하세가와 마리코는 자신의 저서(『인간은 왜 병에 걸리는가』)에서 "인간은 열대우림에서 나와 그늘 없는 초원에서 생활하게 되면서 더위에 적응했다. 이때부터 체모를 줄이고 대량의 땀을 흘리면서 더위에서 살아남은 것이다."라고 해석한다.

문제해설

1. 인간과 침팬지는 DNA 구조가 거의 동일하지만, 실제로는 현격한 차이를 보이는 이유가 인간의 뛰어난 발한 기능이라고 설명하고 있다. 따라서 발한에 대한 인간과 침팬지의 차이라는 (a)가 정답으로 적합하다.

2. 인간이 더운 날씨를 잘 참는 것은 발한 기능, 즉 땀을 잘 흘리는 기능이라고 했으므로 정답은 (b)가 적합하다.

3. 냄새(smell, odor)에 관한 내용은 본문에 등장하지만 이를 인간과의 주요한 차이로 설명하거나 냄새 때문에 땀 흘릴 때 침팬지가 홀로 있기를 원한다는 내용은 본문에서 찾아볼 수 없다. (d)의 경우 침팬지도 땀을 흘린다는 내용은 맞지만 본문에서는 수분이 아닌 지방이 땀샘을 통해 나온다고 했으므로 땀의 역할을 한다고 볼 수 없어서, 하기는 하지만 충분하지 않다는 (d)와 맞지 않는다. 정답은 (c)로, 인간은 땡볕에도 돌아다니지만 침팬지는 그늘에서 쉬면서 더위를 피한다고 했으므로 (c)와 일치한다.

4. 수백만 년 전 열대우림에서 나와 초원에서 생활하게 된 것을 침팬지와 인간을 구분 짓는 신호라고 설명하고 있으므로 그때부터 인간의 진화가 시작됐다는 (a)가 일본 생태학자의 발언을 가장 잘 설명하고 있다고 할 수 있다.

정답　1(a)　2(b)　3(c)　4(a)

Unit 63 | Percentage point
1%의 힘

　퍼센트(percent, 백분율)는 전체 수량을 100으로 잡았을 때 거기서 차지하는 비율을 말한다. 수학이나 과학에서는 물론 실생활에서도 간편하게 상대량을 나타내는 데 쓰일 수 있는 방법이다. 퍼센트의 개념은 고대 그리스인들에 의해 처음 도입되었다. 예부터 100이란 숫자는 한 독립체의 흠 없는 완전한 상태를 의미했기에 100을 기준으로 삼은 퍼센트가 비율의 대명사로 자리 잡은 것은 자연스럽다. "100% 확신한다"고 했을 때 100%는 '완전히' 또는 '전적으로' 확신한다는 뜻이다. 반면에 1%는 아주 작다는 의미로 쓰인다. 토머스 에디슨이 "천재는 1%의 영감과 99%의 노력에서 나온다"고 했을 때의 1%는 거의 가능성이 없거나 무시해도 좋을 만큼 극히 적다는 것을 강조한 것이다.
　그러나 1%는 그렇게 작은 숫자만은 아니다. 비율은 까다로운 개념이다. 퍼센트는 비율이기에 퍼센트가 변함이 없어도 전체 수량이 늘면 그 비율에 해당하는 절대값도 따라서 늘어나게 돼 있다. 200조원의 1%는 2조원이지만 300조원의 1%는 3조원이다. 같은 비율이지만 결과는 엄청나게 달라진다. 또 미세한 수량을 다룰 때 1%는 엄청난 결과의 차이를 불러온다. 정밀기계에서 1%의 오차는 허용되지 않을 만큼 큰 수치이고, 금리 1%의 변동은 세계 경제를 뒤흔들 만큼 위력적이다. 1%의 힘은 여기서 그치지 않는다. 끊어질 확률이 각각 1%인 고리 100개를 연결한 쇠사슬이 끊어질 확률은 63%에 이른다. 1%의 위험도 여럿이 결합되면 전체를 파멸시킬 수 있는 것이다. 반면에 우수한 두뇌 1%가 장래 나머지 99%를 먹여 살릴 수 있다. 1%는 작지만 힘이 세다.

문제해설

1. 이 글은 1%가 작다고 생각되지만 실제로는 그렇지 않다는 것을 강조하고 있다. 따라서 (d)는 정답에서 제외되어야 한다. 본문에서는 1%가 작지 않다는 것을 전체 수치가 커 나가는 경우를 생각해 보거나, 1%의 확률이 여러 개로 이어지는 경우를 산정하고 있다. 따라서 정답은 전체 수치를 고려한 퍼센트의 이해라는 (b)가 적합하다.

2. 금리 1%의 변화는 세계 경제를 뒤흔들 만큼 위력적이라고 했기 때문에 중요하지 않다고 볼 수 없다. (b)와 (d)는 본문에 등장하지 않는다. 정답은 (c)로 두 번째 문단에 설명된 것과 같이 같은 1%라도 총액의 크기에 따라 달라질 수 있다.

3. 1번에서 설명한 것과 같이 1%도 작지 않은 수치라는 것을 지적한 글이므로 (a)와 같이 생각할 수 있다.

4. 총액이 커졌을 경우는 1%라 하더라도 무시할 수 없다고 했기 때문에 (a)가 이를 잘 설명하고 있다.

정답 1(b) 2(c) 3(a) 4(a)

Unit 64 | A different side to drones
드론

　무인항공기 드론을 반대하는 건 시대에 역행하는 듯 보인다. 기술 발전에 둔감해 보일 수도 있고 회의론자로 여겨질 수도 있다. 드론을 가지고 철학적 논쟁을 벌이는 게 어쩌면 이미 의미 없을지도 모른다. 규제가 대거 풀릴 것으로 예상되면서 시장이 이미 움직이고 있기 때문이다. 드론이 긍정적인 목적으로 쓰이는 경우도 점차 늘고 있다. 네덜란드 같은 나라들에서 사용되는 '앰뷸런스 드론'은 (긴급) 현장에 가장 먼저 도착해 의료 장비를 제공한다. 군사적 용도만 강조됐을 때에 비하면 요즘 드론에 대한 거부감은 훨씬 줄어든 느낌이다.
　하지만 최근 미국과 유럽에서 나온 보고서들은 우리가 드론의 사용이나 규제의 효용을 너무 믿고 있는 건 아닌가 하는 우려를 던져준다. 영국 (인권단체인) 리프리브(Reprieve)는 미국이 드론으로 중동의 테러 용의자들을 공격하는 과정에서 천 명이 넘는 민간인들이 숨졌다고 주장했다. 예멘에선 미국의 드론이 한 결혼식장을 공격해 하객과 신부를 포함해 12명이 숨졌다. 미국 언론들이 보도한 연방항공청 자료도 주목할 만하다. 지난 6개월간 드론과 대형 여객기가 충돌할 뻔한 사례가 25건이 된다는 것이었다. 여객기 조종사가 비행 중에 드론을 발견하고 신고한 경우도 193건에 달했다. 항공기 안전도 안전이지만 테러 위험도 생각할 필요가 있다.
　미국 정부의 기본적인 입장은 정교한 규제가 가능하다는 쪽이다. 그러나 총기 규제의 현실을 보면 낙관론이 꼭 좋은 것만은 아니다. 총기 관련 폭력은 예방이 사실상 불가능하다. 사고 후 대처 능력만 키울 뿐이다. 이미 총기가 광범위하게 보급된 상황에서 규제의 실효성은 떨어지기 때문이다. 드론은 대량살상 무기로서 총보다 훨씬 더 위험하다. 총기 규제의 전철을 밟지 않으려면 지나칠 정도로 보수적인 사전 검토가 필요하다. 경제 논리에 휘둘려서도 안 되고 낙관론에 휩쓸려서도 안 된다. 해킹 가능성 등 그 외 기술적 논의도 필요하다. 시장이 먼저 움직이고 규제가 따라 가는 식이 된다면 재앙을 불러올 수도 있다. 당국이 완벽하게 규제할 자신이 없다면 철저히 준비가 될 때까지 엄격하게 규제하는 게 해결법이 될 수 있다.

문제해설

1. 이 글의 전반적인 어조에는 드론의 확산에 대하여 주의가 필요하다는 필자의 입장이 드러나 있다. 본문의 마지막 문장에서 '완벽하게 규제할 자신이 없으면, 철저히 준비가 될 때까지 엄격하게 규제하는 게 해결법'이라고 한 것에서도 역시 단서를 찾을 수 있다.

2. 본문의 첫머리에 '무인항공기 드론을 반대하는 건 시대에 역행하는 듯 보인다. 드론을 가지고 철학적 논쟁을 벌이는 게 어쩌면 이미 의미 없을지도 모른다.'라고 하였으므로 이미 실재하고 확산되는 과정에 있는

드론의 존재 유무에 대한 논의는 의미 없는 논쟁이라고 할 수 있다.

3. 드론의 부정적인 사례를 보여주는 두 번째 단락의 '예멘에선 미국의 드론이 한 결혼식장을 공격해 하객과 신부를 포함해 12명이 숨졌다.'는 내용에서 드론의 문제점을 적나라하게 드러내고 있다. 그러므로 정답은 (d)이다.

4. 드론을 규제해야 하지만, '총기 규제의 전철을 밟지 않으려면 지나칠 정도로 보수적인 사전 검토가 필요하다'는 필자의 입장을 고려하면 완벽하게 규제할 자신이 없는 경우에는 "철저히 준비가 될 때까지 엄격하게 규제하는 게 해결법"이라고 할 수 있다.

정답 1(b) 2(a) 3(d) 4(a)

Unit 65 | A depressing future
우울증

우울증을 앓다 젊은 나이에 세상을 등진 천재 예술가의 경우 그 우울증은 정신병으로보다는 낭만적으로 여겨진다. 우울증을 '마음의 감기'로 비유하기도 한다. 가볍게 스쳐가는 일시적이고 쉽게 치유할 수 있는 증상이라는 것이다. 정신의학자 피터 크레이머는 『우울증에 반대한다』는 책에서 이런 태도를 비판한다. 특히 우울증을 창조성과 감수성의 원천으로 보는 태도를 공격한다. 좌파적 관점에서 우울증은 상업자본주의에 반대하는 소극적 저항쯤으로 여겨진다. 우파들은 정신력을 강조하여 약물치료 같은 손쉬운 처방에 기대지 말라고 한다. 양쪽 모두 우울증을 질병이라기보다는 도덕적·윤리적·미적·지적 속성으로 본다는 것이다.

그러나 우울증은 이미 개인적 질병일 뿐 아니라 사회적 질병이기도 하다. 특히 경제적 풍요와 사회적 좌절과 관련되어 있어서인지 선진국과 자본주의 나라들에서 만연한 질병이다. 먹고 사는 문제가 해결된 후 찾아오는 정신적 공허이기도 하고, 극심한 경쟁 사회에서 일하는 이들에게 나타나는 정신적 특질이기도 하다.

세계보건기구(WHO)는 이미 21세기 인류를 괴롭힐 질병에 우울증을 올렸다. 2020년에는 모든 연령에서 나타나는 질환 중 1위에 오를 것이라는 경고도 내놨다. 『우울증에 반대한다』는 미국의 연간 우울증 관련 비용이 400억 달러가 넘는 것으로 추정한다. 국민총생산의 3%에 이르는 수치다. 『진보의 역설』이란 책에 따르면 미국과 유럽의 단극성 우울증(조증 없는 우울증) 환자는 최근 50년 사이 10배나 늘었다.

문제해설

1. 두 번째 문단에 현대 우울증의 요인들이 등장한다. 먹고 사는 문제가 해결된 후 찾아오는 정신적 공허가 (a), 경제적 풍요와 사회적 좌절에 동반되는 자본주의 질병에 해당하는 내용이 (b)이며, "a psychiatric characteristic that is commonly found among people working in a cut-throat society"에 대항하는 내용이 (d)가 된다. 정답은 (c)로, 본문 서두의 내용을 우울증의 요인으로 잘못 연관시키고 있다.

2. 두 번째 문단의 "... as a mental emptiness that emerges after the necessities of life ..." 부분을 통해 (a)를 추론할 수 있다. (b)는 첫 번째 문단에서, (c)는 마지막 문단에서 사실이 아님을 추론할 수 있으며, (d)에서는 우울증을 근거 없는 것(myth)으로 말하고 있기 때문에 부적절하다.

3. 마지막 문단을 보면 미국과 유럽의 단극성 우울증 환자가 증가한 사실을 언급하고 있으므로 이 사실과 관련된 내용이 적절하다. 따라서 양국이 이 문제를 어떻게 해결하려고 하는가에 대한 (b)가 정답이 된다.

4. 제목이 되려면 '우울증, 질병, 현대' 이 세 가지의 키워드가 포함되어야 하므로 정답은 (d)가 적합하다. 우울증이 새로운 질병은 아니기 때문에 (a)는 부적합하다.

정답 1(c) 2(a) 3(b) 4(d)

Unit 66 | An unnatural disaster
인공지진과 자연지진

9월의 인터넷과 소셜미디어를 들썩이게 한 속보는 단연 지진이었다. 그것도 인공지진과 자연지진이 한꺼번에 들이닥쳤다. 북한에서는 2016년 9월 9일 5차 핵실험으로 규모 5.0의 인공지진이 발생했다. 3일 후엔 경북 경주에서 규모 5.8의 강진이, 정확히 일주일 뒤에는 규모 4.5의 지진이 잇따랐다. 여진은 이후에도 430회 이상 계속되면서 국민을 불안에 떨게 하고 있다. 인공지진과 자연지진은 근본적으로 차이가 있다. 자연지진은 종파인 P파와 횡파인 S파가 함께 나타나지만 인공지진에서는 S파가 거의 관측되지 않는다. 폭발에 따른 음파가 감지되는지 여부도 두 지진을 구별하는 주된 기준 중 하나다. 그럼에도 한번 발생하면 막대한 피해로 이어질 수 있다는 점에서는 다를 게 없다. 철저한 사전 대비가 필수인 이유다.

이번 지진 사태는 우리 사회의 재난 대비 시스템이 얼마나 취약한지 여실히 드러내주었다. 특히 자연지진이 천재에서 끝나지 않고 또다시 인재로 이어졌다는 점에서 심각성을 더하고 있다. 국민안전처는 지진 발생 9분 뒤에야 긴급재난문자를 처음 발송했다. 2차 강진 때 서울 등 수도권엔 아예 문자를 보내지도 않았다. 총리의 첫 지시는 2시간 47분 뒤에야 나왔다. 이 같은 정부의 안이한 초동 대처 속에서 2014년 세월호 참사 이후 그렇게 강조해 왔던 '골든 타임'은 온데간데없이 사라져 버렸다.

야간 자율학습 때 "금방 사라질 지진이니 가만히 있어라"고 했다는 학교는 또 어떠한가. 이 반응은 2년 반 전에 수많은 생명을 앗아가게 한 "가만히 있으라"는 명령을 상기시킨다. 기성세대의 대처에 자라나는 세대가 무엇을 보고 배우겠는가. 급기야 "밤에는 장관을 깨우지 말라"는 기상청 지진 대응 매뉴얼까지 공개됐는데, 그럼 세월호 때

해경을 해체한 것처럼 이번엔 기상청만 없애고 말 것인가. 이러니 울산 태화강의 숭어떼가 일제히 바다로 향하거나 부산 광안리에 개미떼가 출몰한 게 대지진의 전조였다는 등 흉흉한 괴담만 떠도는 것 아니겠는가.

건강을 잃으면 천하가 내 것이라도 아무 소용이 없다. 건강은 우리 삶의 기초이다. 기초가 흔들리면 어떤 탑이라도 버티고 서있을 재간이 없다. 땅이 갈라지고 건물이 무너지는 상황에선 세상의 권세나 금은보화도 소용없다. 지진은 대상을 가리지 않는다. 한나 아렌트는 『예루살렘의 아이히만』에서 인간의 무사유가 악을 만들어낸다고 했다. 과거를 돌아보고 반성하며 미래를 설계하는 '사유'를 망각하고 아무 생각 없이 악습만 반복하는 사회에 대해 경고하고 있다. 자연지진은 자연적인 지진에서 끝내야 한다. 천재보다 백배 천배 더 무서운 게 인재다. 자연지진에 인간의 무사유와 무책임과 무능이 더해져 인공적인 재난 단계로 넘어가는 순간 인공지진 못지않은 재앙이 될 수 있음을 명심할 때다.

문제해설

1. 본문은 2016년 9월 대한민국에서 일어났던 인공지진과 자연지진에 대한 정부의 미숙한 초동 대처에 관해 비판하고 있다. 지진은 대상을 가리지 않으며 자연지진을 막을 힘은 없지만 과거를 돌아보지 않고 악습을 반복한다면 불필요한 피해를 입힌다는 것이 핵심이다. 이러한 사태를 세월호 참사와 비교하며 우리나라의 재난 대비 시스템이 얼마나 취약한지를 보여준다.

2. "밤에는 장관을 깨우지 말라"는 기상청 지진 대응 매뉴얼은 잘못된 기성세대의 대처법 중 하나이다. 이런 매뉴얼을 철저히 따랐어야 한다는 것은 잘못된 진술이다. 또한 이번 사태에서 정부의 미숙한 대처는 얼마나 준비가 안 됐는지를 보여줬으며 여진이 일어난 후 어떻게 대처했는지에 대해서는 본문에 나와 있지 않다.

3. Hannah Arendt의 메시지는 우리 정부가 과거를 돌아보고, 잘못을 뉘우치고 미래를 설계하지 않는다면 악습을 반복할 것임을 전하고 있다.

4. 빈칸 이전 문장에서는 자연지진은 자연지진으로 남아야 하며 천재보다 훨씬 무서운 것이 인재라고 한다. 그러므로 인간의 무사유와 무책임과 무능이 더해지면 인공적인 재난 단계로 넘어갈 것이며 이는 인공지진 못지않은 재앙이 될 수 있다는 말이 빈칸에 들어가야 적합하다.

정답 1(c) 2(d) 3(b) 4(d)

Unit 67 Are electric cars eco-friendly?
전기차가 친환경적이라고?

전력 수요가 증가하면 공급을 늘리면 된다. 문제는 발전 설비를 마냥 늘릴 수 없다는 데 있다. 발전 연료의 90% 이상이 공해 유발 물질이다. 비중이 원자력 30%, 석탄 39.1%, 액화천연가스(LNG) 21.4%, 석유 1.5% 등이다. 신재생에너지의 기술 발전은 더 13년 뒤에도 전체 발전량에서 차지하는 비중이 4.6%에 머물 것으로 정부는 내다본다. 그리고 발전 설비를 늘리려면 주민 반발 등으로 오랜 시간이 걸릴 수밖에 없다. 그러므로 정부는 전력 공급 확대보다 수요 억제에 초점을 맞추고 있다.

그런데 요즘 정부는 친환경적이라며 전기차 확산에 적극적이다. 자동차 업체에 관련 신기술 개발을 독려하는가 하면 전기차 구매보조금을 지원하고 있다. 전기차 자체만 보면 전기차는 어떤 공해 물질도 배출하지 않는다. 하지만 전기차가 쓰는 전기를 생산하기 위해선 발전소는 각종 온실가스뿐만 아니라 방사성 물질도 내뿜는다. 『회의적 환경주의자』의 저자인 덴마크 학자 비욘 롬보르는 "미국이 2020년까지 석유 자동차를 10% 늘리면 대기 공해로 매년 870명 이상이 숨지지만 전기차를 그만큼 늘리면 사망자는 1617명으로 늘어날 것"이라고 말한다. 전기차가 석유 자동차에 비해 효율이 떨어져 사실상 더 많은 환경오염을 유발한다는 논리다.

한국은 아직 발전 설비를 크게 늘릴 준비가 돼 있지 않다. 미세 먼지에 대한 우려가 커지고 있고 고준위 방사성 폐기물 처분장 부지조차 정하지 못하고 있다. 정부는 현재 증가 속도를 고려하면 전기차가 전력 수급에 큰 영향을 주지 않을 것으로 내다본다. 하지만 첨단제품은 어느 순간 수요가 기하급수적으로 증가한다. 이렇게 되면 대규모 정전 사태 위기로 몰릴 수 있다. 발전 설비 확대를 위한 사회적 합의를 이끌어내지 못하면 미래의 전력 대란은 피할 수 없다.

문제해설

1. 질문은 본문의 핵심이 무엇인지를 물어보는 것이며 본문에서 추론할 수 있는 것을 고르는 것이 아니다. 즉 문제의 본질을 잘 파악해야 한다. 첫 단락에서 전력 수요와 공급의 차이에 관한 문제를 제기하고 두 번째 단락에서는 전기차를 사용하면 환경 보호에 도움이 된다는 점이 사실이 아니라는 것을 이야기한다. 또한 마지막 단락에서는 한국에서는 발전 설비를 늘릴 준비가 되지 않은 상태에서 첨단제품 수요가 증가하는 상황이 결국에는 전력 대란으로 이어질 수 있다는 점을 지적한다. 모두 다 종합해 봤을 때 본문은 환경오염에 초점을 둔 것이 아니라 한국의 전력 수요와 공급의 불일치에 관한 내용임을 알 수 있다.

2. 첫 단락에서는 전력 수요가 증가하면 공급을 늘리는 것이 맞지만 주민들의 반발로 인해 수요 억제에 방점을 찍고 있다고 이야기한다. 그러므로 한국 정부가 전력 공급을 확대하려고 노력 중이라는 A의 내용은 틀린 것이다. 또한 정부가 전력 수요가 증가하고 있다는 점을 인지하고 수요를 억제하려는 것이기 때문에 (d)는 답이 될 수 없다.

3. 학자 롬보르에 따르면 석유 자동차가 10% 증가했을 때 매년 870명의 사람들이 공해로 사망한다면 전기 자동차는 같은 수치로 증가했을 때 매년 1617명의 더 많은 사람들이 숨진다고 주장했기 때문에 (d)가 정답이다.

4. 빈칸 이전 문장에서 첨단제품에 대한 수요가 기하급수적으로 증가하

면서 블랙아웃(대규모 정전 사태)의 위기로 몰릴 수 있다는 점을 고려했을 때 첨단제품을 만드는 데 필요한 발전 설비 확대가 보장되지 않으면 미래의 전력 대란을 피할 수 없다고 하는 것이 옳다.

정답 1(c) 2(a) 3(d) 4(b)

Unit 68 UN tide turns against North
지구촌

로마클럽은 1972년에 발표된 『성장의 한계(The Limits to Growth)』란 책을 통해 세계를 충격에 빠뜨렸다. 이 책은 "경제 성장을 억제하지 않으면 21세기 후반엔 천연자원이 고갈되고 인류가 살 지구는 파멸을 맞을 것"이라고 예견했다. 그럼에도, 각국은 앞다퉈 경제 성장에 매진했고 지난주 '지구촌 반상회'라 할 유엔 총회와 '동네 유지 모임'인 G20(주요 20개국) 정상회의에선 지구촌 환경 문제의 해법을 싸고 해묵은 신경전이 재연됐다.

개도국들은 그동안 선진국들이 자원을 남용해온 탓이라고 주장하며, 선진국들은 최근 급성장한 개도국들 책임도 만만치 않다고 비판해왔다. 지난해 식량위기 땐 "인도·중국의 중산층이 고기·치즈 등을 많이 먹어댄 탓", "뚱보 미국인들이 다이어트만 해도 기아 문제가 해결될 것"이라며 양측 간에 유치한 감정싸움이 불붙기도 했다.

그렇게 티격태격하는 사이 지구는 점점 더 골병이 들고 있다. "모든 세계인이 미국인처럼 살려고 한다면 지구가 두세 개는 더 있어야 할 것"이란 세계자연보호기금(WWF)의 경고를 귀담아들어야 한다. 지구는 단 하나뿐이니 미국인도, 인도인·중국인·한국인도 달라지지 않으면 안 된다. 대체 잘사는 나라, 못사는 나라로 편 가르기가 무슨 소용일까? 다들 한마을 주민이고 운명 공동체라는 것을 인식해야 한다.

문제해설

1. 본문을 보면 선진국과 개도국이 지구의 위기를 두고 서로의 탓을 하는 상황을 두 번째, 세 번째 문단에서 말하고 있으므로 정답은 (a)가 된다.

2. 두 번째 문단의 "The starvation problem would be resolved if only obese Americans went on a diet." 부분이 개도국에서 주장하는 내용으로 나온다. 따라서 뚱뚱한(obese, fat) 사람들(Americans, people from developed countries)이 다이어트를 해야 한다는 (b)가 정답이 된다.

3. (b)와 (c)는 본문과 다른 내용이며, (a)처럼 선진국이 주도해서 도와야 한다는 내용도 본문과 다르다. 마지막 문단에서 필자는 지구에 사는 공동 운명체이므로 모두가 변해야 한다고 말한다. 따라서 정답은 (d)가 적합하다.

4. WWF의 "if all people in the world want to live as the Americans do, there would need to be two to three more earths."란 주장은 그런 식으로는 불가능하다는 내용을 설명한 글이므로 가능하다고 설

명한 (c)가 정답이 된다.

정답 1(a) 2(b) 3(d) 4(c)

Unit 69 Dark clouds hang over the peninsula
먹구름

구름을 구성하는 것은 작은 물방울이나 얼음 알갱이다. 빛의 파장이 이런 구름층을 통과하면 광선 속의 색깔이 흩어지는 산란(散亂) 현상이 나타난다. 구름을 구성하는 물질 중에 가장 작은 입자는 파란빛을 산란하고, 가장 큰 입자는 빨간색을 산란한다. 빛이 구름 속의 이런 물질들을 지나면서 가시광선의 일곱 색깔은 모두 산란됐다가 모두 다시 합쳐지면서 흰색을 띤다. 하늘에 떠있는 구름이 흰색으로 보이는 이유다.

먹구름이라고 일컬어지는 적란운(積亂雲)의 양상은 그와 조금 다르다. 이런 형태의 구름은 밀도가 더 높아서 빛이 덜 지나간다. 통과하는 빛의 양이 적어 산란되는 양도 줄어든다. 따라서 구름의 아랫부분이 어둡게 보인다. 이런 이유로 우리가 적란운을 '먹구름'이라고도 부르는 것이다.

먹구름은 자연 현상의 일부에 불과하지만, 어려운 상황이 재난으로 이어질 때에 종종 위기를 일컫는 말로 쓰인다. 사실 많은 문화와 언어에서, 먹구름은 커다란 풍파를 예고하는 어려운 상황을 상징한다. 언론의 예를 보면 '먹구름 증시(證市)', '한국 대표팀에 먹구름' 등의 표현이 좋은 예다.

문제해설

1. 먹구름은 종종 위기를 일컫는 말이라고 했으므로 위기의 상황에 해당하는 보기가 정답이 된다. (c)의 경우 결선에 진출하려면 2골 이상으로 이겨야 하는데 마지막 게임을 1골 차로 이겼다고 했으므로 결선 진출이 불가능해진 상황이 되어 위기 상황이 된다.

2. (a)의 경우 적란운은 빛이 통과하는 양이 적다고 했으므로 흡수한다는 내용과 맞지 않고, (b)의 경우 구름 속에서 빛이 산란되는 것은 맞지만 이것과 무지개의 관련성은 설명되어 있지 않다. 단 가시광선의 빛이 모두 산란됐다가 다시 합쳐져 흰색으로 구름이 보인다는 내용을 설명하고 있다. (c)의 경우 파랑, 빨강 빛 외에도 가시광선에 해당하는 모든 빛이 합쳐져야 흰 빛이 되므로 틀린 설명이 된다. 정답은 (d)로 먹구름은 날씨 외에도 위기를 일컫는다고 했다.

3. 본문은 단순히 기상을 설명한 내용이 아니므로 (b)와 (c)는 맞지 않고, (d)는 너무 단편적인 내용이다. (a)가 기상의 내용보다는 좀 더 포괄적이어서 정답이 된다.

4. 구름과 같이 세상의 몇몇 요소는 문자적(literal) 의미 말고도 비유적(figurative) 의미를 지닌다는 (d)가 정답이 된다.

정답 1(c) 2(d) 3(a) 4(d)

Unit **70** Food for thought for a desolate land
바오밥

'어린 왕자'가 사는 작은 행성에서 바오밥 나무는 공공의 적이다. 거긴 의자를 약간만 움직여 앉기만 하면 하루에 석양을 마흔세 번도 볼 수 있는 작은 행성이며, 성(城)의 크기만한 둘레가 두껍고, 키가 큰 바오밥 나무가 한두 그루만 있어도 재앙이 될 수밖에 없다. 그렇기에 아침에 일어나면 씨앗이 싹을 틔우기 무섭게 뽑아 버려야 한다. 이것은 자고 일어나면 목욕을 해야 하는 것과 같이 중요한 그곳 행성의 규율이다.

반면 지구별 아프리카 사람들에게 바오밥 나무는 음식, 식수, 쉼터, 약을 얻을 수 있는 귀중한 공급원이다. 풍성한 푸른 잎은 유용한 그늘이 되어주고, 줄기는 밧줄과 낚싯줄로 쓰인다. 우기엔 몸통 가득 빗물을 빨아들여 품어 두었다 긴 건기에는 저수지 역할을 한다. 제일 귀중한 자산은 영양분이 풍부한 잎새와 열매다. 특히 과일을 말려서 하얀 가루로 만들면 수프를 만들 때도 사용되고 몇 년씩 저장이 가능하다. 가뭄과 전쟁에 시달리는 많은 사람을 살리는 데 도움이 되는 것이다.

이 나무의 영양학적 가치까지 드러난 건 최근의 일이다. 알고 보니 과육에 오렌지보다 여섯 배나 많은 비타민 C, 우유 두 배 분량의 칼슘이 담겨 있단다. 거기다 비타민 A와 B, 철분도 풍부하고, 열매 속 씨엔 단백질이 가득하다. 황량함과 부족의 땅에 바오밥은 신의 선물임이 확실하다.

문제해설

1. 이 글은 바오밥 나무의 장점에 대한 설명이며, '어린 왕자'는 이 글의 주제를 강조하기 위해 예로 사용한 내용일 뿐이다. (c)는 장점 중 단편적인 내용에 해당해서 적절하지 않고, (d)는 부정적 묘사로 적합하지 않다.

2. '어린 왕자'에 나온 바오밥 나무는 위협적인 존재로 등장하므로 (c)는 바오밥 나무의 좋은 점이라고 할 수 없다.

3. (a)는 첫 번째 문단에서 "On a tiny planet where you can watch the sun set forty-three times" 부분을 통해 알 수 있고, (b)는 두 번째 문단의 마지막 문장을 통해 알 수 있으며, (c)는 두 번째 문단 전체 내용을 통해 바오밥 나무가 아프리카 사람들에게 얼마나 중요한 존재인지 알 수 있다. 정답은 (d)로 바오밥 나무를 뽑는 것이 아니라 씨앗을 뽑는 것이고, 쉽다는 내용은 등장하지 않는다.

정답 1(a) 2(c) 3(d)

Unit **71** Wrangling with nuclear risk
핵실험

1945년 7월 16일 오전 5시, 미국 뉴멕시코 주 알라모고도에서 인류 최초의 원폭 실험이 있었다. 암호명이 트리니티(trinity)인 이날 사용된 20kt짜리 핵폭탄은 사막 위에 거대한 버섯 모양의 구름을 남겼다. 이 폭탄의 위력은 바로 몇 주 후 실전에서 검증됐다. 히로시마와 나가사키에 떨어진 리틀 보이와 팻 맨은 20만 명의 목숨을 앗아갔다.

미국의 핵무기 실험은 구소련과의 냉전이 한창이던 1950년대에 절정에 달했다. 실험은 주로 네바다 주 사막 한가운데 있는 시험장에서 이뤄졌는데, 이 핵실험이 미국의 영화배우 존 웨인의 죽음에 한몫을 했다는 주장이 있다. 존 웨인은 1954년 핵 실험장에서 137㎞ 거리인 유타 주의 평원에서 징기스칸을 소재로 한 영화 '정복자(Conqueror)'를 촬영하고 있었다. 일본 저널리스트 히로세 다카시의 저서 '존 웨인은 누가 죽였나'에 따르면, 향후 30년 동안 전체 출연진과 스태프 220명 중 90명이 암에 걸렸고 그중 46명이 사망했다. 방사능과의 상관관계를 부정하기 힘든 수치이다. 존 웨인은 1964년 발병한 폐암에선 살아남았지만 1979년 끝내 위암으로 죽음을 맞았다. 딕 파웰 감독과 여주인공 수전 헤이워드 역시 암으로 숨을 거뒀다.

미국의 첫 수소폭탄 실험은 1954년 마샬 제도의 비키니 환초에서 이뤄졌다. 폭발 당시 근처 해역을 일본의 참치잡이 원양어선 다이고후쿠류마루(第伍福龍丸) 즉 Lucky Dragon 5가 지나가고 있었는데 낙진을 흠뻑 뒤집어썼다. 이 배는 미 해군이 설정한 안전선 밖에 있었는데도 선원 1명이 사망하고 다수가 두통과 잇몸 출혈 등을 호소했다. 일련의 사고가 핵실험 위험에 대한 주의를 환기한 결과 각국은 1963년 지상-수중 핵실험의 금지 협약에 사인했지만 지하 핵실험은 금지 대상에서 제외됐다. 대기나 해양의 오염과 무관하다는 이유였다. 하지만 지하수나 토양의 오염, 그리고 지진 유발 가능성에 대한 위험성은 여전히 열려 있다.

문제해설

1. 이 글은 핵폭탄의 부정적 측면을 서술하고 있다. 따라서 효용성에 대한 (a)는 정답과 거리가 멀고, (c)는 두 번째 문단에만 해당하는 지엽적인 내용이다. 그리고 (d)에서와 같이 핵폭탄의 역사를 말하려고 한 글이 아니므로 이 또한 적절하지 않다. 정답은 (b)로 실험 중 발생한 낙진에 부작용이 있다는 내용이 두 번째 문단과 세 번째 문단 모두를 설명할 수 있어서 주제로 적합하다.

2. (a), (b), (d)는 사실일 수도 있지만 이 글의 내용만으로는 추론하기 어렵다. 상세한 내용이 본문에 등장하지 않기 때문이다. 정답은 (c)로 핵실험으로 인해 배우 존 웨인이나 일본 원양어선 선원들이 피해를 본 것은 당시 과학자들이 방사능 영향에 대해 충분히 알지 못했음을 알 수 있다.

3. 유타 주의 평원에서 촬영하던 전체 스태프 220명 중 90명이 암에 걸렸다고 나오므로 모든 사람이 암으로 사망했다는 (d)는 본문과 다르다.

정답 1(b) 2(c) 3(d)

Unit 72 | A high-tech, brain-shrinking future
진화하는 인간

요즘 휴대전화로 통화하며 걷는 사람을 거리에서 만나는 것은 너무도 흔한 일이다. 유인원과 같은 크로마뇽인에 이어 한 손을 귀에 대고 걷는 현대인의 모습을 '인류의 진화' 그림에 담아야 하지 않을까 하는 생각도 든다. 최근의 언론 보도에 따르면, 미국의 의사들이 이른바 '휴대전화 엘보' 증후군에 대해 경고하고 있다. 의사들이 이런 걸로 호들갑을 떠는 게 우스워 보이기도 한다. 테니스를 즐기다 테니스 엘보에 걸려 계속되는 통증에 시달리는 것처럼 휴대전화 통화를 오래 하면 손에 통증이 생기고 무감각해지는 게 휴대전화 엘보다. 넷째, 다섯째 손가락이 특히 그렇다.

팔꿈치 통증에 전자파 걱정도 있지만 멀리할 수 없는 게 휴대전화다. 인류에 공간의 한계를 뛰어넘는 능력을 제공하기 때문이다. 여기에다 랩톱 컴퓨터나 무선 인터넷, 자동차 내비게이션까지 가세한 요즘 인간의 능력은 10년 전과 비교해도 엄청나게 커졌다. 이들 휴대용 장치들은 사람의 뇌보다 훨씬 많은 정보를 저장하고, 더 정확하게 기억한다.

최근엔 '뇌-기계 인터페이스(BMI)'라는 새로운 기술이 주목받고 있다. 이 기술은 인간의 뇌에서 나오는 신호를 이용해 로봇이나 기계를 제어할 수 있도록 고안되었다. 유전공학·로봇공학·정보기술·나노기술의 진보가 인간 능력을 더 높은 단계로 끌어올릴지는 알 수 없다. 그렇게 발전된다면 인류는 더 건강하게, 더 오래 살 수 있고 문화적·언어적 장벽도 쉽게 뛰어넘을 수 있게 될 것이다. 자지 않고 먹지 않는 인간이 나타날지도 모른다.

하지만 시간과 장소를 가리지 않고 울려대는 휴대전화 벨소리에 진정한 휴식, 정신적인 자유를 박탈당하고 있는 것도 사실이다. 계산기·사전 덕분에 머리를 쓸 필요가 없다 보니 우리가 기억하는 전화번호 개수는 갈수록 줄어든다. 오스트랄로피테쿠스에서 호모 사피엔스로 진화할 때까지는 인류의 두개골 용량이 늘었지만, 최근 3만 년 동안에는 인간의 뇌 크기가 오히려 10~15% 줄었다는 분석도 있다. 도구나 사회 시스템에 더 많이 의존하면서 뇌 자체의 역할은 그만큼 줄어든 때문인지도 모른다.

인간은 서서히 '사이보그'를 향해 진화하고 있다. 하지만 첨단 디지털 휴대기기를 소유하지 못한 '자연인'은 경쟁에서 도태될 수도 있다. 미래에 대해 예상하는 바보다 상황이 심각해지지 않을까 걱정되기도 한다.

문제해설

1. 휴대전화 엘보는 본문에서 "cell phone gabbers complain of pain or numbness in the hand — especially the pinky and ring fingers"와 같이 설명하고 있다. 따라서 손가락 중 일부에 통증이나 무감각한 증상이 온다는 내용이므로 (d)가 정답이 된다.

2. (a)의 경우 인간의 두뇌가 완전히 쓸모없어진다는 내용이므로 극단적이며, (c)는 본문과 무관하다. (d)도 (a)와 마찬가지로 인간의 두뇌를 불필요하게 만든다고 말해 극단적인 내용이 된다. 본문에서는 뇌에서 나온 신호를 사용한다고 말하고 있다. 정답은 (b)로 마지막 문단의 내용을 통해 알 수 있다.

3. 기술의 진화와 더불어 인간의 두뇌는 더 줄어드는 현상에 대해 언급하고 있으므로 (a)가 제목으로 적합하다. 기술에 대한 내용을 짐작할 수 없으므로 (c)와 (d)는 적절하지 않다.

4. 마지막 문단에 등장하는 "Humans are slowly evolving toward becoming cyborgs." 부분을 통해 기술적으로 진화해가는 인간을 언급하고 있고 이런 점에서 우려되는 부분도 언급하고 있으므로 (b)보다는 (c)가 더 적합하다.

정답 1(d) 2(b) 3(a) 4(c)

Unit 73 | Helping turtles get back on their feet
달려라 거북

거북은 현존하는 파충류 가운데 가장 오래된 동물이다. 가장 오래된 거북은 2억 2,500만 년 전에 출현해 공룡의 멸종과 인간의 진화를 지켜봤다. 거북의 놀라운 생존 비결은 (등과 배의) 단단한 딱지에 있다. 유일한 단점은 기동력이 없다는 점이다.

이러한 거북의 특성은 지역과 시대에 따라 다르게 받아들여졌다. 초기 기독교인들은 딱지 속에 숨는 데 주목해 악과 어둠의 징표로 봤다. 이후 칼뱅파 기독교인들에겐 바람직한 결혼 생활을 상징했다. 그들은 거북에게서 집을 떠나지 않는, 정숙한 여성상을 발견한 것이다. 서부 아프리카 인들은 거북을 교활하다고 보는데, 머리를 숨길 수 있다는 이유로 그렇게 비쳐진 모양이다.

현대인들은 대개 거북에게서 '느림'을 떠올린다. 이것은 이솝 우화 '토끼와 거북'의 영향이 크다. 느리지만 쉬지 않고 나아간 거북이 속도가 빠른 낮잠 자는 토끼를 이긴다는 이 우화의 교훈은 '꾸준히 노력하면 목표를 이룰 수 있다'는 것이다. 하지만 그렇다고 해도 타고난 능력을 지닌 토끼와 달리 갖은 애를 써야 이길 수 있는 거북이 안쓰럽게 느껴진다.

문제해설

1. 이솝 우화에 나오는 토끼와 거북 이야기는 느리지만 꾸준한 것이 결국은 이긴다는 내용이므로 (c)가 정답이 된다.

2. 거북이 노인으로 상징되었다는 내용은 등장하지 않는다. 대신 정숙한 여인이나, 악과 어둠의 상징물, 교활함의 상징이었다는 내용은 두 번째 문단에서 소개되고 있다.

3. 거북이 빨리 기어 다닌다는 내용은 나오지 않으며, 오랜 기간에 걸쳐 살아남은 동물로 나오지만 숫자의 변동은 등장하지 않는다. 그리고 거북이 애완동물이라는 내용은 본문과 무관하다. 정답은 (a)로 거북은 인내를, 토끼는 재능을 이솝 우화에서 상징하고 있다.

정답 1(c)   2(a)   3(a)

Unit 74 | All that glitters is not 'green' growth
'그린 랜드'

'붉은 털 에리크'가 이끈 바이킹족이 아이슬란드를 떠나 그린란드에 정착한 것은 980년이었다. 당시 그린란드는 상대적으로 따뜻한 곳이었고 상당량의 숲으로 덮여있었다. 바이킹족은 땔감을 구하려 나무를 베어내고 가축을 방목하려 목초지를 만들었다. 하지만 수풀이 사라지면서 토양이 침식됐고 농산물 생산도 크게 줄었다. 1300년 이후 지금의 그린란드는 한랭기로 접어들었고 사람들은 굶어 죽어갔다. 18세기 덴마크 사람들이 다시 점령할 때까지 그린란드는 고래와 바다표범을 잡아먹는 이누이트(에스키모)의 세상이었다.

1775년 덴마크 영토로 편입된 그린란드가 지난 일요일 자치권을 얻었다. 230여 년의 덴마크 지배에서 벗어나게 된 이면에는 지구 온난화가 자리 잡고 있다. 온난화로 영구 동토층이 녹으면서 얼음 밑에 숨겨져 있던 귀중한 천연자원이 발견되면서 덴마크로부터 경제적 독립이 가능해졌다. 경작 가능 부지도 지금은 예전의 네 배가 됐다. 이름처럼 다시 '그린 랜드'(Green Land)로 바뀌고 있는 셈이다. 하지만 그린란드가 다시 푸르러지는 것은 인류가 화석 연료를 사용하면서 배출한 온실가스 탓이라 마냥 축하하고 있을 수만은 없다.

특히 그린란드 얼음이 다 녹는다면 해수면이 7m나 올라가고 전 세계 해안의 많은 부분이 바닷물에 잠기게 된다. 방글라데시 같은 나라들은 아예 지도에서 사라질 수도 있다. 특히나, 방글라데시는 빈민국들의 어려운 처지를 부각한다. 방글라데시는 지난해 5월 엄청난 타격을 준 사이클론으로 13만여 명이 희생되고 200만 명의 이재민이 발생했다. 온실가스를 많이 배출하는 나라들은 바닷가에 제방을 쌓고 정확한 기상 예보로 지구 온난화로 인한 희생자가 될 가능성을 줄일 수 있지만, 가난한 나라들은 자연재해에 취약한 처지이다.

문제해설
1. 그린란드가 독립하게 된 이면에는 환경 문제로 대변되는 지구 온난화가 자리 잡고 있다는 것이 본문의 주 내용이다. 따라서 그린란드의 독립을 말하면서 지구 온난화 문제가 빠질 수 없다. 그런 의미에서 독립의 과정을 강조한 (a)는 적절하지 않다. (b) 또한 환경 문제와 결부되지 않아 반쪽의 설명이 되며, (d)의 경우는 마지막 문단에 등장한 지엽적 내용이다. 정답은 (c)로 지구 온난화가 그린란드에는 도움을 주고 있지만 다른 나라(들)에는 주의를 기울이도록 하고 있다는 내용이므로 주제와 적합하다.

2. 방글라데시와 같은 가난한 나라들은 온실가스 배출에 별로 기여하지 않음에도 이에 대한 대비책이 없기 때문에 오히려 그로 인한 피해는 가장 많이 보고 있는 나라이다. 이런 점에서 정답은 (a)가 된다.

3. 두 번째 문단의 "valuable natural resources hidden below the permafrost have been discovered"를 통해 지구 온난화로 인한 기온 상승으로 영구 동토층 밑에 있던 천연자원이 발견되었고, 또한 경작지도 증가했다는 내용이 나오므로 정답은 (c)가 된다.

4. (a)의 경우 에스키모인들이 한동안 살았다는 내용이 나오므로 맞지 않고, (c)의 경우 정부의 정책이 아닌 환경적 요인에 의한 사항이며, (d)의 경우 땔감과 방목을 위한 것이었지 집을 짓기 위한 것은 아니었다. 본문과 맞는 내용은 (b)로 그린란드에 도착한 바이킹족의 산림 훼손으로 인해 결국은 한랭기로 접어들고 사람들은 굶어 죽었다는 내용과 (b)가 부합된다.

정답 1(c)   2(a)   3(c)   4(b)

Unit 75 | Painful patent protection
특허의 역설

독일의 가장 긴 강인 라인강은 중세 유럽 무역의 젖줄이었다. 신성로마제국 황제의 보호 아래 안전하게 운항하는 대가로 상선들은 각 나라를 지날 때마다 통행료를 지불했다. 그런데 13세기 들어 제국의 권위가 약화하면서, 봉건 귀족들이 멋대로 라인 강변에 성을 짓고 제각기 통행료를 걷기 시작한 것이다. 수백 개나 되는 이들 요금소의 횡포에 지친 상선들은 아예 강을 지날 생각을 접게 됐다. 라인강 무역은 쇠퇴했고 덩달아 단물을 빨아먹는 귀족들의 수입도 줄어들었다.

이처럼 여럿이 공공의 자원을 조각조각 나눠 갖게 되면 결국 자원의 존재를 위태롭게 하고 모두가 망한다. 컬럼비아 법대 교수 마이클 헬러는 이에 따른 폐단을 이른바 '반(反)공유재의 비극'이라 일컫는다. 주인 없는 자원을 제대로 쓰지 못하고 낭비하는 것도 문제지만, 라인강 사례 같이 자기 잇속만 차리는 광범위한 소유권 다툼 역시 곤란하단 얘기다. 마이클 헬러는 자신의 저서 『소유의 역습, 그리드락』에서 지나치게 파편화되거나 광범위한 소유권은 결국 산업과 시장을 막다른 골목으로 내몰 수 있다고 주장한다.

현재 생명공학 분야는 특허가 넘쳐난다. 지난 30년간 승인된 DNA 관련 특허만 4만여 개다. 신약을 판매하려는 제약회사들은 보통 수십 개의 특허 보유자를 일일이 접촉해 협상하지 않으면 안 된다. 많은 실험이 특허 보유자들과의 소송 분쟁을 두려워해 실험실을 벗어나지 못하고 사장된다. 사스(SARS·중증급성호흡기증후군)가 맹위를 떨치던 당시 백신 개발이 지지부진했던 것도 그래서다.

비타민 A가 부족한 아프리카와 그 밖의 빈국들의 수백만의 아이들을 구하기 위한 유전자 변형 황금쌀(Golden Rice) 역시 인도적 지원 노력이 없었다면 하마터면 못 태어날 뻔했다. 1999년 과학자들이 (비타민 A를 강화한) 기적

45

의 쌀 개발에 성공했지만 무려 70여 개의 특허 사용 허가를 받아야 하는 난관에 부닥친 것이다. '인도주의적 사용권'을 가진 것으로 재정립한 후에야 그들은 그 쌀을 나눠줄 수 있었다.

문제해설

1. 공공재의 비극과 반대되는 개념으로 반공유재의 비극을 예로 들면서, 주인이 너무 많아도 문제라고 말하고 있다. 대표적인 예로 특허를 들고 있다. 이런 특허를 탐욕이라고 보는 (a)는 지나치고, 특허 등의 권리를 두고 장단기적으로 따지고 있는 득실을 따지는 글이 아니므로 (b) 또한 어색하다. 이 글에서 말하고자 하는 것은 특허 같은 문제가 백신 개발이나 쌀 품종 개발에서 볼 수 있듯이 개발을 막는 역할을 할 수 있다는 (c)가 정답으로 적합하다.

2. 특허의 취득이 이전보다 더 빨라졌다는 내용은 등장하지 않으므로 정답은 (b)가 된다.

3. 각종 특허 분쟁으로 인해 실험실을 벗어나 상용화 단계에 이르지 못하는 경우가 많다는 것이 세 번째 문단의 내용이므로 정답은 (a)가 된다.

4. 주인이 너무 많아 문제가 되고 있다는 '반공유재의 비극'을 설명한 (d)가 정답이 된다.

정답 1(c) 2(b) 3(a) 4(d)

Unit 76 | Humility in the face of pandemics
전염병

1519년 신대륙을 침공해 아즈텍 제국을 정복한 스페인 군의 숫자는 불과 600명이었다. 용맹한 정복자 코르테즈의 수완이 그만큼 탁월했던 것일까, 아니면 당시 아즈텍과 다른 문명에는 없던 총포로 무장한 스페인군의 압도적 군사력에 힘입은 것일까? 스페인의 승리를 도운 이 수수께끼와 같은 '보이지 않는 손'은 다름 아닌 마마, 즉 천연두였다. 아즈텍인들 사이에서 급속히 확산된 천연두가 승리의 요인이었다. 면역력을 지닌 스페인 병사들은 아무런 피해가 없었던 반면, 원주민들은 신대륙에 처음 상륙한 괴질에 속수무책으로 쓰러졌다.

그러니 원주민들의 눈엔 천연두 앞에서도 끄떡없는 스페인 병사들이야말로 '신의 자손'으로 보였고, 그들은 전래 종교를 버리고 기독교를 받아들였다. 멕시코에 처음 전해진 천연두가 남아메리카로 퍼짐에 따라 잉카 제국은 인구가 3분의 1로 줄어들었다. 아즈텍처럼 잉카 제국도 천연두로 힘이 약화하여 1533년 스페인 정복자 피사로의 군대에 굴복하고 말았다.

역사상 가장 가혹한 전염병 피해는 14세기 중세 유럽을 휩쓴 흑사병이었다. 현재는 선페스트로 추측되는 이 공포의 병은 유럽 인구를 절반으로 줄어들게 했다. 흔히 얕잡아 보는 독감 역시 치명적인 병이 될 수 있다. 1918년 1차 대전 무렵 유행한 스페인 독감이 전쟁 사망자보다 더 많은 희생자를 냈다는 사실이 입증한다.

인류의 역사는 전염병과의 투쟁사이기도 하다. 신종 바이러스의 출현은 인류에 막대한 재앙을 입혔을 뿐만 아니라 역사의 물줄기를 틀기도 했다. 그럴 때마다 인류는 재앙을 극복하면서 과학 문명을 발전시켜왔다. 하지만 바이러스도 끊임없이 진화하며, 인간의 혁신과 상관없이 항상 새로운 질병이 존재할 것이다. 더구나 신종플루와 같은 변종 바이러스의 출현은 질병에 대한 현대의 안일함에 경종을 울리게 될 것이다. 우리는 자연의 경고에 귀 기울이고 항상 경계를 게을리 하지 않는 동시에 신종플루와 앞으로 나타날 전염병 앞에서 겸허해져야 할 것이다.

문제해설

1. 두 번째 문단의 서두에 보면 스페인 병사들이 '신의 자손'으로 보였다는 대목이 나오며, 바로 앞부분인 첫 번째 문단 후반에 이유가 등장한다. 스페인 병사들은 면역력을 지녀서 문제가 없었지만 원주민들은 천연두에 속수무책으로 당한 것이다. 따라서 정답은 (c)가 된다.

2. 마지막 문단의 "We must listen to nature's warning and be both vigilant against and humble in the face of the A(H1N1) virus and future pandemics." 부분의 내용을 통해 새로운 질병의 출현, 인간의 나약함과 이에 대한 극복, 그러나 다시 새로운 질병의 출현 등의 연속을 통해 인간이 나약함을 인정하고 겸허해야 한다는 (d)가 글의 목적으로 적합하다.

3. 바이러스가 항상 진화를 거듭한다는 내용은 나오지만, 신종플루가 14세기의 페스트가 진화했다는 내용은 본문에 등장하지 않기 때문에 정답은 (a)가 된다.

4. 천연두가 아니었다면 아즈텍 제국이 그렇게 쉽게 함락되지는 않았을 수 있다. 스페인 군대의 숫자가 불과 600명이었기 때문이다. 하지만 군사력이 압도적으로 앞서있었기 때문에 이를 장담할 수만은 없다는 (c)가 정답으로 적합하다.

정답 1(c) 2(d) 3(a) 4(c)

Unit 77 | Modern-day Medusa stings
해파리

그리스 신화에서 자연을 인격화한 여신 가이아가 만든 괴물 중에는 고르곤이라 불리는 세 자매가 있었다. 막내인 메두사만은 아름다운 용모를 갖고 있었다. 여신 아테나의 신전에서 바다의 신 포세이돈과 사랑을 나눈 탓에 메두사는 아테나의 저주를 받았다. 살아있는 독사 머리카락에 흉물스러운 얼굴을 갖게 된 메두사의 모습은 너무 끔찍해서 그녀를 쳐다보는 사람은 모두 돌로 변했다. 그러나 잘 닦인 자신의 방패에 비친 메두사의 모습만 본 영웅 페르세우스는 이런 운명을 피해 메두사의 목을 자르는 데 성공했다.

하늘거리는 촉수를 가진 해파리는 메두사의 머리와 닮았다. 실제로 라틴어로는 메두사가 해파리를 지칭하는 단어로 쓰인다. 해파리는 산호·말미잘과 함께 자포동물로 분류된다. 몸에 입과 항문을 겸한 구멍이 하나 뚫린 단순한 구조다. 촉수가 먹잇감에 닿으면 수천 개의 세포마다 작은 침이 하나씩 들어 있어 먹잇감에 독침을 날린다. 해파리는 가끔 인간도 공격하는데, 쏘이면 심한 통증을 느끼게 되며, 호흡 곤란과 근육 마비, 심장마비를 겪기도 한다.

중세시대 유럽에서는 자포동물이 식물로 간주됐다. 18세기에는 동물과 식물 중간쯤으로 인식됐고, 19세기에야 비로소 동물로 분류됐다. 해파리의 생활사는 복잡하다. 해파리는 작은 플라눌라로 자유롭게 유영하기도 하고, 단단한 물체의 표면에 붙어 꽃처럼 생긴 폴립으로 자라기도 하며, 원양 해파리가 되기도 하는 등 다양한 형태로 자란다. 스트로빌라의 마디 하나하나가 초기 모습의 해파리로 자라 마침내 독립 개체가 되어 자유 유영하는 어린 해파리가 된다.

요즘 남해안은 해파리 때문에 골머리를 썩고 있다. 국립수산과학원은 해파리 피해가 한 해 3,000억 원을 초과할 것으로 추산한다. 해수욕객이 쏘이는 것뿐만 아니라 그물 훼손으로 어업 피해도 적지 않다. 원전 냉각수 취수도 어렵게 만든다. 해파리는 지중해·북해·발트해·카스피해·멕시코만 등지에서도 골칫거리다. 지구 온난화로 인한 해수 온도의 상승, 육지에서 흘려보낸 오염물질로 인한 부(富)영양화, 해파리를 먹는 물고기의 남획이 원인으로 꼽힌다. 모두 사람 탓이다. 해파리를 뜯어먹는 말쥐치를 방류하고 있지만 적절한 해결책은 아니다. 그렇다고 바다를 메두사로부터 구해줄 21세기의 페르세우스가 없어 안타까울 뿐이다.

문제해설

1. 본문은 해파리와 그 피해에 대해서 다루고 있으므로 (a)가 주제로 적합하다.
2. 마지막 문단에서 말쥐치의 방류는 적절한 해결책이 아니라고 했으므로 정답은 (d)가 된다.
3. 밑줄 친 부분은 메두사에 비유되는 해파리가 문제가 되는데, 메두사를 그리스 신화에서 페르세우스가 처치했던 것과 같은 해결책이 없음을 안타깝게 생각하고 있는 말이다. 실제로 페르세우스와 같은 영웅을 기다린다는 내용이 아니며, 전 세계 바다에 막대한 피해를 준다는 내용도 사실이 아니므로 (d)는 적절하지 않다. 해파리가 더는 피해를 주지 않도록 해줄 수 있는 방법이 필요하다는 (c)의 내용이 더 적절하다.
4. 두 번째 문단 서두에서 "Jellyfish ... which have a single opening into the body which acts as both the mouth and anus." 부분을 통해 해파리는 입과 항문을 겸한 구멍이 하나 뚫린 단순한 구조임을 알 수 있으므로 정답은 (a)가 된다.

정답 1(a) 2(d) 3(c) 4(a)

Unit 78 Lawmakers eclipsed
일식

지구를 포도송이만 한 크기의 구체로 가정하자. 달은 그로부터 약 30cm 떨어진 머루다. 태양은 사람 키만 한 크기로 지구에서 약 50m 떨어져 있고, 약 200m 떨어진 지점에는 멜론 크기만 한 목성이 있다. 천왕성과 해왕성은 레몬의 크기로 각각 1km와 1.5km 정도 떨어져 있다.

해의 지름은 달의 400배, 지구~태양의 거리는 지구~달 거리의 400배다. 지구에서 달과 해의 크기가 비슷하게 보이는 이유다. 지구는 태양을 공전하고, 달은 지구를 공전한다. 태양-달-지구가 일렬로 서게 되면 달이 해의 일부 또는 전부를 가리는 일식 현상이 벌어진다. 어제 태양을 가린 달의 그림자가 지구촌 일부에 드리우면서 약 30억의 인구가 개기 일식을 지켜봤다.

달과 지구의 실제 평균 거리는 38만km이다. 국제선 여객기의 평균 고도가 10km라는 점을 감안하면 그 거리가 얼마 정도인지를 짐작할 수 있다. 그럼에도, 지구로부터 가장 가까운 천체라는 점에서 달은 늘 인류의 탐구 대상이었다. 달은 인류가 발을 디딘 지구 밖의 유일한 천체이다. 올해는 미국의 우주선 아폴로 11호가 달에 도착한 지 40주년 되는 해다.

문제해설

1. 본문에는 금성(venus)에 대한 정보는 없으므로 정답은 (b)가 된다. 태양계의 행성들이 각각 다른 거리로 떨어져 태양을 돌고 있다는 것을 알 수 있으며, 지구가 목성보다 태양에 가깝지만, 일식 때는 태양-달-지구 순으로 배열되므로 달이 태양과 더 가깝게 된다. 그리고 일식은 지구의 30억 인구가 볼 수 있다고 했으므로 모든 지역에서 볼 수 있는 현상은 아님을 알 수 있다.
2. 태양과 그 주위의 행성들이 일렬로 배열되는 일식의 경우 행성의 배열 순서에 대해 묻고 있다. 일식 때는 태양-달-지구 순으로 배열되어야 하므로 태양은 사람, 달은 머루, 지구는 포도로 비유한 (d)가 정답이 된다. 나머지 목성과 천왕성, 해왕성은 각각 멜론과 레몬으로 비유하고 있다.
3. 본문은 하늘의 천체에 대해 설명하고 있지만, 그중에서도 지구의 위성인 달에 대해 주목하고 있으므로 (b)가 주제로 적합하다.

정답 1(b) 2(d) 3(b)

Unit 79 Hats off to Naro's blastoff
우주 개발

19세기 이탈리아의 천문학자 조반니 스키아파렐리가 망원경을 통해 행성을 관측하다가 화성 표면에 새겨진 긴 줄(線)을 발견했다. 아마도 그가 본 건 길이 6,000km의 마리너리스 협곡이었을 것이다. 이 소식은 전 세계에 화성

열풍을 몰고 왔다. 사실상 그 줄이 인공 운하라는 소문이 퍼지면서 화성에도 생명체가 살고 있을 것이란 추측이 확산됐다. 그러나 이는 줄을 뜻하는 이탈리아어 카날리(canali)가 영어의 운하(canal)로 와전되면서 빚어진 해프닝이었다. 하루가 다르게 진화하는 우주과학의 발전 속도를 감안하면 너무도 옛날인 1877년의 이야기다. 하지만 운하까지는 몰라도 화성에 물이 존재했다는 가설은 120년 뒤 화성탐사선이 보내온 사진으로 기정사실화됐다. 물이 있었다는 얘기는 생명체의 존재 가능성과 직결된다.

우주과학에서는 이런 엉뚱한 오해나 상상이 뒤늦게 현실로 실현되는 경우가 있다. 쥘 베른의 『지구에서 달까지』가 발표된 뒤 한 세기가 지나서야 비로소 인간의 발은 달 표면을 밟을 수 있었다. 미지의 세계와 도달하지 못할 것 같은 장소에 대한 동경이야말로 인간 역사의 대부분을 차지하는 상상력의 원천이었다.

물론 인간의 궁금증을 풀자고 우주 개발에 막대한 돈과 에너지를 쏟아 부은 것은 아니었다. 냉전 시기 미·소가 사활을 걸고 우주 개발 경쟁을 펼친 건 우주 개발 기술이 군사 기술과 동전의 양면 관계에 있기 때문이다. 우주 탐사용으로 개발된 기술은 실용적 민수(民需) 기술로 파급됐다. 한때 '우주중계'라 불린 위성방송 기술이나 날씨를 예측하는 기상 관측도 우주 개발 연구의 결과물이다. (뜨거운 물만 부으면 곧바로 한 끼 식사를 해결하는) 동결건조식품, 질병 진단에 쓰이는 단층촬영(CT)이나 내시경 기술도 연원을 따지면 우주 기술에 닿는다.

문제해설

1. (a)와 (c)는 지엽적이어서 주제로 어울리지 않는다. (b)와 (d) 중에서 (d)는 본문의 후반부에 해당하는 내용이므로 (b)가 주제로 더 적합함을 알 수 있다.

2. 마지막 문단을 보면 우주 개발을 통해 군사 기술뿐만 아니라 민간 기술로도 파급될 수 있음을 설명하고 있다. 이 내용을 (b)에서 다시 서술하고 있으므로 정답은 (b)가 된다.

3. 화성에 운하가 있다고 사람들이 생각한 것은 줄을 뜻하는 이탈리아어 카날리(canali)가 영어의 운하(canal)로 와전되면서 빚어진 해프닝이라고 나온다. 따라서 정답은 (c)가 된다.

4. 두 번째 문단의 "The longing for unknown worlds and to go to places that seem impossible to reach have been a source of imagination for much of recorded human history." 부분을 통해 인간은 항상 미지의 세계에 대해 끊임없이 동경한다는 것을 알 수 있으므로 정답은 (a)가 된다.

정답 1(b) 2(b) 3(c) 4(a)

Unit 80 | High hopes for hothouses
비닐하우스

스페인 남부의 알메리아는 1960년대 이탈리아 영화감독들이 '스파게티 서부극'을 촬영하면서 세상에 알려졌다. 이제는 이곳에 있는 비닐하우스로 더 유명하다. 이들 거대 인공구조물은 지구 밖에서도 보인다. 도시의 서쪽에 있는 이 구조물은 서울 절반 규모이다. 이곳은 과학자들에게 지구에 설치된 거대한 거울이나 마찬가지였다. 지구의 햇빛 반사나 복사열의 변화를 측정하는 지점으로 활용됐다.

알메리아 황야는 수백만 톤의 채소와 과일을 생산해 유럽 전역에 수출하는 금싸라기 땅으로 변모했다. 하지만 유엔환경계획(UNEP) '지구 환경 전망 보고서'는 1974년과 2004년의 위성사진을 비교 제시하며 알메리아를 대표적인 환경 급변 지역으로 꼽았다. 지하수와 토양이 오염됐다는 폭로도 이어졌다. 연간 100만 톤에 달한다는 작물 쓰레기는 여전히 골칫거리다.

하지만 흥미롭게도 알메리아 대학 연구진이 비닐하우스를 만들 때 쓰인 인공 재료의 양 때문에 붙여진 이른바 '플라스틱 바다'의 긍정적 효과를 찾아냈다. 약 30년간 스페인 다른 지방에서 기온이 1도가량 상승할 때 알메리아에서는 반대로 0.9도 떨어졌다는 것이다. 연구진은 이것이 비닐하우스가 반사 능력이 가장 높은 빙하처럼 햇빛을 반사해서이며, 이로써 복사열을 줄일 수 있었다고 주장했다. 비닐하우스가 지구 온난화를 줄이는 데 도움을 줄 수 있다는 것이다.

문제해설

1. 알메리아 지방의 지하수와 토양이 농약으로 오염됐다는 것은 사실이나 대량의 비닐하우스 사용으로 인해 다른 지방에 비해 기온이 떨어졌다는 내용에서 지구 온난화를 막을 수 있는 가능성을 모색하는 글이므로 (a)보다는 (d)가 주제로 더 적합하다.

2. "sea of plastic"은 드넓게 펼쳐진 비닐하우스를 지칭하는 말이므로 정답은 (a)가 된다.

3. (a)는 반대로 되어야 맞는 내용이 되며, (b)는 본문에서 서울의 절반 규모라고 했으므로 올바르지 않다. (d)는 본문에서 과거 황야였던 지역이 대량의 채소와 과일을 생산하는 지역으로 바뀌었다고 했으므로 이 또한 맞지 않다. 정답은 (c)로 다른 지역에 비해 기온이 떨어졌다는 내용이 마지막 문단에 나온다.

정답 1(d) 2(a) 3(c)

Unit 81 | X and Y
성별

태아의 성별은 난자와 수정이 된 정자가 X염색체를 가지고 있는지 Y염색체를 가지고 있는지에 따라 달라진다.

Y염색체를 가진 정자가 난자에 먼저 도달하면 아들, X염색체를 가지고 있으면 딸이 된다. 하지만 일부 학자들은 어떤 조건에서는 난자가 X나 Y염색체를 가진 정자 중에 어느 한쪽만을 선택해서 받아들이기도 한다고 주장한다. 여아와 남아의 비율이 일반적으로 100대 105이지만, 어떤 시기에 남아가 훨씬 높게 태어나는 것도 이 때문이라는 것이다. 그래서인지 어떨 때 아들을 가질 확률이 높은지에 대한 연구는 요즘도 계속되고 있다.

2005년 영국의 런던 경제대학원의 학자들은 회계사·기술자·수학자·물리학자는 아들을, 간호·교육 등 남을 돌보는 직종에서 일하는 사람은 딸을 낳는 비율이 각각 높다는 연구 결과를 낸 바 있다. 임신 당시에 부모가 함께 생활하고 있었던 커플의 51.5%가 아들을 낳았고, 떨어져 산 커플은 49.9%만이 아들을 낳았다는 분석 결과도 있다. 뉴질랜드 연구팀은 얌전하고 소극적인 여성에 비해 외향적인 여성들이 아들을 낳을 확률이 높다고 주장했다.

그렇지만 선진국에서는 지난 40년 간 남아 출산율이 꾸준히 줄고 있다. 환경오염을 비롯한 각종 스트레스가 Y염색체를 가진 정자의 활동성을 떨어뜨려, 남아 출생율을 감소시킨다는 설명이다. 콜롬비아 대학의 연구팀은 미혼모가 출산할 때 남아의 사망률이 여아보다 높았다고 보고했다.

> **문제해설**
> 1. 본문은 출생에 대한 환경적, 사회적 요인들에 대해 설명하고 있으므로 (c)가 주제로 적합하다.
> 2. "accountants, mechanics, mathematicians and physicians" 등을 직업으로 가진 이들이 아들을 낳을 확률이 높다고 했으며, "outgoing females conceived more boys than introverted, passive ones."에서는 소극적인 여성보다는 적극적인 여성들이 아들을 낳을 확률이 높다고 주장했으므로 정답은 (a)가 된다.
> 3. 본문에 미혼모의 출산에 대한 내용은 등장하지 않기 때문에 (c)가 정답이 된다.
> 4. 환경오염을 비롯한 각종 스트레스가 Y염색체를 가진 정자의 활동성을 떨어뜨린다는 내용을 통해 (a)의 내용을 알 수 있으며, 마지막 문단의 "we have seen a consistent decline in male birth rates in developed countries in the past four decades." 부분을 통해 (b)를 알 수 있다. 그리고 첫 번째 문단을 통해 여아와 남아의 출생 비율이 특정 조건에서는 달라진다는 내용을 통해 짐작할 수 있다. 정답은 (d)로 미래에 성을 선택할 수 있다는 내용은 본문에 나오지 않았다.

정답 1(c) 2(a) 3(c) 4(d)

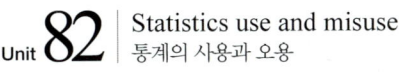

Unit 82 Statistics use and misuse
통계의 사용과 오용

만일 오스트리아의 수사인 그레고르 멘델(1822~1884)이 자신이 몰두하던 정원 완두를 가지고 교배하는 실험을 중단했다면, 세계 유전학에 미친 그의 업적은 달랐을 것이다. 그는 이들 식물의 일부 특성이 특정한 유전법칙을 따른다는 자신의 가설을 증명하고자 무려 15년 동안 완두콩 연구에 매달렸다. 그는 연구 결과의 변화에 따라 번호 순서대로 기록하여 통계를 내 분석하였다. 당시 사람들이 통계에 어두웠기에 사람들은 별 반응이 없었다.

그러다 20세기 초가 되어 멘델이 구상한 개념을 과학자들이 알게 되면서 사후에 그에게 '현대 유전학의 아버지'라는 칭호를 붙인다. 그의 연구를 통해 유전 법칙만이 밝혀진 것은 아니었다. 이들은 실험 결과 비율에 차이가 있음을 발견하고는, 멘델이 자신의 가설을 입증하고자 실험 기록들을 검열하여 삭제했거나 자기 이론과 동떨어진 결과가 나오면 이를 통계에서 제외시켜 버렸을지도 모른다는 의혹을 제기했다.

영국 수학자 찰스 배비지는 자신의 1830년 저서 『영국 과학의 쇠퇴에 대하여』에서 과학자들이 저지를 수 있는 세 가지의 학술 사기를 언급하고 있다. 요리하기(cooking), 다듬기(trimming), 위조하기(forging)라고 표현했다. 여기서 '요리하기'란 자신이 세운 가설에 맞는 값만 취하고, 나머지는 버린다는 뜻이다. 배비지가 더 크게 문제 삼은 건 '다듬기'였다. 측정값이 아주 정확하게 보이게끔 불규칙한 면들을 매끈하게 다듬는 행동이다. 이렇게 위조를 하고 원하는 결과가 나올 때까지 숫자를 다듬는 행태는 사회 통계의 영역에서도 종종 발견된다.

닉슨 행정부의 경제보좌관이었던 케빈 필립스는 닉슨 정부가 경제 지표를 긍정적으로 보고하기 위해 식료품과 에너지 가격을 소비자물가지수 계산에서 제외시켰다고 폭로했다. 미국 경제학자 스티븐 래빗의 책 『괴짜경제학』에는 시카고 공립학교에서 있었던 부정행위 사건이 나온다. 시 당국이 학생 성적이 나쁘면 승진·연봉에 불이익을 주는 정책을 시행했기 때문에, 교사들이 학생들의 시험성적을 조작한 것이다.

> **문제해설**
> 1. 이 글은 과학적 사기에 대해 나열하고 있다. 따라서 주제는 (a)가 적합하다. 나머지 보기들은 모두 단편적인 일부의 내용만을 담고 있어서 주제로 적합하지 않다.
> 2. [3]의 'will contradict'가 'would contradict'로 수정되어야 한다. 과거 시제와 맞춰 글이 서술되고 있기 때문이다. 따라서 과거의 시점에서 '향후 모순될 수도 있는'의 의미를 부여하기 위해서 would를 사용한다.
> 3. 멘델은 현대 유전학의 아버지로 불린다는 내용이 두 번째 문단 서두에 등장한다. 마지막 문단에서 Kevin Phillips는 닉슨 행정부의 부정을 폭로했으므로 밀고자란 의미의 whistleblower는 적절한 단어라 할 수 있다. 그리고 본문의 마지막 부분에서 (d)에 관한 내용이 나온다. 본문과 맞지 않는 내용은 (b)로 세 가지의 학술 사기에 해당하는

요리하기(cooking), 다듬기(trimming), 위조하기(forging) 등을 소개하고 있는데, 이들 중 일부가 서로 유사하다는 내용은 등장하지 않는다.

4. rampant는 만연했다는 의미를 지니므로 '광범위한'에 해당하는 (a)가 가장 유사하다.

정답 1(a) 2(c) 3(b) 4(a)

Unit 83 | Reinventing the wheel
볼펜 · 아이팟 · 신문

인쇄업체에서 일하던 오카다 요시오가 1961년 커터 칼을 발명한 건 절실한 필요 때문이었다. 종이 자르는 일을 하던 그는 면도날이 금세 무뎌져 불편이 이만저만 아니었다. 어느 날 구두 수선공이 유리 파편을 칼날 삼아 쓰는 걸 봤다. 어린 시절 미국 병사들이 조각조각 부러뜨려 나눠주던 초콜릿도 영감을 줬다. 날이 닳으면 끝부분을 툭 잘라내어 사용하지 않은 부분을 쓸 수 있는 칼날을 고안해내게 된 것이다.

헝가리 신문기자 라디즐로 비로는 다 쓴 원고에 잉크를 엎질러 낭패를 본 적 했다. 끈적한 유성 잉크를 쓰면 되겠다 싶었지만 농도가 짙어 펜촉으로 흘러나오지 않았다. 화학자인 그의 동생의 도움으로 그는 1943년 금속 볼 베어링으로 잉크를 밀어내는 방식을 고안했다. 볼펜의 탄생이다. 이를 가장 먼저 사용한 건 영국 공군이었다. 연합군의 2차 대전 승리는 비행 중에도 볼펜으로 또박또박 좌표계에 목표물을 표시할 수 있었기 때문이란 해석도 있다.

이들의 발명은 인류의 삶을 적잖이 바꿨다. 이미 있는 펜과 칼처럼 단순한 물건들을 '다르게' 쓰는 법을 창안했기 때문이다. 정보통신업계에선 이처럼 시스템과 기계를 쉽게 쓸 수 있게 하는 작업의 속내용을 사용자 환경(UI, User Interface)이라 한다. 혁신적 UI는 종종 기술적 진보를 압도한다. 닌텐도사가 2006년에 내놓은 게임기 '위'는 홈 비디오 게임에 완전히 새로운 의미를 더했다. 경쟁사들이 혁신적인 게임 소프트웨어와 게임기 개발에 몰두할 때 닌텐도는 아예 '노는 법'을 바꿔버렸다. 사용자가 자유롭게 몸을 움직여 게임을 즐길 수 있는 무선 게임 컨트롤러를 내놓은 것이다. 위의 세계 판매량은 5,000여만 대에 이른다.

'아이팟'도 역발상 UI의 산물이다. 복잡한 기능은 다 버리고 음향·화질에만 집중했다. 주머니에 쏙 들어가는 날렵하고 심플한 밝은 색 디자인으로 세계 젊은이를 사로잡았다. 애플 최고경영자 스티브 잡스는 신제품을 만들 때 "오직 중요한 건 사용자 눈으로 보는 것"임을 때마다 강조했다. 업자가 아닌 사용자 입장에 서야 혁신의 길이 보인다는 것이다.

문제해설

1. Wii가 인기 있었던 이유는 사용자가 자유롭게 몸을 움직여 게임을 즐

기게 한, 즉 노는 법을 완전히 바꿔버렸기 때문이다. 따라서 정답은 (b)가 적합하다.

2. [2]의 경우 바로 앞 선행사가 사물인 볼펜을 지칭하므로 which나 that으로 변경되어야 한다. [3]의 경우 뒤에 한 개 이상의 품목이 나오므로 복수형인 items로 수정되어야 한다. [4]의 경우 뒤에 added라는 동사가 나오므로 밑줄 친 부분은 앞의 명사를 수식해주는 분사 형태로 수정되어야 한다. 따라서 be동사가 생략된 marketed로 변경되어야 한다.

3. 펜의 발명이 사실은 연합군의 2차 대전 승리를 도왔다고 했기 때문에 방해했다는 (d)의 내용은 사실과 다르다.

4. (b)는 본문의 내용과 다르며, (d)는 본문에 등장하는 내용이 아니다. (a)의 경우도 생각해볼 수 있지만 본문의 내용만을 가지고 추론하기에는 미래 시점의 내용을 다루고 있으므로 제한적인 측면이 있다. (c)의 경우 커터칼을 발명해 자신의 일을 보다 더 쉽게 한 것은 첫 번째 문단을 통해 추정할 수 있는 내용이므로 정답은 (c)가 된다.

정답 1(b) 2(a) 3(d) 4(c)

Unit 84 | Sweetening up lethal diseases
프랑스병

이탈리아 시인 지롤라모 프라카스토로가 1530년에 자신의 시에서 16세기에 '프랑스병'이라고 불린 이 질병에 새 이름을 지어 주었다. 이 질병은 크리스토퍼 콜럼버스의 탐험대가 발견한 신대륙에서 유래했을 것으로 생각됐다. 이탈리아와 독일에선 이 병을 '프랑스병'이라고 불렀지만, 반대로 프랑스에선 '이탈리아병'이란 이름을 붙였다. 동시에 네덜란드에서는 스페인병, 러시아에서는 폴란드병, 터키에서는 기독교도병으로 통했다. 멀리 타히티 섬에서는 영국병이라고 불렸다는 기록이 있다.

이렇게 다양한 이름이 발생한 이유는 쉽게 짐작할 수 있다. 다들 '몹쓸 병을 옮기는 책임'은 적국에 떠넘기고 싶었기 때문이다. 프라카스토로가 이 병에 '시필리스(syphilis·매독)'란 새 이름을 지어 주지 않았다면 유럽 각국은 지금까지도 서로 상대국의 이름을 병 이름으로 부르며 감정다툼을 벌이고 있을지도 모를 일이다. 지난 4월 30일 세계보건기구(WHO)는 현재 창궐하고 있는 국제 전염병에 대해 'SI(Swine Influenza)' 대신 '인플루엔자 A형' 또는 'H1N1'이란 명칭을 공식 사용하기로 결정했다. 이미 널리 쓰이는 SI를 굳이 바꾼 건 불필요한 오해를 막기 위해서다.

병의 이름은 혐오와 공포감을 함께 옮긴다. 20세기 이후 사람들은 병의 이름이 주는 불쾌감을 줄이고자 증세나 원인을 노골적으로 설명하는 이름은 피하는 게 낫다는 결론을 내렸다. 그래서 문둥병은 한센병으로, 노인성 치매는 알츠하이머병으로, 광우병도 변종 크로이츠펠트-야코프병으로 불리게 됐다. 정신분열증도 사회적 편견을 피하기

위해 '도파민 항진증'으로 고쳐 불러야 한다는 주장이 있다. 한국어로는 이미 '지랄'이라는 욕설이 된 병 히스테리가 지금은 간질이라고 불리는 것도 같은 이유다.

문제해설
1. 질병의 이름에 혐오감이나 공포감이 함께 전해지기 때문에 병의 이름이 주는 불쾌감을 줄이고자 질병의 이름을 바꾼다는 내용이다. 따라서 왜 질병들이 중성적 이름을 채용하게 되었는지 설명하는 글이란 내용의 (b)가 정답이 된다.
2. 세계보건기구에서 SI 대신 '인플루엔자 A형' 또는 'H1N1'이란 명칭을 공식 사용하기로 결정했다는 내용이 나오므로 (d)에서 이런 이름을 사용하는 것을 반대했다는 내용은 사실이 아니다.
3. (A)는 바로 앞 conclusion과 동격을 이루는 that절이 오며, (B)에는 바로 앞 disease names를 선행사로 하는 관계대명사가 와야 하므로 정답은 (a)가 된다.
4. 매독이라는 불명예스런 질병이 발생한 이유를 상대국에 떠넘기고 싶어였으므로 정답은 (c)가 된다.

정답 1(b) 2(d) 3(a) 4(c)

Unit 85 | The life-saving act of washing
팬데믹(pandemic)

1346년 그 당시 동서양 교역의 접점이던 크림반도의 항구도시 카파에선 3년이나 이곳을 포위했던 몽골 통치자 야니 벡이 그곳 시민들에게 작별 선물을 남겼다. 느닷없이 의문의 병에 걸려 죽은 군사들의 시체를 성벽 안으로 던져 넣은 것이다. 치명적인 병원균이 그렇게 성 안으로 침투했다. 아시아에서 발생해 실크로드를 타고 날개 돋친 듯 퍼진 흑사병이 마침내 유럽에 발을 내디딘 순간이다. 성곽 안에 피신해 있던 제노바 상인들이 본의 아니게 균의 전파자가 됐다. 이듬해 이들이 고향으로 향하며 들른 항구마다 감염자가 속출했다. 유럽 방방곡곡으로 번진 병은 1년 만에 영국과 아라비아 반도, 나일강 삼각주까지 미쳤다.

신대륙을 빼곤 거의 전 세계를 휩쓴 흑사병은 역사상 최악의 팬데믹(대유행)이었다. 나라마다 3분의 1에서 절반의 인구가 목숨을 잃었다. 사망자가 4,200만 명에 달하고 이 중 2,500만 명이 유럽인이었다. 이 참사는 페스트균을 지닌 벼룩이 쥐의 몸에 서식하고, 이 쥐들이 식량을 쫓아 사람 가까이에 머문 데 기인했다. 그러나 전염이란 개념이 없던 당시 사람들은 원인을 엉뚱한 곳에 돌렸다. 쥐를 박멸하긴커녕 인간의 죄에 분노한 신의 천벌이라며 수만 명이 스스로를 채찍으로 때리는 고행에 나섰다. 마녀 사냥마저 기승을 부렸다. 유대인들이 병균을 퍼트렸단 소문이 돌면서 그들을 산 채로 태워 죽이는 비극이 곳곳에서 빚어졌다.

애꿎은 유대인들이 소문의 희생양이 된 이유 중 하나는 흑사병이 유독 그들만 피해갔기 때문이다. 『탈무드』는 청결을 강조하는 유대교의 전통 덕분이라고 설명한다. 손 씻는 것을 신과 만나는 신성한 행위로 여겨 삼가 지켰다는 거다. 반면 '비누 밑에 돈을 감추면 절대 못 찾는다'는 농담을 할 만큼 여느 중세 사람들은 잘 씻지 않고 살았다.

문제해설
1. 본문은 14세기 흑사병이 퍼지게 된 것을 설명하고 있는 글이므로 (c)가 주제로 적합하다. 어떻게 유대인들은 흑사병에 걸리지 않았는가, 위생이 결정적 구실을 했다는 등의 내용은 부수적인 내용이다.
2. 첫 번째 문단 중 "He catapulted the bodies of his soldiers who had died suddenly from a mysterious disease over the fortress walls." 부분을 통해 병사들의 시체를 성 안으로 던져 전염병을 퍼지게 했다고 나오므로 정답은 (b)가 된다.
3. (A)에는 질병이 특정 지역에 걸쳐 휩쓴다는 내용이므로 'sweep across'가 적절하며, (B)의 경우 ~에 기대어 산다고 할 때 'live on'을 사용하는 것과 같이 이때는 동사만 바뀌어 'feast on'이 된다. (C)는 수동태 표현에 해당하므로 by가 와야 한다. 따라서 정답은 (d)가 된다.
4. 세 번째 문단을 보면 당시 유대인들은 흑사병을 피할 수 있었는데, 이는 손을 잘 씻는 유대교의 전통 때문이었다고 나온다. 따라서 다른 이들보다 유대인들이 더 위생적이었음을 알 수 있다.

정답 1(c) 2(b) 3(d) 4(a)

Unit 86 | Seeking signs of aliens in universe
외계인

1977년 미국에서 태양계 밖의 먼 우주를 탐사하기 위해 떠난 미국 우주선 보이저 1호와 2호에는 황금 도금이 된 레코드판과 재생 장비가 실렸다. 이 레코드에는 당시 지미 카터 미국 대통령과 쿠르트 발트하임 UN 사무총장의 메시지, 그리고 한국어를 포함해 세계 55개 언어로 된 인사말, 베토벤 교향곡 5번에서 호주 원주민의 민요까지 총 27곡의 음악이 녹음됐다. 한마디로 '지구의 소리'가 실린 음반이었다.

이 음반이 실린 이유는 단 한 가지, 외계인이 언젠가는 발견할지도 모른다는 가능성 때문이었다. 물론 33년 전 발사된 보이저 1호와 2호 우주선은 현재 지구에서 각각 115AU, 93AU (1AU = 태양에서 지구까지의 거리) 떨어진 곳까지 날아갔고, 앞으로도 수만 년은 더 날아야 외계 문명이 존재할 가능성이 있는 곳까지 도달할 수 있다. 이 프로젝트는 별 의미 없는 행위 같기도 하지만, 당시 이 계획을 주도했던 천체물리학자 칼 세이건은 "병속에 편지를 넣어 대양에 띄우듯" 해볼만 하다고 주장했다.

저서 '코스모스'로 잘 알려진 세이건은 또 SETI (Search for Extra-Terrestrial Intelligence) 계획을 주도하며 외계인

51

들이 보내올지도 모르는 전자 신호를 포착하기 위해 막대한 예산을 사용했다. 미국 정부는 더 이상 이를 지원하지 않고 있다. 하지만 미국 정부가 1996년 '쓸데없는 낭비'라며 지원을 끊은 뒤에도 세계 125개국의 과학자들이 민간 기구와 후원자들의 도움을 통해 분석을 계속하고 있다.

문제해설

1. 본문의 내용은 외계 생명체와의 접촉을 꿈꾸면서 보이저 1호와 2호에 지구인들의 정보가 담긴 레코드판을 싣고 갔으며, 외계인들이 보낼 수 있는 전자 신호를 연구하는 SETI 프로그램에 관한 내용을 담고 있으므로 (b)에 관한 내용임을 알 수 있다.
2. 칼 세이건이 미 정부를 설득해 결국 보이저 1호와 2호 발사와 SETI 프로그램을 실행한 것을 보면 외계 생명체와의 접촉에 많은 관심을 가졌음을 알 수 있다.
3. 바로 앞 문장에 나와 있는 SETI, 즉 외계 생명체를 찾는 노력을 지칭한다. 따라서 정답은 (a)가 된다.
4. 마지막 문장인 "scientists from 125 countries continue to analyze signals with support from private institutions and donors"을 보면 미국 정부가 SETI 프로그램 지원을 중단한 이후에도 다른 나라의 과학자들이 계속해서 분석을 하고 있다고 나온다. 따라서 (d)의 내용은 사실이 아니다.

정답 1(b) 2(b) 3(a) 4(d)

Unit 87 | The high cost of the patent wars
복제약

발명과 혁신의 중요성이 부각된 건 르네상스 시대부터다. 그 유명한 피렌체 대성당의 돔을 건축한 필리포 브루넬레스코가 사상 첫 특허를 받았다. 돔을 짓는 데 필요한 대리석 운반용 배를 설계한 데 관한 것이었다. 하지만 이 배로 별 재미는 못 봤다. 배는 처녀 출항에서 50t이나 되는 대리석과 함께 침몰해 버렸다.

특허 제도는 나날이 발전했다. 지금은 금전적 이익의 보장 없인 발명도, 혁신도 꽃 피울 수 없다는 상식이 굳어졌다. 그러나 반론도 만만찮다. 돈이 아니라 타인에게 도움을 주려는 착한 마음도 '발명의 어머니'가 될 수 있다는 게 특허 폐지론자들의 주장이다. 특히 제약 분야에서 특허는 '동네북' 신세다. 사람 목숨이 더 중하지 특허가 대수냐며 대놓고 침해한다. 2002년 정부가 나서 무단으로 에이즈 치료제의 복제약을 만든 태국이 그랬다. 국제 사회의 항의가 빗발쳤지만 태국 정부는 약값이 500달러에서 30달러로 뚝 떨어져 더 많은 생명을 살렸다고 맞섰다.

신약 개발에 돈과 시간을 들인 때문인지 특허 침범에 제약사들은 불평을 터뜨린다. 이들 회사는 특허기간이 끝나기 무섭게 값싼 복제약을 시장에 내놓는 업체들에까지도 불만을 토로한다. 미국이 한·미 자유무역협정(FTA)에서 특허 만료 후 복제약 시판을 늦추는 조치를 고집한 건 그래서다. FTA 재협상에서 이 조치의 유예기간이 길어졌다고 한다.

문제해설

1. 이 글은 특허 제도에 관한 글이므로 정답은 (d)가 된다.
2. 이득될 것이 없다면 발명이나 혁신이 활발히 벌어질 수 없을 것이라는 말이므로 'it is ~ that ~' 강조구문을 이용한 (c)가 정답이 된다.
3. 두 번째 문단에 나와 있는 내용으로, 태국의 경우가 정부가 나서서 무단으로 에이즈 치료제를 만들었다는 내용이 나온다. 그리고 항의에 대해서는 더 많은 사람들을 살렸다고 주장했다고 나오므로 특허보다는 사람의 목숨이 더 중요하다는 (d)가 이들의 방어 논리가 된다.
4. 세 번째 문단 초반 "Pharmaceutical companies complain a lot ... because of the time and money they invested in developing a new drug." 부분을 통해 (c)에서 말한 사실을 알 수 있으므로 정답은 (c)가 된다.

정답 1(d) 2(c) 3(d) 4(c)

Unit 88 | The empty seat
빈자리

인도의 수학자 브라마굽타는 서기 600년경 '숫자 0'을 '슈냐(shunya)'라고 불렀다. 슈냐는 산스크리트어로 '공백(空白)'이면서 '부재(不在)'의 의미다. 그가 최초로 공백이란 철학적 개념을 바탕에 0을 '아무것도 없음'을 의미하는 '숫자'로 사용한 것이다. 그 이전엔 0은 그 자체가 하나의 숫자로 여겨진 게 아니라 그저 양이 없음을 표시하는 부호였을 뿐이다.

빈자리의 중요성이 수(數)의 세상에만 국한되는 것은 아니다. '부재'는 인간사(人間事)에서도 물리적인 빈 공간을 넘어 '삶의 의미'요, '자연의 법칙'이기도 하다. 우선 동서를 막론하고 신화(神話)에서 세상의 시작은 무(無)이다. 맨 처음엔 하늘도 땅도 물도 없고 빛도 어둠도 시간도 없었다. 바닥도 천장도 없는 텅 빈 공간, 빈 자리였을 뿐이다. 하기야 137억 년 전의 빅뱅(big bang) 이전에는 우주가 크기 0의 점과 같은 상태였다고 하니 신화의 황당함만 나무랄 일도 아니다.

인간의 참모습과 마음을 추구하는 종교의 영역에서도 비움은 종교적인 단어다. 불교에서 마음은 실체가 있는 게 아니라 허공처럼 텅 비어 있다. 동서남북 어디나 텅 빈 자리가 아닌 데가 없다. 우주 속 무한히 넓은 빈자리가 바로 불교에서의 '공(空)'이다. 그러니 깨달음은 각자(覺者)의 눈에 일체 삼라만상(森羅萬象)은 텅 빈 자리에 존재할 뿐이다.

빈자리는 무엇을 모르는지를 깨치게 하는 자연의 법칙 같은 것이기도 하다. 『생각의 탄생』을 쓴 로버트 루트번스타인은 조각 맞추기 퍼즐을 예로 든다. 완성된 그림 못지않게 빠진 조각이 무엇인지를 보여주는 채워지지 않은 빈

공간 역시 중요하다는 거다. 그건 우리 자신이 모르는 것이 무엇인지 가늠하게 하는 단서가 되기 때문이다. 무얼 봐야 하는지를 알게 되면 빈자리에 들어맞는 조각을 찾아낼 수 있다.

문제해설

1. 본문은 숫자 0으로 시작하지만, 숫자의 의미를 넘어서 0이 의미하는 빈자리(emptiness)를 중심으로 이야기를 서술하고 있다. 과학과 종교에서의 빈자리, 그리고 예술에서의 빈자리를 언급하고 있다. 따라서 (c)와 같이 단순히 숫자 0이 가지는 가치라기보다는 빈자리의 의미들을 주제로 보는 것이 적절하다.

2. 동서를 막론하고 신화에서 세상의 시작은 무(無)라고 했으며, 브라마굽타가 0에 숫자의 의미를 부여했다고 초반부에 설명하고 있다. 그리고 마지막 부분에서 조각 맞추기 퍼즐을 언급하면서 완성된 그림 못지않게 빠진 조각이 무엇인지를 보여준다고 했으므로 이를 통해 (d)를 설명할 수 있다. 정답은 (a)로 빈자리가 항상 물리적 공백을 의미한다고 했는데, 불교와 같은 종교에서는 이것이 물리적 실체를 지칭하지 않는다는 것을 알 수 있다.

3. it이 지칭하는 것은 조각 맞추기 퍼즐에서 빠져있는 부분을 의미한다. 따라서 (b)가 정답이 된다.

4. 수학에도 0이 있다고 했으므로 (a)는 답이 될 수 없으며, (b)는 본문의 내용만으로는 알 수 없으며, (c)의 경우 우주 속 무한히 넓은 빈자리가 바로 불교에서의 공(空)이라고 했으므로 공의 존재를 믿는다고 볼 수 있다. 정답은 (d)로 마지막 문단의 내용을 통해 내용을 유추할 수 있다.

정답 1(a) 2(a) 3(b) 4(d)

Unit 89 Scarier than genetic diseases
유전질환보다 더 두려운 것

최근 개인 유전자 검사가 주목받고 있다. 지난 6월 말부터 의사를 통하지 않고도 소비자가 직접 자신의 유전형질을 알아보는 시대가 열렸다. 방법도 간단하다. 입안 세포를 조사기관에 보내면 된다. 15만원 안팎에 혈당·피부노화·탈모·비만 등 12개 항목에 대한 위험성을 예측할 수 있다. 주로 실생활과 관련된 것이다. 잘못된 분석에 대한 우려 때문에, 암 등 중증질환은 법적으로 금지된 상태다.

본인의 유전정보를 미리 알면 분명 유용하다. 반면 일부 과학자들은 환경이란 변수 때문에 유전자 결정론을 경계한다. 예컨대 일란성 쌍둥이도 성장 과정에 따라 발육에 차이가 난다. 비만 또한 사회경제적 여건이 중요하다. 소득·교육 수준이 낮을수록 과체중으로 고생할 확률이 크다는 연구는 이제 낯설지 않다. 환경적 요인도 후세에 전해진다는 후성(後成)유전학도 있다.

한국인의 술·담배 소비에 경고등이 켜졌다. 통계청의 올 상반기 가계 동향에 따르면, 소득 대비 다른 항목은 대부분 줄어들었는데 주류·담배 평균 소비성향이 전년 대비 7.1% 늘었다. 글로벌 시장조사기관 유로모니터 인터내셔널 조사도 비슷하다. 24개국 가운데 한국인의 술 열량 섭취량은 하루 평균 168㎉로 '술 비만도' 1위를 기록했다. 영광스럽지 않은 수치다. 술과 담배의 사회적 유전이 걱정될 지경이다.

문제해설

1. 본문에서는 주류와 담배 소비에 있어 한국이 24개국 중 1위이며 이러한 소비 성향이 다음 세대로 물려질까 걱정된다는 입장을 취한다. (a), (c), (d)는 본문에서는 찾아볼 수 없다.

2. 첫 단락의 "Due to the concerns for errors in analysis, it is prohibited by law to analyze genetic traits for severe illnesses such as cancer." 문장을 통해 (a)가 정답임을 알 수 있다. 간단한 방법을 통해 위험성을 예측할 수 있다는 점은 긍정적이지만 잘못된 정보를 줄 경우 부정적인 결과를 초래할 수 있기 때문이다.

3. 주류와 담배를 제외한 다른 항목에서는 소비가 줄고 있다는 점이 마지막 단락에서 언급되므로 정답은 (c)이다. (a)는 작년에 비해 7.1% 증가했다는 본문과 반대되는 내용이며, 교육과 소득 수준에 따라 과체중일 확률이 높아진다는 연구는 이미 존재하지만 소득 수준이 낮으면 흡연 및 음주 확률이 높아진다는 점은 찾아볼 수 없기에 (b)도 정답이 아니다. 마지막으로 (d)는 앞서 말한 교육과 소득이 사회경제학적 요인이므로 과체중의 원인을 연구할 때 이러한 점들이 무시된다는 내용은 틀린 것이다.

4. 빈칸 다음 문장에서 일란성 쌍둥이가 다른 체격을 갖게 되는 것은 그들이 다른 환경에서 자라나면 가능한 일이며 유전 정보를 아는 것은 유용하지만 이러한 환경적 요인들도 배제되면 안 된다는 내용의 (a)가 적합하다.

정답 1(b) 2(a) 3(c) 4(a)

Unit 90 Listeria hysteria
리스테리아

리스테리아는 흔히 '유비쿼터스(ubiquitous, 도처에 있는) 세균'으로 불린다. 도처에서 불쑥 나타나기 때문에 그렇다. 토양·물에서도 발견된다. 식물은 흙이나 퇴비를 통해 이 세균에 오염되고, 풀을 뜯어 먹은 가축에 전파된다. 몇몇 저온 살균 처리되지 않은 유제품과 육류 제품을 정기적으로 검사해 리스테리아균의 유무를 살피고 있다. 리스테리아균에 오염된 식품을 먹었더라도 건강한 사람이라면 별 문제가 안 된다. 증상이 없거나 독감 비슷한 증상을 보이다가 이내 치유된다. 사망이나, 생명을 위협하는 심각한 부작용은 주로 노인이나 임산부에게서 많이 나타난다. 이들 그룹에 속한 사람들은 면역력이 떨어지기 쉬워서 리스테리아균에 더 취약하다. 특히 임신한 여성은 건강한 젊은 여성에 비해 리스테리아 식중독에 걸릴 위험이 20배나 높다. 태아를 거부 반응 없이 받아들이기 위해 임신 기간에 스스로 면역력을 낮춘 탓으로 여겨지고 있다. 미국 질병통

제센터(CDC)는 리스테리아 감염을 심각하게 여기며, 이곳 추산에 따르면 미국에서만 해마다 2,500명이 감염되고 이 중 500명이 숨진다.

> **문제해설**

1. (a)의 경우 리스테리아는 모든 사람이 아닌, 특히 노인이나 임산부 등 면역력이 떨어지는 사람들이 걸릴 위험이 크다고 말하고 있다. (b)와 (d)는 본문에 등장하지 않는다. 정답은 (c)로 리스테리아와 같은 일반 박테리아라 할지라도 여전히 위험할 수 있다는 내용이 후반부에 나온다.

2. 임산부는 면역력이 떨어진다고 나오므로 리스테리아에 감염되는 것이 위험하다고 유추할 수 있다.

> **정답** **1**(c) **2**(c)

Unit 91 | The joy of leaving your car behind
차 없는 날

2004년 봄 이탈리아 과학자들은 오랜 숙제를 풀었다. 바로 르네상스 시대의 천재인 레오나르도 다빈치의 자동차를 재현하는 데 성공한 것이다. 그들은 다빈치의 저작 노트 '코덱스 아틀란티쿠스(Codex Atlanticus)'에 나와 있는 설계도대로 나무 자동차를 만들었다. 다빈치의 자동차는 실제 도로를 달리기보다 전시를 하기 위해 고안된 것으로 추정되지만, 과학자들이 마침내 이를 작동할 수 있도록 했다.

자동차가 도로를 달리기 시작한 것은 120여 년 전부터다. (독일의) 카를 프리드리히 벤츠는 1885년 자신이 만든 휘발유 엔진을 단 삼륜 자동차를 개발했다. 1891년에는 네 바퀴 자동차도 만들었다. 본격적인 자동차 시대를 연 것은 미국의 헨리 포드다. 포드 자동차 회사가 1908년에 선보인 모델 T는 튼튼하고 운전도 편리한 데다 가격도 싼 편이어서 중산층도 쉽게 구입할 수 있었다. 모델 T는 1927년 단종될 때까지 1,600만 대나 팔렸다.

미국의 자동차 회사들은 1920년대에 로스앤젤레스 같은 도시의 통근 전차를 사들였다. 이들은 일일 운행 횟수를 줄이면서 전차 이용을 불편하게 만들었고, 결국은 적자를 이유로 전차 운행을 중단했다. 미국의 자동차 문화는 1950년대 전국에 걸친 고속도로 건설로 확고하게 자리 잡았다.

> **문제해설**

1. 본문의 전반적 내용은 자동차에 대한 것이므로 (b)가 적합하다.

2. 통근 전차와 같은 교통수단을 자동차 회사들이 인수해 이용하기 불편하게 만들었다는 내용이 마지막 문단에 등장하므로 정답은 (c)가 된다.

3. (b)는 본문과 무관하며, (c)의 경우 다빈치가 자동차를 고안한 것은 맞지만 현대식 자동차의 등장이 다빈치의 자동차를 모델로 했다는 내용은 등장하지 않는다. 또한 오래 전에 통근 전차의 운행이 중단되었

으므로 (d) 또한 올바른 설명이 아니다. 정답은 (a)로 포드와 같은 자동차 회사가 대량 생산을 통해 미국의 자동차 문화를 만들었다는 내용을 두 번째 문단에서 알 수 있다.

4. 이 글은 자동차가 어떻게 등장하게 되었는가에 대한 내용이므로 (d)가 적합하다.

> **정답** **1**(b) **2**(c) **3**(a) **4**(d)

Unit 92 | A critical look at global warming
온난화 회의론

2003년 여름 유럽은 마치 뜨거운 프라이팬처럼 더웠다. 섭씨 40도가 넘는 폭염 속에 원전은 냉각수가 부족해 어려움을 겪었다. 사람들은 일사병에 시달렸고 수만 명이 더위로 숨졌다. 지구 온난화가 계속되면 이같은 폭염은 잦을 수밖에 없다. 하지만 일부에서는 겨울 한파는 그만큼 줄지 않겠냐고 주장한다. 덴마크의 통계학자인 비외른 롬보르는 2007년 『쿨잇(진정하라)』이란 책에서 "추위로 얼어 죽는 사람이 줄어드는 것 같은 온난화의 좋은 점도 있다"고 주장했다.

하지만, 2001년 『회의적 환경주의자』란 책을 내놓아 세계적인 온난화 논쟁을 불러일으켰던 롬보르의 생각은 그 이후 조금은 달라져 있었다. 2001년에는 온난화의 과학적 근거를 대놓고 부정했으나 2007년에는 온난화 자체는 인정했다. 대신 온실가스 감축에 돈을 쏟기보다는 에이즈·말라리아 박멸에 투자하는 게 효율적이라고 지적했다. 이 같은 변화의 배경에는 2007년 2월 유엔 기후변화위원회(IPCC)가 내놓은 제4차 기후변화보고서가 있었다. IPCC는 전 세계 2,500여 명의 전문가 의견을 종합해 "인류가 온난화를 일으켰다는 데에는 논란의 여지가 없다"고 못 박았다. 이에 회의론자들도 한발 물러설 수밖에 없었다.

요즘 움츠렸던 회의론자들이 다시 목소리를 높이고 있다. 지구 평균기온은 1998년 섭씨 14.5도를 기록한 이래 더 이상 올라가지 않고 있다. 얼마 전에는 저명한 기후학자들이 주고받은 4,000건의 이메일·문서가 해킹돼 온라인에 공개됐다. 메일 중에는 학자들이 온난화에 관한 자신들의 주장을 뒷받침하는, 입맛에 맞는 연구 내용만 골라 발표해왔다는 의심을 받을 내용도 있었다.

> **문제해설**

1. (a)의 경우 세 번째 문단의 "지구 평균기온은 1998년 섭씨 14.5도를 기록한 이래 더 이상 올라가지 않고 있다"는 내용을 통해 짐작할 수 있으며, (b)의 경우 지구 온난화에 대한 논쟁이 계속되는 것을 통해 알 수 있다. (c)의 경우 (b)와 마찬가지로 찬성론자와 회의론자가 각각 그럴듯한 이론들을 주장하고 있음을 알 수 있다. 정답은 (d)로 2007년 유엔 기후변화위원회에서 기후변화 문제에 공통의 의견을 내놓았지만, 지금은 다시 회의론자들이 목소리를 높이고 있다고 했으므로 (d)는 본문의 내용과 맞지 않게 된다.

2. 지구 온난화에 대한 논쟁이 주요 주제이지만 후반에 가서는 회의론자들의 주장을 강조하고 있으므로 정답은 (a)가 적합하다.

3. 앞서 문제에 나왔듯이 지구 온난화 문제는 아직도 논쟁 중인 사항이며, (c)의 경우는 첫 번째 문단에 나타나 있다. (d)의 경우 두 번째 문단에서 온실가스 감축에 돈을 쓰기보다는 에이즈나 말라리아 등에 쓰는 게 낫다는 내용을 통해 알 수 있다. 정답은 (b)로 롬보르의 주장이 사실로 입증되었다는 내용은 등장하지 않았다.

4. (A)의 경우 양보문이므로 과거에는 부정했지만 지금은 인정한다는 내용이 와야 하므로 recognized가 적절하다. 그리고 (B)의 경우 IPCC에서 지구 온난화에 대해 인재가 맞다는 주장을 내놓은 것에 대해 자신들의 기존 입장에서 한발 물러나야 하는 측은 지구 온난화에 회의적인 생각을 갖고 있던 과학자들이므로 (B)에는 skeptical이 적당하다.

정답 1(d) 2(a) 3(b) 4(d)

Unit 93 | Repent, ye carbon emitters
환경 면죄부

지구 온난화 시대의 중죄라 할 탄소 배출에도 면죄부가 등장했다. 탄소를 많이 배출하는 대신 친환경적인 사업에 돈을 내도록 하는 이른바 '탄소 상쇄(carbon offset)' 제도이다. 교통수단 중 가장 많은 탄소를 내뿜는 비행기 여행자들이 주로 산다. 아프리카에 나무를 심고 브라질에 수력발전소를 짓는 데 쓰이며 항공료 외에 10~40달러를 더 지불한다. 죄책감을 덜려는 수요 덕분에 전 세계적으로 이 제도로 벌어들인 매출이 이백만 달러에 달한다.

하지만 탄소배출권이라고 알려진 이 시스템에 대한 비판이 만만치 않다. 중세 때 면죄부가 사람들이 맘 편히 죄를 짓도록 부추겼듯이 탄소 상쇄 제도도 더 많이 여행하고, 더 많이 소비하는 풍조만 조장한다는 것이다.

교토의정서에 따라 2005년 부분 조정된 탄소배출권 거래(cap and trade) 역시 온난화를 악화시키고 있다고 환경 전문가들은 지적한다. 온실가스 배출한도를 넘긴 나라가 한도를 못 채운 나라로부터 배출권을 사들일 수 있게 한 이 제도도 과다 배출국들에 면죄부를 줄 뿐 감축 효과는 미미하다는 얘기다. 나사(NASA)의 기후과학자 제임스 한슨은 런던 타임스지를 통해 "그들은 면죄부를 팔고 있는 것이다. 선진국들은 평소대로 사업을 계속하고 싶어하고 개도국에 푼돈이나 쥐어주면서 면죄부를 살 수 있을 거라 기대하는 것이다. 상쇄와 적응 기금이라는 형태로 말이다."라고 개탄한다.

문제해설

1. 본문은 탄소배출권 제도를 부정적인 시각으로 바라보고 있다. 마치 중세의 면죄부를 발부하는 것처럼 실제로 탄소 배출이 줄어드는 것이 아니라 돈으로 자신의 잘못을 사면 해결된다는 인식이 더해져서 실제 감축 효과는 미미할 것이라고 설명하고 있다. 따라서 실효성이 없이 선진국에서 현재의 생활 방식을 계속 유지하게 할 것이라는 (c)가 정답이 된다.

2. 1번과 같은 이유에서 현재의 탄소배출권 제도는 개선되어야 한다는 (a)가 정답이 된다.

3. 탄소배출권 제도와 면죄부를 서로 비교한 이유는 서로의 취지가 같다고 생각해서이다. 따라서 (b)가 정답이 된다.

4. 본문은 단순히 탄소배출권 제도를 설명하는 데 그치지 않는다. 이런 제도를 통해 중세 시대에 죄를 저지르고도 면죄부를 발부받아 자신의 죄를 탕감했듯이 오늘날의 탄소배출권 제도가 중세의 면죄부가 될 수 있다고 경고하고 있는 글이다. 따라서 정답은 (d)가 된다.

정답 1(c) 2(a) 3(b) 4(d)

Unit 94 | Undersea calamity omen of greater ills
온난화 부메랑

바다 속 열대우림에 비견될 만큼 다양한 생물이 서식하는 산호초가 사막처럼 변했다. 해초들을 사라지게 하고, 작은 생물들의 서식지를 파괴하며, 바다의 아름다운 색을 앗아가버리는 백화 현상이다. 이미 전 세계 산호초의 30%를 죽게 한 백화 현상은 호주의 그레이트 배리어 리프에서 아직도 퍼져 나가고 있다.

전문가들 사이에서도 앞에서 엽록소를 충분히 생성해 내지 못하는 백화 현상이 왜 일어나는지 의견이 분분하다. 육지에서 내려온 오염물질이 원인이라는 의견도 있었고, 아프리카 사하라 사막에서 날아오른 먼지 속의 곰팡이가 원인이란 주장도 있었다.

하지만 대부분 전문가들은 지구 기후 변화로 해수 온도가 올라간 게 가장 큰 원인일 것으로 추정해왔다. 여기에 인류가 내뿜은 이산화탄소(CO_2)가 바닷물에 녹아들어 산성도를 높인 것도 한몫하고 있다는 것이다. 이에 따라 2007년 유엔 정부 간 기후변화위원회(IPCC)는 지구 평균 기온이 1도만 상승해도 전 세계 산호의 80% 이상이 하얗게 변할 것이라고 전망했다. 또 바닷물 산성화가 지금처럼 계속된다면 2050년이면 산호가 10%도 남지 않을 것이란 예측도 있다.

최근 미국 사우스캐롤라이나주 홀링스 해양연구소 과학자들은 의문에 싸였던 백화 현상의 원인을 밝혀냈다. '비브리오 코랄릴리티쿠스'라는 두 얼굴을 가진 단세포 세균이 원인이란 설명이다. 이 미세한 편모는 저온에서는 아무런 해를 끼치지 않지만 수온이 24도를 넘으면 독성 화학물질을 배출해 산호에 스트레스를 준다는 것이다. 온난화는 생태계뿐만 아니라 부메랑이 돼 인간의 삶까지 허물고 있다.

문제해설

1. 이 글은 산호초의 파괴에 대한 내용을 담고 있으며, 그 원인으로 지구 온난화를 지목하고 있다. 하지만 (b)는 지구 온난화만을 언급하고 있으므로 주요 내용인 산호초의 파괴를 설명할 수 없다. 따라서 (a)가 제목으로 더 적합하다.

2. 마지막 문단을 보면 '비브리오 콜랄릴리티쿠스'라는 단세포 세균이 저온에서는 아무런 해를 끼치지 않지만 수온이 24도를 넘으면 독성 화학물질을 배출해 산호에 스트레스를 준다고 나온다. 따라서 올바른 보기는 (b)가 된다.
3. 지구 온난화가 원인이 되어 산호초가 사라지고 있으므로 산호초를 되살리기 위해서는 시급히 조치를 취해야 한다는 (a)가 적합하다.
4. 첫 번째 문장인 "Coral reefs, inhabited by such a rich diversity of creatures that they might be called underwater rainforests," 에 산호초를 물속의 열대우림으로 묘사하고 있다. 따라서 정답은 (d)가 된다.

정답 1(a) 2(b) 3(a) 4(d)

Unit 95 Sky-high dreams
마천루

구약성경 창세기 11장에는 인류 최초의 고층건물인 바벨탑의 건설과 파괴에 관한 이야기가 나온다. 고대 도시 바빌론의 히브리어 이름인 바벨인데, 단일 언어를 사용하는 이곳 바벨 사람들은 벽돌로 탑을 쌓아 하늘에 닿고자 했다. 신에 대한 숭배가 아닌 인간의 영광을 묘사하려 한 바벨탑 건설에 분노한 하느님은 사람들이 서로 말을 알아듣지 못하게 해 공사를 중단시켰다.

성경에는 바벨탑의 높이가 얼마나 됐는지 나오지 않지만 학자들은 6,000m쯤 됐을 것으로 추정한다. 현대적 의미의 마천루가 실제로 세워지기 시작한 것은 1880년대 시카고에 10층짜리 홈 인슈어런스 빌딩이 들어서면서이다. 뉴욕의 상징이 된 엠파이어스테이트 빌딩은 높이가 449m로 1931년 가장 높은 건물의 자리를 꿰찼다.

오늘날의 초고층 건물들은 신의 분노 이상으로 중력을 두려워한다. 높이 솟은 건물을 아래로 잡아당기려는 무자비한 중력을 견뎌내기 위해서는 고강도 콘크리트와 강철이 필요했다. 튼튼한 강철이 없었다면 오늘날의 도시 스카이라인은 없었을 것이다. 벽돌과 석재로도 이론적으로는 1,600m 높이까지 쌓을 수 있지만 실제로는 10~12층이 한계다.

강풍과 지진 같은 환경 요인도 문제다. 50층에 비해 100층에서는 네 배나 강한 바람을 맞게 된다. 건물이 약간씩 흔들리는 것은 견딜 수 있지만 사람이 기거하고 산다면 곤란하다. 수천, 수만 명이 생활하는 마천루를 위해서는 초고속 엘리베이터도 만들어야 하고, 그만큼의 수압을 견딜 수 있는 대량 물탱크도 있어야 한다.

문제해설
1. (a)에서 말하는 환경적 요인으로 바람과 지진 등이 거론되고 있다. 그리고 (a)와 같은 이유에서 여러 요인들이 고려되어야 한다는 (b) 또한 올바른 내용이다. 그리고 엠파이어스테이트 빌딩이 높이 449m라 했으므로 10층짜리 빌딩인 홈 인슈어런스 빌딩보다 더 높다. 하지만

바벨탑이 얼마나 높았는지는 성경에 등장하는 내용이므로 6,000m쯤 됐을 것으로 추측만이 가능하다.
2. 뉴욕에 사는 이들이 높은 건물을 자랑스러워 한다는 내용은 등장하지 않으며, 뉴욕 사람들이 더 높은 건물을 짓는 경우 신의 진노가 내릴 것이라는 것도 본문과 거리가 멀다. 그리고 (d) 또한 본문과 무관하다. 정답은 (b)로 바벨탑이 건설되던 시기에는 신의 진노가 아마도 오늘날의 환경적 요인으로 생각해 볼 수 있다.
3. 이 글은 고층 건물에 관한 것이지만 더 높은 건물을 짓기 위해 경쟁한다는 내용은 등장하지 않는다. 따라서 (d)가 정답으로 적합하다.
4. dialect는 방언이란 말로 (c)를 제외하고 모두 언어나 말, 방언 등을 의미한다.

정답 1(c) 2(b) 3(d) 4(c)

Unit 96 Turn off the lights
빛 공해

1938년 7월 미국 시카고 대학 생리학자인 너대니얼 클라이트먼은 수염으로 뒤덮인 얼굴을 하고 32일 동안의 지하 생활을 보낸 후 동굴에서 나왔다. 동굴 속에서 그는 하루를 28시간으로 정해놓고 생활했지만 새로운 리듬에 끝내 적응하지 못했다. 인체 내부에는 태양이 뜨고 지는 24시간에 맞춰진 강력한 시계가 존재하기 때문이다.

인간뿐만 아니라 동식물들도 태양빛의 영향을 강하게 받는다. 벼·들깨·코스모스 등은 가을철에 매일 햇빛을 받아야 꽃을 피우고 열매를 맺는다. 지난해 3월 영국 로슬린 연구소와 일본 나고야 대학 연구팀은 봄이 돼 새가 짝짓기를 위해 노래를 부르는 것도 태양빛의 영향임을 밝혀냈다. 수컷 메추라기들은 낮이 길어져 빛을 많이 쬐면 뇌 표면의 세포(뇌하수체)가 자극을 받아 호르몬 분비가 늘고, 정소(精巢)가 커져 짝을 찾는 노래를 부르게 된다는 설명이다.

태양에서 쏟아지는 빛 에너지 덕분에 지구 표면은 평균 15도의 기온을 유지할 수 있고, 식물은 광합성을 할 수 있다. 하지만, 생물에게는 태양빛이 없는 밤도 중요하다. 캄캄한 밤은 수컷 반딧불이 암컷에게 자신의 존재를 드러내는 시간이다. 작고 약한 동물이 포식자를 피해 먹이를 구하는 시간이기도 하다.

인간이 만들어낸 인공 빛은 이런 밤의 질서에 영향을 미쳤다. 인공위성에서 내려다 보면 지구의 밤에 새어 나오는 강력한 불빛에 눈부실 정도다. 오랜 지구의 역사를 통해 낮과 밤, 사계절 변화에 익숙해진 생물들이 엉뚱한 계절, 엉뚱한 시간에 밝은 빛을 만난다면 혼란을 겪을 수밖에 없다.

인공 빛은 인류 자신에게도 어두운 문제가 되고 있다. 세계 인구의 3분의 2가량이 별빛으로 가득 찬 밤하늘을 더 이상 보지 못한다. 호주에서는 (자국의 상징인) 남십자성을 하나씩 잃어가고 있다. 국기에 그려진 별을 육안으로 볼

수 없게 된 것이다. 지난해 2월 이스라엘 연구팀은 밤중에 전등이나 TV화면 같이 인공 빛에 노출된 여성들이 가로등 없이 어두운 곳에 사는 여성들에 비해 유방암 발생률이 37%나 높다는 연구결과도 내놓기도 했다.

문제해설

1. 이 글은 빛이 사람과 동물 및 식물에 어떤 식으로 영향을 주는지에 관해 서술하고 있으므로 정답은 (a)가 된다.
2. 본문의 마지막 부분에 빛이 여성의 유방암 발생률과 관련이 있다고 했으므로 건강에 영향을 주지 않는다는 (d)의 설명은 사실과 다르다.
3. 호르몬을 'trigger'한다는 것은 '유발'한다는 뜻이므로 몸속에 화학 물질을 생성시킨다는 (b)가 정답이 된다. (a)는 trigger의 근원적 의미인 총의 방아쇠를 당긴다는 뜻에서 shoot이라는 동사를 사용했지만, 이는 본문의 뜻과는 다르다.
4. 새들이 노래를 부르는 것은 짝을 찾기 위한 것이므로 (A)에는 mating이 적절하며, 식물이 광합성을 할 수 있는 것은 태양의 빛 에너지를 통해서 가능하므로 (B)에는 energy가 적절하다. 그리고 동물들은 지구상에 살면서 계절적 변화에 익숙해졌기 때문에 (C)에는 change가 와야 한다. 따라서 정답은 (a)가 된다.

정답 1(a)　2(d)　3(b)　4(a)

Unit 97 Political deja vu
기시감

가끔씩 눈 앞에서 현재 펼쳐지는 상황들을 전에 한번 본 듯하다는 느낌을 받을 때가 있다. 꿈속에서, 혹은 전생이 있다면, 그곳에서 말이다. 전에 경험해본 듯한 이상한 느낌을 주는 기억들. 이른바 이미 봤다(안다)는 느낌이라는 뜻의 '기시감(旣視感)', 또는 불어로 '데자뷰'로 불리는 체험이다.

일반적으로 기시감에 의한 신비감은 환생과 업(業: 카르마)에 관한 사고로 거슬러 올라간다. 예를 들어 태어난 지 얼마 되지 않은 서구의 아이가 가르치지 않은 불교식의 절을 해 부모를 놀라게 했다가 얼마 뒤 길거리에서 만난 티베트 승려에게 다가가 스스럼없이 다시 절을 했다는 등의 스토리 등으로 발전한다. 그렇다고 환생과 업에 관한 동양적 사고가 이 기시감의 근원이라고 꼬집어 말할 수도 없다. 독일 철학자 프리드리히 니체가 이미 자신의 '영원회귀(永遠回歸)'에 관한 사고를 설명하면서 "세계는 그 자신을 무한히 반복하고 우리가 경험하는 모든 것은 자신의 놀이를 영원히 계속하는 순환"이라고 규정할 때 기시감의 서구적 단초는 나타났다.

기시감은 프랑스 의학자 플로랑스 아르노가 이 현상을 규정했고, 이어 프랑스의 심리학자 에밀 보아락에 의해 데자뷰라는 의학 용어로 정착했다. 최근 미 MIT 대학 신경학과가 이 데자뷰의 신비감을 제거하고 나섰다. 뇌의 작용일

것이라는 추정은 과거에도 있었지만 이번에는 구체적인 뇌 부위를 적시하면서 데자뷰가 신체 이상에 의한 현상이라는 결론을 내렸다.

문제해설

1. (a)의 경우, 마지막 문단에서 미국의 MIT 대학에서 데자뷰 원인에 대해 과학적 추정을 하고 있으므로 논란이 계속될 것 같지는 않다. 하지만 이런 과학적 추정을 데자뷰에 대한 결정적 설명으로 보기에는 충분하지 않기 때문에 정답은 (b)가 적합하다. 그리고 다른 보기인 (c)와 (d)는 본문과 무관하다.
2. 첫 번째 문단에 설명되어 있는 것처럼 어디선가 한번 본 듯하다는 느낌을 데자뷰라고 하므로 정답은 (a)가 된다.
3. 프랑스인들이 처음 데자뷰를 주목한 것이 아니지만, 이 현상을 규정하고 데자뷰라는 용어를 처음 사용했다. 그리고 MIT 신경학자들은 데자뷰가 실제 존재하지 않는다는 것을 증명한 것이 아니라 뇌의 작용에 일환이라는 결론을 내린 것이다. 아이들도 종종 데자뷰를 경험한다는 내용은 등장하지 않으며, 두 번째 문단을 통해 환생과 업과 같은 동양적 사고가 데자뷰의 근원이라는 내용이 있으므로 정답은 (d)가 된다. 동양적 사고뿐만 아니라 서양적 사고에도 데자뷰에 관한 사상이 있음을 본문에서는 강조하고 있다.
4. 제목이 되려면 데자뷰 현상을 가장 잘 설명한 것을 골라야 한다. 데자뷰가 사기는 아니며, 이 글이 프랑스 철학에 관한 내용도 아니다. 그리고 우리가 어디에서 왔느냐를 따지는 것도 아니기에 (d) 또한 부적절하다. 정답은 (c)로 환생과 업에 대한 내용을 데자뷰와 연결해 놓은 내용이므로 보기 중에서는 (c)가 가장 적합하다.

정답 1(b)　2(a)　3(d)　4(c)

Unit 98 Planet's apes in peril
고릴라

고릴라는 이스턴고릴라와 웨스턴고릴라 두 종으로 나뉜다. 털 색깔이 짙은 이스턴고릴라는 아프리카 중부 내륙의 콩고민주공화국에서 살고 있다. 아프리카에서 가장 오래된 국립자연공원인 이 나라 비룽가 국립공원에는 (이스턴고릴라의 아종(亞種)인) 마운틴고릴라 380여 마리가 살고 있다. 전 세계 700여 마리의 절반 가까운 숫자다. 나머지는 르완다와 우간다의 경계에 산다.

비룽가 공원의 고릴라는 주위 인간 사회에 둘러싸여 계속되는 불안정에 고통 받고 있다. 지난 10년 이상 계속되는 내전의 위협을 받고 있는 것이다. 94년 르완다에서 투치족과 일부 온건파 후투족 등 50만 명 이상을 학살했던 후투족 과격파 세력이 잠입해 정부군과 교전을 벌이는 와중에 수많은 고릴라가 희생되었다. 반군은 배가 고프면 고릴라를 잡아먹기도 하고, 정부군이 소탕작전을 벌일 경우 고릴라를 몰살시키겠다는 협박도 한다.

이처럼 추악한 행태가 벌어지는 또다른 요인은 콜탄이란 거무스름한 광물 때문이다. 콜탄을 정련하면 고온에 잘

57

견디는 탄탈(Tantalum)이라는 금속 분말을 얻을 수 있다. 탄탈은 휴대폰·노트북·제트엔진 등에 널리 쓰이면서 수요가 급증해 1㎏에 수십만 원씩 한다. 반군들은 이 콜탄을 암시장에 내다팔아 전쟁자금을 조달하고 있다.

웨스턴고릴라의 아종으로 아프리카 중서부 카메룬·가봉·콩고공화국 등지에 살고 있는 웨스트로랜드고릴라 역시 밀렵과 내전뿐만 아니라 에볼라 바이러스의 창궐, 야자유 농장개발에 따른 서식지 파괴로 위협받고 있다. 전문가들은 웨스트로랜드고릴라가 10만 마리 미만일 것으로 추정한다. 최근 콩고공화국 북부 숲과 습지에서 웨스트로랜드고릴라의 개체 수는 12만 5,000마리 정도인 것으로 조사되었다.

문제해설

1. 반군이 정부군과 대치 중에 고릴라들을 죽였다는 내용은 나오지만 (b)처럼 반군이 승리할 것이라는 내용은 없으며, (c)처럼 고릴라가 안전한 지역을 찾아 떠날 것이라는 내용도 등장하지 않는다. (d) 또한 콜탄이란 광물이 반군의 전쟁자금을 조달하는 데 사용되는 자원이 되고 있다고는 했지만 정부가 이를 사들이지 않을 것이라는 내용은 등장하지 않는다. 고릴라가 내전이나 밀렵 등의 이유로 위협을 받고 있다는 내용이기 때문에 (a)와 같이 상황이 개선되지 않을 경우 멸종할 수도 있다는 추론이 가장 타당하다.

2. 내전을 하면서 잡아먹기도 하고, 정부군에 대한 협박의 일환으로도 고릴라를 죽인다고 했으므로 (d)가 적합하다.

3. 본문은 고릴라들 간의 싸움에 관한 내용이 아니기 때문에 정답은 (b)가 된다.

4. 고릴라들이 처한 실상에 대한 글이므로 (b)와 (c)는 적합하지 않으며, (d)는 비룽가 공원에 있는 마운틴고릴라에만 해당하는 내용이므로 지엽적이다. 따라서 정답은 (a)가 된다.

정답 1(a) 2(d) 3(b) 4(a)

Unit 99 | Kimchi in space
우주식품

미국의 첫 우주인 존 글렌은 1962년 프렌드십 7호에 반유동체인 사과소스를 싣고 갔다. 우주에서도 하루 세끼를 먹는다. 남성에겐 보통 2,200㎉, 여성에겐 2,000㎉의 열량이 제공된다. 맛이나 식감은 대부분 일반식보다는 떨어진다. 우주 식품 제조 시 가장 먼저 고려하는 것은 경량화다. 1㎏을 우주에 올리는 데 5,000만 원이 들기 때문이다. 우주 식품을 동결건조·분말화하는 것은 이처럼 생산비 절감을 위해서다. 우주 식품에서는 위생도 중요하다. ISS 모듈엔 냉장고가 없어 많은 음식을 오래 두고 먹기 힘들어서다. HACCP(식품위해요소 집중관리기준)은 식품 안전과 소비자 보호를 위한 세계 최고 수준의 시스템이다. 그 기원은 우주 탐험에 뿌리를 두고 있으며, 유인 우주비행 시 먹을 음식 준비를 관리하기 위한 것이다. ISS 모듈에 냉장고가 없는 것은 전력이 부족하기 때문이다.

우주 식품의 제공은 미국과 러시아가 양분한다. 미국이 200가지, 러시아가 130가지의 식품·음료를 2008년 1월 국제우주식품 목록에 등록했다. 메뉴엔 별 차이가 없으나 포장재의 종류와 용기의 입구 부분이 다르다. 미국은 알루미늄 포일 등 빛이 통과하지 않는 포장재를, 러시아는 투명한 포장재를 쓴다. 미국산의 용기 입구는 LPG차의 가스 밸브, 러시아산은 휘발유차의 기름 밸브를 연상시킨다. 미국의 우주 식품은 러시아보다 더 잘 밀폐된 용기에 포장된다. 이들 경우에서 보듯이, 우주 식품을 준비하는 것이 지상의 음식 용기와 포장 기술에 큰 영향을 미쳤다.

문제해설

1. 이 글은 우주 식품에 관한 내용으로 경량화나 위생 등에 대해 설명하고 있으며, 미국과 러시아의 우주 식품에 관해 비교하고 있다. 따라서 정답은 (c)가 된다.

2. 미국의 우주 식품이 러시아보다 종류가 많고, 더 잘 밀폐된 용기를 사용하므로 러시아보다 미국의 우주 식품이 더 많이 사용될 것으로 추론할 수 있다. 따라서 정답은 (a)가 된다.

3. 차이가 나는 부분이 포장재 종류와 용기의 입구, 품목 수 등이었으므로 정답은 (d)가 된다. (d)는 언급되어 있지 않다.

4. 마지막 문장인 "the preparation of space foods has greatly contributed to improving the container and packaging technologies of foods on Earth."를 보면 음식 용기와 포장 기술에 영향을 주었다고 했으므로 정답은 (b)가 된다.

정답 1(c) 2(a) 3(d) 4(b)

Unit 100 | A cry for the wolf
늑대의 죽음

어니스트 톰슨 시튼이 쓴 동물 이야기의 고전집『동물기』에는 늑대가 여러 차례 등장한다. 그중에 '배들랜드 빌리'란 검은 목털을 가진 늑대는 몸무게가 63㎏이나 나가고 발자국 길이가 14㎝나 됐다. 그 덕분에 적들(사냥꾼)을 따돌리고 여유 있게 가축을 잡아먹곤 했다. 한번은 끈질긴 사냥개 무리에게 쫓기게 됐으나, 절벽 위로 난 좁은 길로 그들을 유인해 15마리 모두를 하나씩 벼랑 아래로 떨어뜨렸다.

올 2월 미국 스탠퍼드 대학 연구팀은 빌리처럼 북미 대륙에 있는 늑대의 검은 털은 15,000여 년 전의 먼 옛날을 거슬러 올라가면 개의 조상과 이종 교배가 된 결과라는 논문을 사이언스지에 발표했다. 이는 늑대와 개 사이의 유전적, 생물학적 관계를 말해준다.

늑대가 사람을 공격하는 일은 드문 일이다. 개-늑대 잡종이거나 사육 늑대의 경우 어린이를 공격할 때도 있지만,

야생 늑대는 오히려 사람을 두려워한다. 시튼의 책에 등장하는 노련한 늑대 사냥꾼조차 "지금까지 늑대가 사람을 공격하는 것을 본 적은 한 번도 없다"고 말한다. 드물지만 지금도 미국·러시아에는 도시를 배회하며 인간과 공존하는 늑대가 있다고 한다.

하지만 사람들은 늑대가 가축에 막대한 피해를 끼친다며 늑대 사냥을 정당화한다. 캐나다의 환경보호론자이자 작가인 팔리 모왓은 『울지 않는 늑대』란 책에서 "북극의 순록이 줄어든 것은 모피 상인들이 매년 수천 마리씩 남획한 탓인데도, 늑대에게 누명을 씌운다"라며 동물에 대한 인간의 잔혹성과 불필요한 동물의 고통을 고발한다. 80만 년 전 등장한 늑대는 유럽·아시아·북미 지역에 넓게 분포했으나 이제는 서식지 파괴와 과도한 사냥으로 전 세계에 10만 마리뿐이다.

문제해설

1. 저자는 이 글을 통해 늑대의 기원과 특성을 이해시키면서 이를 통해 늑대 사냥 등을 비판하고 있으므로 정답은 (a)가 된다.
2. 야생 늑대가 사람을 공격하는 일은 거의 없다고 했으므로 (b)가 정답이 된다.
3. (b)의 경우 순록이 줄어드는 이유는 모피 상인들의 남획에 의한 것이지 늑대가 원인은 아니라고 마지막 문단에서 밝히고 있다. 그리고 (c)와 (d)는 본문에 없는 내용이므로 정답은 야생 늑대의 수가 줄어들고 있다는 (a)가 된다.
4. 첫 번째 문단에 설명되어 있으며, 절벽 위로 난 길로 개들을 유인해 벼랑 아래로 떨어뜨렸다고 했으므로 정답은 (c)가 적합하다.

정답 1(a) 2(b) 3(a) 4(c)

memo:

1. What's the purpose of the passage?

    (a) To defend wolves

    (b) To track down wolves

    (c) To understand wolves

    (d) To attack wolves

2. What can you infer about wild wolves?

    (a) They are often kept domestically in place of dogs.

    (b) They will not go near humans if they don't have to.

    (c) They attack another wolf if they meet one.

    (d) They are smarter than tamed wolves.

3. Which of the following is true?

    (a) Wolf numbers are decreasing.

    (b) Reindeer numbers are decreasing because of wolf attacks.

    (c) Wolves attack adults instead of children.

    (d) Wolves cause problems wherever they go.

4. How did Badlands Billy escape the hunting dogs?

    (a) He ran faster than them and escaped.

    (b) He convinced them not to kill him.

    (c) He tricked them onto a cliff and pushed them off the edge.

    (d) He attacked them one by one and killed them.

Words & Phrases

tale n. 이야기 fur n. 털 evade v. 피하다, 모면하다 prey on ~을 잡아먹다 chase v. 뒤쫓다
a pack of 한 무리의 persistent a. 끈질긴, 집요한 shove v. 밀치다 interbreeding n. 이종 교배, 품종 간 교배
domestic a. 사육되는, 길들여진 genetic a. 유전의 tamed a. 길들여진 feature v. (~으로) 주연시키다 fatal a. 치명적인
roam v. 배회하다 conservationist n. 보호론자 cruelty n. 잔인함 considerable a. 상당한 reindeer n. 순록
reckless a. 무모한 furrier n. 모피상, 모피공 habitat n. 서식처

문장분석

■ Billy <u>tricked</u> the 15 hounds <u>into</u> <u>following</u> him down a narrow path leading to a cliff and then shoved them over, one after the other. ➜ 〈talk/trick + 목적어 + into -ing〉라는 표현은 '~를 말/속임수로 …하게 하다'는 뜻의 표현이다. 반대의 의미를 갖게 하려면 into 대신에 out of를 사용해 〈talk/trick + 목적어 + out of -ing〉와 같이 표현한다.

홍준기

저자는 시설관리공단 공채시험의 영어과 출제위원을 역임하고, 현재 중앙일보의 영자신문인 Korea JoongAng Daily의 객원해설위원으로 3년여 전부터 지금까지 매주 '리딩스펙트럼' 독해를 연재하고 있다. 또한 최근 국내 최초로 독해지문 전체를 영어로 쓴 '시사독해 실렉션'을 발간, 이 책 내용이 KBS 굿모닝팝스에 게재되었었다. 편입계의 베스트셀러인 '석세스 편입독해'를 비롯, 이 역시 최초로 패러프레이즈 원리를 규명한 편입대비 '패러프레이즈 버스터', '오바마 세계평화연설', '동의어 엑스퍼트', '이재옥 영문법 리스타트' 등을 저술했다. 현재 박문각편입학원에서 디렉터 겸 대표교수로 활동하고 있다.

NEW 리딩 스펙트럼 3 – 자연과학편

발 행 일 2018년 12월 20일(개정신판 2쇄)
저　　자 홍준기
발 행 인 문정구
발 행 처 종합출판 ⅠEnG
출판등록 1988. 6. 17 제 9-175호
주　　소 04002 서울시 마포구 월드컵북로5길 65 주원빌딩(4층)
홈페이지 www.jonghapbooks.com
전자메일 jonghap@jonghapbooks.com
대표전화 02-365-1246
팩　　스 02-365-1248

정가 17,500원

ISBN 978-89-8099-640-7　14740
　　　978-89-8099-623-0　(set)

※ 낙장 및 파본은 바꾸어 드립니다.

「이 도서의 국립중앙도서관 출판예정도서목록(CIP)은 서지정보유통지원시스템 홈페이지 (http://seoji.nl.go.kr)와 국가자료공동목록시스템(http://www.nl.go.kr/kolisnet)에서 이용하실 수 있습니다. (CIP제어번호 : CIP2017005501)」